Millennial Makeover

Millennial Makeover

MySpace, YouTube, and the Future of American Politics

MORLEY WINOGRAD
MICHAEL D. HAIS

RUTGERS UNIVERSITY PRESS
New Brunswick, New Jersey, and London

Fourth printing, 2008

LIBRARY OF CONGRESS CATALOGING-IN-PUBLICATION DATA

Winograd, Morley.
    Millennial makeover : MySpace, YouTube, and the future of American
politics / Morley Winograd and Michael D. Hais.
        p. cm.
    Includes bibliographical references and index.
    ISBN 978–0–8135–4301–7 (hardcover : alk. paper)
    1. Political participation—Technological innovations—United   States.
2. Online social networks—Political aspects—United States.   3. Blogs—
Political aspects—United States.   4. Voting research—United States.   5. Political
parties— United States.   6. United States—Politics and government—Blogs.
7. United States—Politics and government—2001–   I. Hais, Michael D.,
1943–   II. Title.
JK1764.W635 2008
320.97301′4—dc22   2007029658

A British Cataloging-in-Publication record for this book is available
from the British Library.

Visit our Web site: http://rutgerspress.rutgers.edu

Manufactured in the United States of America

CONTENTS

Preface		*ix*
Acknowledgments		*xiii*
Introduction		I

PART I CYCLES OF AMERICAN POLITICS

I	*The Rise and Fall of Political Parties in America*	II
2	*Idealist and Civic Eras in American History*	30
3	*Politicians Love to Talk*	50
4	*Meet the Millennials*	66
5	*Millennials Will Spearhead the Coming Political Realignment*	87

PART II TRANSITION TO A NEW ERA

6	*The Realignment Begins*	III
7	*Winning without the Mother's Milk of Politics*	124
8	*The Technology Tsunami*	140
9	*Social Networks Will Change America's Political Map*	156
10	*Winning the Technology Arms Race*	174

PART III   THE NEW AMERICAN POLITICAL LANDSCAPE

11	*Triggering a New America*	191
12	*Who Will Party with Whom?*	203
13	*Who Will Lead the Realignment?*	220
14	*Rebuilding America's Civic Infrastructure*	233
15	*Public Policy in a Millennial Era*	247
	References	269
	Index	279

PREFACE

IN THE SPIRIT OF OPENNESS and full disclosure that the Millennial Generation treasures, the readers of this book should be forewarned that two life-long Democrats wrote it. Both of us have shared a deep passion for politics and baseball, not necessarily in that order. Along the way, we rooted for the same political party, if not always the same baseball teams. We have also both been fortunate enough to pursue rewarding careers in the private sector.

We did, however, take time out from those more personal pursuits to help orchestrate the successful resurrection of the Michigan Democratic Party after it was buried in the 1972 Nixon landslide. One of us, Mike Hais, supplied the survey research data for Carl Levin's first successful campaign for the U.S. Senate, in 1978, against Senator Robert Griffin, the Republican minority leader. Mike then helped Congressman Jim Blanchard win the state's gubernatorial election in 1982, ending a twenty-year Republican reign. The other author, Morley Winograd, was the state party's chairman from 1973 until 1979, during which time the party recaptured a majority of the state's congressional delegation and, for a brief moment in time, both houses of the state legislature. Together, with the help of the great men and women of the United Auto Workers, we turned the tables on the Republicans and their ticket-splitting strategy, honed to perfection by Governors George Romney and William Milliken in the 1960s and 1970s. We used that approach to elect Democrats by splitting off moderate Republicans from the increasingly conservative candidates the GOP was beginning to nominate, even back then.

After the 1990 midterm elections, the Democratic Leadership Council (DLC) invited Morley, along with Doug Ross, another Michigan Democratic friend, to deliver a presentation entitled "How to Win the White House in 1992." The person sitting next to us taking copious notes was the vice-chair of the DLC, Governor Bill Clinton of Arkansas. As described in *Taking Control: Politics in the Information Age* (1996), Clinton used the speech and the mantra of "Opportunity, Responsibility, and Community" to do what most Democrats, including himself in 1990, thought could not possibly be done.

That book, which Morley co-authored with Dudley Buffa, was also the first to identify an entirely new constituency in U.S. politics, based on the impact of information and communication technologies on how Americans were beginning to work and live. After the book's publication, the Institute for a New California commissioned a series of trail-blazing studies of the California electorate that Mike developed and executed when he was vice president, Entertainment Research, at Frank N. Magid Associates, which identified and profiled "wired workers"—a term that the study made part of the political lexicon of the 1990s.

In 1996, *Taking Control* was brought to the attention of President Bill Clinton. As photographed in *Time* magazine, the president handed a copy of the book to Vice President Al Gore during one of their weekly power lunches and asked him to review its ideas and policy prescriptions. As a result, Morley was asked to assume the position of senior policy advisor to the vice president for the administration's second term, with special responsibility for the National Partnership for Reinventing Government. In that capacity, Morley had an insider's view of the workings of the West Wing, and some of those experiences became the source for a few of the stories we tell in this book.

But despite our personal partisan perspective, in writing this book we have attempted to be as objective as possible. We have not failed to criticize our Democratic allies where we felt criticism was warranted, and we have attempted, along the way, to outline the best strategies that Republicans might pursue to extricate themselves from their current difficulties. We do so for the same reasons that have spurred our interest in American politics for all of our adult lives.

America's identity as a nation comes from its belief in the concept of democracy. Those fundamental values create a common bond that unites an otherwise heterogeneous population. Phrases such as "life, liberty, and the pursuit of happiness" or "in order to create a more perfect union" have been powerful enough to permeate every aspect of American society and make the country's citizens as distinct as if they, like the citizens or subjects of most other nations, shared a common birthplace, race, ethnicity, religion, or language.

Yet the exact nature of American democracy has undergone significant changes during the nation's existence. Each time technology created new economic realities, a new generation of Americans, comfortable in a new world, has forced America to find, within its constitutional framework, the flexibility to change and adapt to those new circumstances.

Today, the United States faces another test of the strength of its democracy from those same twin forces of change. A new generation of Americans, the Millennial Generation, is entering the electorate and workforce in record numbers. Their arrival was heralded by "Baby on Board" signs in minivans twenty-five years ago. Now Millennials are entering young adulthood with a sense of confidence and commitment that reflects their sheltered and yet, at the same time, pressured childhood. Millennials are also the first American generation to be raised with access to the Internet and the incredibly greater communication opportunities the Web offers. Whether they are texting the person sitting next to them in the backseat of a car or IMing a buddy clear across the globe, Millennials are always in touch with their friends. Their team orientation and desire to constantly share information are just two of the Millennial behaviors that are impacting American culture and politics.

This book is an attempt to illuminate Millennial values and behaviors, as well as the technologies that help to create and enable them, for the Baby Boomers and Gen-Xers who are currently running America. In some previous eras, intergenerational misunderstandings and the failure to use new technologies wisely have had catastrophic consequences for American society. Student and racial unrest, barely contained class warfare, and even the Civil War are examples of the failure of America's democratic institutions to manage these discontinuities. In other times, however, the successful integration of a new generation's perspective and the use of new technologies have led to periods of tremendous economic growth and the rebuilding of the country's civic institutions. Victory in the Cold War is the most recent of those happier examples, but others stretch all the way back to the founding of the American democratic republic and to the expansion of the United States to its present continent-spanning boundaries.

Which direction the current confluence of changes in generational attitudes and the introduction of new technologies will take is not yet known. Depending on what America's leaders do to deal with these new realities, the United States in the next several decades could either be infinitely better off or in a much worse position. One thing is certain, however: in less than a decade, the United States will look very different than it did at the turn of the twenty-first century. If Americans are to design a government able to take the United States down the right path and preserve its democratic ideals, it is critical that we understand both the technological changes that are creating new conditions for economic and political success and the very interrelated way in which the new Millennial Generation thinks and behaves. In some small way, the authors hope the data and insights we present in this book begin that journey of discovery and understanding for each of our readers.

Morley Winograd and Mike Hais
August 2007

ACKNOWLEDGMENTS

THE IDEAS, thoughts, and words of this book are most definitely those of the authors. But any work of this scope is, ultimately, a team effort, and for this reason we want to acknowledge a number of individuals without whom this book could not have been written.

We, and anyone who wants to have a clearer understanding of American history and society, owe a large intellectual debt to William Strauss and Neil Howe. Nearly two decades ago we read their well-researched, perceptive, and seminal book *Generations*. It was a "Eureka" moment for us both. That initial reading provided an amazingly clear understanding of the ebb and flow of America's past and its future. At that time, both of us vowed to apply the Strauss and Howe generational framework to the aspect of American life about which we are most passionate—politics. We renewed that commitment following their publication of *The Fourth Turning* in 1997. This book is the fulfillment of that pledge.

As we proceeded, Dr. Elaine Kamarck of Harvard University's John F. Kennedy School of Government freely offered valuable insights and perceptive comments that demonstrated her deep knowledge of American politics and government. We have also had the pleasure of trading political opinions with Dudley Buffa, who provided us extremely useful suggestions on how to organize the book.

We particularly want to thank several institutions and individuals for graciously allowing us full access to high-quality survey data before and during our research for this book. We appreciate the generosity of Dr. David C. King, research director at Harvard University's Institute of Politics. David kindly provided the results of the Institute's excellent surveys of the Millennial Generation and, equally important, his deep understanding of the political attitudes and behavior of this crucial generation of young Americans. We are also grateful to the Pew Research Center for the People and the Press for providing early use of the results of several important studies, and to Jim Albrittain of Pew for tabulating that data so that it met our specific intellectual needs and difficult time constraints.

We owe our largest debt of gratitude to Frank N. Magid Associates, a company widely recognized as the world's most important and influential communications market research and consultation firm. In 2007, Magid celebrated its fiftieth anniversary, marking a period during which it shaped the broadcasting and communications industries to a greater degree than any company of its type. In particular, Mike Hais would like to thank Frank N. Magid, the firm's founder, who was a constant source of knowledge and inspiration during Mike's more than twenty-two years at the company, and Brent Magid, the firm's current CEO, who is guiding the company toward at least another half-century of achievement.

We also want to express our special gratitude to Jack MacKenzie, executive vice president of Magid, as well as president of Magid's Millennial Strategy Program. Jack, a personal friend and former Dodger season ticket co-holder with both of us, counsels many of America's major corporations on the most effective way to communicate with the Millennial Generation. He provided numerous important insights into the behaviors and attitudes of this generation that are so central to this book and to America's future. Jack also generously arranged for us to be able to include, and have full and exclusive access to, the results of questions on three waves of Magid's periodic surveys of the Millennial Generation.

These as yet unpublished surveys were conducted online in January 2006, December 2006, and May 2007, with far larger samples than is normal in commercial market research, thereby permitting us to examine generational political attitudes and behavior with remarkable precision. The first survey interviewed a national sample of 2,468 Millennials, Gen-Xers, and Baby Boomers, enabling us to compare the political attitudes and behaviors of these generations on a wide range of matters. The sampling error for this survey was ±2 percent for results based on the entire sample. The second research wave dealt with political matters in even more detail and was conducted with an online sample of 1,577 American adults. This resulted in a sampling error of ±2.5 percent for results based on the entire sample. Finally, the third round of survey research was completed with a sample of 2,550, producing a sampling error of ±2 percent for results based on the total sample.

Many others at Magid also assisted us in a variety of ways. These include, most notably, Rich McGuire, vice president of Generational Insight, Julie Zipperer, senior administrative assistant, and Charlotte Sundermeyer, director of Data Tabulation.

We also benefited from the understanding that other colleagues showed us as we wrote this book. The wonderful staff at the Center for Telecom Management (CTM) at the University of Southern California's Marshall School of Business not only adjusted their workloads to accommodate the additional time we spent writing the book, but also constantly offered us research tidbits and ideas for consideration. Two colleagues who share a passion for advising government leaders on how to improve their operations, Alan Glassman and Christina Altmayer, made sure that none of our mutual clients suffered from a lack of intellectual attention because of the book. The fact that Alan even found the time to provide the key insight on the best way to tell this story (and to use any Dodger tickets we weren't able to) only underscores what great colleagues they both are. Other colleagues, John Matsusaka, Vice Dean of the Marshall School of Business at USC, and Ivan Rosenberg, the head of Frontier Associates, Inc., provided us with important insights from their research on the topics of direct democracy and leadership, respectively, that helped shape our thinking on those subjects.

But despite all the data we were able to gather on the subject of generational politics, we could not have told the story of Millennials and their technology without the help of people who guided our own education on the subject and who gave us permission to capture those interviews for the book, so that we could tell others what we learned. Beyond the contributions of Jack MacKenzie, our understanding of Millennials was further aided by the intriguing insights of Pete Markiewicz, who provided some of the intellectual content for another great book by Strauss and Howe, *Millennials and Pop Culture*. Pete also connected both of us to the continuing conversation among devotees of *The Fourth Turning*, for which we are especially grateful.

Our journey through the wonders of peer-to-peer technology benefited from the guidance of a number of people who are active in the industry. Dan Schulman, CEO of Virgin Mobile, gave us the key tsunami metaphor that helped crystallize the nature of the technological change the country is currently experiencing. JibJab's CEO, Gregg Spiridellis, taught us the true meaning of intergalactic viral marketing. Ted Cohen took time out from his valuable day as the leading consultant to the digital music industry to make sure we understood just how innocently that industry's upheaval began. Jon Diamond, CEO of ArtistDirect, made certain we had the facts on what the phenomenon of peer-to-peer communications has already meant to record companies, and will soon mean to the entire media industry. And Josh Berman of MySpace and Jordan Hoffner of YouTube took us on wonderful journeys of discovery and understanding in the world of social networking.

Once we understood all that, we were able to learn about the application of these communication technologies to politics from some of the true masters of this new universe. One, Jerome Armstrong, who was there at the dawning of "Netroots" politics, gave us an insider's view of that history and introduced us to Trei Brundrett, who in turn accurately predicted just how this brave new world would evolve and why. They told us about two Millennials whose skills at campaigning through social networking helped them get elected to the New Hampshire state legislature in 2006. That's how we found Jeffrey Fontas and Andrew Edwards, who proved to be every bit as bright and capable as any Millennial can be, and whom we now proudly claim as friends on Facebook. They are joined there by KidOakland, who introduced us to more successful Millennial campaign organizers, this time in Northern California. One of them, Matt Lockshin, is a folk hero in the blogosphere for the successful use of his blog, "saynotopombo," to help elect Jerry McNerney to the U.S. House of Representatives in 2006. He's a special hero to us for quickly finding time to make certain we got that story exactly right.

Others told us stories that were a little more personally painful, out of friendship as well as commitment to the cause. Harris Miller, a long-time friend and co-political junkie for the last thirty years, recovered enough from his 2006 defeat in the Virginia Democratic primary against now U.S. Senator Jim Webb to fill us in on the real story behind that election. Mark Bryan, who bravely tried to get someone in the Democratic Party to use data-mining technologies before the Republicans did, shared with us all the documents and arguments he used in an unsuccessful effort to provide that party with a technological edge they have now lost forever.

But all the data and all the stories would never have appeared in print if it weren't for the efforts of our agent, Ron Goldfarb. From the very beginning, Ron expressed and demonstrated full confidence in our ability to articulate a new way of thinking about American politics in a manner that someone might actually want to read. He worked tirelessly to find just the right publisher, offered sage advice about content and marketing, and, on occasion, managed to calm the worries of two nervous authors. In the end, Ron's efforts on our behalf were at least as much a labor of love as a commercial undertaking. We thank him for that.

For the same reason, we must thank our publisher, Rutgers University Press, and especially its director, Marlie Wasserman. First and foremost, we appreciate Marlie for giving us an opportunity to tell our story and, later, for her thoughtful, perceptive, and helpful comments as we wrote our book. As we worked together, it soon became clear that our book reflected Marlie's interest and concern with America and its politics at least as much as it did her professional responsibilities. Marlie's interactions with us emphasized the warmth, guidance, positive reinforcement, and encouragement that have characterized the way in which the Millennial Generation has been reared (although both authors are well beyond the age of that cohort).

However, none of those feelings of appreciation come close to how we feel about the support we have received from our two spouses during the writing of this book. Bobbie Winograd has earned our eternal gratitude by lending her skills as a proofreader and research librarian to the writing of this book. The interminable hours she spent correcting our writing as well as properly documenting our often obscure sources has prevented us from being embarrassed by the public revelation of just how many mistakes two writers can make. But each of our wives has also played a role in our lives that can only be described in very personal terms.

So, I, Mike Hais, want to thank my wife, Reena, for offering more than a full measure of love, humor, pride, wisdom, and encouragement during the writing of this book and the entire thirty-nine years of our marriage. I greatly appreciate her understanding and forgiveness for the many times during the past year when I may have been around physically but not always intellectually. I am very grateful for her patience in listening to me talk at length about the finer points of generational politics and the many occasions when those conversations resulted in different and better approaches to the subject. Beyond that, the fact that Reena is my very best friend, in fact my soul mate, has added the top and most important layer of happiness and fulfillment to a wonderfully happy and fulfilling life.

And I, Morley Winograd, want to thank Bobbie for forgiving me for breaking my vow never to write another book. Unfortunately, this is only the most recent of many times in our forty-five years of marriage when she has tolerated my pursuit of a dream at the expense of her own wishes and desires. Her unfailing good humor in the face of these flights of personal ambition and her unbelievable ability to be supportive and wise through it all make her a most remarkable woman. No matter what I have done or tried to do in my life, the best thing I ever did, or ever will do, was to take one look at a pony-tailed blonde at a teenage dance party and fall in love with her for the rest of my life.

Finally, for all those we have forgotten to thank, please accept our forgiveness.

Millennial Makeover

Introduction

SINCE THE ESTABLISHMENT of the current two-party system in the United States, American electoral politics have been characterized by a persistent pattern of relatively long periods of great stability in electoral outcomes, lasting about forty years, interspersed with shorter periods of sharp and decisive change. Usually, but not invariably, this realignment makes what had been the minority political party the new majority party. America is now primed for its next political realignment or makeover.

Each of the five major political realignments in U.S. history has been triggered by a crucial event, such as the Civil War or the Great Depression that then became the subject of extensive examination. But the real driving forces behind this constant and predictable shift in the fortunes of America's political parties and in its political institutions and public policy are underlying changes in generational size and attitudes and contemporaneous advances in communication technologies. Technology serves to enable these changes by creating powerful ways to reach new voters with messages that relate directly to their concerns. But without new generations, with their new attitudes and beliefs and a passion for communicating in new ways, advancements in technology would have little impact on political outcomes.

Today, our political institutions face another test from these same twin forces of change. A new generation, Millennials, born between 1982 and 2003, is coming of age in unprecedented numbers. The Millennials bring with them a facility and comfort with cutting-edge communication and computing technologies that is creating the same kind of bewilderment and bemusement that parents of television-addicted Baby Boomers felt in the 1950s and 1960s. Every generation defines itself first by making it clear how and why it is unlike the generation that preceded it. Then, as it moves into positions of power and influence in society, the new generation demands that the nation's institutions change to accommodate its beliefs and its values. The Millennials are about to make those demands on America.

The Millennial Generation is larger than any that has come before it. It is the most ethnically diverse generation in American history. Because of the way in which they have been reared, Millennials are more positive than older generations, both about the present and future state of their own lives and about the future of their country. Recent survey research on the political attitudes of this generation shows a high tolerance for lifestyle and ethnic differences and support for an activist approach by government to societal and economic issues. Unlike the generally conservative Gen-Xers, who immediately preceded them, or the harshly divided Baby Boom Generation, Millennials are united across gender and race in their desire to find "win-win" solutions to America's problems (Frank N. Magid Associates, January 2006).

Millennials are also particularly adept in the use of the new peer-to-peer communication technologies that will increasingly be used to inform and shape American public opinion. Their embrace of this technology began with the original Napster web site that allowed them to share music with all their friends, without regard to copyright laws—and without any cost. Then they made social networking sites like MySpace, an enormously popular way to share personal opinions even in the most intimate detail, online and with their friends. Now they have added video to that extended conversation, making YouTube, a company in existence since only 2005, one of the five most visited sites on the Net. As Millennials become the target demographic for all types of media, this approach to creating as well as absorbing content and information without filtering by experts will soon become the way America prefers to get all of its information.

The presidential campaign of 2008 is the first real test of the willingness of candidates to embrace social networking technologies, and the generation that uses them, as Millennials become a significant portion of the electorate. The initial launches of exploratory committees and official presidential candidate web sites demonstrated a wide range of comfort with "Netroots" campaigning. Most of the major Republican candidates' early web sites failed to go beyond the brochure stage—with appeals for money and volunteers the only interactive aspect, leaving them Internet years behind their Democratic competitors. Within the Democratic field, some, such as Hillary Rodham Clinton, went further than that but still hesitated to venture into the land of peer-to-peer technology, preferring to control interactions through online chats or "American Idol"–like voting for her campaign's theme song. Other Democrats, such as John Edwards and Barack Obama, have actively embraced social networking. Edwards racked up 10,000 "friends" on MySpace within a month of his announcement, and Obama used his web site, built on Facebook's platform, to help secure more money for his campaign from more individual donors than any Democrat in history (Morain 2007).

In 2007, survey research data, as well as the approach and tone of the announced 2008 presidential candidates, provided some clues as to who might be best positioned among the candidates to capture the hearts and minds of a new generation. Senator Obama, the youngest major party candidate, a late Baby Boomer born on the cusp of Generation X, distanced himself from the rest of the candidates in a crucial way that demonstrated his awareness of generational differences and his sensitivity to the concerns and political style of the Millennial Generation. In a YouTube video prior to his announcement, Obama said the country needed "to change our politics first" and "come together around common interests and concerns as Americans," clearly signaling his awareness of the debilitating effect that the Baby Boom Generation's continuation of the culture wars of the 1960s was having on American politics. He and Senator Clinton were the only two candidates from either party who registered significant support from 18- to 29-year-olds in a New York Times/CBS poll in June 2007. But as much fun as it is to speculate which candidate will take advantage of the technological and generational trends impacting the country's mood in order to win the ultimate prize in American politics in 2008, the complexity of current events, candidate missteps, and campaign tactics makes any such speculation a fool's errand.

What does seem clear is that the Democrats' approach to political and societal issues appears more compatible with Millennial attitudes. This is clearly reflected in that generation's perceptions of the two parties and voting results from the 2004 and 2006 elections. The Democratic Party also seems to have taken the early lead in its willingness and ability to use the new communication technology to create a sophisticated, "Netroots" approach to political campaigning. But all of this is just the tip of the iceberg, both in terms of the use of peer-to-peer technology in political campaigns and in the impact that the Millennial Generation will have on American politics.

One way to think about Millennials, in comparison to the two generations that preceded them, is to picture a generational cohort made up solely of Harry Potter and his friends and then to compare those bright-eyed, overachieving wizards with the adults at Hogwarts, who try to mold their upbringing for good or ill. J. K. Rowling, the author of the series that revolutionized the book industry and sparked a desire to read among an entire generation, shows Harry and his team working hard to do their best within the rules set for them to follow and, of course, using their own special ingenuity to save the world whenever necessary. In this reading, Baby Boomers are the teachers and directors at Hogwarts— every one of them individualistic, judgmental egotists who talk more than they act. A few characters such as Hagrid, not in power but always around to try to help, despite less-than-perfect pasts, represent Generation X, the unlucky group sandwiched between two dynamic and dominating generations (Strauss and Howe 2006). As much as *The Wizard of Oz* was an allegory for the politics of the Populist era of the 1890s, the *Harry Potter* series, in spite of its British origin and setting, provides just the right metaphor for understanding contemporary American politics. And while Rowling understands and captures this dynamic perfectly, many other media moguls, authors, and even politicians make the fundamental error of thinking that today's young people think and act just like they did when they were young. Nothing could be further from the truth.

Radio talk-show host Don Imus was surprised to discover how powerful Millennial values have become when his offensive commentary about the Rutgers University women's basketball team was picked up for all to see and hear on YouTube by a young Millennial activist, Ryan Chiachiere, as part of his job monitoring the media. When the high-achieving African American young women on the team had a chance to demonstrate their character and competence in comparison to the self-absorbed, vulgar comments from one of the favorite radio personalities of Baby Boomers and Generation X, the two networks that aired his program gave Imus a permanent time-out for using decidedly not nice words (Cresscourt 2007).

Baby Boomer antiwar activists were also surprised when polling results showed Millennials to be more supportive of the Iraq War effort than any other generation. On the other side of the political spectrum, some conservative Boomers have been forced to change their tune on global warming, in reaction to the strong environmental focus that young people bring to their religious activism. Both sides fail to see just how much endless arguments over ideas and values turn off a generation of activist doers.

No one understood the mores and values of Generation X better than MTV. Yet today, MTV on the Web is an also-ran to MySpace and YouTube for online hits from Millennials. Prominent Generation X authors have bemoaned the habits and lifestyles of a new generation that has abandoned their own cohort's angst and cynicism. One, Jean M. Twenge, even sought to create a new label, which she called "Generation Me," by combining the results from psychological tests of members of Generation X born in the 1970s with Millennials born after 1982. The result was a sensational but undocumented charge that Millennials were the "most narcissistic generation in modern history" (Twenge 2006, 70).

While Twenge argues that child-rearing practices, such as having babies' names spelled out in twelve-inch-high letters in Millennial nurseries, has led to a generation with too much self-esteem and too much focus on "me," virtually all available survey data contradict her conclusions. Millennials, unlike her own Generation X, are much more likely to feel empathy for others in their group and to seek to understand each person's perspective. Ironically, by introducing her unique and elongated definition of a generation's lifespan and in describing her own supposedly superior approach, Twenge exhibits more narcissistic tendencies than the Millennials she purports to describe. But wishing and hoping that the next generation will see the world the way preceding generations see it is a trait not limited to authors with axes to grind; it's an attitude that infects the way politicians and political parties think and act as well.

Historically, as the generational theorists William Strauss and Neil Howe indicate, there have been two types of dynamic generations, which they first labeled "idealist" and "civic" (Strauss and Howe 1991). Both generational archetypes cause political realignments as they assume positions of power, but the differences between them result in two very different types of political realignments. The members of "idealist"

generations strongly adhere to their own personal values and are unlikely
to compromise what they consider to be fundamental questions of right
and wrong. Realignments fueled by "idealist" generations, of which the
Baby Boomers are the most recent example, therefore, result in decades
of political gridlock, atrophy in governmental institutions, and an inability to resolve big societal and political issues and problems. By contrast,
members of "civic" generations tend to be upbeat, optimistic, and group-
oriented. Realignments based on the emergence of "civic" generations,
of which the Millennials and, in the previous generational cycle, the
GI Generation or "Greatest Generation" are prime examples, result in
periods of new governmental and societal institution-building and in the
resolution of major issues and problems.

There are startling similarities between the events of the last dozen
years and earlier periods in our history that preceded the civic realigning
elections of 1860 and 1932. Author Kurt Andersen's description of
America in 1848, the year when the country "came of age," as he
characterizes it, perfectly captures this period just before major changes
engulfed the country:

> Miraculous new communications technologies have suddenly
> appeared, transforming everyday life. Everything is moving discom-
> bobulatingly fast. Globalization accelerates Wall Street booms. Out-
> side San Francisco, astounding fortunes are made overnight, out of
> nothing, by plucky nobodies. The new media are scurrilous and
> partisan. Marketing spin and advertising extend their influence as
> never before. A fresh urban-youth subculture has emerged, rude and
> vibrant, entertainment-fixated and violence-glorifying. Christian
> conservatives are furiously battling cultural decadence, and one
> popular sect insists that the end days are nigh. Ferocious anti-
> immigration sentiment is on the rise. Both major American political
> parties seem pathetically unable to deal with the looming, urgent
> issue of the day. (Andersen 2007)

Twelve years later, in 1860, the election of Republican Abraham
Lincoln forced the nation to confront the Constitution's fundamental flaw
and reaffirm its belief that "all men are created equal." Once the Civil War
ended and the Union and Confederacy were forever reunited as one
nation, the country experienced unprecedented growth, requiring it to

adjust its political institutions in ways that were unimaginable to most Americans in the years preceding the conflict.

Andersen could just as easily have been describing the America of the 1920s as a precursor to the wave of major change that was to sweep the country in the following decade. The 1932 election put Franklin Roosevelt in office, and his Democratic New Deal policies made the federal government the arbiter of social justice, protecting America's blue-collar workers from the ravages of the Great Depression. Once this system of social welfare had been successfully grafted onto the country's constitutional stock, the nation achieved a level of economic, political, and military dominance that could only have been the stuff of dreams during the 1930s.

Andersen's picture of America could also have portrayed the country in 1996, and the technological and generational changes America is about to experience will be just as dramatic and as equally challenging as those of the 1860s and the 1930s. When those changes become pervasive in society, our democratic institutions will have to respond successfully to the resulting pressures on how we manage the country's affairs, or risk a decline in the quality of our lives and in our nation's values. Whether or not America is able to navigate this current period of rapid change will depend upon how quickly our political institutions can adapt to the realities of the twenty-first century and upon the leadership skills of the next president of the United States.

By 2012 the first half of the entire Millennial Generation, approximately 42 million young Americans, will be eligible to vote. The history of political realignments suggests that the realignment shaped in 2008 by this generation's oldest members will be confirmed and solidified when whoever is elected that year runs for reelection. Just as FDR's landslide victory in 1936 made the Democrats the dominant power in American politics for another thirty years, so too will the party that captures the White House in 2008 have a historic opportunity to become the majority party for at least four more decades.

But the stakes for the country in the outcome of the 2008 election are even higher than for either political party. Regardless of which party successfully recombines the four M's of political campaigns—money, media, message, and messenger—to become the dominant party in the coming realignment, the end result will be major changes in the style, tone, and structure of America's government, politics, and society. If past history is any guide, over the next twenty or thirty years, America will positively and forcefully resolve many of the issues and problems that have concerned it for the past four decades. Which path the country takes in resolving these issues will be determined by the choices Millennials and their technologies help America make in 2008.

PART ONE

Cycles of American Politics

CHAPTER 1

The Rise and Fall of Political Parties in America

ON SUNDAY, MARCH 4, 2007, leaders of the African American community gathered in two churches in Selma, Alabama, to commemorate the forty-second anniversary of the attempted march to Montgomery across the Edmund Pettis Bridge by a group of civil rights activists led by the Reverend Martin Luther King Jr. That nonviolent march was met with police dogs, batons, and fire hoses, and its violent ending so horrified the nation that the Voting Rights Act of 1965 was passed within five months of what came to be known as "Bloody Sunday." Since those historic events of March 1965, two generations of Americans had been born into a country profoundly reshaped by the courage and cause that the congregations had come to celebrate and honor.

Gathering in the same churches that were used on that infamous Sunday, Brown Chapel AME and First Baptist Church of Selma, were living heroes of the nation's civil rights movement, including Congressman John Lewis, who was at the front of the Selma marchers on the bridge in 1965, and those who benefited from their leadership, such as Congressman Artur Davis from Alabama's Seventh Congressional District that encompasses Selma. The congregations each had the privilege of hearing from one of the two leading contenders for the 2008 Democratic presidential nomination—Senators Hillary Clinton and Barack Obama.

Senator Clinton is a member of the Baby Boom Generation, most of whose members were in their teens and twenties at the time of the Selma march. This dynamic and idealistic generation forced the country to confront many of its fundamental beliefs about equality, freedom, and opportunity throughout the 1960s and 1970s. Senator Clinton used her remarks to trace the lineage of Selma's "spirit and logic" to the opportunity for her, as a woman, to seek the presidency of the United States—as well as for New Mexico governor Bill Richardson, a Hispanic, and Senator Barack Obama, an African American, to do the same. She even pointed to a childhood memory of her pastor giving her "a chance to see this phenomenon," the Reverend Martin Luther King Jr., in Chicago, in January 1963. King's speech, she recalled, was on the importance of "Remaining Awake through a Great Revolution," and she took his message on the importance of involvement to heart.

What she didn't talk about was her own political ideology at that time. After seeing Dr. King, she was still motivated to campaign for Republican Barry Goldwater's presidential candidacy in 1964. She did so in spite of the fact that Goldwater based his campaign on his opposition to the Civil Rights Act, enacted that year, which guaranteed blacks legal access to public facilities throughout the country.

But Senator Clinton was not being duplicitous or insincere in the remarks she delivered in Selma. Her clarion call to continue the march "for freedom, justice, opportunity and everything America can be" was very much in line with her generation's commitment to using ideals as the driving force to provide meaning in their lives. The impulse was the same whether it was being exercised by a young woman caught up in the Republican politics of her parents, or the questioning college student who as she matured became just as ardent on behalf of liberal causes, such as civil rights, women's rights, and the anti-Vietnam War movement. For an idealistic Baby Boomer of that era, it was not really a stretch to move from being a conservative Republican to a liberal Democrat in less than five years.

Senator Obama took a different approach to tracing his lineage to the events at the Edmund Pettis Bridge in 1965. He told his audience, in cadences that fit comfortably in that Sunday's church setting, that President John F. Kennedy, as part of the ideological war with Communism, had instituted an exchange program for young Africans to visit the United States so they could see that America was not the nation of hate and discrimination that Bloody Sunday seemed to portray. One of the people selected by the State Department was the son of a houseboy in British colonial Kenya. While in this country he met a woman from Kansas, and their son grew up to become a U.S. senator.

Barack Obama told his Selma audience that his mother's family could trace its American lineage back to "a great, great, great, great grand-father who had owned slaves." This heritage allowed him to make it clear to the audience that he owed his very political existence to that historic day forty-two years ago in Selma. "Don't tell me I'm not coming home when I come to Selma," he shouted to a crowd enraptured with this personal testament to what its sacrifices had made possible.

But the main theme of Obama's remarks on that Sunday was even more poignant and biblical. He compared the efforts of those who led the civil rights movement to leaders of the "Moses Generation" who had led the Hebrew people out of slavery in Egypt. "We are in the presence today of a lot of Moseses, giants whose shoulders we stand on, who battled for America's soul." But, he pointed out, the Bible makes it clear that God did not let Moses cross the River Jordan to see the Promised Land before he died. Instead, all of Moses' generation, and its children as well, had to wander in the desert until a new generation, which Obama called the "Joshua generation," was born. Once that generation was ready to lead the Israelites into battle, they were given permission to enter the land of milk and honey and to engage in the great civic endeavor that created the kingdom of Israel. Obama pointed out that those who followed the heroes of the civil rights movement were very much like that "Joshua generation." The newer generation owed a debt to their own "Moses generation" and to its ideals of "liberty, equality, opportunity and hope" that could never be fully repaid. Nevertheless, it was only the members of a "Joshua generation," who had the new skills and focus needed to close the "gaps" in "educational achievement, health care, empathy, and hope" that still permeated American life.

Obama's remarks were not only politically effective, but insightful in ways that many in his Selma audience and TV viewers across the country may not have appreciated. After first paying homage to the Baby Boomers of the "Moses generation," whose idealism was the spur for the civil rights movement, Obama pointed to the work of another, older generation, the GI Generation, whose values of sacrifice and discipline he constantly praised. His identification of gaps that the "Joshua generation" needed to close between the promise of the civil rights vision and the reality of today's America echoed John F. Kennedy's campaign assertion of a "missile gap" with Russia. Senator Obama's call to "ask not just what our government can do for us, but what we can do for ourselves" had an even more direct connection to the inaugural address of the first GI Generation president of the United States.

Whether Senator Obama was aware of it or not, his remarks in Selma referred to an explanation of American political history based on the concept of generational cycles. According to this explanation, every eighty years or so a civic-oriented generation, like the one he called the "Joshua generation," reappears in America. This civic generation sets about the task of rebuilding or repairing a society that seems to have lost its way, after a period of upheaval caused by the idealistic fervor of a "Moses generation" (such as the Baby Boomers in America's current generational cycle). Although Obama didn't mention it by name, there was another generation in addition to those of Moses and Joshua. This cohort, like all the Israelites, was made to wander in the desert for forty years because the Lord was punishing them for their sins. It, too, has a parallel in America's current generational cycle, Generation X—a generation whose members often felt as if they had to endure a nomadic existence without guidance or support from their parents or from society as a whole (Strauss and Howe 1991, 1997).

But, as Senator Obama realized, the generational cycle of American politics is about to turn again. The newest version of a "Joshua generation" is starting to emerge and make its mark. The two people who literally wrote the book on America's generations, William Strauss and Neil Howe, call this most recent incarnation of a rebuilding civic generation the Millennial Generation (1991, 1997, 2000). The Millennials, whose members were born in the period from 1982 to 2003, possess all the characteristics of the previous "Joshua generations" in American history. By identifying with the rising Millennial Generation, Senator Obama was not only deferentially and personally assuming the mantle of the civil rights movement, he was also speaking to a new generation ready to leave its own distinctive mark on American politics.

THE PERSISTENT PATTERN OF AMERICAN ELECTORAL POLITICS

Since the establishment of the current two-party system, American electoral politics have been characterized by a cyclical pattern of relatively long periods of stability in election outcomes interspersed with shorter periods of decisive and sharp change. While some sort of national crisis that galvanizes the electorate seems to trigger the suddenness of these shifts, the real causes of the phenomenon are the very same underlying generational changes that Strauss and Howe (and the Bible) first described, coupled with significant changes in communication technologies that together cause a dramatic shift in the nation's political dynamics. These forces are now of sufficient size and momentum that the presidential election of 2008 will see a major movement away from our most recent period of relative political stability. America is about to experience another electoral upheaval, or realignment, just as it has every forty years or so throughout its history.

The longer, relatively stable eras in American politics have consistently been eight to ten presidential election cycles (32–40 years) long. During each of these time periods, one political party dominated national politics by winning about three-quarters of the presidential elections contested in that era. Overall, the dominant party in each cycle has won 34 of the 45 (76%) presidential elections contested since 1828. Broadly, there have been five such eras of party dominance in U.S. history:

- 1828–1856—Democrats won 6 of 8 presidential elections (75%)
- 1860–1892—Republicans won 7 of 9 presidential elections (78%)
- 1896–1928—Republicans won 7 of 9 presidential elections (78%)
- 1932–1964—Democrats won 7 of 9 presidential elections (78%)
- 1968–2004—Republicans won 7 of 10 presidential elections (70%)

But what distinguishes each era goes beyond the domination of the electoral process by one of the political parties. During each period the two parties were supported by different electoral coalitions, as specific regional and demographic groups gravitated toward one party or the other. For instance, the Republicans retained their political dominance in the realigning election of 1896, but with a coalition of interests built around the country's emerging industrial economy, not the agricultural and mercantile interests of their previous coalition. Each period was also characterized by unique issue concerns and public policy outputs. For example, certain eras saw a focus on what today would be called social issues; others centered on economic matters. Likewise, certain periods led to an expansion of federal government power and involvement in America's society and economy, and others led to a contraction of federal activity.

Each of these eras of relatively stable party dominance has ended with a sharp and decisive change in electoral results. Political scientists call these periods of major electoral change "critical" or "realigning" elections. Since the patterns underlying these major changes seem to take two or three presidential elections to emerge and fully develop, they are more accurately characterized as "eras."

Historically, American electoral realignments have occurred about thirty-six years apart, centering on the presidential elections of 1828, 1860, 1896, 1932, and 1968. For the most part, these realignments have led to installation of the weaker party during the previous era as the dominant party of the new era. That is what happened in 1828, 1860, 1932, and 1968. But a change in party dominance, while the norm, has not occurred in all realignments. In the era that began in 1896, the Republican Party continued to win most presidential elections, as it had in the earlier era, but with a higher level of electoral support, a changed voter coalition, and a different policy focus than had previously been the case. If these nearly two-century-old cycles of political and electoral ebb and flow hold true to form, America's next political realignment, or makeover, is now under-way and will gain even further momentum in the next few elections.

REALIGNMENT THEORY EMERGES

In 1948, all signs, including most polls, pointed to a Republican vic-tory. The charismatic Franklin Roosevelt, with his radio voice that, according to his GOP opponents, had mesmerized the electorate into voting for Democrats, was dead. His successor, Harry Truman, a decid-edly uncharismatic former Kansas City machine politician, whose faults the Republicans tried to capture with the slogan "To err is Truman," seemed like a much easier person to defeat than FDR. The major crises that had attached Americans to Roosevelt, the Depression and World War II, had ended successfully, presumably enabling voters to return control of the national government to the Republican Party that had largely con-trolled it for the preceding seven decades. Furthermore, in the 1946 midterm elections, the Republicans had swept to victory, capturing con-trol of both houses of Congress for the first time since 1930. The results of the 1948 campaign seemed so pre-ordained that the *Chicago Daily Tri-bune* heralded Truman's defeat in its first post-election headline, even before all the results were in.

But Tom Dewey never became president, and the Democratic victory compelled historians and political scientists to move away from analyzing the outcomes of elections based on candidate personalities and the particular issues of the times, and to search instead for broader explanations. The result was realignment theory, which gave observers a means of viewing and interpreting American elections by seeing them not as almost totally unconnected, idiosyncratic events, but as part of broader historical patterns (Rosenof 2003).

Among the first to mention these cycles were the Arthur Schlesingers. Arthur Schlesinger Sr. described alternating eras throughout American history of "liberalism" (emphasis on advancing public purposes) and "conservatism" (emphasis on the freedom to pursue private interests) (1922). Arthur Schlesinger Jr. built on his father's work and wrote in 1986 about the cyclical recurrence of historical periods of "public energy" and "private interest."

In 1955, political scientist V. O. Key coined the term "critical election" to designate a specific election in which electoral patterns change dramatically for several decades. Key described the cycles of long-term stability and periodic, quick, decisive change that have characterized American electoral history and listed the "critical elections" that had occurred to that point. His work became the foundation upon which all subsequent realignment analyses, including this book, were built (Key 1955).

How to Recognize a Realignment When You See One

Many of the early analyses of realignments conducted in the 1950s and 1960s were based on examinations of the Democratic New Deal realignment of the 1930s, and utilized data from voter attitude studies conducted each presidential election year by the University of Michigan Survey Research Center, beginning in 1948. These analyses led to broad agreement among early observers about the primary features of the recurring cycles of stability and sharp change, which have characterized America's elections and political system almost since its beginning.

As noted, in the earlier periods of electoral stability, the dominant political party won about 75 percent of presidential elections. Furthermore, the percentage of the national presidential popular vote received by each of the major parties varied only slightly across each period of electoral stability. Historically, the dominant party has won, on average, about 51 percent of the national popular vote during each such era; and its vote in most elections throughout a stable era ranged by no more than four or five percentage points from that average.

Those election outcomes were attributed to what was seen as the most powerful explanation of voting behavior—party identification. The percentage of Americans who identified with, and normally voted for, the candidates of each party remained broadly constant throughout each stable era, as did the set of regional, racial, ethnic, religious, and social class groups that together formed each party's voting coalition. In this formulation, most people developed their identification with a political party, usually that of their parents, at a young age. That identification provided a lens through which politics was viewed and interpreted and a guide to shape voting choices. Because party identification rarely changed throughout the lives of most individuals, the identifications provided a significant degree of inertia to electoral results and, in effect, kept the stable eras in place (Campbell et al. 1960, 1966).

From the 1930s through the early 1960s, for example, about half of the electorate identified themselves as Democrats, around a third as Republicans, and a quarter as Independents. During this period, Democratic identifiers and voters were disproportionately southern whites, northern Catholics and Jews, blacks, and those with blue-collar occupations. The smaller, less diverse set of Republican identifiers and voters were centered among northern white Protestants, especially those with white-collar jobs. Because the number of identifiers in the Democratic coalition was consistently larger than that of the Republicans, the Democratic Party was able to dominate national politics throughout this period.

The early analysts also broadly agreed about the characteristics of the realignments that inevitably ended each stable era.

First, realignments were seen as comparatively rare events. At the time in the 1950s and 1960s when analysts first began to study realignments, there was consensus that there had been only four previous realignments throughout two centuries of American history, centered on the presidential elections of 1828, 1860, 1896, and 1932.

Second, in comparison with the periods of broad stability, realignments were quite brief. At first, observers suggested that single decisive elections produced realignments. Later, analysts came to believe that the trends underlying and producing realignments more likely took place over the course of several elections and should be referred to as realigning "eras" rather than realigning "elections."

For example, many observers believe that the Civil War realignment began with the emergence of the Republican Party in the mid-1850s and culminated with the election of Abraham Lincoln in 1860. Analysts also say that the New Deal realignment properly began in 1928 with the Democratic nomination of Al Smith, a Roman Catholic. That event brought many eastern and southern European immigrants into the electorate as Democrats. The realignment was then cemented in place in 1936 with a vote that was based far more strongly on social class voting than in previous elections. The Republican realignment of the late 1960s is seen by many as actually starting in 1964, when five Deep South states voted for Republican Barry Goldwater. However, in comparison to eras of political stability, realignments were seen as short in duration, spanning no more than two or three presidential election cycles, or eight to twelve years.

Third, analysts believed realignments were precipitated by the disruption of the long-standing distribution of party identifiers, and the resulting coalitions that had underpinned the previous period of electoral stability. To an extent, members of some groups that had previously identified with, and voted for, one of the parties moved toward the other. Perhaps more frequently, groups that had been relatively inactive politically came into the electorate in large numbers to support one of the parties, giving that party a decisive edge in an otherwise closely divided electorate. For example, there is evidence that, in the realignment of the 1930s, black voters deserted the Republican Party, which they had preferred since the time of Abraham Lincoln, and moved toward the Democrats. And many eastern and southern European Catholic and Jewish immigrants and their children began to vote for the first time during this era—the vast majority of them for the Democrats.

Finally, realignments are temporally associated with a severe social or economic crisis, such as the Civil War or a major depression, events seen as necessary to disrupt the standing party and group identifications that underpinned the eras of stability. Because they were linked to major crises, realignments were also seen as events in which issue-voting was preeminent and voter turnout increased substantially.

Due to this linkage to national crises and issue voting, realignments have resulted in major changes in public policy. The realignment of the 1930s instituted more than three decades of governmental activism in issue areas as diverse as the economy, race relations, and international affairs. All these progressive ideas stood in sharp contrast to the laissez-faire economic policies that dominated American politics in the decades following the realigning election of 1896, and the policies of limited governmental regulation and low taxation since 1968.

Realignment theory also pointed to the remarkable regularity of such makeovers throughout American history. Broadly, political realignments have taken place in the United States every thirty-two to forty years. They have occurred with such regularity that it seemed highly unlikely in the 1950s and 1960s for the phenomenon to be simply coincidental. Political observers waited with great expectations for the cycle to repeat itself in the late sixties or early seventies.

THE END OF REALIGNMENT THEORY AS WE KNEW IT?

In some important ways, what happened in a series of presidential elections, centering on that of 1968, did indeed fit the tenets of realignment theory. The previously weaker political party, in this case the Republicans, won seven of ten presidential elections, ending a similar string of Democratic presidential election victories that had started in 1932. Moreover, as in previous realignments, the contours of the voting coalitions of the two parties were altered on a long-term basis. The once solid Democratic South now became the solid Republican South. The Rocky Mountain and Prairie West, which in the realignments of the 1890s and 1930s had been strongly Democratic, became overwhelmingly Republican. The Northeast, especially New England, and the upper Midwest, which had been the most Republican regions of the country in earlier realignments, now became the country's most strongly Democratic. In the terminology of today's television networks, the red states became blue states and the blue states became red states.

At the same time, in a number of other significant respects, the political dynamics that began in 1968 did not resemble those of the New Deal realignment, or perhaps earlier ones. In previous realignments the newly dominant party won control of both the presidency and Congress from the start. By contrast, the Democrats generally continued to control both houses of Congress from 1968 until 1994.

Moreover, the influence of party identification seemed to change after 1968. In earlier eras the large majority of Americans identified with one or the other of the two political parties. Starting in 1968, however, increasing numbers of Americans identified themselves as Independents, while the number seeing themselves as Republicans or Democrats declined. In the attitude surveys of the 1950s and early 1960s, about one-quarter of the electorate identified themselves as Independents. By 1972, more than a third claimed to be Independents, and, beginning in the late 1980s, four in ten did so.

Also, while the Republican Party won most presidential elections after 1968, it never established a lead in party identification. Through the early 1970s, Democratic identifiers outnumbered Republicans by about a 1.6:1 ratio. From the 1980s into the first decade of the twenty-first century, slightly more than a third of Americans consistently identified themselves as Democrats, slightly less than three in ten as Republicans, and a plurality of nearly four in ten as Independents. In this environment, split-ticket voting became far more common than before, and the importance of candidate imagery, issues, and ideology gained in importance in shaping voting decisions, while that of party identification receded.

All these factors, along with a sharp decline in voter turnout, appeared to undercut the validity and usefulness of realignment theory in explaining electoral outcomes and understanding their meaning in American history. Because what happened in 1968 and the decades that followed was so different from what had occurred in the 1930s, many observers doubted that a "realignment" had even taken place. Writing in 1991, political scientist Everett Carll Ladd said that for many, waiting for the next realignment had become as frustrating as "waiting for Godot" (Shafer 1991). Or as columnist David Broder wrote in 1978, "We are now in the fifth decade since the last realignment—two or three elections past the point at which the cycle should have produced a new mandate and a clear governing coalition" (Lipset 1978).

There are two basic approaches taken by those who have attacked realignment theory. David Mayhew dismisses realignment theory almost entirely as a useful means of viewing American elections and politics (Mayhew 2002), a criticism that one defender of realignment theory labels as overly rigid and "hyperquantitative," for ignoring evidence other than voting results as indicators of possible realignments (Paulson 2007, 12). The other, more indirect criticism of realignment theory maintains that the period since 1968 is one of electoral and party "dealignment" rather than realignment. For this reason, the second set of critics argue that a theory based on the concept of realignment neither accurately describes nor explains what happened in American politics in the last third of the twentieth century, and perhaps at other times as well (Burnham 1970; Ladd 1978).

The most cogent current defender of realignment theory, political scientist Arthur Paulson, acknowledges that the characteristics of the electoral changes that have occurred during and after the late 1960s were different from those of the 1930s. However, he says all criticisms of the theory "share two faults in their approach to realignment. They attribute to realignment theory observations that are not necessarily definitive of the concept of realignment, or essential to the theory; and both treatments render the concept of realignment ahistorical" (2007, 11). In other words, Paulson maintains that the critics misstate at least some of the key elements of realignment theory and do not properly view American elections from a broader historical context.

Paulson does acknowledge the "dealignment" and "disaggregation" that have characterized American elections during the last three decades, but labels this as "realignment by other means" (11). He states that electoral realignment and disaggregation are not mutually exclusive and that dealignment is not necessarily an irreversible process. Paulson summarizes his argument this way: "However altered the form of its appearance, realignment remains a useful analytical tool. Regardless of terminology, very significant electoral change in the 1960s and another wave of change that seems to be developing at the turn of the century would indicate that a periodic sea change in aggregate voting behavior remains characteristic of the American political system" (20).

Paulson also points out that what happened in the 1960s and beyond does have many of the characteristics of realignment as it is described in the original theory. In fact, he argues, this era marks the "most compelling electoral realignment in American history" because of the decisive inversion of party electoral coalitions, as the South and Prairie and Rocky Mountain West became the most Republican regions of the country and the Northeast and upper Midwest the most Democratic. Paulson further points to a major change in America's "policy agenda" as the country shifted from New Deal liberalism to conservatism in most areas as another indication of realignment. Finally, he argues that the realignment was eventually completed, however long it may have taken, when it moved from the "top" (the presidency) in 1968 to the "bottom" (Congress) in the 1994 midterm elections (2007, 23–25).

A Better Realignment Theory Emerges

Paulson is right. Realignment theory remains meaningful and useful. Massive electoral and political change or realignments have occurred throughout American history and are very likely to occur again in the very near future. These realignments have taken place on a regular or periodic basis that is too obvious to ignore or to attribute simply to chance. They have resulted in major transformations of party voting coalitions and public policy.

The critics also have a point. Not all realignments are the same. Most, but not all, have reversed the fortunes of the political parties, making the formerly weaker of the two the dominant one. Some realignments have resulted in long-term increases in voter participation, and others have produced declines. Some realignments have enhanced the importance of political party identification as a factor shaping voting choices, and others have lessened its importance. Some have led to increased straight-ticket voting, and others to greater split-ticket voting. And while all have resulted in important policy changes, the direction and type of those changes vary from one realignment to another.

But the theory of political realignment is actually strengthened, not weakened, when it is reexamined and reformulated to take into account these differences, so that all the historical facts once again fit the general theory. To do so requires bringing to the surface, and carefully examining, the underlying forces that regularly and consistently reshape American politics.

Technological + Generational Change = Realignment

Historically, most realignments have been temporally associated with some of the major crises in American history: the Civil War, the

Depressions of 1893 and 1929, and the racial, anti–Vietnam War, and countercultural ferment of the 1960s and 1970s. However, while these crucial events triggered the specific timing of the realignments, underlying changes in generational size and attitudes and advances in communication technology are the real driving forces of this constant, and predictable, shift in the fortunes of America's political parties.

Technology serves to enable these changes by creating powerful new ways to reach new generations of voters with messages that relate directly to their concerns. But without the emergence of new generations with new attitudes and beliefs, as well as a passion for using these new technologies, neither the telegraph and telephone of the nineteenth century, nor the broadcast media of radio and television in the twentieth century, nor even this century's Internet and mobile communication capabilities would be able to make any real difference in American politics. To understand why America's political cycles exist and will persist, it is particularly important to understand the cycles of generational change that underpin and ultimately produce political realignments.

GENERATIONAL CHANGE IS THE KEY TO POLITICAL REALIGNMENT

While a few of the earliest realignment theorists believed that realignments were largely based on the massive conversion of voters from one party to the other, it soon became clear that the emergence into the electorate of large numbers of new voters, most of whom are young and identify with and vote for the candidates of one party, is what really underpins America's political realignments.

Samuel Lubell (1952), in a chapter entitled "A Little Matter of Birthrates," provides a colorful portrait of the way in which the emergence of a large new generation can sharply alter the political order. He describes the coming-of-age of the large GI Generation, in particular the ethnic, heavily Catholic and Jewish component of that generation and how this sizable generation identified with and voted for Franklin Roosevelt and other Democrats, thereby overwhelming the smaller and more Republican older generations. He quotes from his 1940 conversation with John Kryzinski, a Buffalo tavern keeper and Democratic precinct captain, who clearly saw in microcosm how this new, large generation was turning things around politically: "Out in ritzy Humboldt Park they get two voters to a family. I get six out of my house. I got neighbors who give me eight" (1952, 52). What happened in Buffalo in the 1930s has happened almost universally in every realignment, before and since.

The writings of seminal generational theorists, William Strauss and Neil Howe, are particularly useful in providing an understanding of the impact of generational change on electoral realignments. In their books *Generations* and *The Fourth Turning*, Strauss and Howe describe a recurring cyclical pattern of four generational types that has existed throughout American history. Each generation, in particular those that have been born since the United States became an independent country, is, on average, a bit more than twenty-two years long, meaning that each complete cycle is about eighty-eight to eighty-nine years in length. According to Strauss and Howe, America is now in its fifth historical generational cycle, the "Millennial Cycle," which began around 1967 and won't be complete until about 2050 (1991, 1997).

With one exception, the nineteenth-century cycle that Strauss and Howe call the Civil War cycle, each cycle has consisted of four generational types that recur in the same order. Each generational type has a characteristic set of attitudes and behaviors that is broadly similar, regardless of where in American history it appears.

- "Idealist." This is a "dominant and inner-fixated" generational type. Idealists are reared in an indulgent manner and are driven throughout their lives by their deeply held values. Baby Boomers are the Idealist generation in America's current Millennial generational cycle.
- "Reactive." A recessive generation that, because of its unprotected rearing, is more often than not criticized and condemned; it tends to become alienated, risk-taking, entrepreneurial, and pragmatic in adulthood. In the current generational cycle, Generation X represents the Reactive type.
- "Civic." A generational type described as "dominant and outer-fixated." The members of this generational type are reared in a highly protected manner so that an orientation to societal challenges, problem solving, and institution building marks their adult lives. The Millennial Generation is the Civic generation of the current cycle, as the GI Generation was of the previous one.

- "Adaptive." Another "recessive" generation type, but one raised in an overprotected and suffocating way, which tends to make them risk averse, conformist, and inclined toward compromise. In the current generational cycle, the members of the Adaptive Generation are children born since 2003 and still too young to be in kindergarten. They have not yet been given a specific name. In the previous generational cycle, the Silent Generation, born from 1925 to around 1945, the only generation in U.S. history to have failed so far to elect a president from its own generation, was the Adaptive type.

It is not a coincidence that all U.S. political realignments have occurred in what Strauss and Howe label the second and fourth "turnings" in generational cycles. These are periods in which the more "dynamic" or "dominant" and outgoing generational types—the moralistic, value-driven "idealists" and the problem-solving, constructive "civics"—are entering positions of influence and eventual control as young adults.

One feature that all the eras of dynamic change have in common is that they were invariably preceded by greater-than-average population growth for their era, both from births and immigration. That, in turn, gives the two "dynamic" or "dominant" generational types the numbers to alter the political process and to produce electoral realignments.

While throughout the course of U.S. history birth rates have drifted downward, they have normally risen in the decennial censuses taken about twenty years before the realigning generations first came of age politically (for example in 1910 for the GI Generation, in 1950 for the Baby Boomers, and in 1990 for the Millennials). Consequently, all the generations leading the way in political realignments were at least 15 percent and sometimes as much as 60 percent larger than the generations preceding them in the generational cycle.

Similarly, the two or three decades before realignments have generally been characterized by rising immigration. As a result, the generations that are born and come of age in the generational cycle before the realigning generations, that is, the parents or grandparents of the realigning generations, have typically contained the greatest percentages of immigrants.

WHAT A DIFFERENCE AN ARCHETYPE MAKES

But there are also important differences between the two types of "turnings." The realignments induced by the rise of "idealists" and those produced by the emergence of a "civic" generation have far different results both in the attitudes and behavior of the electorate and in public policy. Idealist realignments tend to be associated with the very elements that many of the critics of realignment theory describe as "disaggregation" or "dealignment." Within the electorate, these involve increased independent party identifications and split-ticket voting, low voter turnout, negative attitudes toward politics and political institutions, and a focus on divisive social issues involving such concerns as substance use, sexual behavior, and socially acceptable roles for women and men. In the public policy arena, idealist realignments tend to lead to gridlock, limited use of and even decline in the national government, and greater economic inequality.

By contrast, civic realignments are characterized by enhanced party identification and straight-ticket voting, rising voter turnout or stable turnout at high levels, positive attitudes toward politics and political institutions, and a focus on broader societal and economic concerns rather than social issues involving personal morality. This type of realignment results in public policies that rely, to a significant degree, on the national government to deal with major societal and economic concerns, institution building, and a greater degree of economic equality.

To fully understand the differences between idealist and civic realignments, it is important to note that the two types of realignments are not historically linked to, or inevitably associated with, either of America's political parties. Both the Democratic Party (1828) and the Republican Party (1896 and 1968) have led previous idealist realignments. Likewise, both the Republicans and the Democrats have spurred and been the beneficiaries of civic realignments in the past—the former in 1860 and the latter in 1932. It is their differential impact on such factors as voting participation, attitudes toward the political process, and public policy, and not their partisan direction that distinguishes idealist and civic realignments from one another. Depending on the way in which the two parties position themselves on issues and the type of candidates they nominate, either party (or perhaps even a brand new one)

TABLE I

Major Characteristics of Idealist and Civic Realignments

	Idealist Realignment	Civic Realignment
Attitudes and Behavior of the Electorate		
	Independent party identification and split-ticket voting	Identification with specific political parties and straight-ticket voting
	Declining and low voter turnout	Rising voter turnout and/or maintenance of turnout at high levels
	Negative attitudes toward politics and political institutions	Positive attitudes toward politics and political institutions
	Focus on divisive social issues, often involving personal lifestyle, such as substance use, immigration, feminism, and sexual behavior	Focus on broader societal and economic issues
	Exclusionary racial and ethnic concerns	Inclusive racial and ethnic concerns
Public Policy Outputs		
	Gridlock, limited expansion or decay of political and governmental institutions	Greater ability of political process to deal with major concerns and institution building
	Greater economic inequality and relatively large income and wealth disparities	Greater economic equality and relatively small income and wealth disparities

could lead an idealist or civic realignment in the future, just as they have in the past.

Nor are the two types of realignments tied to any particular ideology. To use contemporary terminology, they are neither inherently liberal nor conservative. In idealist eras, politics are primarily driven by politically centered efforts to achieve or defend deeply held values above all other political goals. This means, for example, that disputes over appropriate sex roles for women, or race relations, have featured idealists on both sides. On one side, there were idealist liberals who, among other things, battled for equal employment opportunities for women, abolition of slavery, or racial equality. Against them stood idealist conservatives, who contended, for example, that the most appropriate and important roles for women are homemaking and motherhood, or that slavery and/or racial segregation was the natural and appropriate order of things. And it also means that during the civic era after World War II, for instance, conservatives such as Barry Goldwater and liberals such as Hubert Humphrey could support with equal vigor the maintenance, or even the growth of, federal institutions, such as the military, the space program, and the interstate highway system, especially if those institutions could be tied to major causes such as the Cold War against Communism.

The accompanying table outlines the differences between idealist and civic realignments along the two critical dimensions in which they differ and makes clear the historical validity of a revised realignment theory that accounts for these differences. The similarities and differences in civic and idealist realignments explain a great deal about the history of American politics and, at the same time, provide a powerful lens for examining its future.

CHAPTER 2

Idealist and Civic Eras in American History

THROUGHOUT ITS HISTORY, America has experienced major political upheavals, or realignments, about every four decades. These realignments are caused by the coming of age of a new generation and the development of a new communications technology that is particularly appealing to the emerging generation. The differing characteristics of the emerging generation produce two very distinctive types of political realignments: civic and idealist. A civic realignment is strongly centered on cooperative efforts to resolve societal problems and build institutions because those are the typical attitudes and values of a civic archetype generation. Idealist realignments, in line with the beliefs of that generational archetype, are driven by attempts to use the political process to achieve or defend deeply held personal values above all else.

While in certain respects what happens during and after civic and idealist realignments is similar, in many other important ways the results that flow from the two types of political realignment are very different. In seeking to understand these similarities and differences it is important to remember that neither type of realignment refers to a particular partisan or ideological direction. Throughout the course of American history, the Democratic and Republican Parties have both led idealist and civic realignments. Both liberals and conservatives have, at various times, supported the strong political adherence to personal values that characterize idealist eras and the problem resolution and institution building that mark civic eras. But the similarities and differences between the two types of realignments do reveal what will happen to the nation's politics during the next three or four decades, no matter which candidate or party takes advantage of the changes that are about to occur.

REALIGNMENTS BRING PEOPLE
TO THE POLLS

Because of the sheer size of the realigning generations, and also because the realignments are triggered by major societal crises, both idealist and civic realignments are often accompanied by a sharp initial increase in voter turnout. In 1828 nearly 60 percent of the voting-age population turned out at the polls, up sharply from about 25 percent in 1824. In the civic realigning era centering on the 1860 election, voter turnout rose from 70 percent in 1852 to 79 percent in 1856 to 81 percent in 1860. Turnout also increased in the next idealist realignment in the last decade of the nineteenth century, rising from 75 percent of the voting age population in 1892 to 79 percent in 1896. In the New Deal realigning era, participation rates rose from only 49 percent in 1924 to 57 percent in 1928 before falling back to 53 percent in 1932 and then rising to 57 percent again in 1936. Voting participation did not increase in 1968, but it did remain at nearly the same relatively high percentage of the voting population (61%) that it was in both 1960 (63%) and 1964 (62%). The percentage of voting-age Americans who cast presidential ballots in 1968 was greater than it had been in 1956 (59%), and well above what it was in 1948 (51%). Based on these historical precedents, voter turnout is likely to rise, in 2008, as it did in 2004 and 2006, and to maintain that level of participation, or even rise again, in 2012.

REALIGNMENTS BREAK UP THE OLD GANGS
AND CREATE NEW ONES

The idealist realignments of 1828, 1896, and 1968 and the civic realignments of 1860 and 1932 all led to the creation of a clear and stable set of party coalitions, which held together for decades until they were once again altered in the next realignment. In the 1828 realignment, Andrew Jackson's agrarian Democrats, centered in the South and West, were the heart of Old Hickory's constituencies, while the commercial and industrially oriented Whigs, centered in the Northeast and especially in New England, fought him tooth and nail. These two coalitions differed not only in the economic interests they represented but also in the more traditional values Democrats endorsed in contrast with the Whig's promotion of modern values (Lipset 1978).

The coalitions shifted somewhat in the 1860 civic realignment. The South, especially with the end of Reconstruction, became overwhelmingly

Democratic, while the New England states were as reliably Republican. With an eye to winning the West's political loyalties, Lincoln's Republicans passed legislation such as the Homestead and Land Grant College Acts, which successfully brought that region into their coalition. The Northeast, upper Midwest, and border states were more competitive, but the first two regions were generally Republican and the latter leaned Democratic until the idealist realignment of 1896.

That realignment essentially recreated the coalitions that had first appeared in 1828 and which had been greatly weakened in the civic Civil War realignment. The Republican coalition, once again, centered on the urban industrial states of the Northeast, in particular those of New England and the upper Midwest. The Democrats dominated the South and, thanks to the rhetoric and easy money policies favored by William Jennings Bryan, became strong in the Plains and Rocky Mountain states. In this realignment, as in the first idealist realignment, the Democrats continued to reflect tradition and the Republicans modernity.

The New Deal realignment, centered on the 1932 presidential election, also led to the alteration of old voting coalitions and the building of new ones. At its outset, the South and Rocky Mountain West were the most strongly Democratic, and the upper Midwest and especially New England were the most Republican regions. But reflecting Industrial Age economic divisions, in this realignment the new coalitions also had class as well as regional components. A large majority of blue-collar workers allied with the Democratic Party, while white-collar workers attached themselves to the Republicans. Catholics, Jews, and African Americans became key members of the Democratic coalition, and northern white Protestants tended to be Republicans.

The idealist 1968 realignment completely turned America's electoral map around, reversing the coalitions of the earlier idealist realignments of 1828 and 1896. The South and West became the Republican heartland, and the Northeast and upper Midwest the strongest Democratic regions. In one sense, things did remain the same as they had been earlier: the South and West were the regions of traditionalism and the Northeast and upper Midwest the centers of modernity. As a result of this realignment, however, the Democrats became the party that embraced modern mores, and their opponents, this time the Republicans rather than the Whigs, became the party that promoted traditional values.

There was movement within the electorate in 1968 as well. The class-based New Deal coalition established in the 1930s bent and in many instances broke. Jews and African Americans increased their already strong ties to the Democrats, with the latter group becoming about 90 percent Democratic. Catholics, a group that was about as loyal to the Democrats in the New Deal coalition as were Jews and African Americans, became an evenly divided set of swing voters after 1968, an important component of what were frequently referred to, in the 1980s, as "Reagan Democrats." Meanwhile, white Protestants, especially Evangelicals, identified and voted Republican even more strongly than before. Instead of a clean demarcation based upon social class, after 1968 Republican support became greatest among those with moderate incomes and education levels. Meanwhile, Democrats did best among both the very poorest and least educated and those with higher incomes and postgraduate education. The emphasis on social issues, such as abortion, helped to drive apart the class basis of American political coalitions and establish ones built more on faith and values than economic interests.

Party coalitions will almost certainly shift once again in the coming civic realignment, just as they have in all previous realignments. From a regional perspective, this most likely means that the South, which has often voted in opposition to much of the rest of the country, will likely remain a GOP stronghold. The Northeast, upper Midwest, and Pacific Coast states may well increase their support for the Democratic Party. The decisive region, as it has been in several previous realignments, may be the western states, especially those in the Southwest. The coming realignment will also have a clear ethnic component as America's growing Hispanic and Asian populations choose a party. But in the end, all this movement will be based, as it always has been throughout U.S. history, on the coming of age of a new generation—this time the Millennial Generation. As Millennials firm up what will become a lifelong allegiance to one of the two parties, they will put in place partisan coalitions that will shape American politics and government for the next forty years.

Voters Stay Interested in Civic-Era Politics

While all realignments are initially accompanied and produced by increased turnout, voter participation eventually declines significantly after idealist realignments but remains at high levels or even increases after civic realignments. After the idealist 1828 Jacksonian realignment, voting participation steadily dropped from a high of about 80 percent in the 1840 presidential election to a low of less than 70 percent in 1852. Similarly, voter participation declined almost immediately after the idealist 1896 realigning election. Starting in 1900, the percentage of the voting-age population that cast ballots declined every presidential election over the next three decades, eventually falling from 79 percent in 1896 to only 49 percent in 1924. Finally, as with all other idealist realignments, voter turnout began to drop sharply immediately following the 1968 presidential election, falling by more than five percentage points in 1972 and eventually reaching the same low point in 1996 as in 1924.

By contrast, voter turnout remained at high levels throughout the thirty to forty years following America's two previous civic realignments. From 1860 through 1892 electoral turnout dropped below three-quarters of the voting-age population in only two elections, and then only slightly—1864 (74%), as a result of the inability of many soldiers to vote during the Civil War, and 1872 (71%), when three southern states did not participate in that year's presidential election. In the New Deal realignment, turnout rates actually increased after 1932 and, with one exception (1948), remained at around 60 percent through 1968, peaking at 63 percent in the tight Kennedy-Nixon race of 1960.

The United States should experience continued high levels of voter participation for at least the next two or three decades, as the Millennial Generation joins the electorate in unprecedented numbers and votes at rates comparable to, if not greater than, their generational predecessors. Many different groups and causes will try to claim responsibility for this reversal in civic life, but generational cycles should be given most of the credit.

IDEALISTS ARE INDEPENDENT DIVIDERS; CIVICS ARE PARTISAN UNIFIERS

Divided control of the national government was more frequent after the 1828, 1896, and 1968 idealist realignments than at other times in American history, although the timing of divided government was different in each of the three eras. After the 1828 idealist realignment, divided government increased markedly beginning in the 1840s. While the same political party controlled the presidency and both houses of Congress in six of the seven Congresses from 1829 to 1842, starting in 1843 there was divided government in six of nine Congresses. Divided government was less frequent following the 1896 idealist realignment than after any other of that type, occurring in only four of eighteen Congresses from 1897 to 1933. Three occurred when the era's dominant Republican Party split, leading to the rise of the Progressive Party and the election of Democrat Woodrow Wilson in 1912 and 1916. The final occurrence of divided government in this idealist period took place in its last Congress, elected in 1930 on the cusp of the coming New Deal realignment. By contrast, divided government was the norm from the very beginning of the idealist realignment centering on the 1968 election. It existed in fourteen of the twenty Congresses during this era, primarily because the South continued to elect conservative Democrats with great seniority to Congress early in the era, even after that region had become strongly Republican in most presidential elections.

After civic realignments, unified government is the norm. Divided control of the national government did occur from time to time during the period of close elections following the Civil War realignment of 1860, but it was rarer than in the previous idealist era. From 1861 through 1895, the same party controlled the presidency and the House of Representatives in twelve of eighteen Congresses. Almost all instances of divided government during this period came in sessions of Congress that met after midterm elections when the party that did not hold the presidency made sufficient gains in House campaigns to gain control of that body. In years when both the president and the House were elected, the same party won the presidency and House in eight of nine elections. The one exception to all this actually proves the rule. It occurred in 1876, at about the midpoint of that idealist political era, when Democrat Samuel Tilden won the presidential popular vote and the Democrats won the House, but Republican Rutherford Hayes won the presidency as a result of a Republican compromise with southern Democrats that ended Reconstruction. There would only be one other electoral vote winner and popular vote loser until the 2000 election, more than halfway through our most recent idealist era.

After the civic New Deal realignment, unified government was particularly prevalent, existing in fifteen of nineteen Congresses from 1933 to 1969. The first exception was the Republican Congress elected in 1946, when voters answered affirmatively to the Republican campaign slogan, "Had enough?" The others occurred in the last three Congresses of the Eisenhower administration when voters said that they still "liked Ike" but adhered to the norm of the New Deal era by electing Democratic Congresses in 1954, 1956, and 1958.

Idealist realignments lead to an increase in the number of voters who label themselves Independents and an increase in split-ticket voting, sometimes leading to the temporary rise of third parties. Civic realignments, by contrast, lead to an increase in the frequency with which voters identify with one of the two parties and in straight-ticket voting. University of Michigan Survey Research Center data indicates that independent identifications increased from around a quarter of the electorate after the New Deal realignment to about four in ten after the idealist 1968 realignment. The frequency of split-ticket voting also doubled during that period—from about a third of the electorate in 1956 and 1960 to two-thirds in 1972. Finally, around four in ten voters considered themselves to be strongly identified with one of the parties during the civic New Deal alignment of the 1950s and early 1960s; in 1972, after the occurrence of the idealist realignment of 1968, only a quarter did so (Nie, Verba, and Petrocik 1976).

Without survey research data, we cannot be certain about the distribution of party identification or the frequency of split-ticket voting in the aftermath of the two earlier idealist realignments. However, one analyst, using data from University of Michigan surveys conducted in the 1950s and 1960s, estimates that there were about the same percentage of Independents in the electorate in the 1920s as in the 1980s, in each case about twenty years after an idealist realignment (94). Given the frequency of divided government starting in the 1840s, it is reasonable to assume that attachments to the two parties weakened and split-ticket voting increased in the decades after the 1828 idealist realignment as well.

With a civic realignment now on the horizon, the same political party is likely to enjoy majorities in both houses of Congress and gain control of the presidency much more frequently than in the past forty years. Which party that will be remains to be seen.

GOVERNMENT IS GOOD IN CIVIC ERAS,
BAD IN IDEALIST ONES

Attitudes toward virtually all political institutions become more negative over time as a result of idealist realignments. They become more positive following civic realignments. In the late 1950s, nearly thirty years after the civic New Deal realignment and about a decade before the idealist 1968 realignment, more than two-thirds of Americans held positive attitudes toward at least one of the political parties. By 1972, a majority had negative perceptions about both the Republicans and Democrats. Toward the end of the New Deal era, two-thirds of Americans also believed that public officials care what most people think and eight in ten felt that government is run for the benefit of all. In 2006, two-thirds believed that special interests, not the people, usually get their way in government, and only one in ten said that politicians care about what people like themselves think (Frank N. Magid Associates, January 2006). Without polling data, it isn't possible to know exactly how upbeat voters in the middle of the nineteenth and early twentieth centuries were about government and politics. However, the drop in voting participation during those periods certainly suggests the likelihood that feelings of political efficacy declined at those times as well. If America's history is a guide, as hard as it is to believe during the current idealist setting of discouragement and disdain for politics and government, the coming civic realignment will lead to more positive attitudes toward the country's national institutions.

These negative attitudes during idealist eras toward political institutions, including political parties, also create a fertile field for third-party movements. The Populist Party in the late nineteenth century and George Wallace's American Independent Party in 1968 gained strength as a civic era came to a close and a new idealist generation first began to make itself felt in national elections. Wallace indicated his disdain for the two major parties by proclaiming, "There ain't a dime's worth of difference" between the Democrats and Republicans. Both Wallace and the Populists found energy for their rebellion against the elite from the same type of voter—what we have referred to as "traditionalists" (especially from rural areas, small towns, and the South and/or West). They were on the side of the "little guy" who worked hard for a living, as opposed to, in the words of Wallace, "pointy headed intellectuals who can't even park a bicycle straight," "bearded, briefcase totin' bureaucrats," and student protestors who "if they lay down in front of [his] car, it would be the last time they laid down in front of anybody's car." The earlier Populist rebellion had an equally emotional tone, excoriating Wall Street bankers, or "Shylocks," who made money by manipulating money. One Populist leader urged farmers to "raise less corn and more Hell" and another demonstrated how he would "stick a pitchfork in Grover Cleveland's ribs."

By contrast, the Progressive/Bull Moose (1912) and Perot (1992) candidacies occurred near the middle of idealist eras. Ralph Nader's quixotic Green Party candidacy in 2000 was closer to the end of one. But all three had a quieter tone and a more reformist approach than the more visceral Populist and Wallace rebellions against elitist culture and economics.

Regardless of their tone, however, third-party movements have occurred more frequently in idealist than in civic eras. Most likely because voter ties to the major parties are softer in idealist than in civic eras, third parties have also had a larger impact on electoral results in the former than in the latter. In several idealist-era presidential elections, those of 1912, 2000, and, according to some observers, 1992, third-party candidates siphoned off enough votes from one of the major parties to deny that party's nominee a victory he may well have won otherwise.

Third-party protests do occasionally rise in civic eras, although less frequently than in idealist eras. Examples are the Greenback Party in 1880 and the Progressive and State's Rights Parties in 1948. In neither instance did the third (or fourth) parties deny one of the major parties a presidential victory. This is because voter ties to the major parties are especially high in civic eras, making most voters unwilling to desert the party with which they identify.

CIVIC REALIGNMENTS LEVEL THE ECONOMIC PLAYING FIELD

History clearly shows us that economic disparities increase after idealist realignments, no doubt helping to fuel some of the third-party movements the country has witnessed. But these disparities decrease after civic realignments, dousing the flames of third-party rebellion and reinforcing allegiances to the two dominant parties.

Although economic data from pre–Civil War days is very sketchy, there is evidence that income and wealth disparities increased after the idealist realignment of 1828, peaking in the 1850s. These disparities were directly related to the era's central issue, slavery. During the 1850s, at a time when the soon-to-be Confederate states represented less than a third of the U.S. population, nearly 60 percent of those in the country's top economic tier were southern planters who owned large numbers of slaves.

The data is much clearer for the two idealist eras, beginning with the 1896 and 1968 presidential elections. In fact, the gap between rich and poor Americans was never as large historically as it was in the thirty years following the 1896 realignment. In 1917, the top 10 percent of American wage earners received 40 percent of the country's aggregate income, a number that rose to 46 percent in 1928. Data presented by Kevin Phillips, an architect of the Republican realignment of 1968 but a critic of Reaganomics in the 1980s, indicates that the wealthiest 0.5 percent of U.S. households held nearly one third of the country's wealth in 1929; the top 1 percent possessed nearly half (Phillips 1990). This was the highest degree of economic inequality at any point in U.S. history.

Income and wealth disparities were almost as large after the idealist 1968 realignment as they were after that of 1896. In 1968, the top fifth of U.S. households received about 43 percent of the country's aggregate income and the top tenth received 32 percent. Over the course of the next forty years that percentage moved steadily upward; by 2005, the top fifth of households were receiving 50 percent of aggregate income, the highest in any year since 1967. From 1968 to 2005, the share of aggregate income received by the bottom three-fifths of American households fell from 33 percent to 27 percent. By 2001, the top 1 percent of Americans held nearly 40 percent of the country's wealth, almost equaling the economic disparities of the Roaring Twenties. And the top fifth held more than 90 percent of the nation's wealth, leaving the bottom 80 percent with less than10 percent.

By contrast, economic disparities lessened after the civic realignments of 1860 and certainly that of 1932. After the Civil War, the main contributor to a more equal distribution of wealth was emancipation that stripped southern planters of their valuable human property. By the time of the New Deal, detailed economic statistics were being kept, leaving no doubt about the greater degree of economic equality following the Great Depression and the election of Franklin Roosevelt. The percentage of aggregate income received by the top 10 percent of wage earners dropped from around 45 percent in the late 1920s to just over 30 percent from the mid-1940s through the 1960s. And the 40 percent-plus share of the nation's wealth held by America's richest 1 percent fell to less than 30 percent by 1949.

Concern about the degree of economic inequality in the United States continues to rise among voters as we approach the next civic realigning election. Whoever wins the presidency in 2008 will need to deal with the issue, either through increased taxes on the wealthy or through expanded economic opportunity for the less fortunate, or with a combination of both approaches. In any case, the result, as in all previous civic eras, will be a greater level of economic equality in America than we have experienced in the last few decades.

SOCIAL ISSUES LOSE THEIR PUNCH IN A CIVIC ERA

Concern with social issues involving matters of personal lifestyle, morality, and religious belief emerges with greater force in the eras ushered in by idealist realignments and recedes from the political scene in eras that begin with civic realignments.

Concern over substance use is clearly far greater in idealist eras. The American Temperance Society was formed in 1826, two years before the 1828 idealist realigning election, and within ten years had 8,000 local groups and 1,500,000 members, about a quarter of the adult white population at the time. The same concern reemerged with even greater force in the late nineteenth century, with the formation of the Women's Christian Temperance Union and the Prohibition Party, finally culminating in the passage in 1917 of the Eighteenth Amendment enacting Prohibition.

Within months of the civic realigning election of Franklin Roosevelt, the Twenty-first Amendment repealing Prohibition was proposed and ratified. This event was presaged when Herbert Hoover, a Prohibition supporter, was booed and greeted with chants of "We want beer!" at a World Series game in 1931.

The last twenty-five years of the twentieth century were marked with the expenditure of large sums on the "War on Drugs," by both Democratic and Republican administrations; First Ladies imploring potential drug users to "just say no"; and a large increase in the number of Americans incarcerated for selling and using narcotics. This concern is likely to lose salience in the politics that will follow the next civic realignment.

Attention to the place of women in American society is also greatest in idealist eras. The word "feminism" entered the language after the idealist realignment of 1828. In 1848, Elizabeth Cady Stanton and Lucretia

Mott organized the first major attempt to fight for women's suffrage. In the 1850s, Amelia Bloomer created the clothing article that bears her name in an effort to blend Victorian concepts of modesty with expanded notions about acceptable feminine activity. After declining during the Civil War period, the struggle for women's suffrage began anew around the time of the 1896 realignment, reaching a peak in the first two decades of the twentieth century with the passage of the Nineteenth Amendment that allowed women to vote for the first time across the entire country.

But the push for women's rights also tends to slow considerably after civic realignments. A nine-page online "History of the Movement" devotes one brief paragraph to the women's rights activities of the post–Civil War period and one more to those from the 1920s into the 1960s (National Women's History Project 2007). Similarly, an *Information Please* timeline prepared for Women's History month in March 2007 describes the 1869 founding of the National Woman Suffrage Association by Susan B. Anthony and Elizabeth Cady Stanton. The timeline mentions no other events until 1890, on the eve of the next idealist realignment. For the three decades from the 1930s into the 1960s, the timeline mentions only three events. By contrast, eight are listed for the idealist 1900–1921 period and nineteen for that of the 1960s and 1970s (Imbornoni 2007).

Concern with the role of women emerged again forcefully in the 1960s, coincident with that decade's idealist realignment and with a new name that better reflected the politics of the era—women's liberation. The National Organization for Women was founded in 1966 to take the lead in what was now referred to as the "women's movement." This time the issues were broader than voting rights and concerned the position of women in the economy, education, religion, athletics, the family, and even the military. But this issue, too, is likely to fade from the top of the political agenda as the most gender-neutral generation in the nation's history helps to bring about the next civic realignment.

Disputes concerning the primacy of biblical creation or Darwinian evolutionary theory have also risen after idealist realignments and receded during civic eras. In the civic era after the Civil War, Darwinism was broadly accepted as a provocative idea, and America's industrialists used the notion of survival of the fittest to justify the accumulation of great wealth. By contrast, about three decades after the idealist 1896 realignment, the Scopes monkey trial captivated the nation, as an aging William Jennings

Bryan defended traditional beliefs against the modernist Clarence Darrow. From the 1950s and early 1960s perspective of a civic era, *Inherit the Wind*, first a Broadway play and later a Hollywood movie, made Matthew Brady (Bryan) look like a tragic buffoon, but to many Americans in 1925, Bryan was indeed doing God's work.

Few who watched that picture in the 1960s would have predicted that the issue of evolution versus creationism would emerge once again as the twentieth century ended; just as few would predict today that it will soon fade in relevance in our nation's political debate. But if history is any guide, it will. In the presidential primary debates leading up to the 2008 campaign, no Democrats took a stand against evolution, but almost all of the Republican candidates put their faith exclusively in the biblical story of creation. If history runs true to form, the question won't even be asked in the presidential debates of future civic-era campaigns.

In the next civic era, campaign consultants and political parties that have made a living using "wedge issues" to divide the electorate will have to learn a new playbook. Campaigns that engage the electorate on the great economic and foreign policy issues of the day and offer positive, partisan solutions to address them will get a much more attentive hearing from a civic-era electorate than from a campaign built on the ideological divisions of the preceding era.

CIVIC ERAS UNITE AMERICA
IN MORE WAYS THAN ONE

Ethnic and racial conflict is more pronounced after idealist realignments, generating policies in this area that are often hostile and exclusionary. The nation, however, tends to relax after civic realignments, shifting to more inclusive public policies.

In response to the immigration to the United States of millions of Irish and German Catholics, anti-immigrant activity became an important feature of U.S. politics for the first time after the idealist realignment of 1828. An anti-immigrant group, the Order of the Star Spangled Banner, and a third political party associated with it, the American (or Know-Nothing) Party, emerged to win fifty-one House seats in 1854 and eight electoral votes in 1856.

In 1831, less than three years after Andrew Jackson became president, William Lloyd Garrison published the first edition of *The Liberator*, an act credited with igniting the abolitionist movement. Later that year, Nat Turner led the largest slave rebellion in American history. Neither met with immediate success. Garrison was held in contempt and harassed as much in his native New England as in the South, and Turner was captured and executed after the suppression of his rebellion. But despite these initial failures, the actions of both men started a growing wave of antislavery activity that three decades later was the primary factor ending America's first idealist era.

Ethnic and racial conflict was also a prominent feature of the social and political environment during and after the idealist realignment of 1896. Anti-immigrant agitation reemerged in the last two decades of the nineteenth century, eventually bringing immigration to an almost complete halt through a 1924 law that imposed strict, low nationality quotas on immigration, especially from eastern and southern Europe and Asia. This idealist era was also one in which the Jim Crow laws that gave legal backing to segregation were enacted, and the lynching of blacks rose to historically high levels. While the political deal that ended Reconstruction in the 1870s let the white South handle race relations as it pleased, the creation of a legal system of segregation was not sanctioned by the Supreme Court until *Plessy v. Ferguson* in 1896, the year of an idealist realigning election.

During this era the southern states also enacted various laws—literacy tests, poll taxes, and grandfather clauses—preventing most African Americans from voting. In every year during the 1890s there were at least one hundred lynchings, mostly of blacks. The Ku Klux Klan was revived in 1915, an organization that in this idealist era's incarnation was anti-Catholic, anti-Jewish, and anti-immigrant, as well as anti-black. It came to control several state governments and march 250,000 of its members down Pennsylvania Avenue in Washington, D.C., in 1925. All this was memorialized and endorsed in America's first blockbuster movie, *The Birth of a Nation*, a technologically superb motion picture released in 1915, filled with white supremacist propaganda.

The next idealist era centering on the 1968 election also saw an increase in ethnic and racial concerns, and sometimes violence. Urban riots became regular summertime occurrences in cities across the country during the mid- and late 1960s, events that were endorsed by idealist, value-driven, uncompromising young black leaders like Stokely

Carmichael, H. Rap Brown, and Huey Newton. The reaction of many white Americans was just as vigorous and sometimes violent as well. Concern with racial turmoil and fears of crime were factors ending the old civic New Deal political order and helped Richard Nixon's law-and-order campaign bring about a Republican-dominated idealist realignment, starting in 1968—a realignment driven by an effort to extend and protect traditional values that were as deeply held as those of the young black radical separatists.

Today, concern with immigration, primarily from Latin America but also from Africa and Asia, is increasing once again. Critics such as Pat Buchanan and Lou Dobbs warn of the negative impact of immigration on America's culture, economy, and, after September 11, 2001, its security. In 2005, legislation was enacted to erect a fence along part of the U.S. border with Mexico, and two years later Congressman Tom Tancredo formally announced his run for the Republican presidential nomination, basing his candidacy almost entirely on a tough anti-immigration stance. The emotion surrounding this issue is very typical of idealist eras, especially ones that are ending.

Ethnic and racial concerns take a different form during eras begun by civic realignments. Befitting the strong group and institution-building orientation of civic generations, civic realignments lead to an inclusive rather than an exclusionary approach to immigration and race relations. The political tactics used to achieve these goals tend to be legalistic, legislative, and nonviolent. In the decades after the civic 1860 realignment, immigration was generally welcomed, even though these "new immigrants" were largely composed of eastern and southern European Catholics and Jews, different from the northern and western Europeans of the "old immigration." In part, the new immigrants were welcomed because they staffed the factories and mines of the country's burgeoning industrial economy, but also because American society was seen as a "melting pot" in which immigrants benefited from but also strengthened the alloy of American life. Emma Lazarus wrote her paean to the "huddled masses yearning to be free" squarely in the middle of this civic era, a poem that changed the symbolic meaning of the Statue of Liberty to one that welcomed immigrants as well as celebrated American freedom.

In the early part of the civic New Deal era, there was initial resistance to significantly changing the restrictive immigration policies of the

1920s. President Franklin Roosevelt feared driving a wedge into the New Deal coalition and losing southern support for his economic and international policies over the issue. Even as late as 1952, the McCarran-Walter Immigration and Nationality Act extended the quota policies of the previous idealist era. But in 1965, as this civic era drew to a close, that law was amended to eliminate nationality quotas and greatly expand the number of immigrants allowed to enter the country.

Civic eras have also placed a greater emphasis on more inclusive approaches in race relations. In large part, of course, the Civil War was fought to end slavery in America. The postwar policy of Reconstruction was designed to incorporate the newly freed Negro population into the country's economic and political life; and for awhile it had some success in doing so, permitting blacks to vote and, for the first time ever, providing them with agricultural land and public education. But weariness with the tensions of the Civil War and its aftermath ended Reconstruction in favor of an accommodating political arrangement between northern Republicans and southern Democrats.

In the New Deal era, FDR was often reticent to endorse new civil rights measures for the same political reasons that concerned him in dealing with immigration policy. After World War II, led by older members of the GI and Silent Generations, a new civil rights movement emerged, using the courts, legislation, and nonviolent action by idealist Baby Boomers, both black and white, to end segregation in the South. The first visible step in this direction, the desegregation of big league baseball in 1947, took place outside the political arena but had far-reaching consequences. Starting with President Harry Truman's executive order in 1948 integrating the armed forces, continuing with the *Brown v. Board of Education* decision in 1954 that legally desegregated public schools, and the enactment of several civil rights laws in the 1960s designed to desegregate public facilities and housing and to ensure blacks the right to vote, this civic era was one strongly characterized by political and governmental efforts to include African Americans in all phases of American life.

With the most ethnically diverse and gender-neutral generation in the nation's history about to enter the electorate in large numbers, American politics is about to renew its cyclical rhythm and return to policies of inclusion and tolerance on issues such as immigration or civil rights. While ethnic and racial issues will likely arise from time to time during the coming decades, those issues will usually be resolved in favor of a more open and equal society.

GOVERNMENT IS WHERE THE ACTION IS IN CIVIC ERAS

Historically, civic realignments have led to institution-building and the greater use of the national government to deal with societal concerns and to stimulate the economy. Idealist realignments have led to eras in which the national government's growth did not keep pace with the over-all growth of the economy. Government was rarely seen as an economic spur or as a major source of societal change and problem resolution during those eras.

The Jacksonian Democrats, who dominated the idealist realignment of 1828, saw themselves as the protectors of traditional state's rights and resisted almost all efforts to strengthen the national government. The Democrats fought, usually with success, to keep the federal debt low. That era was the only one in American history to end with a smaller fed-eral debt than when it began. From his battle against the National Bank to his refusal to enforce a Supreme Court decision prohibiting the removal of Indians from land in Georgia that went against his vision of states' rights, Jackson's efforts to restrain the national government are leg-endary. During this era, Democrats also resisted most efforts to use the national government to support economic expansion. There was some governmental activity of this type, but it was the state governments, often controlled by the opposition Whigs, that were most active in supporting the new canals and railroads of the era.

The next idealist era, beginning with the 1896 election, did include about a decade of reformist policies in the Theodore Roosevelt and Woodrow Wilson presidencies, although it is not entirely coincidental that both men had the support of only a minority of voters through much of their administrations. Roosevelt expanded federal regulation of business trusts, railroads, and the food and drug industries and created the national parks, often over the objections of other leaders of his own party. His call for a "New Nationalism" that would promote the "public welfare" over property rights was several decades before its time and didn't become part of our nation's policies until his cousin Franklin brought about a new civic era. More in tune with the idealist era, and with the traditions of the

Democratic Party of that time, were the "New Freedom" policies advocated by Woodrow Wilson, which argued that America would best advance if the national government promoted economic competition through a combination of low tariffs and banking reform. But even more in tune with the tenor of their times were the small government, low taxation, high tariff, and pro-business policies of "Old Guard" conservative presidents like Taft, Harding, and Coolidge.

Similarly, the administrations of the five Republican and even the two Democratic presidents who served during the period after the idealist realignment of 1968 did not produce any major new federal programs. Instead, the Republican administrations, particularly those of Ronald Reagan and the two George Bushes, endorsed policies of limited regulation and low taxation, especially on corporations and better-off Americans, as the best stimulus for economic growth.

After an early attempt by President Clinton to create a federal program to pay for medical care for all Americans met with overwhelming rejection, and particularly after the Republicans gained control of Congress in 1994, his administration curtailed any major efforts to expand the national government. Liberal Baby Boomer pundits roundly criticized Clinton for playing "small ball" politics, as if most voters were prepared to support anything more. Instead, one of his administration's proudest achievements was a balanced budget, hearkening back to Jacksonian promises of the end of the national debt. Vice President Al Gore led an effort to "reinvent" government, but just a few years later, the inability of the national government to effectively deal with the ravages of Hurricane Katrina and to provide adequate medical care to veterans and wounded soldiers from the war in Iraq suggested that some of the reinvented agencies atrophied again as soon as even this minimal attention to their work disappeared.

By contrast, the eras that started as a result of civic realignments were characterized by a belief in the national government as a stimulus for economic growth and a solution to America's problems. Even as it fought the Civil War and instituted the first federal income tax to pay for it, the Republican government of Lincoln's first administration adopted policies such as the Homestead Act, the Morrill Land Grant College Act, and the Pacific Railway Act. These policies contributed significantly to the westward expansion and economic growth of the nation and, at least, temporarily moved the western states into the Republican electoral column.

The use of the federal government and its growth after the New Deal civic realignment indelibly branded the Democratic Party as the party of "big government." During the 1930s the national government assumed a major role in helping Americans to cope with the Great Depression and, later, in regulating and managing the economy so that such an event would not happen again. After World War II, through the GI Bill of Rights and in Lyndon Johnson's Great Society programs enacted just before this civic era came to a close, the federal government pursued policies designed to enhance the economic opportunities and economic status of all Americans. The United States also clearly assumed a role of international leadership, producing for the first time a major and permanent growth of the nation's military forces. Even during the Eisenhower administration, the one Republican administration during the New Deal civic era, there was no scaling back of the national government; if anything, the creation of the interstate highway system and the space program further strengthened the federal government and its institutions. By contrast, when Bill Clinton declared in his 1996 State of the Union address that the "era of big government is over," he correctly characterized the nature of the idealist era in which he was governing, even if his pronouncement failed to remove the big government stigma from the brand of his Democratic Party.

But activist government is due for a comeback. Even though how the government operates to achieve large national goals will be as different in the next civic era as the New Deal was from its predecessors, the pattern will be the same. In the next civic era, voters, especially Millennials, will once again demand an activist role for the national government, in order to meet the new challenges the country will face.

Both public policy and voter behavior differ in significant ways between realignments that are driven by the arrival in the electorate of an idealist generation, such as the Baby Boomers, and those caused by the coming of age of civic generations, such as the GI Generation and, soon, the Millennial Generation. Both types of realignment, however, are enabled by the invention and deployment of new communication technologies that change the way political campaigns are conducted and enhance their capacity to reach and involve voters. The youngest generation's interest in, and facility with, these new technologies further enhances its role in leading each change in the political cycle. It is, therefore, no coincidence that in every realigning era the nation has also experienced the growth and success of new communication technologies, which have in turn helped to shape election results and define the fortunes of political parties.

CHAPTER 3

Politicians Love to Talk

POLITICAL REALIGNMENTS OCCUR on a regular basis in American politics when a major event or crisis triggers a reassessment of America's direction. The triggering event touches off a wave of renewed interest in the political process, especially by a large new generation of voters eager to be heard. The resulting political debate and election outcome sets the general course of public policy for four decades, until a new wave of change causes the country to alter its course again.

For that debate to take place and have the impact it must have on the nation's political psyche, as many people as possible must actually be involved in the conversation. But how involved the electorate can be is limited, at least in part, by the capacity and reach of the communication technologies of the particular era. Fortunately for America, the long waves of technological change and innovation (Atkinson 2005) that have occurred in American history have oscillated in harmony with its generational cycles, so that as the nation finds the need to confront new challenges, the ability to debate those questions in wider and wider circles with more and more information has also been possible. Each time the country faced fundamental questions about who it was as a nation, and what values it stood for, the country was able to harness the newest in communication technologies to meet the demands of its political discourse.

A HOUSE DIVIDED AGAINST ITSELF CANNOT STAND

In the middle of the nineteenth century, the ability to communicate the same information at the same time almost anywhere in the country played a key role in America's debate over its most enduring political contradictions. The first practical application of Samuel F. B. Morse's "electric invention of the telegraph," on May 1, 1844, was to send news of the nominees of the Whig convention in Baltimore to Washington, D.C. The government-sponsored telegraph line used for that transmission was officially inaugurated later that month from the Supreme Court's chambers with a message that asked provocatively, "What hath God wrought?" The answer was swift in coming.

By 1850, there were over twenty companies operating more than 12,000 miles of telegraph lines in the United States. Following what today would be a familiar "s-shaped" growth curve, the technology created whole new employment categories that filled twelve pages in the 1852 U.S. census. Jobs, such as pole climbers, key operators, and messenger boys, who scrambled to get messages from the end points of the telegraph operator's network to the specific residence or business for which the message was intended, were opened up to young men and, in the case of telegraph operators, women across the country. In an attempt to pack as much information as possible into a very expensive communication medium, just as Millennials do today when sending text messages, entire new acronyms and abbreviation schemes came into being, with their own decoding books to translate them back into English for the uninitiated (Standage 1998).

By 1858, when Abraham Lincoln engaged in his famous debates on slavery with Democratic senator Stephen Douglas, the telegraph operators' dots and dashes that captured their words were quickly set into type in every Illinois newspaper. Senator Douglas was a national figure, actively brokering compromises between the North and South designed to preserve the country's original balance between states permitting and prohibiting slavery. Lincoln was a relatively unknown figure, recently embraced by the newly formed Republican Party, who had challenged Douglas's approach by famously declaring in the state's capital of Springfield, "A house divided against itself cannot stand." When the two candidates agreed to debate that proposition in each of the seven congressional districts in Illinois, the entire nation was able to read their arguments in hometown newspapers. But whether or not the information was accurate depended on the point of view of both the newspaper editor and the reader.

The 1850 census counted over 1,600 party-affiliated newspapers and fewer than 100 "independent" papers across the United States. By 1870, almost 90 percent of the daily newspapers in the fifty largest U.S. cities were affiliated with one of the two political parties. Just as present-day Americans choose to watch cable television news networks based upon party and ideological identifications—conservatives and Republicans preferring the Fox News Channel and liberals and Democrats preferring CNN—so, too, did mid-nineteenth-century Americans decide which newspaper to read based on their own partisan leanings. Parties effectively used the newspapers who supported their policies to reinforce party preferences, provide "talking points" to party leaders and loyalists, and, most important, to mobilize voters.

Here, for example, are excerpts from the coverage of the first Lincoln-Douglas debate, held on Saturday, August 21, 1858, in Ottawa, Illinois, from the Democratically oriented *Jacksonville Sentinel*, compared to the article from the *Daily Pantagraph*, a Republican newspaper in Bloomington, Illinois.

The *Sentinel* headline dramatically states its judgment on the outcome: "The 'Dead Lion' Skins the 'Living Dog.'" The story begins by contrasting the relative support of the two candidates as they initiated the contest: "Douglas was met and escorted by an immense procession, bearing flags, banners, mottoes, &c., to the Geiger House, where he was welcomed in a neat address by Hon. W. H. W. Cushman. Mr. Lincoln came in on the cars and was escorted to a hotel by his friends."

To prove its point that Douglas, at least in its opinion, had completely won over the crowd of some 12,000 people, the *Sentinel* concluded its own reporting and then borrowed a dispatch from the *Chicago Times* to describe the end of the three-hour discussion:

> At the conclusion of Douglas' reply the shouts of the multitude were tremendous and two-thirds of the meeting surrounded him and escorted him in triumph to his quarters.
>
> Lincoln in the meantime seemed to have been paralyzed. He stood upon the stage looking wildly at the people as they surrounded the triumphant Douglas, and, with mouth wide open, he could not find a friend to say one word to him in his distress. It was a delicate point to republicans who had witnessed his utter defeat, and who knew how severely he felt it, to offer him condolence, or bid him hope for better success again. The only thing they could say was that Lincoln ought not to travel round with Douglas, and had better not meet him

any more. When Douglas and the Democrats had left the square, Lincoln essayed to descend from the stage, but his limbs refused to do their office. In this extremity, the Republican Marshal called half a dozen men, who, lifting Lincoln in their arms, carried him along.

In the Republican-oriented *Pantagraph*, the end of Lincoln's address is met with much greater acclaim: "Three cheers were proposed and given with tremendous volume—followed by three more, and then three more, extending to all parts of the public square." Undoubtedly their description of Lincoln being carried off the stage in triumph would not have had quite the spin it was given in the *Chicago Times* either.

In fact, the *Pantagraph* was so enamored of the clarity of Lincoln's remarks that it printed them in their entirety over the course of four days, August 25–28, complete with annotations on crowd reaction and commentary. "Laughter and applause" at the beginning turned into "cries of yes, yes, and applause" as Lincoln advanced his arguments, which were later greeted by "loud cheers," and ultimately led to "great cheering" being heard in the public square. The *Sentinel* preferred to quote Douglas's arguments in its coverage and to reference Lincoln's remarks only by way of setting up the alternative. So Lincoln's most famous utterance up until that time was dismissed in its reports as "his doctrine of a house divided against itself, etc."

Meanwhile, the arguments that Lincoln advanced to cheers in the *Pantagraph* were variously described by the *Sentinel* as "a few loose and floundering observations" leading to an "attempted explanation of his slavery extermination platform [which] was especially lame, weak and inefficient" because it was based upon "the miserable sophism, then, that slavery is about to be made national, and perpetuated." They did promise the reader they would print the entirety of Douglas's half-hour reply to Lincoln in the next day's edition, but for the time being, all the reader needed to know was that "Mr. Douglas' reply was scathing and crushing. He made the 'woolfly' at every clip, and as an intellectual effort, as a model of terse argument, crushing facts and cutting invective."

The Media as Intermediator

Our ability to read every word of the Lincoln-Douglas debates on the Internet, as taken from the contemporary newspaper stories and commentaries of 1858 that so perfectly captured the pulse of the country in the heat of this critical debate, was made possible by the Robert McCormick Foundation. McCormick's grandfather, Joseph Medill, made the *Chicago Tribune* the mouthpiece of the Republican Party in the mid-1850s and provided invaluable aid to Abraham Lincoln in his quest for the presidency. With the power to shape public opinion in their hands, owners of newspapers in America's swelling urban centers (and the political party leaders allied with them) had the ability not just to report events, but to shape them.

Perhaps the most notorious of these early media magnates was William Randolph Hearst, whose sensational, if not downright erroneous, coverage of the sinking of the USS *Maine* in Havana harbor and other supposed Spanish atrocities visited upon the Cubans helped lead the United States into war. The Spanish-American War also gave Teddy Roosevelt a heroic image that he used to launch his national political career, enabling him to obtain the vice presidential nomination on the Republican ticket of 1900 with President McKinley, over the objections of the incumbent and his supporters. But the epitome of political communication technology and campaign organization for its time occurred four years earlier, when both sides put their best weapons on the field of battle to determine once again what type of country America was to become.

AMERICA REALIGNS ITSELF
FOR THE TWENTIETH CENTURY

Because of a series of economic depressions, or panics, in the years immediately prior to 1896, economics became the central issue of the realigning presidential election that year. The inherent conflicts between the interests of farmers, miners, and laborers—the heart of the country's agrarian economic past—and the manufacturers and owners of capital—the leaders of America's industrial economic future—became the center of the campaign's debates.

The debate began when the words of a young Nebraska congressman, William Jennings Bryan, made the telegraph wires hum with reports of his eloquent summation to the Democratic convention on the need to, in effect, inflate the value of the nation's currency by having it backed not only by gold, but silver: " Having behind us the producing masses of this nation and the world, supported by the commercial interests, the laboring interests, and the toilers everywhere, we will answer their demand for a gold standard by saying to them: *you shall not press down upon the brow of labor this crown of thorns, you shall not crucify mankind upon a cross of gold*" (Whicher 1953, 36).

William Randolph Hearst's newspapers were particularly praiseworthy in their reporting of the candidate and his principled stand on behalf of the working class. One of the reasons for the magnate's efforts on behalf of the nation's downtrodden might have come from his family's holdings in mining properties, estimated by some at the time as worth between twenty and forty million dollars. Hearst, along with other "Silver Kings," would have seen the value of their metal double if Bryan's proposal had become law. They invested over $289,000 in securing delegates to the Democratic convention who were pledged to bi-metallism and gave generously to the campaign once it was underway (Whicher 1953). Whatever Hearst's motivation, Bryan and his rhetoric became the subject of fawning articles in every one of the eighteen cities where Hearst published at least one newspaper—from the *New York Morning Journal* in the East to the *Chicago Herald and Examiner* in the heart of the Midwest, and all the way out West to the *San Francisco Examiner*.

The Republicans, who had expected the campaign to be about the merits of higher protectionist tariffs, were completely surprised by the national frenzy touched off by reports of Bryan's speech and subsequent nomination as the Democrat's presidential nominee (five ballots and twenty-four hours later). Their own candidate, Ohio governor William McKinley, predicted, " This money matter is unduly prominent. In thirty days you won't hear anything about it" (38). Luckily for the Republicans, they had plenty of time to regroup and counterattack. Using the efficiencies made possible not only by the telegraph but also by the newly invented telephone, Mark Hanna, an industrialist and chairman of the Republican National Committee, organized the most expensive political campaign the country had ever experienced. The cost of the campaign, estimated to be somewhere between six and ten million dollars, was paid for by a gentlemen's agreement among the trusts that each would contribute one-quarter of one percent of the market cap value of each company to the Republican Party's campaign coffers (Croly 1912).

The campaign built upon and refined the national campaign strategies originally used by Andrew Jackson in the realigning election of
1828, when the ability to move people more quickly over greater dis-
tances produced truly national campaigns for the first time (Jamieson
1992). "The transportation revolution made it possible to organize politics on a national basis, with wide-ranging campaign tours and 'monster'
rallies, and the proliferation of newspapers enhanced the role of the
partisan editor who fanned the flames of party feeling" (Morison,
Commager, Leuchtenburg 1977).

Determined to persuade voters about the dangers of "cheap money,"
Hanna organized an "exhaustive and systematic educational canvass of
the country." Fourteen hundred speakers were enlisted to spread the
word, while party operatives distributed the message, using 275 different
pamphlets and leaflets, written in ten different languages. The most popular piece was a forty-page "conversation" on the issue of whether the
country would be better served with a weak currency that lessened the
crushing debt loads of many farmers and workers, or with a strong currency that would ensure the financial reputation of the country's bonds,
issued at that time by private bankers (Croly 1912). With Republican
support no longer assured in what had been safe states, the RNC's army
of canvassers distributed over 125 million pieces of literature, the vast
majority in the critical western plains and midwestern states lying
between the "Y" of the Missouri and Ohio Rivers (Whicher 1953).

The results of this massive canvass appeared to stem the tide by
October, even as the Democrats responded with their best weapon—the
rhetorical genius of their nominee. Bryan embarked on a 100-day cross-
country campaign, making six hundred appearances in twenty-seven
states while traveling over 18,000 miles, something that was only made
possible by the completion of the nationwide railroad network in the
decades after the Civil War. It is estimated that Bryan ended up being
heard by five million Americans in the course of the campaign, a feat that
was never achieved again until radio became a force in American political campaigns (Whicher 1953).

While Hanna did not use the railroad to take McKinley to the voters, he did use it to take the voters to McKinley. Hanna persuaded
Republican-affiliated railroad executives to provide excursion tickets to
voters who could then listen to McKinley speak from his front porch and

respond to their carefully screened and pre-submitted questions. Each such gathering, the equivalent of town hall events in modern-day campaigns, was dutifully reported by the Republican press without as much as a whisper of their rehearsed nature. As contrived as this technique seems to modern-day observers skilled in detecting spin and false modesty from candidates, it adhered to the traditions of nineteenth-century politics, which considered it unseemly for a candidate to show that he actually wanted the office for which he was running (Croly 1912).

Bryan broke decisively with this tradition, creating the most emotional campaign the country had witnessed in thirty-six years: "I would rather have it said that I lacked dignity than that I lack backbone to meet the enemies of the Government who work against its welfare in Wall Street" (Whicher 1953, 46).

The intensity of the campaign produced a record turnout. More people voted for Bryan, 6.5 million, than had ever voted for a Democratic presidential candidate. But it wasn't enough to beat McKinley, who received 7 million votes and won the Electoral College decisively (271–176), albeit with slim majorities in many of the contested states (Whicher 1953). In the end, the organizing genius of Mark Hanna, combined with the industrial-age technologies of its day, created the epitome of what a national campaign should be and would be about—organized canvassing, using communication technologies to track progress, and enormous sums of money spent on informing the voters and getting them out to vote—and all of it concluding with hoopla and parades to assure wavering supporters that victory was just ahead if they remained steadfast in their support for the party of their choice. All that was needed was a way to reach all the voters all the time, at a cost even a Democratic campaign could afford.

MASS MEDIA FOR THE MASSES

The answer to the Democrats' prayer appeared as the Republican hegemony over American politics that flowed from the election of 1896 was at its zenith. "Wireless telegraphy," now known as radio, was originally conceived as a way to eliminate the need to string wires to connect each part of the network. But its larger potential was apparent to Pittsburgh inventor George Westinghouse. His engineers invented the vacuum tube in 1906, a breakthrough as important to the Industrial Age as microchips and transistors (which ultimately replaced tubes) were to the Information Age. Radio not only eliminated the need for telegraphic wires, but it also eliminated the need for any middleman, such as a news-paper editor, to collect, edit, and shape the information before it was relayed to the ultimate recipient. Using this new architecture people could hear exactly what was said, when it was said, wherever it was said.

Frank Conrad, chief engineer for the Westinghouse Corporation, began "broadcasting" not only information about wireless equipment but also music from his phonograph collection. The show was so popular that a Pittsburgh department store began advertising radio sets, the iPods of their day, so people could hear the music Conrad was playing. Conrad's boss soon realized the company could sell a lot of radio sets by broad-casting music, news, and information free of charge to anyone with a device within range of its signal. Westinghouse applied for, and was granted, the first commercial radio license in the United States. His sta-tion, KDKA, went on the air on November 2, 1920, just in time to report the results of the presidential contest between Warren Harding and James Cox in its first official broadcast (KDKA 2007).

KDKA created the concept of regular programming. Miraculously, every individual within range of the station's signal could listen to the same programming simultaneously. It was an instant sensation. Between 1923 and 1930, 60 percent of American households bought a radio (Robertson, Garfinkel, and Eckstein 2000). To eliminate the resulting chaos on the airwaves, the government passed the Radio Act of 1927, which required anyone who wanted to broadcast on a particular fre-quency at a particular time to obtain a license from the federal govern-ment. The Federal Regulatory Commission required the licensee to serve "the public interest, convenience and necessity." The regulations that followed enabled two new networks, NBC and CBS, to become the dominant source of news and information on the radio within a decade (Streeter 2007).

Radio became a national medium for advertising that exploded in popularity just as manufacturers were looking for a way to reach all their customers at once; meanwhile, candidates hungered for the efficient reach it could provide to their campaigns. In 1919, Woodrow Wilson became the first president to speak to the small number of Americans who had radio sets, and four years later Calvin Coolidge's State of the

Union address was the first to be broadcast. The ability of radio to reach the masses meant that, by the end of his term, Coolidge had spoken to more Americans than had all his predecessors combined. And in 1928, Republican Herbert Hoover and Democrat Al Smith became the first presidential candidates to use commercial network radio as part of their campaigns (Jamieson 1992).

Hoover won the election, but with the onset of the Great Depression, America faced its darkest economic hour. In 1930 the president asked radio and movie star Will Rogers, a Democrat, to assure the nation that the end was not near. Whatever Rogers's achievement in the task, it could not save Hoover's presidency, which came to a crashing end with his defeat in 1932 by Franklin D. Roosevelt, whose soothing radio presence allowed him to communicate directly and effectively with the American people. The heated oratory, partisan journalism, and armies of party precinct workers of nineteenth-century campaigns yielded to candidates with the best radio voices, those who could take advantage of the economies of scale that broadcast media brought to political campaigns. No longer dependent on the intermediate filtering of the news by defenders of the status quo, Roosevelt could and did take his campaign for a New Deal directly to the American public. Americans liked what they heard, and the Republican Party and its establishment allies suddenly found themselves out in the political cold.

By 1932, more than 18 million American households had radio sets, greater than twice the number in 1928. And in spite of the ravages of the Great Depression, the number of U.S. households with radio sets climbed to almost 23 million by the time of Roosevelt's reelection in 1936. In 1935, the proliferation of radios enabled approximately sixty million Americans to listen to FDR's "fireside chats."

Radio required delivery skills that were new and different from the loud, dramatic, and florid oratory of previous eras. It demanded a calm, cool, reassuring manner of speaking and delivery; Roosevelt clearly had those skills. James Farley, FDR's postmaster general and, in modern terms, his political director, recognized the importance of Roosevelt's ability to effectively use radio in the president's landslide victory in 1936, which firmly cemented the New Deal realignment. "The influence of the radio in determining the outcome of the 1936 election can hardly be overestimated," noted Kathleen Hall Jamieson. Radio enabled Roosevelt "to overcome the false impressions created by tons of written propaganda put out by foes of the New Deal. No matter what was written or what was charged, the harmful effect was largely washed away as soon as the reassuring voice of the President of the United States started coming through the ether into the family living room" (Jamieson 1992).

LET'S ALL GO TO THE MOVIES

"Talkies," first marketed in 1927, were the 1920s' mirror image of being able to watch TV shows on an iPod; they added sound to what had been a strictly visual medium. Instead of people waiting for theater or vaudeville productions to make a stop in their small town in order to get a glimpse of what folks in the big city were seeing, they could each pay a nickel to watch the movies. Performers with both visual presence and strong voices, such as Gloria Swanson and Lionel Barrymore, became Hollywood celebrities—which means, to quote Roxee in the musical *Chicago*, set in the Roaring Twenties, "somebody everyone knows."

In the late 1930s through the 1940s, motion pictures supplemented but did not replace radio as a medium of political communication and persuasion. For a brief period, the movies in effect served as a way station between radio and television. Politicians used campaign-sponsored "documentary" films as well as the popular, appealing, and ubiquitous theatrical newsreels (the latter serving as a form of free media), just as TV newscasts are now used and valued by political campaigns. Movie audiences of the 1930s and 1940s reacted openly to the political action that loomed large on the silver screen. A September 1936 Peter Arno cartoon in the *New Yorker* depicted several dinner jacket- and fur coat-wearing Republicans attempting to persuade some friends: "Come along. We're going to the Trans-Lux to hiss Roosevelt."

Name recognition, as we say today, became the goal of every politician. Scrambling to get close to celebrities, careful to cultivate the newspaper pundits or bloggers of their day, and ever conscious of their on-air personalities, politicians of the early twentieth century realized that America, which was rapidly becoming one nation in terms of popular taste, could become one nation in terms of popular opinion as well. That future became reality when the broadcast media industry was able to add the pictures of television to the sound of radio.

"IT'S HOWDY DOODY TIME,
BOYS AND GIRLS"

Just as the telegraph grew 600-fold in its first decade, television usage exploded in living rooms across America from 1950 to 1960. During the 1950s, the number of television sets in American homes grew even more exponentially than had radio in the 1930s. In 1950, there were fewer than four million TV sets in U.S. households. That number increased more than twelve-fold by 1960, as Americans bought nearly 10,000 television sets per day from 1954 to 1956 (White 1960). From a novelty found in 11 percent of American households in 1950, television became a necessity by 1960, with 88 percent of American households owning at least one TV set. In 1968, the year at the center of the country's next electoral realignment, almost 57 million American households had a television set.

Ironically, the first presidential candidate to recognize the power of television was not Republican Richard Nixon, who was raised in the heart of California's television culture, but Boston-bred John F. Kennedy. In an election as close and as dubiously counted as the presidential contest of 1960, any single event can be credited for causing victory or defeat, but historians generally attribute Nixon's poor performance against the telegenic JFK in the first televised presidential debates in American history as the point at which the Kennedy campaign truly caught fire. Nixon and his political staff had ignored the suggestions of the campaign's TV advisors about Nixon's schedule on the day of the debate, the makeup he wore, and the lighting on the set. As a result, viewers perceived Nixon as pale, haggard, and sweaty, while the less experienced Kennedy looked fresh and confident. Those who listened to the debate on radio thought Nixon had bested Kennedy, but the greater number of Americans watching on television came away with the exact opposite impression (Jamieson 1992).

Nixon learned his painful lesson on the power of television. In 1968 he brought his television advertising talent, who had previously been hired as outside consultants, directly into the campaign apparatus. Their essentially independent operation became the stuff of legends. Joe McGinniss, a journalist whom the Nixon team allowed to observe the campaign from the inside, later wrote an exposé of its inner workings that suggested its television operatives packaged and sold Richard Nixon as a commodity, implying that voters were given a questionable, if not false, picture of the candidate (McGinniss 1969).

Neither critics nor admirers of the Nixon TV team, however, attempted to deny the effectiveness of their efforts in minimizing the candidate's weaknesses, maximizing his strengths, and reflecting and meeting the concerns of the American electorate in the turbulent late 1960s. Nixon appeared on the primetime TV comedy "Laugh In." His Democratic opponent, Hubert Humphrey, chose not to appear on the show because he believed it would make him look unpresidential. But Nixon's appearance seemed to humanize a candidate with a reputation for stiffness, perhaps just enough to turn the election in his favor and to end nearly forty years of Democratic electoral dominance. From that campaign forward, television consultants and media experts would have the most important seat at the campaign strategy table.

Facility with the medium of television continued to reinforce the Republican advantage in national campaigns that Nixon first established in 1968. The less-than-flattering image of Michael Dukakis riding in a tank, which showed up in a Republican TV commercial in 1988, and the audible sighs and aggressive body language of Al Gore in his first debate with George W. Bush in 2000 are only two examples. Indeed, in the latter campaign, polling indicated that support for Gore rose between the debates but fell immediately after the next debate. And of course, no one was more skilled at the use of television than Ronald Reagan, in both his presidential campaigns and his two terms in office.

Beyond boosting Republican presidential candidates, television also contributed significantly to the ticket-splitting and rise of independent party identifications that followed the realignment of the late 1960s. Television made it possible for individual candidates at all levels to run "candidate-centered" campaigns separate and apart from their own political parties. Encouraging ticket splitting and appealing to Independents became a staple of both Democratic and Republican campaigns, especially after 1968 (De Vries and Tarrance 1972). For example, Republican moderates George Romney and William Milliken used this strategy to win the governorship in heavily Democratic Michigan in the 1960s and 1970s, while Democrats successfully employed it in the campaigns of James Blanchard and Jennifer Granholm in a later era of Republican dominance in the state.

BACK TO THE FUTURE WITH RADIO

In the late 1980s and early 1990s, Republicans also developed a facility for using an old medium, radio, in a new and different way—talk shows targeting conservative Republican audiences, the most notable of which was hosted by Rush Limbaugh. George W. Bush was so intent on recruiting his audience that he reportedly carried Limbaugh's bags up the stairs to the Lincoln Bedroom in the White House. Talk radio audiences were indeed united in their conservative beliefs. Limbaugh referred to his listeners as "ditto heads" and the listeners, in turn, often greeted Limbaugh with the salutation, "Dittoes, Rush."

Conservative talk radio did much to reinforce its listeners' ideology and mobilize their votes for Republicans, while Democratic on-air imitations proved pale and unpersuasive. Talk radio was given credit for helping Republicans capture control of Congress in the 1994 midterm elections, something that finally moved the realignment that began in the late 1960s from the top to the bottom of the federal government.

As late as 2003, it was talk radio hosts in California, John Kobylt and Ken Champiou, who ignited a successful recall campaign against the incumbent Democratic governor, Gray Davis. The previous year, Davis had run television ads in the primary designed to defeat a Republican moderate, former Los Angeles mayor Richard Riordan, in his race against the more conservative and lesser-known opponent, Bill Simon. The strategy succeeded in that Simon defeated Riordan for the Republican nomination but never really stood a chance against Davis in the general election. That matchup, however, also led to a very low turnout that, while reelecting Davis, also helped to set a low threshold for qualifying a recall petition on the ballot. Since the number of signatures required for such an effort is determined by multiplying a fixed percentage times the number of votes for governor in the previous election, Davis's tactic in 2002 helped to sow the seeds of his own destruction in 2003.

Davis also lent support to two issues that helped to create the climate for a successful recall. He used an increase in the tax that Californians pay to obtain a license plate for their car or truck each year to help close the state's budget gap, and he supported the idea of issuing driver's licenses to undocumented immigrants. During the recall itself, this latest battle over immigration became the number one reason for voting among 17 percent of the state's electorate. As often happens with an election near the end of an idealist era, this was the highest mark for the immigration issue since 1994, when Republican governor Pete Wilson used the issue in TV ads to scare Californians into voting for his reelection (Pincus 2003). Talk radio lit the match on this dry kindling by asking its listeners to go to their station's web site, download a petition to recall the governor, and get their neighbors to sign up. The more than two million daily listeners to talk radio across the state downloaded 100,000 petitions in the first month. The fire was unstoppable as the ditto heads easily gathered enough signatures to force a vote on whether to retain the governor who had been handily reelected the previous year (Fox 2003). On November 4, 2003, for the first time in California history, a sitting governor was removed from office, and Arnold Schwarzenegger, the star of the movie *The Terminator*, became the new governor.

THE NEXT BATTLEGROUND

Each political party is able to learn from the other, and no advantage in campaign technology lasts forever. Twenty-four years after Nixon's "Laugh In" appearance, candidate Bill Clinton borrowed a page out of Nixon's playbook to revitalize his stalled presidential primary campaign, donning sunglasses to play the saxophone on Arsenio Hall's late night television show. Today, appearances with Jay Leno or David Letterman or even on "Saturday Night Live" have become *de rigueur* for anyone aspiring to the presidency. It is a standard way to boost a candidate's "Q" score (a Hollywood measure of a celebrity's—or politician's—audience familiarity and favorability) and reveal the real person behind the podium, just as candidates publicized their log cabin frontier roots in Lincoln's day.

While it is true that each time a new form of communication technology has appeared, the first candidate to figure out how to maximize its impact in campaigns has triumphed, it is also true that the ultimate winner of the campaign technology arms race has not always been the first to use the medium well. Sometimes the party that has suffered defeat from the initial use of the technology has learned from that experience and gone on to master the technology, using it to help regain power.

The next round of that competition will be fought not only over the nation's airwaves, but also on the Internet. The battle will often be fought on social networking sites like MySpace and Facebook. A major tactic will be to show an opponent's mistakes in full-motion video on YouTube or similar sites the day they occur. The competition will require the ability to master the speed and tone of conversations conducted every moment of the day and night, using the very latest in mobile and high-speed broadband technologies. In short, it will be a battle to win the hearts and minds of a new generation inextricably intertwined with all these new technologies—the Millennials.

CHAPTER 4

Meet the Millennials

A NEW GENERATION ARRIVES on the scene about once
every twenty years, and every time it does, older generations struggle to
understand how "these kids today" think and behave. While every generation is unique, many of the clues to understanding its members' behavior can be found by taking a longer historical view and noting recurring
patterns of child rearing and parental attitudes toward their children,
which play such an important role in establishing each individual's belief
system. Of course, not every member of any given generation exhibits
the archetypical behavior of their cohort, but survey and aggregate data
do reveal clear behavioral tendencies that define a given generation. So,
too, does the popular culture's portrayal of young people and their parents, a favorite subject of both television sitcoms and movies. Looking at
both the social research data and media portrayals of each generation
helps to draw a clear picture of Millennials and how they differ from
Baby Boomers and Generation X.

MILLENNIALS ARE A LOT LIKE
THEIR GREAT-GRANDPARENTS

The Millennial Generation was born in the years 1982 to 2003. Millennials are the children of Baby Boomers and Gen-Xers, but in many
key respects they are more like their GI Generation (Tom Brokaw's
"Greatest Generation") grandparents and great-grandparents than they
are like their own parents. The parallels between the Millennial Generation and the GI Generation (born in the years 1901 to 1924) provide us
a glimpse into how Millennials might influence America and its future.

Millennials are the largest and most racially diverse generation of
Americans ever. About 40 percent of Millennials are of African American,

Latin American, Asian, or racially mixed backgrounds, compared with nearly 25 percent of the two next older generations. Twenty percent of Millennials have at least one parent who is an immigrant.

While nearly 90 percent of the GI Generation was white, it was also diverse by the standards of its era. Many were immigrants themselves or the children of Catholic and Jewish immigrants from southern and eastern Europe who composed the last great wave of Europeans to enter the United States in the late nineteenth and early twentieth centuries. The ethnic diversity of the GI Generation is reflected both in the sneering comment of Adolf Hitler that the United States was a "mongrel nation" incapable of successfully waging war and the Hollywood movies that frequently depict American World War II fighting units as comprising soldiers of widely varying ethnic and regional backgrounds. Neil Simon's semi-autobiographical comedy *Biloxi Blues* perfectly captures the moment in American history when members of the GI Generation came out of their ethnic enclaves and lost their cultural innocence in the forced solidarity of boot camp.

Both the GI and Millennial Generations were also large in comparison with the generations that immediately preceded their own. There are now twice as many Millennials as Gen-Xers and already a million more Millennials alive than Baby Boomers—a gap that will only increase over the next several decades as the Baby Boomers age and die. In 1930, when the GI Generation was poised to start making its mark on American society and politics, there were nearly as many members of that generation living at that time as there were members of the two previous American generations combined. Then, just as now, the sheer numbers of that generation allowed its beliefs and attitudes to become the dominant style of its era.

There are also parallels in the societal, economic, and political settings in which the GI and Millennial Generations grew up and came of age. In both settings, labeled idealist eras, there was loud demand for limiting immigration to protect American culture, values, and jobs, even as both generations were significantly changing those very values and culture. Both eras also featured widespread exhortations and major governmental expenditures to eliminate potentially addictive substances: the struggle to enact and enforce Prohibition during the GI Generation's youth, and the War on Drugs in the time of the Millennials. Economically, both eras were marked by modest recoveries from the troughs that had occurred during the previous generation's coming of age, recoveries that were most clearly distinguished by rising stock markets and also by sharpening economic inequality. The childhoods of both the GI and Millennial Generations were marked initially by the United States reducing its involvement in international affairs. For the GI Generation it was the end of World War I and the rejection of the League of Nations and foreign alliances, and the end of the Cold War for the Millennials. However, in both eras events—specifically the rise of fascism during the 1930s and the attacks of 9/11 and the growing threat of terrorism and Islamic extremism—eventually forced Americans to pay greater attention to events in the world than they might otherwise have preferred.

As the GI Generation emerged into young adulthood, it confronted the major economic collapse of the Great Depression and, a decade later, the beginning of World War II. Of course, whether the Millennials will have to face crises of that magnitude remains to be seen, but it is interesting to note that survey results indicate that Millennials (and older generations) have every expectation that they will.

BABY BOOMER, GEN-X, AND MILLENNIAL CHILDHOODS

Each generation of Americans is born into a social environment characterized by distinctive values about marriage, family, and children. As generational theorists William Strauss and Neil Howe remind us, these values are not constant, but instead recur over time, in cyclical fashion corresponding to the emergence and maturation of each new American generation. These domestic values shape how each generation is reared as children and teenagers, and they remain through adulthood, midlife, and old age. The values contribute strongly to the distinctive lifelong attitudes and behavior of each generation in areas as diverse as politics and governmental organization, economics, participation in and attitudes toward particular occupations, appearance and sex roles, the rules for acceptable social interactions, the subjects and writing styles of both fiction and nonfiction authors, and, of course, music and popular entertainment (Strauss and Howe 1991).

During the past six decades, as the three most recent American generations—Baby Boomers, Gen-Xers, and Millennials—developed and emerged as distinctive generations, these values, attitudes, and behaviors involving marriage, family, and children have changed sharply. And these changes are clearly reflected in a wide range of demographic data.

Baby Boomers were born in the years 1943 to 1960, according to Strauss and Howe, or 1946 to 1964 according to most other observers. They came of age in America during an era when the large majority of adults were married; birthrates and live births were high; divorces very rare; couples married and had their first children at historically young ages; women stayed at home to care for their families, rather than joining the labor force; and the movement from central cities to the suburbs began in earnest.

Census data tell us that in the 1950s, when most Baby Boomers were children, more than two-thirds of American adults were married; live births were at their highest level (about 25 per 1,000 women); and divorce rates were at their lowest level (2.3 per 1,000 population in 1955, falling slightly to 2.2 in 1960) than at any time during the past century. The actual number of births increased annually after 1945 and peaked at just over 4.3 million in 1957. In 1955 the median age at which males first married was 22.6 years. The average female married in that same year at an age (20.2) when, before the passage of the Twenty-sixth Amendment to the Constitution, she was too young to vote. During the Baby Boom era, the average age of a first-time mother was a historically low 21 years.

Most Boomer era households were supported by just one wage earner, and most married women stayed at home. In fact, during the 1950s only a third of all women, and a quarter of married women, participated in the labor force. On a personal level that meant that Baby Boomer children, like their Silent and GI Generation parents, spent about five hours per day with an adult role model, who was more often than not their mother (Manning, Field, and Roberts n.d.).

Finally, with the building of communities like Levittown and the interstate highway system, Baby Boomers and their parents became America's first large group of suburbanites. From 1940 to 1960, the percentage of Americans living in suburbs doubled, from 15 percent to 30 percent—the largest such increase in U.S. history. According to numerous observers, among the many supposedly deleterious effects of increasing suburbanization was the weakening of close-knit extended families. This phenomenon was poignantly portrayed in *Avalon*, Barry Levinson's autobiographical

1990 movie about the disintegration of his large, fractious, but loving Baltimore Jewish family.

All this was to change sharply for Generation X (those born in the years 1961 to 1981 according to Strauss and Howe, but between 1964 and 1982 according to other observers). Baby Boomers were born and came of age in an era of apparent stability in both American society and family life. Gen-Xers, who were born to older members of the Silent Generation or to younger Baby Boomers, were children during a time of both societal and domestic instability. The years from the mid-1960s through the early 1980s were marked by declines in marriage and birth rates and increases in divorces and out-of-wedlock births. To the extent that people married and had children at all, they did so at an older age than previous generations, as increasing numbers of women entered the labor force.

By the end of the 1970s, the number of adult Americans who were married fell to barely six in ten; the number who had never married rose to about three in ten as older married persons died and relatively few younger ones replaced them. During the 1960s and 1970s birth rates fell from their peak of nearly 25 per 1,000 women to just over 15 per 1,000 by 1980. Annual live births declined consistently during the late 1960s and early 1970s. They eventually reached lows of about 3.1 million per year from 1973 to 1976, a trend that caused hospitals across the United States to curtail or eliminate their maternity services. In 1965, when the first Gen-X babies were born, the median age at which males first married was about 23 years, and for females it was 22. Over the next twenty years, it rose by three years for both sexes. During the two decades when Gen-Xers were born, whether for reasons of economic necessity or self-actualization, the percentage of women in the labor force crossed the 50 percent threshold for the first time in U.S. history, other than briefly during wartime emergencies.

The movement to the suburbs continued unabated, and even increased in the wake of racial tensions and the deterioration of central cities. In 1970, when the first Gen-Xers were about six years old, a slight plurality of Americans (38%) lived in the suburbs for the first time in U.S. history. And, by 1980, as the last Gen-Xers were being born, 45 percent of Americans were suburbanites.

The amount of time Generation X children spent with significant adult role models dropped to about fifteen minutes a day. This was colorfully illustrated by the 1990 movie *Home Alone*, in which eight-year-old Kevin (Macaulay Culkin) is mistakenly left behind when his family leaves on a European vacation and is not even missed until his parents have arrived in Paris. Of course, like other self-reliant Generation X role models, Kevin demonstrates his ability to defend his suburban Chicago home from woefully incompetent robbers, without any help from the police or other adults, all of whom are portrayed in the movie as completely clueless.

When the Millennial Generation came onto the scene in the 1980s and 1990s, American patterns of domestic behavior changed once again. A number of the trends that had begun during the years Generation Xers were born were reversed. The average age at which Americans married, after rising consistently and significantly from the 1950s to the mid-1980s, stabilized or even declined slightly, to around 27 years in the late 1990s. After rising steadily to a 1980 peak of 5.2 per 1,000 population, the divorce rate fell steadily to a low of 4.2 in 2000. The birthrate ticked up a bit during the 1980s (to about 16 per 1,000 for white women and 22 per 1,000 for African Americans at the end of that decade). This caused the annual number of births to increase consistently through the 1980s, finally reaching four million in 1989, nearly as many as during the 1950s Baby Boom and holding at that level throughout the early 1990s.

Some things did not revert back to the patterns of previous eras, however. The number of American adults who had ever been married continued to fall (to around 55% in 2000), and the percentage of women involved in the workforce continued to rise (60% in 2000), despite the call of religious conservatives and talk show hosts, such as Dr. Laura Schlessinger, for moms to stay at home. And yet the amount of time children spent with significant adult role models rose to several hours each day. While this was not a full rebound to 1950s levels, it was accompanied by a concerted effort of parents to provide "quality time" interactions with their kids and involve fathers in the lives of their children more than ever before. The Millennial Generation became the first one to experience the concept of co-parenting, with both fathers and mothers playing an equal role in their children's upbringing.

Finally, due to continuously rising housing costs, the growth of ever more far-flung suburbs (categorized as exurbs) continued in metropolitan areas across the United States, so that by 2000 fully half of all Americans lived in the old suburbs or the new exurbs.

POP CULTURE CAPTURES THE
COMEDY OF IT ALL

The values embodied by these shifting behavioral patterns were portrayed and transmitted with great clarity and humor in the popular culture prevalent during the development and coming of age of each of the last three American generations. Nowhere are these trends better portrayed than in that staple of American television, the situation comedy.

Perhaps no sitcom captured the complete texture of the America into which Baby Boomers were born better than "I Love Lucy." The prevailing wisdom about the place of women's place in society was portrayed by Lucy Ricardo's consistently foolish attempts to enter the workplace (such as the iconic inability of Lucy and her best friend, Ethel Mertz, to keep up with a chocolate candy factory assembly line), and the recognition at the end of each episode that Lucy's true role is that of a homemaker. The importance of motherhood was captured in Lucy's teary-eyed announcement of her pregnancy to her husband, Ricky, and the birth of baby Little Ricky (an episode that set TV ratings records that stood for years). The show also captured America's changing residential demographics with the Ricardos' move from their Manhattan brownstone to the Connecticut suburbs.

With few exceptions (Jackie Gleason's "The Honeymooners" being the most notable), nearly all 1950s sitcoms that aired during the childhoods of the early Baby Boomers portrayed wholesome, white, middleclass nuclear families. The Andersons in "Father Knows Best," the Cleavers in "Leave It to Beaver," and the Nelsons in "The Adventures of Ozzie and Harriet" appeared to reside in small towns or new suburbs. They were headed by craggy, strong, and wise GI Generation fathers who held some type of white-collar job and a gentle, warm, stay-at-home mom who never seemed to have a hair out of place even during the most stressful of situations. The Baby Boomer children in these sitcoms (Beaver Cleaver and his older brother, Wally; Betty, Bud, and Kathy Anderson; and David and Ricky Nelson) were attractive, occasionally mischievous, but never really bad, and were generally obedient. Dad, and to a lesser extent Mom, managed to resolve all the not-too-serious problems confronting the family with little difficulty. Mom provided comfort, care, and compassion; but Dad was clearly the boss of the family—a wise if somewhat distant figure to whom the kids turned for advice. To the extent that discipline was needed it was Dad's job to provide it, usually through strength of character, not an iron fist.

"Father Knows Best" went off the air in 1960, "Leave It to Beaver" in 1963, and "The Adventures of Ozzie and Harriet" in 1966, just as the last Baby Boomers and first Gen-Xers were being born. As a result, it is not known if in later years any of the TV Anderson, Cleaver, or Nelson children became rebellious young adults in conflict with their GI Generation parents, like so many real-life young adult Baby Boomers. However, after soaring to success as a recording star, in real life Ricky Nelson did, in fact, rebel and experiment with alternative lifestyles and drugs.

On the cusp of the generation change between Baby Boomers and Gen-Xers, the character of the families portrayed in sitcoms began to change, reflecting the transformations that were occurring in American society. Many of the more popular of them ("The Andy Griffith Show," "Bachelor Father," "Family Affair," "The Courtship of Eddie's Father," "My Three Sons," "The Partridge Family," and "Julia") portrayed families headed by single parents, although, due to network concerns about audience sensibilities, most of them were widowed rather than divorced. A few others, such as "The Brady Bunch," portrayed blended families. Once again, however, the parents were most often widowed, not divorced.

The life situations and problems confronting these sitcom families on the cusp of generational change were occasionally a bit more socially complex than those dealt with by the families in the 1950s programs. For example, in one episode of "My Three Sons" the head of the household, Steve Douglas (Fred MacMurray), was required to convince a judge of the viability of his legally adopting Ernie into a household with no women present. And the Brady family from time to time, at least gently, dealt with issues such as women's rights, sex roles, and even ethnic relations and interracial adoption when a white neighbor's family adopted black children. Still, in the end, societal conflict and tension were minimal in these transitional domestic situation comedies, with the focus being primarily on matters such as dating, sibling rivalry, homework, and the normal family issues of the era. The single parent or blended family invariably managed to successfully resolve most of these by the end of each half-hour episode.

By the middle of the 1960s and into the 1980s, the years in which Generation X was born and maturing, situation comedies had to embrace the full sweep of the changes that were occurring in America to

remain relevant. Perhaps the program that best, and certainly first, captured the varied social transformations of that era was "All in the Family,"
the greatest sitcom hit of the early 1970s and the fourth most popular TV
show of all time ("Greatest Shows" 2002). The protagonist of "All in the
Family," a member of the GI Generation, Archie Bunker, futilely
attempted to stem the tide of change inundating his working-class home
and railed against his rebellious Baby Boomer daughter and son-in-law's
politics and lifestyles. In contrast to Ward Cleaver's proud service as a
Seabee, Archie's military participation, in what he constantly referred to
as "W-W-Two, the Big One," was a source of ridicule (he was a quarter-
master in the Army Air Corps and received a shrapnel wound in his rear
end, not in combat but in an accident). Reflecting the tumultuous cultural politics of its era, the show consistently broke new ground, dealing
with and debating issues such as racism and homosexuality, while also
making it okay to talk about rape, impotence, and breast cancer during
the "family hour" on network television. By the end of the show's run, as
the first Millennials were being born, even Archie's long-suffering wife,
Edith, joined the side of women's libbers when, after years of being told
to "stifle" herself during discussions with Archie, she fights back and sur-
prises both him and herself by telling him to "stifle" during an argument.

The shows of the era in which Gen-Xers were being reared and
coming of age were set in varied locations, but only rarely in traditional
domestic settings. Among other places, they occurred at a Twin Cities TV
station ("Mary Tyler Moore"), a radio station ("WKRP in Cincinnati"),
a New York cab company ("Taxi"), an Atlanta interior decorating studio
("Designing Women"), a New York courtroom ("Night Court"), the
office of a Chicago psychologist ("The Bob Newhart Show"), a Phoenix
diner ("Alice"), and a Boston bar ("Cheers"). In many of them, visits to
the houses or apartments where the protagonists presumably received
their mail were rare and fleeting; the real homes of the lead characters
and their real families seemed to be located in the places where they
worked, partied, or drank.

Moreover, most of the adult characters on situation comedies no
longer were middle-class men who went to the office and middle-class
women who stayed home. Jobs ranged up and down the occupational
spectrum from psychiatrist, judge, and attorney to loading dock foreman,
cab driver, and mail carrier, and from gainfully employed to chronically

unemployed to retired. And, it wasn't only men who worked outside the home. Most notably, Mary Tyler Moore, who portrayed suburban house-wife and mother Laura Petrie in the mid-sixties "Dick Van Dyke Show," was reincarnated in 1970 in a program that bore her name. As Mary Richards, a young woman far more dedicated to her career as a TV news producer than to a search for a husband, she served, along with Marlo Thomas in "That Girl," as a role model for other "liberated" young women across America.

Across all the varied locations and occupations portrayed in the Gen-X era situation comedies, there were a couple of major consistencies—ongoing marriages were few and far between, and children were equally rare. Robert Hartley (Bob Newhart) and his wife, Emily (Suzanne Pleshette), had no children, and Vera, the wife of Norm Peterson (George Wendt) in "Cheers," never appeared on camera during the entire run of the show (Norm would often expend major effort to hide from her). Even among other situation comedies, there were few married couples. Divorced, widowed, and certainly single characters were far more com-mon. Tommy, the son of the widowed Alice on the show of that name, was one of the very few children who appeared regularly in sitcoms of this era. Among the only other children who surfaced occasionally were those of divorced barmaid Carla Tortelli (Rhea Perlman on "Cheers"), whose kids, in accord with the frequently negative perceptions held of children during this era, were marginal juvenile delinquents.

The children who did have significant roles on any of the 1970s and early 1980s sitcoms rarely lived in a conventional or traditional family setting. Typical were the daughters of Ann Romano (Bonnie Franklin) in "One Day at a Time," an Indianapolis homemaker who surprised her husband by filing for divorce so that she could pursue a career in adver-tising and raise her daughters on her own. That wasn't easy. Ms. Romano consistently found herself confronting issues such as teenage suicide, drug use, and premarital sex as she attempted to hold her family together in a difficult environment. (In an ironic real-life parallel to the show, Macken-zie Phillips, the actress who played the older Romano daughter, had to be written out of the show occasionally because of substance abuse problems.) In the later 1980s, married families who had children began to reappear in situation comedies with greater regularity, but at least initially those were anything but the placid, happy, and well-adjusted families of the 1950s sitcoms. In keeping with common Generation X perceptions about marriage and children, the relationships between spouses and between parents and children were often harsh and caustic. In "Married . . . with Children," husband and father Al Bundy, a marginally capable women's shoe salesman, and his wife, Peggy, a sarcastic, vulgar woman with an out-of-date, brassy, red bouffant hairdo, more or less attempt unsuccessfully to rear an attractive, promiscuous, dim-witted daughter and a bright, snotty, unpopular son.

Sitcoms that portrayed Generation X as it matured into young adulthood depict a generation unable to hold a job and hesitant to commit to marriage and children. In "Seinfeld," a sitcom said to be "about nothing," a commentary on the presumably empty lives of young adult Gen-Xers, the characters seem to drift aimlessly between jobs. The six attractive stars of "Friends" substitute their friendships with one another for their families. None of the friends ever seem to have any clear occupational successes. In fact, one of the program's standing gags is that none of the others can determine just exactly what Chandler Bing's (Matthew Perry) job actually is.

The Gen-Xers in these enormously popular shows had infrequent interactions and strained relationships with their Silent Generation or Boomer parents. Jerry Seinfeld's parents have moved to a condo in Florida and only come into his life occasionally to whine and carp at him. His friend George Costanza has a similar relationship with his own parents. On "Friends," Monica Geller's parents selfishly spent the money that they had supposedly set aside to pay for Monica's wedding in order to buy a beach house for themselves. And Chandler Bing's father, a transvestite with an act in Las Vegas, is supposedly the cause of Chandler's own dubious sexuality. All of the parents are weird; none of them have a relationship with their children that is helpful in any way.

Although most are physically attractive, the Gen-X young adults are no more successful in their personal lives than in their careers. In both "Seinfeld" and "Friends," the characters seem to drift almost aimlessly between "romantic" engagements, sometimes with one another and sometimes with others outside the friendship circle. In "Friends," the on-again off-again relationships between Ross and Rachel and between Chandler and Monica play out with almost excruciating slowness, before the latter couple finally marries and eventually adopts twins. Ross and Rachel break up, presumably for the last time, only to come together in the show's final episode, aired as the last of the Millennials were being born.

The transition out of Gen-X sensibilities into a new era first surfaced in the appropriately titled situation comedy "Family Ties" during the late 1980s, as television audience parents began to rear their Millennial children. It had a more conventional and pleasant domestic lifestyle. While most of the Keaton children are clearly Gen-Xers, their parents are former Baby Boomer flower children. She is a self-assured woman and a successful architect, and he is the idealistic director of a public TV station. Both are liberal Democrats. Their eldest son, Alex (Michael J. Fox), on the other hand, like so many Gen-Xers who followed, is a conservative Republican who admires Richard Nixon and Ronald Reagan. His first sexual encounter is even with a girl who shares his passion for Milton Friedman. But the Keaton's younger daughter, Jennifer, is actually an early Millennial, embodying the characteristics of that generation—a positive, upbeat attitude linked to academic achievement. As a member of the Millennial Generation, many of whom later came to identify with the Democratic Party, she also successfully but lovingly resists Alex's efforts to convert her to conservative Republicanism.

The situation comedy that captured Millennial-era family life, child-rearing practices, and childhood experience to the greatest extent was "The Cosby Show," which initially aired when the first Millennials were being born. While this means that most of the children on the show would have been Gen-Xers, Cliff and Clair Huxtable reared them as if they were Millennial children. In fact, some of the most prevalent attitudes toward parenting exhibited by Boomers and Gen-Xers seem to be lifted straight from the behavior of the show's lead characters. Although Cliff and Clair have high-powered, demanding professional careers, they both devote a lot of time and attention to their children. Cliff is as involved in child rearing as Clair. The parents have clear beliefs and set the standards for family behavior, but they are friends of their children rather than the somewhat distant authority figures of the Baby Boomers' GI Generation parents or the adversarial or detached Silent and Boomer parents of Gen-Xers. Finally, in spite of the constantly expressed wishes of Cliff and Clair that their children get out of the house and live on their own, at one time or another all the Huxtable children boomerang back home; eventually the elder Huxtables have to assume a significant role in the rearing of their Millennial granddaughter.

Overall, the most popular television situation comedies since the 1950s have perceptively portrayed the demographic trends and domestic lives of the Baby Boom, Gen-X, and Millennial Generations with amazing accuracy. In so doing, they have provided a clear reflection of the behavior, attitudes, and values that will continue to influence and shape the roles played by each of these three contemporary generations in American society and politics.

The Care and Feeding
of Millennial Children

Attitudes toward marriage and children and the domestic behavior that results from those beliefs have changed significantly across the lifespan of the three most recent American generations. As both demographic data and our excursion into Television Land clearly indicate, the newest group of children, the Millennials, unlike the Gen-Xers before them, were wanted and valued. During much of the 1960s and 1970s, having and rearing children was something to be delayed or even avoided, an attitude that accompanied the development of "the pill" and the *Roe v. Wade* decision.

At a global and societal level, overpopulation was perceived as a threat to the environment, leading to an excessive consumption of governmental services and economic and natural resources, a fear that was nonexistent in the growth-oriented, can-do, postwar Baby Boom era. It is hard to even imagine a GI Generation father agonizing about bringing another child into a world threatened by war and overpopulation, as did Archie Bunker's Boomer son-in-law, "Meathead," in "All in the Family," when he was informed by his wife of her possible pregnancy.

At a personal level, children were frequently seen as hindering opportunities for personal and career growth, especially for women. Several of the more popular movies during that era portrayed children as uncontrolled savages (*Lord of the Flies*), promiscuous sexual predators who led proper and conservative older men astray (*Lolita*), possessed by the devil (*The Exorcist*), and even the spawn of Satan (*Rosemary's Baby*).

By contrast, a drop in the use of birth control and abortion and a decline in divorce rates accompanied the arrival of the Millennials.

The statistics verifying these changes are clear. The rate of abortions per 1,000 women dropped steadily from a peak of 29.3 in 1980 and 1981, when the final Gen-Xers were being born, to a low of 21 as the final Millennials were coming into the world in 2000. The absolute number of abortions reported in the United States declined from a high of over 1.3 million through the 1980s to a low of about 300,000 in 2005. As indicated, divorces per 1,000 adults fell from 5.2 in 1980 to 4.2 twenty years later.

Living a life that didn't involve rearing children was seen as selfish and incomplete, for straight and gay couples alike. Movies such as *Three Men and a Baby* and *Jerry McGuire* portrayed children as gifts from God, necessary to give meaning to the empty lives of formerly dissolute and self-centered Baby Boomers and Gen-Xers. The career arc of television actor John Ritter clearly illustrates the shift of Baby Boomers and Gen-Xers from young adults who studiously avoided marriage and parenthood to dedicated spouses and, especially, parents. In the 1970s situation comedy "Three's Company," his first major television role, Ritter played Jack Tripper, a twenty-something Baby Boomer who attempted to "date," but definitely not commit to, every attractive woman who came within his view. In his final TV role, "8 Simple Rules for Dating My Teenage Daughter," which originally aired in the 2002 and 2003 television seasons, Ritter portrayed Paul Hennessy, a middle-aged father who dedicates much of his life to protecting his Millennial daughter from latter-day Jack Trippers.

The perception of Millennials as wanted, necessary, and valued, in turn, led their parents to adopt child-rearing practices and advocate public policies emphasizing protection, structure, and positive reinforcement. A 2005 study presented to the Texas Association of College Technical Educators indicated that over 9,000 books were written about self-esteem and children during the 1980s and 1990s as Millennials were born and came of age. This contrasts with the fewer than 500 books written on the subject during the 1970s when Gen-Xers were being reared (Manning, Fields, and Roberts n.d.).

And parents took the message to heart. The average score on the Coopersmith Self-Esteem Inventory test was higher for Millennials ages 9 to 13 in the mid-1990s than for 73 percent of all Gen-Xers of the same age in 1979. Two comments from Millennials about their childhood capture the approach perfectly. "My mom constantly told me how special I was. No matter how I did, she would tell me I was the best," nineteen-year-old Natalie recalled. Kristen, age twenty-two, said her parents were always "telling me what a great job I did and repeatedly telling me I was a very special person" (Twenge 2006, 58).

The need to protect precious Millennial children was visibly reflected in the arrival of "Baby on Board" bumper stickers in 1982, at just the time the first cohort of Millennials was being born. Play dates and organized recreation, lessons in sharing nicely, and tutoring to ensure the school readiness of four- and five-year-olds replaced the home-alone lifestyles of the "latchkey kids" from an earlier generation. To maximize the self-esteem and social integration of their Millennial children, Baby Boomers and especially Gen-Xers now supervised contests where, regardless of abilities, all children participated, scores were not kept, winners or losers were not determined, and everyone got a trophy just for showing up.

These attitudes toward children were quickly translated into political behavior. A sense that public schools were failing their students became pervasive, and school bond initiatives, which as often as not failed at the ballot box in the 1960s and 1970s, passed with much greater regularity in the last decade of the twentieth century. In California, the state where the tax revolt of the 1980s started with the enactment of Proposition 13 in 1978, the passage rate in school bond referenda increased to about 75 percent in the late 1990s and the first years of the twenty-first century, up from the 50 percent or less it had been a decade or two earlier. Moreover, in 2000, the California electorate voted to reduce the threshold needed to increase school taxes from a two-thirds supermajority to 55 percent, thereby ensuring even greater spending on the state's public schools in the future.

During the 1990s and into the first decade of the twenty-first century, standardized tests to measure the success of students, teachers, and schools were endorsed by politicians of both political parties and instituted, over the objections of teachers' unions and school administrators, in states across the nation and eventually at the federal level. Charter schools, a new type of school that received public funds but was freed from many regulations and encouraged to use innovative teaching methods, also came into existence, despite the objections of the entrenched educational establishment. The use of vouchers that would permit parents to spend public dollars to educate their children in schools of their own choosing, public or private, was widely advocated, especially by political conservatives; such proposals generated even more opposition from those who felt they knew how to educate a child better than the dedicated parents of Millennials.

A sense that child abuse and sexual exploitation were widespread and needed to be dealt with vigorously became a staple in political campaigns and TV news programs alike. In the 1990s, most states established data banks containing the names of persons who had ever been convicted of sexual abuse, and such persons were prohibited from living near schools or parks where children were likely to be found. Several times a year, television programs such as "NBC Dateline" could ensure high ratings by airing sting operations, depicting local police departments across the country arresting dozens of potential online sexual predators. Amber alerts on freeways everywhere encouraged the entire country to join in the apprehension of those who would steal children from parents.

THE RESULTS OF ALL THAT CAREFUL CHILD REARING

In large part as a result of their protected, structured, and positively reinforced upbringing, the Millennials are an exceptionally accomplished, positive, upbeat, and optimistic generation. Juvenile crime, teen pregnancy, and abortion rates are substantially lower and standardized academic performance test scores are higher among Millennials than they were among both Baby Boomers and Gen-Xers. The number of violent crimes annually committed by juveniles in the United States rose steadily during the 1970s and 1980s, peaking at just over 1 million in 1993 and 1994, a time when most Gen-Xers were in their teens and early twenties. By contrast, violent crimes committed by juveniles fell to around 300,000 in 2002 and 2003, when most Millennials were in their teens and early twenties. Over the same period, homicides involving juveniles dropped from more than 3,500 per year to less than 1,500. Moreover, in spite of the widespread publicity and fear engendered by tragic and spectacular events, such as the murder of twelve students by two of their classmates at Columbine High School near Denver in 1999 and of thirty-two students and teachers by an alienated student at Virginia Tech in April 2007, crimes committed in schools also declined sharply as Millennials came of age. This led one contemporary educator to claim that children were now safer in the schools than they had been at any time since the 1960s. It should be noted that these absolute drops in juvenile crime occurred even though there were twice the number of Millennial teenagers as there had been Gen-X teenagers.

The positive lifestyles of Millennials in comparison to the older Baby Boomers and Gen-Xers are reflected statistically in other areas. Data collected by the Guttmacher Institute, America's foremost organization dealing with reproductive matters, indicate that the teenage pregnancy rate rose by more than 20 percent from the time the last Baby Boomers entered their teens (early 1970s) to the time that the greatest number of Gen-Xers were in theirs (early 1990s). It then declined more than 35 percent from that peak in the first years after 2000. Over the same period, the teenage abortion rate more than doubled at first, and then fell by 50 percent. Similarly, data collected by the U.S. Department of Education indicate that both the reading and mathematics achievement levels of American children were consistently higher in the early years of the twenty-first century than they had been at any point during the previous thirty years, as American primary and high school students read more and took higher-level math courses.

The positive behavior of Millennials is clearly reflected in their characteristically upbeat and optimistic attitudes. Survey research results from 2006 indicates that two-thirds of Millennials rate their own lives as "excellent" or "pretty good," well above the numbers of Gen-Xers and Baby Boomers (57% each) who felt that way. Millennials are also much more likely to expect that their lives will be better ten years in the future (82%) than either Gen-Xers (75%) or Baby Boomers (58%) (Frank N. Magid Associates, January 2006). And, lest it be thought that these numbers simply reflect a greater optimism of young people regardless of generation, Pew Research Center surveys indicate that Millennials are more upbeat today than Gen-Xers were at the same age in 1990, more frequently believing that they live in an exciting time, have greater sexual freedom, and have a greater chance of buying a house and bringing about social change (2007).

The optimistic life expectations of Millennials cross socioeconomic and ethnic lines. According to Strauss and Howe, "Among those [Millennials] in families earning less than $30,000, 54 percent believe the world holds 'many opportunities' for me. Among those in families earning over $75,000 that proportion rises to 78 percent. More than four in five (including 95 percent of Latinos and 97 percent of African Americans) believe they will be financially more successful than their parents, a percentage that rose sharply in the '90s" (Strauss and Howe 2006, 84).

Moreover, the Millennial Generation seems less bound by the sex role expectations of earlier generations. For the first time in American history, equal numbers of males and females are graduating from college and attending professional schools. Beginning with the passage of Title IX in 1972, requiring equal access and support for women in school sports, some conservatives have even claimed that the way in which Millennials have been reared is "girl centered" and injurious to boys.

The result of all these changes in the way Americans raise their children has created a very close, positive, and indeed friendly relationship between Millennials and their parents, unlike that of the rebellious Baby Boomers and the neglected and misunderstood Gen-Xers of generations past. Half of all Millennials say they see their parents in person every day, and, aided by widely available and relatively inexpensive cell phone service, nearly as many (45%) talk with their parents on the phone daily. Virtually all do so at least weekly. One in five communicates with them by email at least occasionally. These incidences of ongoing parent-child contact are well above those for all older generations of Americans (Pew Research Center 2007a).

The Millennials have a strong group and community orientation and a clear tendency to share their thoughts and activities with others—friends, teachers, and parents. This is considerably different than "it's all about me" Baby Boomers and the cynical individualism of alienated Gen-Xers. Among teen and young adult Millennials, group dating and clubs have replaced the singles bars of the two older generations as the most popular social venues. Even in education, group study sessions and shared learning are the preferred way to gain knowledge.

Lengthy group cell phone rounds of Instant Messaging ("IMing") and wide-ranging continuous text messaging "conversations" have become increasingly important in how Millennials communicate with one another. About half of Millennials report that they have in the past twenty-four hours sent or received an email (50%) and/or a cell phone text message (51%), and almost a third (30%) an instant message. The Millennials use of the latter two media clearly dwarfs that of all older generations. In addition to simply sending messages on the Internet and cell phones, most Millennials (54%) use Internet social networking sites, such as Facebook or MySpace, that allow users to come together online around shared interests or causes. Virtually all (80%) Millennials over the age of fourteen have created a personal profile on at least one of the social networking sites, and they use these sites constantly to stay in touch with their "friends"—three-quarters of Millennials update their social networking site at least weekly (Pew Research Center 2007a).

Volunteerism and community service programs are now a recognized aspect of the curricula of most public schools, and, in turn, have been internalized as a part of the attitudes and lifestyles of most Millennials. A January 7, 2007, PBS program entitled "Generation Next" (its label for the Millennial Generation) indicated that 80 percent of Millennials had participated in some type of community or societal improvement program during the previous year.

MILLENNIAL MOVIES AND MUSIC

All these Millennial traits and characteristics are now being reflected in a variety of popular culture media, from movies to music, for and about Millennials. The Millennial Generation's values and behaviors were captured perfectly in *The Devil Wears Prada*, the first Millennial example of that American cinematic staple, the coming-of-age movie. Andy Sachs (Anne Hathaway) is a true Millennial, different from the lead character of previous coming-of-age movies about other generations. From her androgynous first name to the classic scene where she leaves the table during dinner with her father (who doesn't seem to mind) to take an important cell phone call from her boss, Andy could only be a Millennial.

If anything, her character far more closely resembles another Andy (Hardy), the lead character of the most representative of GI Generation coming-of-age movies, than she does any other more recent leads in this genre. She differs from Benjamin Braddock (Dustin Hoffman) in *The Graduate*, the depressed, Boomer rejecter of his parent's "plastic" values, as well as from the neglected, misunderstood, but entrepreneurial Gen-Xer Joel Goodsen (Tom Cruise) in *Risky Business*, in several key ways. First, there is the ethnic and gender-preference diversity of her friendship group (an African American woman, a gay man, and her somewhat scruffy but sensitive boyfriend who is pursuing a career as a chef). There is also the fact that she is a young woman who can reasonably aspire to having both academic and career success and a happy relationship (and presumably marriage) with her boyfriend.

There is quite a contrast between how the lead characters in the Baby Boomer and Gen-X coming-of-age movies relate to their friends and the relationships that both Andy Sachs and Andy Hardy have with their clean-cut, attractive, and upbeat peers. Benjamin Braddock appears to have no friends at all and Joel Goodsen literally profits from his friends by providing a "for hire" outlet for their sexual appetites, using his parents' empty house as his place of business (in true Gen-X fashion, his parents had left Joel at home alone while they went on vacation). For both Andys, by contrast, their friends are critical sources for advice, support, validation, and the accomplishment of both personal and broader goals.

They both also have strong and positive relationships with their parents and the other adults in their lives, all of whom provide a level of friendship and guidance that is at least as important and valuable as that provided by their peers. For Andy Hardy these highly important adults are his strong, wise father, his gentle, loving mother, and his practical maiden aunt schoolteacher who lives in the Hardy home. Even though Andy Sachs's parents are divorced, it is clear that her mother and father both love her and are involved in her life.

Finally, the two Andys, after some struggle, eventually live for and by their ideals. They do what is right for both them and for the group, but they manage to do so politely and in a way that leaves their relationships with others intact, in Andy Sachs's case, even with the Devil herself.

A generation's music also evokes the mood and character of that generation, reinforcing a sense of time and place whenever it is heard in a movie or TV show. Indeed, the distinctiveness of each succeeding generation is captured in its music as much as in any other part of pop culture.

Music becomes identified with a generation when its members are in their teens and twenties. Sometimes, as in the case of today's Millennials, a generation's tastes evolve as it grows up, which provides insights into its fundamental attitudes and beliefs as it matures. For instance, teen Millennials in the late 1990s and the first years of the twenty-first century screamed for carefully packaged boy bands, such as 'N Sync and the Backstreet Boys, just as any five- to twelve-year-old girl today can sing from memory the songs and quote every line of dialogue from Disney's *High School Musical*. While the specific subject matter—winning and sharing boys, friends, and love—may not be distinct from the themes of the music of other generations, the technical sophistication and tone of the production marks it as unique to this time and this generation.

The optimistic outcomes and spirit of Millennial "tween" music were powerful enough to sweep away such vestiges of Gen-X culture as the dark, macabre Goth look, which officially ended with the post-2006 Christmas season closing, in malls across America, of Hot Topic stores, the chief purveyor of that genre's music and clothing (York 2007).

Although "tweeny" pop may be the favorite musical genre of many of the youngest Millennials, when Internet blogger Peter Savich listed the dominant musical genre for American generations stretching back to the Missionary Generation (the last previous incarnation of an idealist Generation, represented by the Baby Boomers in the current generational cycle), his list captured a new category of Millennial musical taste not even in existence in the 1990s: Mashup. A quick glance at his list helps put this in perspective:

- *Ragtime*—Missionary Generation (late 1890s)
- *Big Band Jazz*—Lost Generation (1920s)
- *Swing*—GI Generation (mid-1930s)
- *Rock 'n' Roll*—Silent Generation (early to mid-1950s)
- *Psychedelic Rock*—Baby Boomers (mid- to late 1960s)
- *Hip Hop, Rap*—Generation X (mid-1980s)
- *Mashup*—Millennial Generation

None of the earlier generations could even have conceived of, let alone produced, a genre such as Mashup, which consists of the combination (usually by digital means) of the music from one song with the a cappella version of another—with the music and vocals frequently belonging to completely different genres. Mashup, as a dominant musical form, awaited the emergence of the digital technology that made combining musical types easy to accomplish and a generation proficient in the use of that technology—not to mention the willingness to ignore the copyright violations this and other forms of peer-to-peer (P2P) communication make possible.

The Millennial Generation acquired a unique set of attitudes and beliefs in its childhood. The upbeat optimistic attitudes of Millennials, their ethnic diversity and openness to nontraditional sex roles, their strong connections to family and friends, and their concern for the wider community will bring major and long-lasting changes to American society and politics in the years just ahead, just as each major generational and technological shift has done in the past.

CHAPTER 5

Millennials Will Spearhead the
Coming Political Realignment

THE CLEAR PATTERN of American political history sug-
gests that the United States is on the brink of its next electoral realignment. This same pattern also suggests that the Millennial Generation will
determine the direction that realignment will take. Its presence was barely
felt in the 2000 election, when the very first young adults born into this
civic generation became eligible to vote, but the number of Millennials
participating in elections has grown steadily ever since.

The size of the youth vote began to increase after 9/11. Galvanized by
the terrorist threat to the country and later by the Iraq War and other major
issues facing the country, the interest in politics and voting among young
Americans continues to increase as the United States moves toward its next
civic realignment. Survey data indicate that Millennials are significantly
more likely to be very interested in keeping up with national affairs than
their Gen-X counterparts had been in the late 1980s (36% vs. 24%) (Pew
Research Center 2007a). In the 2004 presidential election, the voter
turnout of 18- to 24-year-olds rose eleven percentage points over what it
had been in 2000. This compared to a four-percent increase among voters
over 25 (Cannon 2007). Thirty-two percent of 18- to 24-year-olds told
Harvard University's Institute of Politics that they planned on voting
in the 2006 congressional elections. That promise was borne out with a
24 percent increase in voter turnout among this age group in comparison
to its level four years earlier. And contrary to popular belief, more than
twice as many Millennials have voted for a political candidate as have voted
for an "American Idol" contestant (Abcarian and Horn 2006).

By 2008, almost half of the largest generation in American history
will be eligible to vote, making Millennial attitudes and beliefs the key to

understanding how much the dynamics of American politics will change before the first decade of the twenty-first century is over.

THE MORE A GENERATION CHANGES, THE MORE IT REMAINS THE SAME

There is a widely held belief that people invariably think and act one way when they are young, but then sharply alter their beliefs and actions in a predictable manner as they age. In the political sphere, for example, some would argue that it is normal for people to hold extreme or radical views when they are young and become increasingly conservative as they age. Aristide Briand, the French prime minister during World War I, expressed this belief succinctly, "The man who is not a socialist at twenty has no heart, but if he is still a socialist at forty he has no head." Similar sentiments have been attributed to Winston Churchill and George Bernard Shaw, among others.

For the most part, however, survey research suggests that this conventional viewpoint is wrong. While it is true that on certain specific questions people's opinions may change as they gain whatever wisdom comes from experience, it is also true that most people rarely change the fundamental patterns of perceptions, beliefs, and attitudes they learn when they are growing up. Instead, people use those familiar patterns to sort through the swarm of information that they encounter as they grow older, retaining much of that which reinforces their belief system and discarding most that does not. Some of the very earliest research on American political behavior, such as Bernard Berelson, Paul Lazarsfeld, and William McPhee's classic study of voting in the 1948 election, demonstrated the existence, importance, and imperviousness to change of those long-standing patterns of perception, belief, and attitude.

While those experiences and beliefs are not identical among individuals, survey researchers and ethnographic observers are able to measure the attitudes and behaviors of individuals within the same age cohort who together compose a generation that is, taken as a whole, clearly distinct from the generations that came before and those that will come after. There is evidence in support of those distinctive and relatively immutable generation-based patterns in a wide range of surveys today.

For instance, survey data collected by the Pew Research Center in March 2007 demonstrates clear distinctions in the attitudes of specific

American generations toward God and religion, attitudes that do not change significantly as members of those generations grow older. The study shows that while Americans overall have retained certain core religious values, these basic beliefs are held with less intensity than they were twenty years ago. Since at least 1987, around eight in ten Americans have agreed that they "never doubt the existence of God," that "prayer is an important part of their daily lives," and that "we will all be called before God at the Judgment Day to answer for our sins." The numbers holding these underlying beliefs have varied within normal statistical range across the past two decades, but strong agreement with each of them is down by about ten percentage points during the same period. A closer examination of the data reveals that, especially since the late 1990s as the last of the Gen-Xers and the first of the Millennials began to come of age, this decline is mostly caused by differences in generational attitudes toward religion.

Overall, only 12 percent of Americans describe themselves as atheist or agnostic or don't identify with any particular religious tradition. This number is up by just four percentage points since 1987. But age differences in lack of religious belief or affiliation are striking. Within the oldest American generations, the last remaining members of the GI and Silent Generations, just five percent are secular or unaffiliated. That number rises to about one in ten among Baby Boomers to 15 percent of Gen-Xers, and nearly one in five (19%) among Millennials—almost four times the percentage of nonbelievers as existed within the GI and Silent Generations.

As the Pew Center makes clear, the greater religiosity of today's elderly is not at all a matter of people becoming more traditional or religious as they grow older: "The number of seculars within each generational group is about the same in 2007 as it was 10 or 20 years before. . . . People have not become less secular as they have aged" (Pew Research Center 2007d, 31). Instead, the country has become proportionately more secular over the last forty years because generations characterized by life-long, strongly held religious beliefs matured and died and were replaced by new generations with equally long-lived, but less intense, religious faiths.

Unique and life-long sets of generation-based behavior and attitudes exist in the political realm as well. America's last political realignment in the late 1960s produced a number of significant attitudinal and behavioral patterns in the electorate that are characteristic of all idealist realignments. These include, among other things, a major decline in the extent to which voters identify (especially strongly) with one political party, a concurrent increase in the number who say they are Independents, an increase in split-ticket voting and a decline in straight-ticket voting, and a drop in the number of voters who have positive perceptions of the political parties.

All these changes were tied to and produced by the rise of a new generation of voters, the Baby Boomers. When the young Baby Boomers entered the electorate during this idealist realignment, many said they were Independents, and most of those who did identify with a political party did so only weakly. Many Boomers also tended to vote split tickets and to express negative opinions about the political parties. Even as they aged, Baby Boomers persisted in their tendencies to identify as Independents or, at most, identify weakly with a party, to split their tickets, and to hold unfavorable attitudes toward the parties (Nie, Verba, and Petrocik 1976).

Survey data from that realigning era also clearly indicates that, in spite of the rise of the ticket-splitter Baby Boomer voters, members of the electorate who had been voting for several decades or more generally tended to think and act as they always had. They continued to identify with the same political parties to the same extent, and with the same degree of strength, as they had before the realignment. And they voted a straight ticket and expressed favorable attitudes toward at least one of the political parties more often than the new generation of voters.

As a result, Baby Boomers thought Pat Paulsen's campaign for president in 1968, which mocked both political parties, was hilarious and on target in its spoofing of the emptiness of American politics. Meanwhile, members of the GI Generation didn't get the joke and thought Paulsen's campaign and the reaction of Boomers was one more example of the younger generation making fun of America's most precious traditions.

A 2004 AARP survey of the three oldest living generations (the GI, Silent, and Baby Boom) provides additional evidence that the attitudes and behaviors of the older and more "established" GI Generation voters remained constant for decades after the 1968 realignment. The GI Generation was more likely than either of the other two younger generations to identify with either the Democratic or Republican Parties (the greatest number of them remaining Democrats seven decades after the New Deal realignment of the 1930s), and also to say that they always, or nearly always, vote for the same political party. While a majority of the Baby

Boomers and half of the Silent Generation agreed that America needed a strong third party, only a third of the seventy- or eighty-year-old GI Generation did so (Love 2004).

The perceptions and attitudes through which the members of an emerging young generation interpret politics stem from the way they were reared, the common experiences that they share with others in their generation, and the events occurring in the wider world around them. However, as they age, the members of the once-emerging generation use their initial perceptions, attitudes, and behavioral patterns to help them more successfully interpret, respond to, and cope with new political events. The longer these perceptions and attitudes are held, the more useful they become and the more firmly they are held and protected—even when new, contradictory information and perceptions produce cognitive dissonance.

As a result, the hardest voting behavior for political campaigns to change is that of the most elderly in the voting population, something corporations and broadcasters also acknowledge when they rarely pitch their advertising campaigns at anyone over forty-nine years old. Members of the electorate are most easily persuaded when they are young, before their beliefs harden into attitudes they will retain throughout their lives. Whichever party wins the hearts, minds, and votes of Millennials during the next few elections will, therefore, achieve a competitive advantage that will last for the next forty years.

MILLENNIALS ARE AN OPTIMISTIC BUNCH

As with all other generations, the Millennials hold distinctive political attitudes and demonstrate patterns of political behavior that will persist throughout their lives. Any forecast of America's political future has to take account of the values and political beliefs of this emerging new generation, especially in contrast to the attitudes and behavior of the two largest older generations in the current electorate. Of course it is impossible to predict with absolute certainty the precise identity of future candidates or the exact form issues may take in the future. But knowledge and understanding of the political profiles of these three generations, especially the Millennials, does provide a much clearer sense of what to expect in America's next civic realignment and the decades that will follow it.

Millennials are more upbeat and optimistic about their own lives than older generations. About two-thirds of Millennials rate their own lives as either "excellent" or "pretty good" (65%). By contrast, a smaller number of both Baby Boomers and Gen-Xers (57% each) rate their own lives as "excellent" or "pretty good." Seventy-four percent of Millennials expect their lives to be even better in five years, as compared with 59 percent of older Americans (Pew Research Center, January 2007). An even greater percentage (81%) of Millennials expect things to be better for them in ten years, while only 58 percent of Boomers and 75 percent of Gen-Xers think that their lives will be better ten years from now (Frank N. Magid Associates, December 2006).

Of course, some would argue that all young people are more optimistic about their lives, but that the "school of hard knocks" will eventually turn them into "hard-headed realists." However, surveys tell us that Millennials are more upbeat today than Gen-Xers were twenty years ago, when they were the age that Millennials are now. For instance, 64 percent of Millennials believe that they live in an exciting time, whereas only 50 percent of Gen-Xers thought so when they were in their late teens and early twenties. In addition, Millennials are more likely to believe today that they have a greater amount of sexual freedom than Gen-Xers did at a comparable age, in 1987 (66% vs. 54%). Millennials also think they have a greater chance of bringing about social change (56% vs. 48%) and a better chance of buying a house (31% vs. 28%) than the young Gen-X group did twenty years ago (Pew Research Center 2007a).

This high degree of personal optimism, especially about the future, extends to almost every aspect of life, especially those related to economic status. Millennials are more likely than either older generation to believe that they will have the right amount and quality of education to succeed in life and find good jobs, that they will always have interesting and fulfilling careers and be sufficiently well-off while working, and that they will be able to afford good health care, own a home, and then retire comfortably (Frank N. Magid Associates, December 2006).

MILLENNIALS THINK POLITICS CAN MAKE THINGS BETTER

Millennials, like most Americans, are not happy with the present political and societal situation in the United States—nearly two-thirds

(62%) of all Americans and 60 percent of Millennials say that things in America are currently "off track." However, survey research shows that Millennials disagree with their elders in their level of faith in the political process to resolve problems and improve things. Their greater personal optimism makes Millennials, by a margin of almost twenty percentage points, less likely than other generations to agree that special interests rather than the people always get their way in American politics. By similar margins, they are more likely to reject the ideas that politicians don't care what everyday people think; that people who work hard and play by the rules never seem to get ahead in America; and that politicians are more concerned with their own parties than the entire country (Frank N. Magid Associates, December 2006). Millennials are also much more likely than older generations to believe that the government is run for the benefit of all the people (51% vs. 36%) (Pew Research Center 2007d).

Millennials, also to a greater degree than members of older generations, have confidence in the federal government and are more likely to favor a clear, rather than ancillary, role for it in American life. A decisive majority (64%) of Millennials disagrees with the statement, "When the federal government runs something it is usually inefficient and wasteful," while 58 percent of older generations agree with that harsh appraisal. Millennials are also substantially less likely to believe that the federal government should run only those things that can't be run at the local level (63% vs. 71%).

These more favorable Millennial Generation attitudes toward the federal government are not simply a matter of "normal" youthful liberalism. Millennials today are far less likely than Gen-Xers were in the late 1980s to believe that the federal government is usually wasteful and inefficient (32% for Millennials, 47% for young Gen-Xers) and that it should do only what can't be done at the local level (63% vs. 76%) (Pew Research Center 2007a).

More important, Millennials, to a greater extent than other generations, are confident that the American political process and political institutions will be able to handle the major challenges they expect to occur in the coming decades. When asked about the likely resolution of a range of major events or crises, from economic collapse to environmental and health disasters and from terrorist attacks to a world war, a majority of

Millennials believes that one of the political parties or both will be able to effectively deal with each. In particular, to a greater extent than either Gen-Xers or Baby Boomers, Millennials name one party as being most likely to resolve virtually every concern rather than saying that both parties are equally likely to do so. By contrast, the two older generations that together dominated an idealist era in which Independent identifications, ticket splitting, and negative perceptions of political institutions were the norm find it more difficult to choose between the two political parties (Frank N. Magid Associates, December 2006). Millennials are ready for America's two-party political system to meet the challenges of the future in the same way it was able to handle the crises that faced earlier generations during and after the civic realignments of 1860 and 1932.

MILLENNIALS WANT EVERYONE TO SUCCEED, WITH THE GOVERNMENT'S HELP

Historically, civic realignments lead to greater reliance on government, especially the federal government, to deal with economic and social welfare issues and to favor policies that are designed at least to produce a greater degree of economic equality among Americans. One of the indications that such a realignment is coming is the recent rise in support for such policies.

Since 1994, the year in which Republicans wrested control of both houses of Congress from the Democrats, there have been significant increases in the percentage of Americans who believe that "the government should take care of people who can't care for themselves" (from 57% to 69%), "the government should guarantee every citizen enough to eat and a place to sleep" (59% to 69%) and "the government should help more needy people even if the national debt increases" (41% to 54%). Since 1996, the number favoring a smaller government that provides fewer services has fallen from 61 percent to 45 percent, while those preferring a bigger government providing more services have increased from 30 percent to 44 percent. Finally, since the mid-1990s, two-thirds of Americans have consistently favored federally guaranteed health insurance for all citizens, even if it means raising taxes.

The Millennial Generation, with its strong group orientation, is leading this growing support for increased federal economic and social welfare activities. Millennials are more likely than older generations to believe that the government should take care of people who can't take care of themselves (73% vs. 68%), help more needy people even if the national debt increases (59% vs. 54%), and to support federally guaranteed health insurance for all citizens even if this requires raising taxes (73% vs. 66%). The Millennial Generation is also far more favorable toward a bigger government that provides more services than are older Americans (69% vs. 39%) (Pew Research Center 2007d).

MILLENNIALS INCLUDE EVERYONE IN THEIR GROUP

The previous civic realignments of 1860 and 1932 ultimately led to more inclusive racial attitudes and policies. Based on the changing attitudes of Americans, the next one is likely to be no exception.

The great diversity of the Millennial Generation and its experiences growing up in a multiracial society is reflected in their relatively color-blind attitudes on racial relations. The number of Americans who agree with the statement "It's all right for blacks and whites to date each other" has nearly doubled over the past twenty years (from 48% in 1987 to 83% in 2007) (Pew Research Center 2007a). Among Millennials, the level of agreement, 94 percent, comes about as close to unanimity as any survey will find. As Justin Britt-Gibson, a twenty-five-year-old African American, wrote in the *Washington Post*, "I'm used to displays of warmth between interracial couples being ignored or barely noticed. They're hardly on our [Millennial] minds at all" (Britt-Gibson 2007).

Currently, a very large majority, 82 percent of all Americans (up from 72% in 1987), disagrees with the statement, "I don't have much in common with people of other races." Among white Millennials, 49 percent, as compared with 24 percent of people in their age group in 1987, completely disagrees with the statement (Pew Research Center 2007a).

Americans are also increasingly favorable about governmental and social policies intended to promote racial inclusiveness. Support for affirmative action programs to help blacks, women, and other minorities get better jobs and education rose from 58 percent in 1995 to 70 percent in 2007. The numbers who favor improving the position of blacks and minorities by giving them preferential treatment has also increased during the past two decades (from 24% in 1987 to 34% in 2007). Leading the way, a large majority of Millennials endorses affirmative action programs

(82%) as compared with two-thirds of older Americans. More strikingly, most Millennials also support racial preferences (54%), compared with less than a third of older generations.

These attitudes, however, do not reflect a Pollyannaish perspective on the state of race relations in America. While a plurality (49%) believes that there has been real improvement in the position of black people, a large majority of Americans (62%) also rejects the contention that discrimination against blacks is rare in America today (Pew Research Center 2007d).

COMING TO A CONSENSUS ON IMMIGRATION

Considering the intensity of the current dispute over immigration, it seems difficult to believe that concern with that issue will recede any time soon. However, if previous civic realignments are any guide, the nation will soon come to a consensus on this issue with an approach that favors inclusion rather than exclusion.

While a large majority of Americans (75%) continues to agree with the broad statement "We should restrict and control people coming into our country to live more than we do now," that number has dropped from 82 percent in 1994. Moreover, only a declining minority of Americans endorses the more stringent solutions currently being advanced to deal with illegal immigration. The numbers who favor building a fence along the Mexican border to prevent illegal immigrants from entering the United States is down, from 54 percent in 2006 to 46 percent in 2007. A consistent six in ten of all Americans favor a program that would allow undocumented immigrants who have been in the United States for several years to gain legal working status and the possibility of future citizenship (Pew Research Center 2007d).

To a considerable extent, these changes stem from the emergence of a diverse young generation, the Millennials, which holds far more positive attitudes toward immigrants and their impact on society than older generations. A majority of Millennials (52%), in contrast with only 39 percent of older Americans, believes that "immigrants today strengthen our country because of their hard work and talents," rather than being "a burden because of their impact on jobs, housing, and health care." Similarly, two-thirds of Millennials, compared with just under half of all others, feel that the growing number of immigrants strengthens American society rather than threatens our customs and values. As a result, the Millennial Generation is more likely than other generations to endorse a program that would allow undocumented immigrants to gain legal status and citizenship (65% vs. 59%) and to reject a fence along the Mexican border (54% vs. 48%) (Pew Research Center 2007d).

MILLENNIALS ARE LESS HUNG UP
ON SEXUAL ISSUES

Like earlier idealist realignments, the most recent one has been marked, and perhaps even defined, by sharp disputes over social issues. The cultural intra-generational wars of the Baby Boomers over issues such as the role of women in American society, abortion and birth control, and appropriate sexual behavior have come to define the meaning of the words "liberal" and "conservative" in our current political lexicon, to the degree that differences over federal economic policies defined the terms in the four decades after the New Deal realignment. But based on our country's history, the coming civic realignment will shift the attention of most Americans from these issues to other, more pressing matters. Indeed, survey research indicates that the shift is already in progress, with the Millennial Generation leading the way.

For example, Americans are increasingly tolerant of homosexuality, in part because nearly half say they have a close friend or family member who is gay (Pew Research Center 2007d). The increasing tolerance of gays is clearly reflected in popular culture. From Jerry Seinfeld saying on his 1990s sitcom that he is not gay but hastening to add, "—not that it's a bad thing," to the favorable treatment of gays in TV programs such as "Will And Grace," gays are increasingly part of the pop cultural mainstream. After the Boston Red Sox won the World Series in 2004, five players on the team were given a makeover on "Queer Eye for the Straight Guy." Nothing of the sort was even remotely imaginable during the nearly one hundred years since the team had last accomplished that feat.

Pop culture reflects public opinion or it wouldn't be popular. At the most basic level, a majority of Americans (51%) now agrees, "Homosexuality is a way of life that should be accepted by society." More specifically, over the past twenty years the number agreeing with the statement "School boards have the right to fire teachers who are known homosexuals" is down by nearly half (from 51% to 28%). In 1987, close to half of Americans (43%) believed "AIDS might be God's punishment for immoral sexual behavior," but now less than a quarter (23%) do (Pew Research Center 2007d).

While embracing nondiscrimination toward gays, generally, a majority of Americans remain against gay marriage. About eight in ten (but only two-thirds of Millennials) have "old-fashioned values about family and marriage." Still, opposition to gay marriage has fallen from 65 percent in 1996 to 54 percent in 2007.

It is Millennials who are leading this trend toward greater tolerance of gays. About six in ten (58%) believe that homosexuality is an acceptable lifestyle and that gays and lesbians should be permitted to adopt children (61%). Less than one in five Millennials hold that AIDS is God's punishment for sexual immorality. A large majority (71%) opposes the firing of teachers who are known homosexuals. Among this generation, a solid majority (61%) even thinks that gay marriage should be permitted (Pew Research Center 2007d).

Once again, Millennials do not hold these tolerant attitudes simply because young people invariably are liberals who will transform into conservatives as they age. In the words of the Pew Center, "The generation gap on this issue was relatively small in the 1980s; young people were only slightly more supportive of gays. But by 2003, young people's views on this issue were significantly different from their older counterparts" (Pew Research Center 2007a).

Similarly, Americans have increasingly accepted an expanded role for women. Currently, three-quarters reject the statement, "Women should return to their traditional roles in society," with a slight majority (51%) disagreeing completely. But generational differences in this area are particularly striking. The GI and Silent Generations came of age and lived much of their adult lives in an era when sex roles were sharply defined. Only about four in ten members of these older generations completely reject the idea of women returning to traditional roles. Baby Boomers and Gen-Xers are evenly split on the question. By contrast, more than six in ten Millennials, and more than two-thirds of Millennial women, are opposed to this notion. A generation raised in the most gender-neutral environment in the nation's history is not about to accept the notion of limiting people's lives based on their gender.

However, there is one social issue—abortion—on which there are no significant differences between Millennials and older generations. Like other generations, about a third of Millennials now believe that abortions should generally be available with no restriction. Just over half say that abortions should be limited in some way, primarily confined to cases involving rape, incest, or a threat to the life of the mother. A bit fewer than one in five believes that abortions should not be allowed at all (Pew Research Center 2007d).

These results suggest that abortion is not viewed so much as an issue of women's rights as it is a conflict between public morality and individual freedom. On balance, most Americans now come down on the side of individual freedom. The number who favor making it more difficult for women to obtain abortions has fallen from nearly half of the public in 1985 to about a third in 2007. And about half of all Americans, including six in ten Millennials, favor permitting women to obtain the "morning-after" pill without a doctor's prescription (Pew Research Center 2007a).

The contest for attorney general in Kansas in 2006 captured this change in attitudes in the American heartland. Voters in that state chose former Republican-turned- Democrat Paul Morrison as their attorney general over the Republican incumbent, Phill Kline. During his time in office, Kline subpoenaed medical records of women who had abortions, forced healthcare providers to report sexual activities of girls under sixteen, and encouraged the anti-evolution actions of the state board of education (Slevin 2006). It was all too much even for the voters of this solidly "red" state, and America's tradition of individual freedom trumped these attempts to have the state's coercive powers used to define personal morality.

In all, it is clear that Americans, especially the emerging Millennial Generation, have become increasingly tolerant of homosexuality, supportive of gay rights, and positive about an expanded role for women in our society and economy. Even on the more divisive issue of abortion, most Americans do not favor its elimination or even placing major new restrictions on it. As the more socially tolerant Millennial Generation becomes a larger portion of the electorate, the power of social issues to drive our political debate will wane. The result will surprise only those who don't pay attention to the historical pattern of civic realignments.

MILLENNIALS WANT TO STAY INVOLVED
IN THE WORLD AND HAVE OTHERS
JOIN THEM

The civic realignment of the 1930s took place at a time when the country was almost totally focused inward on the disastrous economic conditions the country was experiencing. George Washington's admonition to avoid "entangling" foreign alliances seemed even wiser in the aftermath of World War I, which cost over 50,000 American lives but failed to make the world "safe for democracy." By the end of Franklin Roosevelt's second term, however, the country was sharply divided about the role and place of the United States in the world, as indicated by the passage in the House of Representatives, by only a single vote, of the Selective Service Act of 1940, which instituted a peacetime military draft for the first time in U.S. history.

This division was apparent in both the public opinion polls and the attitudes of individual Americans at that time. Members of the young civic GI Generation felt the conflict especially acutely—no one more than young Nile Kinnick of Adel, Iowa, an All-American football player at the University of Iowa and the winner of the 1939 Heisman Trophy, for whom the university's football stadium is named. Kinnick was initially an isolationist, as were many others of his generation, especially those from the small towns of the Midwest. The conclusion of his December 1939 speech accepting the Heisman award, given about three months after the outbreak of World War II in Europe, reflected his isolationist beliefs: "I thank God I was warring on the gridirons of the Midwest and not the battlefields of Europe. I can speak confidently and positively that the players of this country would much more, much rather, struggle and fight to win the Heisman award than the Croix de Guerre" (Baender 1992). By August 1941, Kinnick, seeing the dangers posed by fascism overseas, passed up an opportunity to enter law school and, instead, enlisted in the Navy reserve. He was activated four days before the attack on Pearl Harbor. At about the same time that Kinnick enlisted, Charles Lindbergh gave an isolationist speech before an America First meeting in Des Moines that blamed the Roosevelt administration, the British, and the Jews for attempting to push the United States into the war. By contrast, in a letter written to his family Kinnick expressed his changed attitudes toward American intervention in World War II: "There is no reason in the world why we shouldn't fight for the preservation of a chance to live freely. No reason why we shouldn't suffer to uphold that which we want to endure. May God give me the courage to do my duty and not falter" (Baender 1992). As with other members of his GI Generation, Kinnick's devotion to his duty came at a high cost; he died in June 1943, when his carrier-based plane crashed into the Caribbean.

While some, like Nile Kinnick, resolved their own personal struggles over American intervention in foreign affairs even before the attack on Pearl Harbor, that event was sufficiently traumatic to change the country's attitudes on this subject, not only for the duration of World War II but also for the next several decades. Americans of all political stripes and both major parties became fully committed to a foreign policy based on activism, international alliances, and military strength. Even former isolationist leaders, such as Senator Arthur Vandenberg, perceived a need for an activist U.S. foreign policy in the years following World War II and strongly supported such initiatives as the Marshall Plan, NATO, and the U.S. entry into the United Nations.

Support for an activist, interventionist foreign policy was so widespread that for decades after the end of World War II each political party sought to portray the other's presidential candidate not as a quick-on-the-trigger war monger, but as too weak to defend America's interests in the Cold War against Communism. In his 1960 presidential campaign, John Kennedy criticized the Republicans for allowing a "missile gap" to develop that would presumably leave the United States vulnerable to the Soviet Union, and Republican candidates both before and after 1960 attacked Democrats as "soft on Communism."

This bipartisan support for an internationalist foreign policy disappeared during the idealist realignment of the late 1960s as Baby Boomers helped to divide the nation, as well as their own generation, over the Vietnam War. The peace symbol became the icon for many in the new generation, even as many others of the same generation joined the newly formed Young Americans for Freedom (YAF). That organization helped Barry Goldwater win the Republican presidential nomination in 1964, explicitly rejecting the older, moderate Republicans who had dominated that party's power structure in the post-FDR era. For the next forty years, the Republicans would seek to define Democrats as the party of military weakness and their own party as the only one prepared to fight for the country's values of freedom and democracy, anywhere in the world.

Now, on the cusp of another political realignment, the question of the extent and character of America's role in the world has come, once again, to center stage in the nation's political debate. Survey research does suggest that on balance and at least at a broad level, almost all Americans still favor an activist international role and foreign policy for the United States. Nearly nine in ten (86%) currently agree that "it's best for the future of our country to be active in world affairs." This number is basically unchanged over the past twenty years, although the percentage strongly agreeing has fallen somewhat since the immediate post-9/11 period, from 49 percent in 2002 to 42 percent in 2007.

A concurrent drop in support for the Iraq War almost certainly led to this overall decline in the intensity of support for international activism. The number believing that it was the right decision to use military force against Iraq fell from 74 percent in the days immediately following that incursion to a low of 40 percent in January 2007. Support for continuing troop deployment in Iraq dropped almost as far, from 64 percent in September 2003 to 41 percent in early 2007. By the end of 2006, a majority (57%) believed that the Iraq War had made America *less* secure. In early 2007, half felt that our presence in Iraq had hurt rather than helped in the war on terrorism (50% vs. 36%), a very sharp reversal from the early post-invasion period, when two-thirds had held the opposite belief. Given these sharp declines, it is perhaps surprising that endorsement of an activist role for America in the world has not fallen even farther than it has (Pew Research Center 2007d).

While a large majority of Americans continue to support an interventionist foreign policy, although perhaps with less intensity, what have changed are attitudes toward the type of international activism that the public would like to see. Recent surveys suggest that most Americans now favor a foreign policy based on a more nuanced use of the military and a greater reliance on multilateral alliances than that often pursued by George W. Bush's administration. The number agreeing that the best way to ensure peace is through military strength fell from 62 percent in 2002 to just 49 percent in early 2007. Over the same period, agreement with the proposition "We should get even with any country that tries to take advantage of the U.S." dropped from 61 percent to 40 percent. Willingness to at least sometimes endorse preemptive military action against countries that may seriously threaten the United States but have not yet attacked us also declined, from 67 percent immediately after the invasion of Iraq to 55 percent four years later (Pew Research Center 2007d).

By contrast, in late 2006, a majority of Americans agreed that America's security depends on "building strong ties with other nations" (55%) rather than "its own military strength" (35%). These numbers shifted significantly from a near-even split six months after 9/11, when 44 percent said that America's security depends on building ties with other countries, and 41 percent said it depends on our own military strength (Greenberg Quinlan Rosner Research 2006). Clearly, this shift occurred primarily because most Americans no longer believed that the Iraq War had enhanced the country's security or had helped in the struggle against terrorism.

None of this should be taken to indicate that in their growing opposition to the war in Iraq, Americans had somehow become less patriotic or anti-military. Unlike the flag-burning ceremonies and the hateful epithets directed at those in uniform that polarized the country in the 1960s, today Americans are united in their support for America's fighting men and women. Nine in ten considered themselves very patriotic in early 2007, the same percentage as twenty years ago and a couple of months after 9/11. Similarly, 84 percent now say that have a favorable opinion of the military. That number is about ten percentage points higher than in the late 1980s and is consistent with what it has been since the early 1990s, except right after 9/11 when it temporarily rose to about 95 percent (Pew Research Center 2007d).

While Millennials are as activist or interventionist as older Americans, they are more supportive of using multilateral and internationalist approaches in asserting and advancing America's interests in the world. By early 2007, Millennials had become as opposed to the Iraq War as other generations. But, perhaps, because of their greater diversity and tolerance, younger Americans are more supportive than their elders of globalism or, more specifically, of the "world becoming more connected through greater economic trade and faster communication" (Pew Research Center 2004). Millennials are also far more likely than other generations to believe that America's security depends to a greater extent "on building strong ties with other nations" (64%) as opposed to "its own military strength" (29%). This was more than twice the margin of support for a multilateral approach than among all Americans (53% vs. 38%) (Greenberg Quinlan Rosner Research 2005).

The greater support of Millennials for globalism and multilateralism and reluctance to rely primarily on the military for national security does not mean that they are a dovish generation as were many Baby Boomers during the Vietnam War. Quite the contrary. Just before the outset of the war, younger people were more supportive of military action against Iraq than other Americans. However, even then, Millennials were far more skeptical than other generations that the Iraq War would help in the war against terrorism (Pew Research Center 2002). There is no strong anti-war or isolationist movement centered among the younger generation, as occurred in the previous idealist realigning era. If anything, to the extent that there is a well-organized anti-Iraq War movement, its most visible members are Baby Boomers like Cindy Sheehan or the Gen-X executive director of MoveOn.org, Eli Pariser.

A survey of the activists in antiwar candidate Howard Dean's 2004 presidential campaign bears this out. Young voters were represented among Dean activists to no greater extent than they were among all Democrats. By contrast, Baby Boomers were substantially over repre-sented. More to the point, among Dean activists, Millennials were actu-ally more supportive of the Iraq War than older activists: six in ten, as compared with a third of Baby Boomers, believed that U.S. troops should be kept in Iraq until the situation in that country stabilizes. Millennial Dean activists were also much more supportive of the use of preemptive military force than Boomer Dean activists (31% vs. 13%) (Pew Research Center 2005).

In sum, Millennials are not a generation of isolationists or pacifists. Most of them express support for the broader war on terrorism and for an activist American role in the world. While a sizable number of Millennials oppose certain policies, such as the Iraq War, they are no more likely to do so than older generations. Instead, the Millennial Generation, like the last civic generation, the GI Generation, favors concerted collective action to deal with international security. They will coalesce around a clear approach to this issue when events and the right leader lead them, and thereby our country, to a consensus.

MILLENNIALS ARE A MORE DEMOCRATIC GENERATION—SO FAR

It seems hard to believe that about seven in ten American voters perceived only "a fair amount" or "hardly any difference" between the two political parties during the past two decades, at time in which Republicans almost invariably labeled their Democratic opponents as ultra-liberals, and Democrats returned the favor by constantly referring to Republican candidates as extreme right-wing conservatives. The tendency of generations to stick with the opinions they form in their youth is the only rational explanation for this phenomenon. But as this latest idealist era draws to a close, these perceptions are giving way to the more partisan point of view that is closer to the norm in a civic era.

Voters increasingly perceive major differences between the two parties. In late 2006, nearly four in ten voters (38%) saw a great deal of difference between the two parties—the largest number holding that perception in at least two decades. The number was about fifteen percentage points higher than it was in the late 1980s and early 1990s (Pew Research Center 2007d).

This change is being led by Millennials, who are much more likely to focus on differences between the parties than their elders. When asked to indicate the importance of various factors in shaping their votes in the 2006 midterm elections, Millennials placed greater significance on their feelings about the Republican and Democratic Parties. By contrast, Gen-Xers attributed more importance to the positions taken by candidates on issues when deciding whom to vote for, and Baby Boomers saw the personalities and abilities of the candidates as more important (Frank N. Magid Associates, December 2006).

Furthermore, the early election results in this realigning era suggest that the Democrats have a clear leg up in the competition to win the hearts, minds, and votes of this more partisan generation. The first small segment of Millennials who voted in the 2004 presidential election were, along with a dwindling number of members of the GI Generation, the only generational groups that cast more ballots for John Kerry than George Bush. And, according to CNN exit poll data, in the 2006 midterm elections, Millennials voted for Democratic House candidates over Republicans nationally by a wide margin (60% vs. 38%). While majorities of other generations also participated in the 2006

Democratic sweep, their level of support for the Democrats was narrower, around 1.2:1.

The support for Democrats in the 2006 elections is reflected in other more fundamental and potentially more lasting ways. With the help of Millennials, in early 2007, exactly half of the American electorate (50%) identified to some degree as Democrats. By contrast, just over a third (35%) of the electorate identified to at least some extent as Republicans. This represented the largest Democratic margin over Republicans in party identification in at least two decades, and perhaps since the early 1970s. As recently as December 2004, a month after George W. Bush's reelection, the Democrats held a narrow 48 percent to 43 percent edge. In October 1994, on the eve of the Republicans' sweeping midterm election victory that gave them control of Congress, the two parties were tied at 45 percent each in party identification (Pew Research Center 2007d).

At the moment, this Democratic Party identification advantage results more from Republican losses than large Democratic gains. A significant portion of Democratic identifiers in the Pew results are Independents who lean to the Democrats rather than voters who are firmly committed to that party. But, as V. O. Key pointed out (1960), voters more often act rationally in retrospect by turning against a party that has displeased them in the past rather than by voting for a party that might potentially please them in the future. This is beginning to happen to George W. Bush and the Republican Party as America moves toward its next era of political realignment.

Once individuals take on a party identification, they don't often change it and, as a result, a rising new generation spearheads major shifts in party identification and the political realignment that flows from it. This makes the results from exit polling on Election Day in 2006 especially dangerous for the Republican Party and its future. Among 18- to 29-year-old voters, most of whom are Millennials, 43 percent identified as Democrats and only 31 percent as Republicans. By contrast, in all other age groups, the division in party identification was essentially even, as just over one-third of all older generations identified with each of the two parties.

But the trends underlying this data are even more potentially damaging to the Republicans. Party identification distribution among 18- to 29-year-olds in 2002, when most in that group were Gen-Xers, was 39 percent Republican and 37 percent Democratic. The distribution began to shift in 2004, when Millennials first began to make their presence felt, with Democrats taking a small edge (37% vs. 34%) over the Republicans (Keeter 2006). If the trend continues at that rate, in 2010, when all members of this age group will be Millennials, Republicans could face an almost 2:1 deficit in party identification among 18- to 29-year-olds. Indeed, in early 2007, the ratio of Democratic to Republican identifiers was 1.75:1 within the Millennial Generation (Pew Research Center 2007d).

The trend away from the Republicans and toward the Democrats among young Americans has persisted, albeit with little notice, for at least fifteen years. In 1991, when 18- to 25-year-old voters were entirely comprised of Gen-Xers, a majority (55%) identified as Republicans, more than ten percentage points above the level of Republican identifiers among older voters. The level of Republican identification among young adults has steadily declined ever since, so that by 2007 only 30 percent of 18- to 25-year-olds, all of whom are Millennials, saw themselves as Republicans, while 52 percent said they were Democrats (Pew Research Center 2007d).

Survey results demonstrate that this movement in party identification is also consistent with the liberal and conservative images of the two parties. While self-perceived conservatives outnumbered liberals by almost a 2:1 margin (33% vs. 18%) among older voters, the number of self-perceived liberals and conservatives was essentially equal (26% vs. 27%) among Millennials (Pew Research Center 2007d).

The Democratic advantage in party identification among Millennials is clearly reflected in their attitudes toward American political institutions. Not surprisingly, in early 2007, a majority of Millennials (57%) had favorable perceptions of the Democratic Party and unfavorable impressions of the Republican Party (52%). Most Millennials (55%) also held favorable attitudes toward Congress, now controlled by the Democrats, while two-thirds (65%) disapproved of George W. Bush's performance as president. On all these dimensions, Millennials were more positive than other generations about the Democrats and less favorable toward the Republicans (Pew Research Center 2007d).

Still, the political party that will benefit from the coming realignment is not preordained. The Democrats are currently more comfortable with government as a means of dealing with societal concerns and with lifestyle diversity, positions that mesh better with Millennial Generation political attitudes. However, the Republicans also have a history, albeit more distant, of societal activism and libertarian tolerance that stretches back from Dwight Eisenhower to Theodore Roosevelt to its founding hero, Abraham Lincoln. The campaigns, candidates, and events of the rest of this decade will determine which party gains the life-long allegiance of this new generation and, with it, a dominant advantage in the next civic era of American politics.

PART TWO

Transition to a New Era

CHAPTER 6

The Realignment Begins

THE SHIFTING OF THE EARTH'S CRUST that creates the destructive power of a tsunami can be detected long before the waves crash onshore and sweep away everything in its path. Sometimes, the first tremors start so far out to sea that they remain unmeasured and unnoticed until it is too late. More often, the sensitive monitoring devices that scientists have placed on the constantly moving ocean surface can give those in the path of the oncoming disaster sufficient warning to take cover on higher ground, so that they can return and rebuild after the waves have receded. With pressure continuing to build toward America's next political realignment from the twin forces of generational and technological change, some politicians are beginning to sense that the ground is shifting beneath them as well. Those who are moving to higher ground and experimenting with new ways to be successful in this emerging landscape are much more likely to survive, and even thrive, when the full force of the waves of change arrive on shore and transform America and its politics.

EARLY WARNING SIGNS

The first tremor on the political Richter scale was recorded on November 3, 1998, when that year's congressional election campaign ended in a way few had anticipated. Traditionally, the party holding the presidency has lost, on average, twenty-nine House seats in the second term of a president. The reason for this pattern is generally attributed to the public getting weary of the incumbent and signaling its desire for change by taking out its frustrations on congressional candidates of the president's party. One month before the 1998 election, the Republican-controlled House of Representatives had authorized an impeachment inquiry to determine if President Clinton had lied under oath about his sexual relations with Monica Lewinsky in the White House. The action was designed to turn out Republican voters in record numbers by underscoring the need to restore moral virtue to Washington. The inquiry provided raw meat for the congressional campaign, leading previously independent or ticket-splitting voters to choose sides in the great debate that engulfed the country over whether the House should impeach the president and if the Senate should convict him and remove him from office.

But the outcome was hardly what Republicans, or many Democrats, for that matter, expected. The architect of the Republican campaign, Speaker of the House Newt Gingrich, resigned his post and retired from Congress when the American public, instead of ratifying the Republican jihad, turned out in great numbers to support Democrats, allowing the party to pick up five seats in the midterm election. It was only the second time since the Civil War that the party of an incumbent president was able to pull off such a feat (the other being the initial ratification of Franklin Roosevelt's New Deal realignment in 1934).

To celebrate his triumph and to get started on the 1999 budget, Clinton scheduled a cabinet meeting one week after Election Day. It was the first since January 23, 1998, when Health and Human Services Secretary Donna Shalala had left the Cabinet Room and told reporters on the White House lawn that she had chastised President Clinton for his dalliance with Ms. Lewinsky. Now, for the November meeting, the entire cabinet was in attendance and every seat that ringed the room behind the conference table was filled with administration staffers from the highest level.

Chief of Staff John Podesta called the meeting to order and, after being delayed by a critical call from Saudi Arabia about developments in Iraq, the president entered the room from the door leading to the Oval Office. He quickly surveyed the crowd of his newly inspired cabinet and staff. "Do you think we can get anyone else in here? I wonder how full the room would be if we hadn't won the election?" That was enough of a zinger that some audible dissents could be heard from some in the room. They assured him they would all have been there no matter the election returns.

After a little more of this almost friendly jousting with his cabinet members, many of whom had found it inconvenient to campaign too aggressively during the fall, the president returned to the historic nature of the election. He said he had done some research on midterm elections over a year before, and that the Democratic gain in the House was the first time the incumbent party had been able to pull off that feat in the sixth year of an administration since 1822. Among modern presidents, the previous best performance had been in 1986, when the Republicans lost only five seats during the Reagan administration. The lesson that Clinton drew from all this was that second-term presidents lost popularity because "the incumbent had begun to run out of ideas and the public started looking around to see what was new." To prevent that outcome, he told everyone in the room to continue thinking of new ideas. "In fact," he said, "I would be very disappointed if we weren't proposing new ideas on the day before we left here." Clinton fully intended to govern from a position of strength for the next two years and stick it to his Republican enemies in any way he could. The partisan cultural wars that had begun full force in the 1968 idealist realignment election, and that Gingrich had reignited, were to continue with all the force each side could muster.

Two years later, Vice President Al Gore decided to go the president one better. Attempting to catch the draft from this political storm, Gore sought to harness the potential of a newly energized Democratic base by returning to the party's nineteenth-century populist roots. While Clinton's friends in the pro-business Democratic Leadership Council looked on aghast, Gore assailed traditional corporate targets, such as the energy and pharmaceutical industries, with as much zeal, albeit with somewhat less effective rhetoric, than William Jennings Bryan had employed one hundred years before. Even as his top campaign aides bickered endlessly about whether to pursue a base-turnout strategy or a campaign to win over Independents, Gore stayed on the course he had chosen at the Democratic National Convention in Los Angeles—to play up his southern family roots and appeal to the power of "the people versus the powerful" to keep the good times rolling. True to the traditions of the Democratic Party, he spent Election Day morning in the rain in Iowa shaking hands with union workers as they arrived for the first shift. He then flew to Florida for one final campaign stop before going home to Nashville to see if his strategy had worked.

The answer, of course, turned out to be long in coming, and a crucial part of it only barely arrived in time. As Gore's motorcade left downtown Nashville for the War Memorial Plaza, where a chilled and wet crowd awaited his concession speech, a message flashed across one of his aides' Blackberry. As common as these devices are today, in 2000 Gore and his inner circle of campaign aides were among the few people who actually used them. Back then, Blackberries were nothing more than pagers with a thumb-operated keyboard attached. But Gore enjoyed using it to stay in touch with his wife—texting her, for instance, even as his campaign advisors clamored for his attention during the final campaign debate's rehearsal. Now the message coming from the staff back at headquarters was that the continuing vote tallies in Florida were no longer assured. Something had dramatically changed there, and the Sunshine State, rather than being placed in the Republican column, was now considered too close to call. As a result, the staff members watching the returns on television in the middle of the night at campaign headquarters were now urging Gore not to concede, even though he had already told George W. Bush he would. Arriving behind the stage where the crowd had gathered, Gore then placed another call to the future president of the United States, informing him that he was withdrawing his offer of concession.

Although few if any political observers recognized it at the time, that moment was the beginning of the end of the era of independent or ticket-splitting voting. Partisan feelings, long suppressed in an indifferent or indecisive electorate, took strong root, as the actual vote count took more than a month to resolve (if it ever truly was). The public demanded a constant stream of current information about each twist and turn of the recount drama. Viewership surged at CNN, MSNBC, and the Fox News Channel as each competed to present the latest, most "fair and balanced" news stories from Florida. No such inhibitions existed on the Web, however, where a frontier style of journalism created a free-for-all of opinions, often disguised as fact. By the time the Supreme Court decided the final results of the recount, those generating "new news on the Net" had found an audience that would stay loyal to their favorite partisan sources long after Gore finally conceded in mid-December (Chait 2007).

One of the most distinguishing characteristics of civic realignments is the highly partisan nature of the electorate during such eras. The bitterly contested, still disputed election of 2000 created precisely those feelings on the part of both Gore and Bush supporters, cementing in place one of the key building blocks required to build the foundation for politics in a civic era.

SORTING OUT THE VOTERS

The highly charged partisan atmosphere in the nation temporarily evaporated in the smoke and flames of the terrorist attacks on 9/11. With the nation under siege, leaders in both parties immediately closed ranks in response. Senate Democratic Majority Leader Tom Daschle even hugged George Bush after the president's special address to Congress nine days after the attack. But the feeling of bipartisan solidarity didn't last long. Soon, both sides were back to pursuing electoral strategies built on the "politics of polarization."

William Galston and Elaine Kamarck, two of the premier election analysts in the Democratic Party, used that phrase as the title of their post-2004 election analysis. They pointed out that the nation's increasingly partisan attitude was not a result of any sudden shift in the overall ideological composition of the electorate. Using data drawn from national exit polls, they wrote, "In 2004, the electorate was 21 percent liberal, 34 percent conservative, and 45 percent moderate. That is practically a carbon copy of the average over the past thirty years—20 percent liberal, 33 percent conservative and 47 percent moderate—with remarkably little variation from election to election" (Galston and Kamarck 2005, 3).

Rather than a shift in the overall ideological orientation of the electorate during the first two elections in the new millennium, there was instead a "great sorting out," to use another phrase from Galston and Kamarck, of ideologically based partisan loyalties within the electorate. Eighty-five percent of self-perceived liberals voted for Democratic nominee John Kerry in 2004; only 72 percent of them had voted for Jimmy Carter in 1976. Similarly, 84 percent of self-perceived conservatives voted for George W. Bush; only 70 percent of them voted for President Gerald Ford twenty-eight years earlier (Galston and Kamarck 2005). In order to encourage a strong turnout by the core base of their party, strategists in both parties, but especially the Republicans, encouraged this ideological polarization, with campaigns devoted to those issues that most divided America, especially social issues such as abortion and homosexuality, that had come to redefine the meaning of the words "liberal" and "conservative." For the Republican Party that dominated this idealist era, the partisan base was increasingly built on conservative, white Evangelical Protestants, a group that came to comprise nearly 40 percent of Republican voters and identifiers nationally (Smith, Keeter, and Green 2006).

On one level, the strategy was successful, especially so for the Republican Party. The GOP was able to parlay its appeal to religious conservatives into presidential victories in most elections after 1968 and in control of Congress after 1994. As recently as 2000, those who voted for George W. Bush listed his position on abortion as the most important issue shaping their voting choice—more important even than Bush's stance on taxes and social security (Pew Research Center 2000).

But for many other potential voters, the shrill ideological positioning and negative campaigning of the two parties may have been a major turnoff. As the parties rallied their respective bases, voting seemed to become an inside and unappealing game for many Americans who did not strongly identify with either party. Overall voting participation in presidential elections dropped steadily election by election, from 61 percent in 1968 to only 49 percent in 1996. The one exception to this downward trend was in 1992, when the independent candidacy of Ross Perot gave a temporary voice to some of those left out of the political process. Turnout rose by about five percentage points, only to decline to an all-time low four years later when Perot, though still a candidate, was no longer a significant factor.

Although the polarization strategy seemed to enable Republicans to maintain their hold on the White House and both chambers of Congress in 2000 and 2004, beneath the apparently tranquil surface major changes were occurring in the electorate. Just as Herbert Hoover's victory in the 1928 presidential election disguised the beginning of the end of one era of idealist Republican dominance, George W. Bush's reelection in 2004 may have masked the end of another.

2004 IS BEGINNING TO LOOK A LOT LIKE 1928

The signs that point to the initial stage of an impending realignment can be seen in some of the data that was buried by the story of these seemingly overwhelming Republican victories. After decades of decline, voter participation rose significantly in 2004 (by 5.3 percentage points over 2000), just as it did in 1928 (by 8 percentage points from 1924). This suggests both the arrival of a new generation of voters and the reactivation of some previously disenchanted nonvoters. The 60.7 percent turnout among eligible voters in 2004 was the highest since the realigning 1968 election. John Kerry received 59 million votes, 8 million more than Al Gore in 2000. But George Bush increased his popular vote total from 50.5 million in 2000 to over 62 million in 2004, thereby winning reelection, albeit by the narrowest margin of any incumbent president in the nation's history. More women than men voted, and African Americans voted in almost the same percentages as whites, demonstrating the broad nature of the electorate's newfound interest in political participation (Committee for the Study of the American Electorate 2005).

Both the 1928 and 2004 elections also saw important shifts in the composition of the electorate. In 1928, it was the arrival of new ethnic voters, primarily Catholics and Jews, who were inspired by the Democratic candidacy of Al Smith, which led to Democratic victories in the formerly rock-ribbed Republican states of Massachusetts and Rhode Island. The 2004 election saw the beginning of a trend of less intensely religious Christians of all denominations, as well as those of non-Christian faiths and secular voters, toward the Democrats and away from the Republicans, a trend that continued in 2006. Together, these three groups constitute an increasingly larger share of the American population and electorate, thanks to the increasing number of Millennials with their less intensely religious attitudes. Between 2002 and 2006, the Democratic share of the congressional vote rose by twelve percentage points among those who never attend religious services and by eight points among those who attend no more than a few times a month. Over the same period, Democrats registered similar, or even larger, gains in their electoral advantage among Jews (25 percentage points), other non-Christians (7 points), and those unaffiliated with any religion (10 points). By contrast, the voting preferences of the more intensely religious, especially white, evangelical Protestants changed little, remaining solidly Republican. This prompted the Pew Research Center to speak of a "God Gap" in voting and to ask, unlike many other observers who saw danger for the Democrats in their lack of appeal to religious conservatives, if it wasn't the Republican Party that was "hurt because it failed to appeal to voters beyond the traditionally religious" (Keeter 2006).

The 2004 electorate also displayed the highest level of partisan, straight-ticket voting behavior in over forty years. While approval ratings of the incumbent president always differ between voters identified with either the Democrats or the Republicans, these partisan feelings reached unprecedented levels in 2004. Until that time the difference had never been greater than 70 percentage points. But, in 2004, Gallup polling recorded an average difference of 79 points over the course of election, and the difference reached an all-time high of 83 points in October. The voters' opinions of the job Bush was doing as president translated directly into how they cast their ballots for congressional candidates, with almost 90 percent voting a straight ticket. This represented the lowest level of ticket-splitting behavior ever recorded in fifty years of National Election Study (NES) survey statistics (Jacobson 2007).

All these recent phenomena—increased partisan loyalties, straight-ticket voting, and voter turnout—are leading indicators of civic electoral realignments. America's electorate was beginning to shift its voting behavior and its attitudes about politics. A political era dominated by the cultural wars of the Baby Boomers was coming to an end.

MAKING WAVES

In 2006 the shift happened, sending shockwaves throughout the political establishment. Campaigns that attempted to use social issues involving personal lifestyles to divide the electorate and to pit groups of Americans against each other found that such appeals, though previously successful, had lost much of their power. Meanwhile, campaigns that used new, more efficiently targeted media to generate volunteers and to per-suade new voters to join the electorate enjoyed surprising success. The four M's that determine election victories—money, media, message, and the messenger—were being redefined for a new era.

With Republicans in control of all three branches of the federal gov-ernment and holding a majority of governorships and state legislatures as well, a quick glance at the surface of the political ocean in 2005 would not have suggested anything dramatic was about to happen. Indeed, the large waves of change that were about to engulf the nation's capital were so far offshore that, after the 2004 election, the Democratic Party estab-lishment immediately fractured over what strategy to pursue to counter what appeared to them as the arrival of Karl Rove's prediction of long-term Republican hegemony.

Defeated presidential primary candidate Howard Dean took over as chair of the Democratic National Committee the next year. He prom-ised to take the party's message to all fifty states, regardless of previous partisan voting history, recruiting organizers from his failed 2004 presidential bid who had the ability to get people involved in politics through online interaction—the so-called Netroots—as well as through more traditional ways of organizing grassroots campaigns. By the end of 2005, Dean and the DNC had placed a total of 183 such organizers in state party operations around the country (Kamarck 2006). The more pragmatic and battle-tested Democrats in Congress thought the idea was as crazy as Dean himself appeared following the infamous scream in his concession speech the night of the Iowa caucuses. Charles Schumer, chair of the Democratic Senatorial Campaign Committee, and his counterpart in the House, Rahm Emanuel, wanted to concentrate instead on recruiting candidates who could be sold to more conservative and independent voters in key states and districts, and then focusing their money and energy on those contests.

Dean's strategy was based upon a belief that the electorate was ready to vote for old-time Democratic liberalism for a change; Schumer's and Emanuel's strategy was based on a belief that a majority of the country was locked into the conservative philosophy of the Republican Party. They believed that Democrats had to find ways to mitigate that tendency in order to win. Luckily for the Democrats, both strategies had a chance to succeed, thanks to the ineptitude of the Bush administration and a new surge of Millennial voters coming into the electorate.

MOVING A HOUSE

The official Democratic campaign to regain a majority in the House of Representatives was called "Red to Blue" (R2B) to dramatize the type of political change the politically savvy Emanuel hoped to accomplish in each of the contests. It started by promoting thirty-three House candidates that the Democratic Congressional Campaign Committee (DCCC) thought could win. All the Democrats needed was a pick-up of fifteen seats to make California's Nancy Pelosi the first woman to serve as Speaker of the House.

The strategy of localizing the campaign by matching the candidate's profile with that of the district, not the ideological beliefs of most Democrats in Washington, was clearly evident in these selected districts (Bendavid 2007). In North Carolina's Eleventh District, for example, Emanuel convinced Heath Shuler, a former football player, to run;

Shuler's conservative instincts were strong enough that he refused to commit to voting for Pelosi for Speaker should he and the Democrats triumph. The dedicated liberals in the college town that was part of this Smoky Mountain district were left to mutter privately about Shuler's positions on issues, and to determine for themselves if party victory was more important than ideological purity (Shuler 2006).

Other candidate profiles reflected a similar propensity on the DCCC's part to find some kind of heroic quality in their candidates. Another sports hero was Baron Hill, a former congressman and basketball player who was a member of Indiana's sports Hall of Fame, now seeking to regain his seat in Indiana's Ninth Congressional District. In Pennsylvania, Jason Altmire, a local football star, was selected to run in the suburbs and towns north of Pittsburgh. Seven Democratic candidates had distinguished war records; seven others had police officer or law enforcement backgrounds. Five had distinguished themselves in nonprofit causes, such as Patty Wetterling, who was instrumental in creating the nation's Amber Alert system after her own eleven-year-old son was abducted at gunpoint. Ten of the other candidates were local officeholders looking to move up the elected official food chain, a relatively low number compared to most crops of challengers in other years.

While this strategy may have been merely a defensive move by the DCCC, in anticipation of Republican attacks on their candidates' patriotism, the net result was a mosaic of messengers or candidates with a dimension that Emanuel hadn't focused on. The life stories of many of these candidates had the potential to appeal to the newest members of the 2006 electorate, Millennials, who place a great deal of importance on service to one's country and community.

Once the DCCC had selected challengers whose profiles would appeal to voters in their districts, the campaign then asked the candidates to focus on raising the money necessary to get their messages out in the general election. The first qualification for getting more support from the DCCC was the ability to raise sufficient funds to blanket each district with television ads. A July 18, 2006, DCCC press release trumpeted the overall lead the Democrats held in fund-raising in these key races and further broke out the numbers for all to see. Twenty of the candidates had already raised the key threshold for support set by Emanuel: $1 million by June 30, 2006. Five of the candidates had raised between $10,000 and

$50,000 more than their opponents; six had outraised their opponents by $50,000 to $100,000, seven by between $100,000 and $200,000, and eight by more than $200,000. If money and the right messenger were the keys to victory, the Democrats were in great shape.

THE HOUSE'S FOUNDATION CRACKS

Despite the well-planned and professionally organized campaign, which benefited from the added momentum that flowed from the country's hostility to the course of the war in Iraq, Emanuel's thirty-three Democrats didn't do as well as might have been expected in the general election. Of the original Red to Blue candidates the DCCC helped with money and campaign advice, only seventeen were victorious. This alone would have been enough for the Democrats to take over control of the House for the first time in twelve years. But in addition, there were thirteen other Democratic victories on election night in 2006, featuring candidates not originally on the R2B list. Of the thirty Democrats elected in previously Republican districts, there were almost as many who won following Dean's strategy as Emanuel's. Thirteen candidates who moved to new and higher ground in their campaign messages and utilized online media to reach new voters efficiently became upset winners on election night.

Given the impact that local issues and personalities have on the outcome of individual congressional campaigns, there are inherent limits to interpreting the aggregate results of any off-year election. This is true even when issues such as the war in Iraq dominate the national debate. But there were some common threads in this midterm election that yield a few clues about developing trends, which will become even clearer in the 2008 presidential campaign.

First, the 2006 electorate seemed particularly interested in candidates whose life stories were authentic narratives that demonstrated a commitment to their team or their community or their country. Interestingly, of the fourteen military heroes or crime fighters on R2B's first list, only half were victorious. Toughness alone was not what voters were looking for. Meanwhile, nine of the winners among the thirteen who didn't make the Democratic leadership's original short list had professional careers as doctors, teachers, or scientists, including three attorneys who had not held political office before. Combining the community service professionals, the sports heroes, and the former members of the military or crime fighters who were victorious, there were nineteen Democratic candidates who won by using stories of personal service and community to overcome the politics of polarization used by their opponents.

All of these nineteen winning messengers brought a positive message to their campaigns about the ability of political institutions, particularly Congress, to effect meaningful change. Candidates with this type of campaign theme included Dr. Steve Kagan in Wisconsin, whose web site immediately involved the viewer in his plan for a "Healthy America"; Nancy Boyda, a pharmaceutical chemist in Kansas, whose strictly home-grown campaign in 2006 cost her half the amount of money she spent in a losing effort against the same incumbent in 2004; or David Loebsack, a Cornell College of Iowa political science professor, who biked and walked his way across the length of his rural district to defeat a thirty-year Republican incumbent, while barely spending enough money to have to file with the Federal Election Commission. In those races, and others like them, money was not the secret to the candidate's success. Their winning margins came from the use of a new message, highly partisan yet at the same time positive, about America and its future, that was more in alignment with a shift toward civic-era attitudes among the electorate.

The different outcomes in these potential takeover contests also suggested a geographic contour to the changes coursing through the electorate. Even after accounting for specific district characteristics, such as those with open seats or with Republicans embroiled in scandal, Democratic challengers outside the South did as well in districts with smaller cities or towns as they did in predominantly suburban districts. Candidates who connected with the economic concerns of their constituencies by talking about the growing inequality of wealth in America and/or the impact of a global system of trade on local jobs fared particularly well. In fact, economic concerns, which historically rise near the top of the electorate's issue agenda in civic realignments, were considered more important than the war in Iraq, terrorism, or "values" issues by congressional voters in every part of the country except the South, according to CNN exit polling data.

It was also better to be a Democratic challenger in the East or Midwest (where more then three-fourths of such challengers were successful) than to take on a Republican incumbent in the South (50 percent) or

West (40 percent). A map of the districts that switched from red to blue in 2006 suggests that the "great sorting out" is working its way from the East along the St. Lawrence Seaway, to the Midwest and across the northern tier of Plains states, down through the Mississippi Valley. As the Northeast completed its long-term movement from a Republican bastion to a reliably, if not overwhelmingly, Democratic region, a growing sea of blue districts also began to emerge along the country's midwestern watersheds. If these trends continue into the 2008 election, more states in more parts of the country will be in play than in recent presidential elections, another traditional characteristic of a realigning election.

The midterm elections of 2006 provide evidence of a changing electorate looking for new messages from a new type of messenger. In accord with earlier periods in American history, winners were more likely to have conveyed a positive, civic purpose in their campaigns than the more ideological and divisive appeals of their opponents. But another, equally important change in campaign dynamics also became apparent in analyzing the outcomes of the congressional campaigns in 2006. For the first time since broadcast media came to dominate political campaigning in the twentieth century, money was no longer the absolute key to victory.

CHAPTER 7

_____

Winning without the Mother's Milk of Politics

_____

POLITICAL ANALYSTS, steeped in the strategies of television campaigning and polarization, generally attributed the Democrats' 2006 victories to the fund-raising of the Democratic Congressional Campaign Committee and the work of Congressman Rahm Emanuel in recruiting the right candidate for each district. Indeed, immediately after it became clear that the Democrats had succeeded in taking over Congress, one of the best-known consultants in the party, James Carville, suggested that Howard Dean should resign as DNC chair because his fifty-state strategy had deprived some Democratic candidates of victory by not providing them with the money necessary to win ("Odd Attack" 2006). DNC members predictably ignored such foolish advice and reelected Dean, but the argument that "whoever has the most money wins" still persists.

Federal Election Commission post-election data allow us to test this hypothesis in forty-nine marginal districts. The numbers, which show the expenditures of each candidate as well as those of each party's congressional campaign committee in individual races (but, it should be noted, do not show what was spent by outside interest groups), demonstrate that money still provides some advantages in a campaign—but not nearly as much as commonly believed.

It is true that those Democratic challengers whose campaigns raised more money than their Republican opponents or at least matched them dollar for dollar did have about a 70 percent chance of winning in this Democratic year. When the Republican candidate raised more money, the Democrats' success rate dropped to less than one in two, suggesting some relationship between victory and dollars but hardly a perfect correlation. Certainly, a Democrat's chances of winning became progressively worse as the money gap widened; but, thanks to the DCCC's district-by-district targeting, that disadvantage occurred in only half the races in the Democrats' potential pick-up districts in 2006. Whether the funding arrived in the campaign first and eventually led to victory or whether the relative financial parity of most campaigns was an effect that followed the candidate's ability to generate support without a lot of early DCCC money is much more difficult to determine. But almost every study suggests that there is a point at which simply throwing money at a campaign provides increasingly less value to the candidate (Kamarck 2006).

In addition, one post-2006 campaign study made clear that more than just money and campaign ads were behind the Democrats' congressional victories. Elaine Kamarck analyzed the average increase in Democratic votes in the thirty-five contested congressional districts where Dean and the DNC had placed one of their organizers for at least a year and compared it with the average Democratic vote in those districts in the previous midterm election in 2002. She found that the average Democratic vote increase in those districts was 9.8 percent, more than twice the 4.7 percent increase that Democrats enjoyed in all contested congressional campaigns in 2006. In other words, over and above the general trend in the electorate that favored Democrats in that year, the ability to add Netroots efforts to traditional grassroots campaigns doubled the Democratic advantage (Kamarck 2006).

Of course, in many of those districts, the DCCC could also take some credit for their contribution in money and traditional campaign advice, since there was much overlap in where campaign resources were targeted. But, Kamarck's study points out, the impact of money was much less than traditional wisdom would suggest. Candidates in those races that benefited from Dean's fifty-state strategy, and who received less than $10,000 in contributions from the DCCC, were still able to increase the average Democratic vote total by 7.4 percent, well above the average Democratic lift of 4.7 percent. Receiving more than $10,000 from the DCCC but less than $100,000 enabled those with Dean's organizers to increase the Democratic vote from 2002 by almost the same percentage (8.4%). The impact of DCCC money only really became apparent when the amount was larger than $100,000 but less than $200,000. In those districts that received both that amount of money from the DCCC and the benefit of Dean's Netroots organizers, the Democratic vote increased

by a full 13 percent over 2002, 8.3 percentage points more than the average Democratic performance in 2006 (Kamarck 2006).

While money might be the mother's milk of politics, in an age of relatively inexpensive online communication, there is more than one way
that campaigns can skin the campaign cat to get their candidate's message
to the voters. The conventional wisdom on the role of money and media
in campaigns is rapidly becoming outdated.

NETROOTS DISRUPTS AMERICAN POLITICS

Indeed, the most revealing insights into what political campaigns
might look like in the future were to be found in congressional races
where Democratic candidates managed to win despite having much less
money to spend than their Republican opponents, and with little or late
support from one of Dean's fifty-state strategy organizers. In those races,
the candidate had to find a new formula for victory, or else the traditional
weapons of a late twentieth-century political campaign—large amounts
of money spent on broadcast media focusing on the most divisive social
issues in our political debate—would have doomed the challenger's
quixotic campaign to defeat.

The most dramatic example of this new formula for victory was the
campaign of Carol Shea-Porter, a former social worker and community
college political science professor in New Hampshire's First District. As
Dean pointed out after the election, she won without any financial help
whatsoever from either the DCCC or the DNC. Her campaign raised
slightly less than $300,000 and was outspent by her incumbent opponent
three to one. Adding in the fact that she was only one of four women to
defeat a male incumbent in the entire country, it is understandable why
so many national Democrats were surprised to find her on the winners'
list the day after the election.

Her victory was very much a family affair. Of the two television ads
she was able to produce and air, one featured her eighty-three-year-old
mother explaining why life-long Republicans such as herself should vote
for her daughter. Shea-Porter used lessons learned from her GI Generation father, who fought in World War II, and from her husband, who
served in Vietnam, to explain her anti-Iraq War position. In her other
commercial, she said that wars should only be fought when they are
"morally justifiable and even then only as a last resort."

While Shea-Porter certainly took a strong antiwar stance, she grounded her campaign's overall message in the context of the economic inequalities that troubled Yankee voters in New Hampshire. She said her goal was to represent the "'bottom 99 per cent' in her state and her country—those Americans who do not worry about the vagaries of the stock market or whether they can afford a bigger yacht, but whether they will have enough money for pizza for their family on a Friday night" (Mehren 2006). And when anyone suggested her new position in Congress would cause her to lose that focus, she cited the presence of her Millennial teenage son, who was still living at home, as the best guarantee such a thing would never occur. Her focus on family was tailor-made for Millennials able to vote in her district. Her campaign's emphasis on the need for greater economic equality was the perfect message to deliver to an electorate undergoing a civic realignment.

With limited funds, the challenge was to get this message out to voters scattered up and down the length of the western half of New Hampshire. Shea-Porter's solution was to use the extensive grassroots networks in that politically savvy state in combination with new online networks, or Netroots, to make sure her campaign for change was heard. With an entirely volunteer staff operating initially out of her house, she was able to handily defeat the State Assembly majority leader in the primary and then to oust the incumbent Republican congressman in the general election. Shea-Porter's belief in the power of Netroots to undercut the monetary advantage of those who depend on broadcast media was made abundantly clear when, after her election, she declined the help of Emanuel and the DCCC for her 2008 reelection campaign.

Clear across America, another congressional candidate also leveraged the power of the Internet to build a volunteer force that toppled a seemingly unbeatable Republican opponent who also had a lot more money to spend. That challenger also had a Millennial story to tell. Jerry McNerney first decided to run against Congressman Richard Pombo in California's Eleventh District when McNerney's son, Michael, phoned his father before the 2004 primary. He pointed out that there was no Democrat listed on the ballot to challenge the "number one enemy of the environment" in the Congress of the United States. As a wind energy engineer, McNerney had dedicated his life to preserving the environment, and his son's call made it clear to him that he "had to stand up" for what he believed in by taking on the quixotic quest to beat Pombo in his own backyard. He won the Democratic nomination in 2004 as a write-in candidate, but Pombo trounced him in the general election, 61 to 39 percent.

Few people gave McNerney much of a chance to win in 2006. But first, Pombo faced primary opposition from two Republicans: one who didn't like the congressman's ethics, and another, much better known, former congressman and anti-Vietnam War presidential candidate Pete McCloskey, who saw the race as yet another cause in his long quest to moderate the worst instincts of the Republican Party. Together the two Republican challengers held Pombo to 61 percent of the primary vote, a relatively weak showing for a candidate with his standing in Congress.

But Rahm Emanuel and the DCCC weren't about to wait for the outcome of the Republican primary before recruiting a candidate that meshed with their national strategy—someone who could raise a lot of money and appeal to the more moderate Republicans in the district who didn't support Pombo in the primary. Neighboring congresswoman Ellen Tauscher, the vice-chair of the Democratic Leadership Council, helped her colleagues recruit Steve Filson to run against McNerney in the Democratic primary. He had just the résumé the DCCC was looking for: an Eagle Scout, service in the Navy, and the ability to raise money. Filson and the DCCC were so sure that he would scare off any other primary opposition that they didn't even bother to consult with local party leaders about the race before he announced he was running. Assuming that Emanuel's formula was the winning one, he made little effort to reach out to the grassroots activists who had supported McNerney in 2004; when he did his efforts only got him in more trouble. At one meeting he described the stakeholders of the Democratic Party as elected officials and failed to even mention grassroots activists at all (Matt Lockshin interview 2007).

But the Bay Area has long enjoyed a tradition of grassroots political activism, much of it centered around progressive causes, and they were not about to abandon the district's nomination to the establishment's candidate quite so readily. One of the leaders of this loosely organized network, Vicki Cosgrove, was particularly vocal in her support for McNerney. When others looked for guidance on whom to support in the primary, she made it clear that she was "sticking with Jerry; he's my guy," and that others should too (Babaloo 2007).

The challenge for McNerney's supporters was how to connect this dispersed and diverse group into an effective force in the primary. While Cosgrove and her friends were good at using email to coordinate work in the Bay Area on behalf of antiwar causes and candidates, they needed some way to connect their interests in this race with the weaker and more traditional Democratic Club structure in other parts of the district. United mostly by their desire not to let the DCCC tell them whom to nominate, these activists got online and on the phone to convince others to get involved and then made sure that they did.

In addition, a young Millennial "cusper," twenty-four-year-old Matt Lockshin, decided to start a blog designed solely to enable Pombo's defeat, saying he was "inspired to find a way to empower normal people to make meaningful change. . . . I also thought we [the Democrats] should be running and supporting candidates in red areas [of California]." The "saynotopombo" blog regularly deconstructed the conventional wisdom that McNerney had no chance; Lockshin also provided news from the grassroots about the campaign and made it easier for activists to get involved. By telling everyone when phone banks or door-to-door canvassing would be taking place in the sprawling East Bay district, and urging everyone to send money if they couldn't spare their time, Lockshin's blog successfully translated the interests of online Netroots activists into effective, offline grassroots action.

Filson raised twice as much money as McNerney did, even though the latter's money came from many more individual donors. But Filson's money and résumé was not enough to secure the nomination. The energy of McNerney's activists easily carried him to victory in the primary. The result made headlines in the nation's liberal blogosphere, and provided further momentum for the campaign as the general election began. Using extensive email lists and the passion of his supporters, McNerney suddenly became the favorite in a series of Netroots contests designed to spotlight potential Democratic takeover contests. Newly energized by the blogosphere, and more tightly linked than ever before, the campaign was now ready to take on the toughest challenge of all.

McNerney organized a general election campaign that made the race a tossup by October 2006. The basic plan was to maintain focus on grassroots campaigning, using online communications to recruit volunteers to knock on as many doors in the tri-valley area east of the

San Francisco Bay as they could, along with the Central Valley towns of Tracy and Stockton. McNerney's call to make the San Joaquin Valley "the Silicon Valley of renewable energy" provided a clear contrast with Pombo, who had introduced bills in Congress to repeal the Endangered Species Act and sell off national parkland.

Having sat out the Democratic primary, environmentalist groups decided they couldn't pass up this opportunity to take on their most dedicated antagonist in the general election. The Defenders of Wildlife Action Fund, the political action arm of the group by the same name, led their efforts. Every time they found a potential volunteer online, they could point them to the "saynotopombo" blog, which told its readers how to join the growing grassroots effort. Even though there was no formal direction or control from on high between Lockshin's blog, the Defenders of Wildlife, and the campaign itself, the three independent efforts produced as well-oiled a political machine as the district had ever seen.

In Internet marketing terms, the campaign "went viral." Each activist recruited other friends to join the cause, creating a snowball effect as the momentum and excitement grew. "Saynotopombo" continued to lower the barrier to entry into the campaign by supplying information and encouragement to volunteers all over the Bay Area. In the final days of the campaign, the Defenders of Wildlife bussed in all the like-minded activists that they had identified in Berkeley, Oakland, San Francisco, and other areas near McNerney's district, where they knocked on 12,000 doors in one weekend—spreading the word about just what kind of congressman Pombo really was.

The incumbent, meanwhile, employed the more traditional campaign weapon—television attack ads, paid for with large amounts of Washington lobbyist money. By the end of September, Pombo had received almost $400,000 for his campaign war chest from the National Republican Congressional Committee, while the DCCC, after McNerney's primary victory, sent him a nice check and wished him luck.

One of Pombo's TV commercials showed individual veterans questioning McNerney's patriotism in light of his antiwar views. The power of the ad was weakened considerably, however, when the "saynotopombo.com" blog pointed out for all to read that among the ostensible volunteers in the ad was a paid staff person from Pombo's campaign. The volunteer nature of McNerney's campaign continued to make a clear statement to the voters about the differences in values and authenticity between the two candidates, which was more than a match for the other side's money.

Once the district showed up on the national radar screen as a potential win, money and visits from national Democrats poured in for the final weeks of the campaign, so that in the end the winner was outspent by the incumbent by only $1 million—$4.8 to $3.8 million. McNerney's campaign focused on an issue of broad concern, the environment, a subject upon which over 85 percent of Democrats and Independents agree (even two-thirds of Republicans think of themselves as pro-environment) (Pew Research Center 2007a). That focus, combined with his use of the Net to attract and motivate people to join his grassroots campaign, allowed McNerney to easily defeat one of the masters of the politics of polarization, 53 percent to 47 percent. The incumbent even lost his hometown thanks to the hard work of Martha Gamez, who ran the entire grassroots effort out of her garage in Tracy, California (Lockshin interview 2007).

McNerney's campaign completely reshuffled the "four Ms" of political campaigning that hold the keys to victory—money, media, message, and messenger. It focused on issues of broader societal concern, not on the politics of polarization. It used online media to raise money and help build a network of grassroots supporters. In the words of Matt Lockshin, "McNerney supporters viewed his first run against Pombo as a demonstration of McNerney's character . . . in terms of moral courage and toughness." It was a candidate profile that meshed perfectly with Millennial voters' positive attitude toward politics and political institutions, which McNerney was able to energize during the campaign. In the end, the combination brought down an incumbent who epitomized the dying idealist era of American politics, even though the winner was significantly outspent.

SWITCHING THE SENATE

Over on the Senate side, Chuck Schumer's challenge seemed even more difficult than Rahm Emanuel's. He, too, began by focusing on candidate recruitment and fund-raising, needing a net gain of six seats to take control of the upper chamber. Like Emanuel, Schumer was not afraid to face down Democratic Party ideologues if he felt his chances of winning would be better with a candidate more suited to a specific state's ideological profile. In Pennsylvania, he recruited the state treasurer and former auditor general Bob Casey Jr. to take on one of the most ideologically conservative Republican senators, Rick Santorum, despite the fact that the National Abortion Rights Action League (NARAL) was strongly opposed to Casey's pro-life position.

In Ohio, the Democratic Senatorial Campaign Committee (DSCC) shoved aside a darling of the liberal blogosphere, Paul Hackett, a veteran who had helped ignite the anti-Iraq War movement with a surprisingly good showing in a special congressional race in 2005, in favor of long-time congressman Sherrod Brown, whose liberal credentials were impeccable but who was a relative newcomer to the world of Netroots politics. In Missouri, Schumer worked hard to convince State Auditor Claire McCaskill to risk her political career against the darling of the right wing, incumbent senator Jim Talent. All three recruitment efforts, along with a nasty primary challenge that threatened to weaken Republican incumbent Lincoln Chafee in Rhode Island, gave the Democrats a real shot at four of the six seats they needed to take control of the Senate. But any other wins would have to come from states in the upper South or western Plains, neither of which had been friendly territory to the Democrats in earlier elections.

Ohio and Pennsylvania proved to be relatively easy pickings in the general election, with economic angst, antiwar fever, and, in Ohio, Republican scandals providing the momentum. The Missouri campaign was one of the most bitterly contested elections in the state's history—in a state known for its hammer-and-tongs style of political warfare. Senator Talent's campaign manager said the election was about "God, guns, and babies," and the Republicans spent over $23 million to make sure Missourians knew McCaskill was on the "wrong" side of every one of those issues.

McCaskill's strategy was to place on the ballot two propositions designed to energize the electorate around economic and health care issues. One would raise the state's minimum wage; the other would overturn the state's total ban on stem cell research, in favor of making legal, in Missouri, any such research that was federally approved. Talent's campaign gleefully attacked both, calling the proposal to raise the minimum wage to $10 per hour "excessive by any stretch of the imagination." Talent's campaign manager was sure the voters would maintain the state's ban on stem cell research, reminding an interviewer on PBS's "News Hour," "We're in the Bible belt."

McCaskill countered with an emotional ad that gave personal witness to the cause of stem cell research to save lives, featuring an appeal by actor Michael J. Fox, whose tremors from Parkinson's Disease were all too evident in the commercial. The spot was eventually viewed over two million times on YouTube (Poniewozik 2006). On the fiscal side, McCaskill campaigned in her ads against "economic elites, who issue no bid contracts to their friends, pay themselves excessive executive compensation, and destroy competition and jobs" through industry consolidation and outsourcing.

In the end, McCaskill matched Talent almost dollar for dollar; the bitter campaign failed to generate any increase in turnout; and, by the narrowest of margins, McCaskill defeated Talent and his ultra-conservative, social-issue agenda. In exit polls, Missourians ranked economic concerns as their top issue, not values or even the war in Iraq. By a margin of 60 to 37 percent, McCaskill carried the 45 percent of voters who told CNN's exit pollsters that economic concerns were "extremely important." The bellwether state of Missouri chose the economically oriented civic-era messages of McCaskill over the tried and true social issues from an earlier, dying era.

YOUTUBE SHAKES UP THE SENATE

Still, none of this would have altered the balance of power in Washington were it not for the Democrats' surprising victories in Virginia and Montana. There, the Democratic campaigns shifted the ground and the ground rules, changing the message and the media from what their Republican opponents had come to expect. Along with a consistent drumbeat against the war, the campaigns focused on the issue of economic fairness and accountability for fiscal integrity in Washington (Webb and Tester 2006). When their opponents tried to use the old-time religion of divisive issues to protect their incumbencies, the Democratic campaigns countered with a brand new tactic—live video of their opponent's mistakes, posted and spread instantaneously on one of the newest and most popular social networking web sites, YouTube. "User-generated content" suddenly became a far more potent campaign weapon than the slick ads created by media consultants.

Jim Webb is hardly a true-blue liberal, but Virginia is hardly a blue state. A former Republican, he served as secretary of the navy during the

Reagan administration and previously expressed himself in decidedly nontraditional Democratic terms on issues such as the ability of women to serve in the military and gun control. Webb's candidacy was initially promoted to the DSCC by two Nebraskans, not only former senator Bob Kerrey, a Democrat, but also an incumbent senator, Chuck Hagel, a Republican. Still, once Webb defeated a more liberal Democrat in the primary, long-time activist and high-tech executive Harris Miller, the DSCC decided to pour resources into his campaign, at least to bloody one of the Republican Party's potential presidential candidates, Senator George Allen (Miller interview 2007).

The Webb campaign received an unexpected boost on August 11 when the senator was captured on camera using what many considered a racial slur. Allen began his remarks at an informal outdoor gathering that day by announcing that his campaign was going to be about "positive, constructive ideas." To demonstrate his sincerity, he addressed S. R. Sidarth, a young man of Indian descent who was filming the event and whom Allen knew worked for the Webb campaign. "Welcome to America and the real world of Virginia," he said, referring to Sidarth as a "macaca." It might have been a small story, easily fudged and forgotten in previous campaigns, but this year was to be different. Sidarth brought the video back to the Webb campaign office, where the campaign, lacking any other distribution methodology, decided to post it on YouTube. The spectacle of a senator belittling a young, dark-skinned man and apparently even challenging his immigration status was riveting when the event was captured live. The resulting swarm of publicity made YouTube a must-see site not just for Virginians, but for anyone involved in political campaigns across the country for the rest of the campaign.

Allen remained befuddled by the power of YouTube and his state's newfound interest in inclusive ethnic and racial policies. After he denied that he had known "macaca" was considered a racial slur, it was reported that Allen's mother was an immigrant from Algeria where the term was so used, making his denial seem more implausible. In addition, it was revealed that his mother was Jewish, a fact not widely known until then. Rather than shrugging off this disclosure as of only mild interest or as a source of pride, as it had been with similar revelations involving John Kerry and Madeleine Albright, Allen appeared to be embarrassed. He lamely attempted, in scenes once again captured on video, to deny knowledge of his Jewish lineage by telling jokes about his mother serving him ham sandwiches when he was a boy.

These and other video clips unalterably changed not only the debate in the campaign—and with it the polls that had previously shown Allen coasting to reelection—but also the level of voter interest. Turnout rose by 14.6 percent compared to 2002, reaching the highest level for a midterm election in Virginia's history. The increases occurred predominantly on college campuses and in inner-city neighborhoods in Richmond and Norfolk (Cannon 2007; Center for the Study of the American Electorate 2006). According to CNN exit polls, nonwhite voters, who made up 21 percent of the Virginia electorate, provided Webb his victory margin. In addition, Virginia's heavily Millennial university towns—Charlottesville (where Sidarth attended the University of Virginia), Williamsburg, Radford, and Fredericksburg—turned out in record numbers. Eighteen- to twenty-nine-year-olds provided Webb with his widest margin of support, 4 percent, among all age groups and represented 12 percent of all the votes cast. Overall, Virginia voters told exit survey researchers by a wide margin (56 to 39 percent) that they favored offering most illegal immigrants legal status rather than deporting them, and two-thirds of those favoring a more tolerant approach voted for Webb. Furthermore, while exit polls showed Webb losing among the state's Christian voters, he gained his slim margin of victory from an overwhelming advantage among non-Christians of many faiths.

Despite having outspent his opponent by almost three to one, Allen couldn't overcome the damage done to his image by the power of recordings made on a video cam and posted on the Internet for all to see. The posts had created a buzz in the mainstream media and among voters that grew in intensity in ways that could not have been foreseen only months before. When it was over, the Republican Party had been saved the embarrassment of having George Allen actually seek its nomination for president, an outcome for which it had YouTube and its viewers to thank.

In Montana, the Democratic primary featured a true hero of the Democratic blogosphere, the president of the state senate, Jon Tester. His election to the state legislature, in a district that typically voted 60 percent Republican, had made him an early favorite on blogs like DailyKos and MyDD. He started out the primary as the underdog, however, against rising political star John Morrison, the state's auditor controller and insurance commissioner and the son of a Montana Supreme Court justice (Armstrong and Zúniga 2006). Tester's campaign combined old-fashioned farmhouse-to-farmhouse campaigning with the very latest in Netroots organizing to build his support initially. After Morrison's personal indiscretions became public during the campaign, Tester was able to claim a surprisingly easy primary victory.

The general election campaign used a civic-era political message and the latest in campaign tactics—the video stalker—to bring an organic farmer from Montana to the U.S. Senate, tipping the balance of power back to the Democrats on the morning after the general election. Tester's stock-in-trade was a standing-up-for-the-underdog populism reminiscent of another prairie Democrat, William Jennings Bryan (Armstrong and Zúniga 2006, 165). This message contrasted nicely with stories of multi-million dollar payoffs orchestrated on behalf of the incumbent, Conrad Burns, by convicted influence peddler Jack Abramoff. The taint of scandal caused Montanans to take a second look at their three-term senator. What they saw on a seemingly never-ending series of YouTube videos was not pretty.

An early favorite was a video of Burns slowly falling asleep at a Montana farm bill hearing in August. Tester had hired a twenty-four-year-old Millennial, Kevin O'Brien, to go to every Burns event and bring back clips of the senator in action so they could provide them to local political TV reporters. But then another Millennial campaign staffer, Andy Tweeten, suggested he could use his iBook computer to "mashup" the video with some music and titles and post them on YouTube. The video was viewed 75,000 times, five times more than any canned commercial that either campaign posted on the same site (Schatz 2006).

Later, when Burns jokingly interrupted a campaign speech to provide instructions to "Hugo, the nice little Guatemalan man who's doing our painting for me in Virginia," the whole incident was quickly posted on YouTube. His remarks were then incorporated into regular TV ads by the Tester campaign, which talked about how it was "wrong for a senator to make jokes about illegal immigration" in the context of stories that the original YouTube videos had created. When Burns made comments suggesting that those who drove taxis during the day in Washington, D.C., were "terrorists at night," the whole damning process started all over again.

Voter turnout surged in Montana, especially among Millennials. Thanks to the same-day registration laws of the state, 18- to 24-year-olds voted in record numbers, helping to increase overall turnout in the state by 7.6 percent from 2002 (Cannon 2007; Center for the Study of the American Electorate 2006). Exit polls showed Tester getting his largest margin over Burns, 8 percent, from voters under thirty, who made up fully 17 percent of Montana's electorate in 2006.

More than half of Tester voters told exit pollsters their votes were mainly against Burns, with only about a third of all Montana voters believing Burns had high ethical standards. Burns spent almost twice as much as Tester in order to blanket the television airwaves in Montana with his own version of the truth. But in the end, the incumbent discovered the ancient wisdom of Tammany Hall's Boss Tweed: "I don't care a straw for your newspaper articles; my constituents don't know how to read. But they can't help seeing them damn pictures" (Huffstutter 2006, 12). The voters believed what they saw on the Net and subsequently gave Burns the boot. In the end, neither he nor Senator Allen could fake authenticity.

A New Formula for Victory

The 2006 elections demonstrated the potential power of campaigning in ways that were clearly different from the politics of the last four decades. Candidates who delivered a message that focused on the need for greater economic equality and ethnic inclusiveness did surprisingly well. Many, though not all, were able to defeat well-funded campaigns by opponents who sought to maintain the divisions between right and left, red and blue, and liberal and conservative by attacking the patriotism, faith, or values of their Democratic opponents. Some Republican members of the U.S. House of Representatives were able to fend off strong Democratic challenges in states like Ohio, Kentucky, and New Mexico, and the Democrats' attempt to win an open Senate seat in Tennessee in the person of Congressman Harold Ford fell short. Overall, however, Democrats were able to use a new combination of the four Ms of political campaigns to wrest control of Capitol Hill from a Republican campaign built on the tactics and issues of a dying era.

Indicative of a coming civic realignment, the old idealist value-related issues of immigration, abortion, and gay rights were consistently rated as less important by voters in exit polls on Election Day 2006. Furthermore, when voters were asked to express their opinions on these social issues, most actually came down on the more liberal side of the debate.

The shift in message was especially effective when it was coupled with the use of the Net, not only to raise money but also to create a less filtered dialogue between the candidate and the voters. The results were particularly impressive among young people. Voters under thirty preferred Democrats over Republicans for the House by a stunning 60 to 38 percent margin, the largest by far of any age group. This Millennial advantage was present in every region of the country, most notably in the East, 74 to 25 percent, and the West, 63 to 33 percent. The margin represented a 6 percent drop for Republicans among all voters under thirty, and an even greater 10 percent drop among young white voters (Greenberg Quinlan Rosner Research 2006).

The fact that these voting results are supported attitudinally across a range of survey questions suggests that what happened in the 2006 midterm elections was more than a temporary deviation from the norm; they presage major changes in American politics. In spite of their reputation for lacking political knowledge, most Americans are well aware of what took place on Election Day 2006. Large majorities know that the Republicans controlled the U.S. House (80%) and Senate (75%) before the midterm election and that the Democrats won control of the House (79%) and Senate (70%) after it. Moreover, a clear plurality of Americans (46%) and Millennials (48%) were happy with the results of the election, twice the numbers expressing dissatisfaction (Frank N. Magid Associates, December 2006).

Finally, voters are optimistic about what will come from the Democratic victory. Millennials, the generation on the verge of spearheading a civic realignment, are especially positive. They believe the Democratic congressional victory will result in an "improvement" in every one of a number of specific issues—the war in Iraq, national security, the economy, taxation, immigration, political corruption, government spending and the federal debt, and societal values. While the members of other generations expect an improvement in most of these issue areas as well, Baby Boomers and Gen-Xers actually predict the Democratic win will lead to setbacks on taxes and immigration (Frank N. Magid Associates, December 2006).

But midterm elections can only presage political realignment; they cannot make it happen. Before a new generation of voters and their technologies transform American politics, the country will need to experience a presidential campaign that uses all the tools and tests all the messages that were merely experiments in 2006. Before that happens, an entire industry of television ad producers, political pollsters, and campaign consultants, not to mention candidates and campaign committees, will have to adjust quickly to this rapidly evolving new world, or drown in the waves of change that will engulf them.

CHAPTER 8

The Technology Tsunami

THE 2006 ELECTIONS DEMONSTRATED the combined
power of generational and technological change to produce new winners
with new ideas and new ways of winning. This wave of change is washing
over the social and political landscape of America, threatening to sweep
away businesses, power structures, and institutions that were built on the
beliefs and technologies of a previous era. Already, the music industry's
business model has been completely disrupted, in the last decade, by its
customers' extensive use of peer-to-peer technology (P2P). Around
97 percent of the songs stored on the more than 100 million iPods in use
today were either copied illegally or ripped from personal CDs with no
compensation to the record company (Wingfield and Smith 2007; Smith
2007). Similar disruptions in the way all entertainment industries do business are becoming evident, as people watch their favorite TV shows on
their iPods or download first-run movies to watch on their PCs in the
comfort of their homes. Since Washington, as one wag put it, is "Hollywood for ugly people," the power brokers and pundits who currently lead
our national political debate are also feeling the changes that those in the
music, television, and movie industries are unsuccessfully trying to resist.
And, just as each of the key entertainment industries are being forced to
find new ways to relate to their customers in an Internet era, political parties, candidates, and campaigns will have to find new ways to communicate their messages and promote their messengers to voters—if they want
to win elections in the twenty-first century.

SMALL INNOVATIONS PRODUCE
LARGE CHANGES

The source of this radical shift in power begins with the underlying
architecture of the Internet, which permits the high speed, or broadband,

coupling of computers and computing devices of all types, with anyone and everyone throughout the world, whenever and however they wish to be connected. The Internet's method for addressing and sending packets of information, generally referred to as Internet Protocol (IP), allows messages of any size to be switched through the network in order to arrive at the appropriate destination so long as the network has the capacity to carry them, even if some delay is experienced along the way. Unlike the switched telephone networks that were the dominant technology of the twentieth century, IP networks do not require any "intelligence," or sophisticated software, in the network to accomplish this task. Instead, each router simply reads the address header in the message and sends it to the next available router stop along the way, until it reaches the final destination. This shift in the fundamental architecture of communication networks, therefore, places all power in the hands of the user—the one initiating the message. It takes power away from those such as the old AT&T, which used to be able to "gate," or limit, traffic on the network, based upon the need for the traffic to stay within the capacity of the very sophisticated switching software used to create a virtual, dedicated connection each time a user wanted to communicate with another user.

The potential of the Internet to change the world of communications was recognized early in the 1990s. Dan Schulman, then an up-and-coming executive at AT&T, later the CEO of Virgin Mobile USA, warned his colleagues as early as 1996 that the Net was creating a "tsunami of change, unseen and unfelt now, but sure to wipe away the world as we know it when it arrives." Initially its arrival in "dial up" mode did shake up the world of "brick and mortar" retail businesses. It also created the email phenomenon known in the industry as a "killer application," because the ease and convenience of sending messages electronically made everyone want to get his or her own address on the Net. Both these changes were captured in the first movie romance built around the Internet, *You've Got Mail*. In 1998, teenage Millennials and their Gen-X parents could both find something to like in the dual tensions of the movie's plot as Meg Ryan falls in love with Tom Hanks online. Hanks also turns out to be a threat to her small neighborhood bookstore because he runs a very 1990s big box, small service, price-focused bookstore chain. (The movie itself was a remake of the 1940s hit *The Shop Around the Corner*, starring Jimmy Stewart and Margaret

Sullavan, that entertained the GI Generation with its portrayal of a romance initiated through letters exchanged through a "snail mail" post office box.) Still, the impact of the Internet on American business in the 1990s was more a story of dot.com boom and bust than it was the earth-shattering, life-changing event that people like Schulman had predicted.

Then came broadband, and with it the ability to download larger and larger files, at faster and faster speeds. The Center for the Digital Future has been studying the behavior of Internet users and non-users since 2000. Its research shows that when people have continuous access to the Net, and the ability to quickly download content to their computing device, their use of the Net changes completely. As Jeff Cole, the Center's director, put it after reviewing the results of their 2004 study, "The 'always on' feature of broadband will have significant effects on Internet use, creating change for users that is almost as great as the difference between Internet access and not having access at all." Ever since 2004, when this phenomenon first became large enough to be measured, broadband usage, or "penetration," has been steadily increasing in the United States. About two-thirds of American households have Internet access, and about half of those access the Web at broadband speeds (Pew Research Centerl 2007b). Instead of "going on line" in concentrated, short spurts of time, which was the case in a dial-up world, broadband Internet users incorporate being on the Net into their daily activities, making the Net more of an integrative experience than a disruptive one, to use Cole's terminology. In particular, the Center's 2004 study showed that broadband users spent more time on the Net—"doing their job from home, instant messaging, playing games, seeking entertainment information, using online auctions, and downloading music"—than did those who used a dial-up modem to access the Net. Furthermore, the increasing speed at which consumers and businesses can acquire their information using a broadband, always-on connection enables them to download larger and larger files, which in turn makes the Net a new channel for distributing entertainment and information of all kinds. And, for most Millennials, it is this world of broadband access to the Internet that is the only world they have ever known.

But computers linked at broadband speeds to other computers on the Net can do one more thing that most futurists failed to anticipate.

With the right software, one computer can link directly to another and use the information on the second computer's hard drive as if it were its own. No intermediary authority needs to take the file from one computer and then prepare, or package, it for transfer to another. Instead, each computer acts as a "peer" of the other, as the two become virtually one computing device while exchanging data. This is as significant a step in the evolution of modern-day computing as was the jump from hominids to *Homo sapiens* millennia ago. Once computers gain this simple capability, they can talk to any other computer with the same code on IP networks, just as language expanded the social circles of our prehistoric ancestors, and no authority or gatekeeper can prevent them from doing so.

Skype, a communication service company now owned by eBay, uses this technology to allow people to talk to each other (in the old-fashioned manner) for no additional cost over their computers. There is no network intelligence in the system that is required to set up the call, keep it up, take it down, and thereby bill the caller based upon the length of time of the connection. The concept, known technically as Voice Over Internet Protocol (VOIP), is actually quite easy to implement, compared with the bandwidth needed to download larger files such as music or video; but the concept is the same regardless of the content being "peered." Since the Internet connection is prepaid as a flat fee in one's monthly Internet access, it seems to most people, especially Millennials, that anything else done online is, or at least should be, free.

All information technology architectures, or designs, influence how we think we should communicate and share information. Initially, IBM's mainframe architecture suggested that information needed to be centralized in a special place, guarded by people with unique and esoteric skills, whose permission was required to gain access to the knowledge only they could extract. Later, Apple personal computers, or those built on the "Wintel" platform (Windows software from Microsoft operating or running on an Intel chip), completely undercut that design, nearly driving IBM into bankruptcy. Enterprises linked desktop computers, or "clients," over local area networks to decentralized mini-computers, or servers, and empowered teams of "wired workers" to accomplish their own goals using information that was literally at their fingertips (Buffa and Winograd 1996).

Today, P2P architecture places all power in the hands of the users, creating an ethos and a belief system that they are, and ought to be, free to do whatever they wish with any information they can find. Since no permission is required to interact with anyone else and there is no intermediary gating the nature of that interaction, there doesn't seem to be any reason to have rules that would limit such interactions. P2P architecture truly empowers the user, creating a mindset that resists any attempt of any kind to control what is shared, whether it comes from a music industry magnate, publisher, or political power broker. And Millennials have experienced the power of this new architecture more than any other generation.

MILLENNIALS LOVE THEIR PEERS' MUSIC

The first industry to be rocked by the application of P2P technology was the music business. Recording studios, which had controlled the selection and distribution of artists and their music almost since, as the song says, "Edison invented sound," suddenly discovered that they had lost much of that power because of this new technology.

It all began innocently enough with the creation of the MP3 file protocol in the mid-1990s. MP3 offered a superior format for compressing CD-quality audio files for downloading to a computer or to other digital playback devices. (Ironically, MP3 is actually an acronym for "*Motion Picture Expert Group-1 Audio Layer III*, named after the industry working group that created this standard, which was intended to expand the market for CDs by incorporating compressed video into the product.) By 1999, more than one-third of all audio files on the Net were in this MP3 format, ready to be downloaded to Millennial laptops whenever their users desired. Those files took up very little space on a hard drive, so customers could have thousands of songs if they wanted to, each one a perfect digital copy of the original file (Short and O'Brien n.d.).

The first company to popularize the MP3 format and take advantage of its commercial potential—named, appropriately enough, MP3.com—was co-founded by Michael Robertson. Robertson deliberately set out to use the "Power of the Net to change the system" (Short and O'Brien n.d., 9). In 1999, his company, in partnership with the bricks-and-mortar retailer Best Buy, sponsored a national tour led by rock stars

Alanis Morissette and Tori Amos that featured a few of the more than 10,000 Indie bands that had put their songs out on the Net in MP3 format, independent of the Big 5 record companies.

EMI Group, Warner Music Group, Bertelsmann, Sony, and Universal Music Group considered Robertson's efforts more of an annoyance than a major threat, however, since the total Indie market that year represented only about 15 percent of all music sales. It consisted mostly of artists whose recordings were thought to be too far beyond mainstream taste to be profitable for the major labels. The music industry was built on proven performers with mass appeal whose blockbuster sales paid for the high manufacturing and distribution costs that had become prevalent in the industry.

By signing with a major label, musicians paid a steep price for their chance at fame. Typically, artists gave up all their intellectual property rights, a practice sometimes referred to as "intellectual gillnetting," in return for about 10 percent of the retail revenue from a $15 CD. This financial arrangement, combined with the artistic insensitivity and bottom-line orientation of many of the large labels, caused other artists, particularly those in the emerging world of hip-hop and rap, to use their individual fame to also go the Indie route. All these factors made the MP3 distribution alternative increasingly attractive.

MP3.com's business plan was designed to take advantage of the disconnection between those who created the content and those who marketed it. The site went live in November 1998 and had over 10,000 visitors on its first day—all happily sampling and downloading whatever music they liked—without any cost whatsoever. In less than a year, it became one of the most popular sites on the Web, with more than 20 million songs downloaded, 18,000 artists' music available, and 300,000 unique visitors a day (Short and O'Brien n.d.).

The site was a powerful marketing and promotional tool designed to be friendly to both the creators of the content and their listeners, encouraging as much interaction as possible and thereby allowing them to learn with each click of the mouse what each wanted from the other. This model of closely linking the production of content with the consumer, in some cases even melding the two to create a "prosumer," is what all Internet businesses strive to emulate today. The rapid learning occurring from the "short feedback loops" inherent in the design accounts for the way such businesses grow so rapidly, creating new phrases, such as "Google it" or "I TiVoed it," seemingly overnight. The model holds just as much promise for any industry, be it automobile manufacturing or political campaigning—if it has the courage to give up control in return for success.

TRYING TO PUT THE DIGITAL GENIE BACK IN THE BOTTLE

The music business was in no mood for such a revolution. Robertson, a classic entrepreneurial Gen-Xer and a strong believer in the power of P2P computing, told the world, "Technology is a steam roller. You either drive it or it runs you over" (Short and O'Brien n.d., 2). But his own music world was run over by U.S. copyright laws. One of his offers, "Instant Listening," allowed customers who could prove they had already purchased a particular CD to listen to MP3.com's version free of charge. To help acquire some of these titles for their servers, MP3.com purchased a record store and ripped all the CDs in it into the MP3 format. All the record companies sued, and the resulting multi-million-dollar settlements for copyright infringement helped to bring about the eventual demise of MP3.com, ending the first phase of the music industry's evolution (Ted Cohen interview 2006).

Those who founded Napster, in May 1999, thought they had overcome all these problems by launching their MP3 file-sharing business using P2P communication technology architecture rather than the "client/server" design that MP3.com employed. Instead of "owning" any music on their site, Napster simply allowed those who downloaded a simple piece of software from their site to exchange files of recorded music with any other user willing to share his or her favorite tunes. Since Napster was merely a technological conduit for this transfer and never possessed the actual music files, its owners believed they were fully within their legal rights to encourage the exchange by providing lists of files available for copying from PCs around the world.

Ted Cohen, now a key strategist for digital music businesses, was among those in the 1980s who participated in discussions on the music industry's digital future, and who failed to imagine a world in which people didn't go to a central site to get the information or files they wanted in order to copy them. When Cohen first realized what Napster had done, his reaction was "Wow!" The record industry was even more surprised—but considerably less impressed.

Within six months of Napster's launch, the music industry, faced with a dramatic decline in the sale of CDs, sued to shut the service down. The lawsuit was filed just as Cohen and others were toasting Napster at the WebNoize Conference in November 1999. Hillary Rosen, head of the Recording Industry Association of America (RIAA), announced the lawsuit from Washington, D.C., as she addressed Napster's interim CEO, Eileen Richardson, in front of a raucous and unsympathetic audience.

The RIAA argued that Napster's active encouragement and enablement of the transfer of such protected material constituted a violation of its members' copyrighted intellectual property, under the provisions of the Digital Millennium Copyright Act (DMCA) passed the previous year. The lawsuit dragged on for years, while more and more Napster users, most of them Millennials, discovered the joy of sharing songs without cost with their friends or even strangers who happened to share their tastes in music. As the battle wended its way to the Supreme Court, the on-again, off-again settlement negotiations finally came to a head. Napster offered to pay the industry one billion dollars per year to compensate for any lost royalty revenues, in return for the end of all legal challenges to the most successful use of P2P technology to date (Cohen interview 2006).

Noting that the amount was to be permanently capped, the RIAA, unwilling to lose its control over music production and distribution, declined the settlement offer and decided to take its chances with the Supreme Court. Despite losing its case in all the lower courts, the RIAA won the only victory that counted—a decision from the Supreme Court that ultimately allowed it to shut down Napster's P2P file-sharing business and that of all its clones.

The music industry, which by then had grown as cocky and isolated as any Tammany Hall politician, then decided to sue its customers to make sure they stopped misbehaving. In September 2003, just as the last of the Millennials were born, the RIAA issued subpoenas for illegally downloading songs off the Internet to a group of P2P users, including a twelve-year-old girl whom they accused of being a modern-day pirate. Certain that an aggressive enforcement of copyright laws would bring their customers to heel, the RIAA continued such lawsuits against people like sixteen-year-old Michelle Santangelo of New York and ten-year-old Kylee Anderson of California, as well as college students throughout the country, attempting to corral all its future customers and to demand payment for each song they had "illegally" downloaded (Newton 2007).

The effect of this legal war was to create a permanent mindset on the part of the Millennial Generation that entrenched special interests would stop at nothing to prevent them from sharing information on the Net that was, or at least ought to be, inherently "free." Along the way, the struggle helped make Millennials suspicious of all elites attempting to control what they were allowed to know, whether it was the latest Indie band or the real story behind a political debate.

Peer-to-Peer Pressure Is Irresistible

Like other attempts to put the technology genie back in the bottle, the RIAA's victory was short-lived. Music lovers, especially younger ones, having become accustomed to sharing their music without cost or restriction, didn't just suddenly stop accessing MP3 files because they couldn't find the music easily on Napster. For one thing, every CD or MP3 file could be "ripped" onto their own computers' hard drives, at which point they were free to transfer them over the Net to the computer of any friend who wouldn't have to buy the source CD at all.

Even the wildly popular iPod turned out not to be the solution to the record industry's problems. The iPod, with its simple one-dial interface, was an overnight sensation. Its easy-to-use iTunes software, which enabled the transfer over the Internet of any song in the iTunes store to the iPod, was DMCA-compliant because Apple used its own proprietary Digital Rights Management (DRM) protocol, FairPlay, to prevent songs from being played on any other MP3 device. Essentially, Apple had re-created MP3.com's client/server architecture, but with this very important added feature to make it all legal. It was also very popular. In the first eight months of the product's launch, 25 million songs were downloaded, and the iPod became the "must have" gift for Christmas in 2003 (Healey 2003).

But the users of P2P technology refused to settle for any form of centralized control over how and when they got the music they wanted to hear. By early 2007, sales of CDs were off 20 percent from a year earlier (Smith 2007). Practically all the damage could be attributed to declining music purchases by Millennials, who bought one-third less music between 1989 and 2004, with their share of all music purchases dropping to just 11 percent (Strauss and Howe 2006).

Jon Diamond, CEO of ArtistDirect, Inc., which operates the second-largest music/content destination on the Web as well as Media Defender, the leading Internet Privacy Protection (IPP) company, estimated that over 90 percent of all songs acquired on the Net in 2006 were downloaded through the use of P2P file sharing networks. iTunes sales of two billion songs in 2006, through its online portal, represented about 88 percent of the legally downloaded music sold in the United States. But that same year, Diamond points out, "Americans initiated tens of billions of requests for illegal P2P music file transfers. In any given month there are 300 million users of such services on the Net, or about 10 to 20 million simultaneous users at any given moment, depending on the time of day" (interview 2007). And the number of such users continues to grow.

Based on matching the song titles requested with the IP address of the requester, Diamond estimated that the vast majority of these file-sharing requests were generated by Millennials, exercising what they saw as their inalienable right to share everything with everyone. The CEO of eMusic.com, David Pakman said, "Most of the youth of today has decided not to buy music anymore. They might steal it or listen over the Internet, but no one has yet figured out a way to monetize what they are doing" (Semuels and Quinn 2007).

And in February 2007, Apple's Steve Jobs suggested the industry acknowledge reality, forget about the whole idea of DRM, and return the industry to its MP3 roots (Wingfield and Smith 2007). In an open memo to the industry, Jobs pointed out that only about 3 percent of the music on any individual's iPod was actually purchased through the iTunes store anyway. Within a month, one of the major record companies, EMI, agreed; its "DRM-free" music became available at iTunes, albeit for a slightly higher price. The files were not, however, in the easy-to-use MP3 format, signaling the continuing desire of the music industry to try to find some way to control, or, as Millennials might say, harass, its customers. But if the industry has any hope of ending the rampant piracy that dominates the distribution of music, it will eventually have to make the experience of buying music online easier for its customers than "ripping it off," to paraphrase iPod's original commercial.

Of course, Jobs's proposal was met with great trepidation by those with a stake in the old ways of doing business. Hillary Rosen, who by then had become a consultant in the industry, suggested that "for the labels, it feels like jumping off a cliff" (Quinn, Semuels, and Chmielewski 2007). Her comment was reminiscent of the famous scene in *Butch Cassidy and the Sundance Kid* when the two heroes are contemplating jumping off just such a cliff to escape the posse that has encircled them. Butch (Paul Newman) suggests they jump, but Sundance (Robert Redford) protests: "I can't swim." Butch's response became a classic rejoinder to anyone afraid of the future. "Are you crazy? The fall'll probably kill you." Whether the fall from power does, in fact, kill the four record companies still in business, or whether they learn how to swim in the rapid waters of P2P technology, remains to be seen. What is certain is that they are only the first of many leaders in the media and entertainment industries to be faced with the life-threatening pressure that comes from P2P technology and the users it empowers.

YOU'RE NEXT, KID

The recent history of the record industry will inevitably be repeated with other entertainment media, as communication and computing infrastructures become able to handle more and more digital data, at lower and lower prices. Already the fastest growing types of files being swapped in the world of P2P users are television shows. Even as the popular press gushes over the decision by Disney to allow iPod owners to download the newest episode of "Grey's Anatomy," movies that haven't even been released yet are being watched on Millennials' laptops in dorm rooms around the country. Each day more than 30 million requests for movies circulate on file-sharing networks around the world. On the first day of a major film's release in the United States, approximately 5 million searches will be launched on the Net by people seeking to download a copy illegally (Diamond interview 2006).

An analysis of actual traffic on the Internet provides an even clearer picture of the popularity of P2P sharing of digital content. Worldwide, about 55 percent of all Internet traffic is P2P-oriented, and 61 percent of that traffic is in video files, typically television shows or movies. Only one percent is VOIP (Telegeography 2007). The 10 to 20 million people engaged in P2P file sharing at any given moment in time far overshadows, for instance, the 2 million unique visitors to YouTube during an entire day (Diamond interview 2006). Some in the industry can already see the handwriting on the wall. Dick Wolf, the producer of such successful shows as "Law and Order," told the *Wall Street Journal* that, after watching the file-sharing behavior of his teenage son, he thought the TV industry as we know it has five or at most ten years to live (Steinberg 2006).

The movie industry, which represents a significant next step up on the scale of digital files, will be the last form of entertainment to be forced by the pressure of P2P technology to find new ways to deliver its product to its customers. But with the irresistible force of the Millennial Generation's penchant for sharing everything, it will also have to make peace with the power of technology to enable that very activity, if it wishes to remain in business. Jack MacKenzie, an expert on Millennial media behavior, points out that one of the reasons for the recent decline in movie theater attendance is the conflict between the norms of behavior expected of movie-goers and Millennials' social style. "The first things they tell you when you go to a movie is to turn your cell phone off and don't talk. You might as well tell Millennials to not even bother showing up" (interview 2007).

Even more fundamental to the worrisome future of today's media industry is the penchant for civic-era generations to reject the dominant popular culture of the time. Idealist Baby Boomers thought of rock groups like the Beatles as allies in a rebellion against the establishment. Hippies gained global notoriety as the Beatles' hit song "All You Need Is Love" was released in June 1967, at the height of that year's "Summer of Love." But Millennials, just like their GI Generation predecessors, focus their youthful attention on the tone and content of America's culture, not the moral authority of the political establishment. Strauss and Howe's observation about the way different generations react to the world they inherit captures the media industry's problem perfectly: "Millennials will rebel against Gen-X styles and attitudes, correct for Boomer excesses, and fill the role vacated by the GIs" (1996, 48).

THE SHIFTING POWER EQUATION

The new facts of life were apparent to at least some of the industry moguls gathered in Davos, Switzerland, for the annual World Economic Forum in January 2007. The theme of the conference, "The Shifting Power Equation," said it all. It took a leader from the Silent Generation,

Rupert Murdoch, to put things most bluntly. "It's so pluralistic. We [the big companies] all have less power, much less. We just have to let this go. We can't reverse it. We're in the very early stages of it" (Szalai 2007). He wasn't a Johnny-come-lately to the party, either, having said as early as 2005, "Young people don't want to rely on a Godlike figure from above to tell them what's important. . . . They want control over their media, instead of being controlled by it" (Anderson 2006, 37). Then he plunked down $580 million for MySpace, just to show he wasn't afraid to put his money where his mouth was.

His fellow panelist at the Davos gabfest, Bill Gates, talked about how much impact the Internet was having on television viewing habits, especially among young people:

> I'm stunned how people aren't seeing that with TV, in five years from now, people will laugh at what we've had. The rise of high-speed Internet and the popularity of video sites like YouTube has already led to a worldwide decline in the number of hours spent by young people in front of a TV set. In the years ahead, more and more viewers will hanker after the flexibility offered by online video and abandon conventional broadcast television, with its fixed program slots and advertisements that interrupt shows. Certain things *like elections* [emphasis added], or the Olympics really point out how TV is terrible. You have to wait for the guy to talk about the thing you care about or you miss the event and want to go back and see it. Internet presentation of these things is vastly superior. (Szalai 2007)

Murdoch also acknowledged that News Corporation's Fox News Channel's attempts to influence popular opinion on the war in Iraq had been a failure, due to the power of the Internet to provide alternative viewpoints directly to the voters. Murdoch may be, in fact, the last in a long line of media barons who have attempted to use their control of the distribution of information to direct the course of American politics and policy. But, as with his predecessors, he has found that advances in technology had eroded the ability of those in power to stay there.

EVERYONE WANTS TO BE A PRODUCER

The power of the broadcast media masters to influence politics is under attack from a medium that many of them don't understand. They are fighting a guerrilla war with candidates who dog their opponents with hand-held cameras to catch the latest faux pas and put it on YouTube for everyone to see. After 150 years of increasingly centralized control over the creation and distribution of news and information, the Net and P2P technologies suddenly present an opportunity for power to flow in the opposite direction. With MySpace and other social networking tools, each voter can become his or her own campaign office and flood the nation's political speech with unfiltered ideas from every corner of the country.

Even as the political establishment joins movie moguls and TV executives in fighting a rearguard action against this trend, do-it-yourself video, or "user-generated content," is eating away at the very foundation of its fortresses. This is occurring to such an extent that *Time* magazine's "Person of the Year" award for 2006 went to "you"—that user reflected in a mirror on the magazine's cover who happily uploads the latest version of what passes for creativity on YouTube.com.

YouTube's popularity exploded as spectacularly as a Mentos mint plopped into a bottle of Diet Coke. Traffic zoomed from about 300,000 viewers per day to over two million on December 14, 2005, when YouTube posted a video clip of a skit entitled "Lazy Sunday" from NBC's previously passé "Saturday Night Live." Suddenly, SNL was popular again, thanks to this new form of video distribution (MacKenzie interview 2007). By enabling people to simply and easily upload and download video clips, the founders of YouTube created a whole new sharing experience for their Millennial audience, and along the way they created a business that they sold to Google for $1.6 billion.

As high-speed broadband penetration approached the 50 percent mark among American households with Internet connections, and digital video recorders (DVRs) were incorporated into standard offerings from TiVo or the local cable company, commercial skipping became a habit as well. Advertisers began to switch their media buys from broadcast television to "click through" ads on Google, Yahoo, and other Internet search sites. Suddenly, the Net was awash in money, testing new ways to gain the attention of users, or "eyeballs," as the industry so pointedly put it. The upfront television ad buy of major consumer goods manufacturers began to drop in 2004, as a brave new world of targeted advertising, where the message was only seen by those most likely to be interested in it, began to emerge. Nike, one of the most successful brands in the world, pulled part of its advertising business from the agency that had been a critical partner in creating that success because the company didn't think the advertising

firm had the skills necessary to continue to build the brand in this new
world of digital media (Vranica 2007). By 2007, Google was hosting seminars for political consultants, where its newly formed sales team, dedicated to selling ads to campaigns, explained the intricacies and nuances of
"click through" ad buying (Puzzanghera 2007).

For politicians, these changes in television viewing habits, and their
impact on advertising strategies, are particularly troublesome. The most
recent survey of Internet user behavior, by Jeff Cole's Center for the Digital Future, showed that people are no longer turning off their televisions
to browse the Net. Instead, they are relegating TV to a background
sound, looking up occasionally from their laptops to see a particularly
dramatic or visually interesting moment, but otherwise content to have
the sound, not the picture, be the reason for including the television as
part of their online, multi-tasking world.

Furthermore, the cost of video editing is falling so quickly that
someone with a little knowledge of the technology can create television
ads using FinalCutPro software on a MacPro in his apartment on a Sunday afternoon. That's what Phil de Villas, aka "parkridge47," did in March
2007 when he created the first presidential campaign commercial to go
viral. Entitled "Vote Different," it cast Hillary Clinton as Big Brother in a
mashup of an Apple iPod ad that was in turn an echo of Apple's legendary
1984 Super Bowl commercial attacking IBM's centralized mainframe
dominance. The ad urged its viewers to support Barack Obama as a ges-
ture of defiance to the political establishment. Almost three million people viewed it on YouTube before the month was out. While Obama could
truthfully deny his campaign had any part in its creation, no media consulting maven could deny that the number of its viewers, compared to its
cost, completely upset the economics of traditional television production
and distribution (Goldstein 2007).

These developments present the possibility of an end to the ever-
rising cost of thirty-second television campaign commercials, and the
time-consuming and potentially corrupting need to raise the money to
pay for them. They also pose a direct threat to the prime seat at the table
that media advisors have held in every national campaign since Richard
Nixon's in 1968. Democratic media consultants, in particular, would be
threatened by any move away from paid media to digital campaigns that
use the free distribution channels of the Net. Unlike their Republican

brethren, who have settled for fixed fees for their services, Democratic consultants, such as Bob Shrum, have traditionally taken at least a 10 percent cut of all money spent on television advertising by the campaigns they are advising—even as they urge their clients to spend more money on TV. In Al Gore's 2000 presidential campaign, this arrangement netted Shrum and his firm about $5 million. Even when the arrangement was modified by John Kerry in 2004 to a mix of fixed and commission payments, Shrum's firm walked away from the losing effort with about $8.35 million in its pocket. The advisors convinced the Kerry campaign to spend three times the money Gore had paid out on television ads—none of which were as devastating, or as powerful, as the Swift Boat ads launched by Kerry's opponents. The group behind those ads bought a minimal amount of television time to air them. The buy was designed, from its inception, as merely the easiest way to gain attention to the ad before it moved onto the Net, where it could do real and lasting damage (Dickinson 2007).

The power of viral marketing is being recognized in corporate campaigns, such as Nissan's launch of its new Sentra, which, in order to reach its target demographic, used video of a Millennial living in the car for a week. But this idea has been slow to penetrate the control-oriented world of political consulting. "There's little impetus to try anything new," says Joe Trippi, a recognized visionary in the use of the Internet in political campaigns, first for Howard Dean's 2004 bid and later for John Edwards in 2008. "You can't get a 10 percent commission on a million people viewing something for free on YouTube" (Dickinson 2007).

Peer-to-peer communications will upset the balance of power in the world of hand-to-hand political combat in 2008 even more than it did in 2006. Victory will no longer automatically go to the candidate with the most money, especially if the campaign has the wrong media advisors. Instead, candidates will have to create political content that people surfing the Net will want to watch. New, more authentic messages, delivered by credible messengers, will provide a competitive advantage over the techniques for selling a candidate that have been honed over the last forty years. Just as the entertainment industry has seen its entire world turned upside down by the power of P2P technologies, the political world is about to be shaken to its core by the arrival of these new capabilities for reaching voters, especially the generation that uses them every moment of every day.

CHAPTER 9

Social Networks Will Change America's Political Map

MOVING FROM A BROADCAST entertainment architec-
ture, with its centralized control over both the production and distribution of content, to the decentralized, user-driven structure of the Net
was not easy to accomplish for many in the media industry. "I want my
MTV" was the emblematic 1980s mantra of Gen-Xers, who demanded
their parents give them access to that cable channel and its music. But
today, MTV's corporate parent, Viacom, struggles to find the right formula for attracting Millennials to its web sites (Karnitschnig 2006). The
idea that the Internet was just another distribution channel for the type
of programming that had made Viacom so successful with Generation X
was firmly fixed in the company's underlying strategy.

In March 2007, Viacom's owner, Sumner Redstone, made it clear just
how much he believed in the old model by suing YouTube's new owner,
Google, for $1 billion in damages for alleged copyright violations. Via-
com could have joined its media brethren at NBC Universal and News
Corporation in their efforts to create a rival to YouTube's video-sharing
web site, one that would fully respect the intellectual property rights of
all the media companies involved in this new venture. But Redstone preferred the RIAA's "sue 'em" strategy instead. "It's hard for us to believe
[Google] has any desire to protect our content," remarked Viacom's chief
executive, Philippe Dauman, summarizing the motivation for the lawsuit
(Delaney and Karnitschnig 2007). Completely missing from this statement is any acknowledgment that viewers on YouTube might have
something of their own to contribute to the site's content. But Viacom,
unwilling to give up the control it felt was necessary to make money from
its investments in its existing properties, in effect sacrificed the

potential brand loyalty of an entire generation just to preserve the value of what it could control today.

Political campaigns are the equals of any media company when it comes to wanting to run things from the top and control every aspect of the product they are selling. As Joe Trippi, Howard Dean's campaign manager in 2004, wrote, "Most campaigns do everything in their power to control every element of the candidate's image and message, from the clothes he wears to each word out of his mouth" (2004, 109). As a consultant to Silicon Valley start-ups, Trippi could see that the notion of running a campaign from the bottom up would require an "open source" approach, with control located, if at all, in the swarm of contributors to the campaign's efforts rather than at its headquarters. But, as he pointed out to Dean, attempting such a feat would be like "jumping from a fifteen-story building" and trusting the front line troops would be there to catch you. In a DeanNation blog posted in May 2003, Trippi wrote, "Every political campaign I have ever been in was built on the top-down military structure. . . . This kind of structure will suffocate the storm [groundswell of support], not fuel it. . . . The important thing is to provide the tools and some of the direction . . . and get the hell out of the way when a big wave is building on its own" (119). The idea, as the Dean campaign itself proved, is easier to articulate than to execute. But those candidates who master the art of putting the voters in charge of the campaign will be rewarded with victory.

CHANGING THE MAP ONE STATE AT A TIME

Those who cut their teeth in 2004 on this new way to involve the voters soon found themselves in demand by all of the 2008 presidential campaigns. Mark Warner, who left the governor's mansion in Virginia in 2005 to explore a presidential run (which he ultimately decided against), recruited one of the more prominent members of the Dean campaign, Jerome Armstrong, who had coined the term word "Netroots" in 2002 to describe the growing community of people who became politically active through online interaction. Armstrong was hired for what turned out to be a one-year test of the ability of online campaigning to build support for a relatively unknown presidential candidate. Warner, who had co-founded Nextel and invested in other Internet start-ups before he became governor, fully appreciated the potential of this new approach to campaigning. Joining Armstrong at the center of the candidate's Netroots activities was Trei Brundrett, whose knowledge of peer-to-peer technologies may have even surpassed Armstrong's. With Warner's full support, the two Net organizers set out to build upon what the Dean campaign had done and, in particular, to take advantage of social networking sites that weren't widely used in 2004.

In 2006, the pair created a web initiative to complement Warner's "Forward Together" political action committee, designed to attract interest and build a network of future volunteers and supporters. Their idea was a contest among Democratic congressional candidates in Republican districts called "Map Changers," a name given to Warner by a Missouri Democrat in reference to Warner's impact in helping to change red districts to blue. The contest rules were simple: an individual visiting the web site would "vote" for a Democratic challenger as a sign of support, at the same time submitting his or her name, email address, and zip code to the Warner PAC web site. That data, of course, was invaluable to the nascent Warner effort, while the winning congressional candidates would receive Warner's time and help in raising money. After an initial round of voting, the ten candidates with the most online votes won a contribution from Forward Together. Then, in the final round of the contest, those ten competed to see who would get Warner to come to the candidate's district and headline a fund-raiser for the campaign. In effect, Brundrett and Armstrong had created an incentive for the Democratic candidates to self-organize and create networks of political activists that might in turn help Warner in his own possible presidential run. The idea proved so successful that it was repeated for legislative candidates in the two key early presidential contest states, Iowa and New Hampshire (Brundrett and Armstrong interviews 2007).

In New Hampshire, two nineteen-year-old Millennials running for the state legislature, Andrew Edwards and Jeffrey Fontas, were among the top five online vote getters, each receiving a $1,000 check from Warner's PAC. Edwards attends Worcester Polytechnic Institute when he is not engaged in politics. Fontas majors in political science at Northeastern University, which allows him to count his time in the state legislature as his "co-op" semester of work (interview 2007). The account of their winning the Map Changer contest can still be read on their October 2006 blog postings. Having won the money, they asked their friends and supporters for ideas on how best to spend it in their campaigns. In the end, each opted to use the winnings from his online campaigning to buy the fundamentals of offline grassroots campaigns—lawn signs, literature, and local advertising.

But their skill in social networking was the key to winning Warner's contest. Edwards and Fontas each created a group on Facebook's social networking site specifically for his campaign and encouraged friends from around the world to join. Facebook's platform, or operating system, allows users to join or create any group that might be of interest—from a particular band or musical genre to a candidate or a political party or anything in between. Fontas and Edwards sought to streamline the process of mobilizing people they knew only through the Internet by making clear their groups' purposes: "Fontas for State House" and "Edwards for State Representative."

When the Forward Together contest was announced, they decided to use the site's NewsFeed feature to round up support. NewsFeed is designed to tell each user what is going on in a community that a member has joined, either by signing up for a group or by "friending" another user. News about the community shows up on the profile page of all members of the community for other friends to see whenever they check their profile. Normally what passes for community news is information about who is "friending" whom, what parties people went to the night before, or who has just posted pictures that others should view. But Edwards and Fontas grasped the potential for this feature to be used in their political campaigns long before most campaign gurus had even heard of the concept.

They both began by posting a "note" about the Map Changer contest on their personal profile, which meant that each of their friends or members of their group received notice of the contest as one "story" in that community's NewsFeed. But the two social networking gurus went one step further, using the "tagging" function within the Facebook platform as well. Technically, a "tag" is metadata, or "information about information," created when a user labels a particular piece of data, such as a photo, with information that will help categorize the item so it will be easier to find again. By mentioning each of their friends in the note, thereby "tagging" them, the note automatically appeared in all their friends' NewsFeeds as well, so that people with whom neither of them were friends but who were "friends of their friends" also heard about the contest. By using the platform, or operating system, of Facebook's site, the news about the contest "spread like wildfire" (interview 2007).

This frenzy of social networking was enabled by the Warner web site, which provided "widgets," or small Web-based applications, that each contestant was able to import to his own web site and include in the "post" or "note" about the contest. The widgets told visitors who clicked on them how to vote in the Map Changer contest and why they should vote, and also provided a sample ballot that could be copied to any other web site for further sharing. Based on his Dean campaign experience, Armstrong designed the Map Changer contest to provide contestants with the tools they might want to use to assist their individual organizing efforts, but he left it up to each participant to decide how best to spread the word and gain support (interview 2007):

Edwards's and Fontas's creative use of Facebook's NewsFeed application didn't end there. For instance, Edwards placed a notice on his campaign profile site of the contest but treated it as an "event." Under NewsFeed's rules, this meant that each person invited to the event was sent an "invitation" to attend, or, in this case, to vote. The friends then either had to RSVP, in effect voting for Edwards in the contest, or take some other affirmative action to remove the invitation from the member's personal profile. He used this particular feature to avoid constantly emailing people to ask for their votes, which would have been viewed as a violation of Net etiquette. After the contest, he underlined the importance of these social networking features for his contest victory. "The News-Feed, coupled with features like Notes and Media sharing, is such a perfectly integrated system to disseminate information. It's already *the* tool, in fact" (interview 2007).

Edwards had more than 150 friends in his campaign Facebook group at the time of the contest, and Fontas had more than 250. Starting from that core, the two candidates then reached out to other Facebook users and traditional sources of online Democratic support, such as DailyKos. com, to get people to vote for them in the Map Changer campaign. Not satisfied with those efforts, the two candidates posted a plea for votes on the "Something Awful" forum, a comedy web site filled with messaging pranks, digitally edited pictures, and humorous movie reviews. The idea to use this particular site came from Fontas, who constantly checked the site's forum for news updates and commentary and posted his own thoughts about the news on the site for his fellow news addicts to read. However, in order not to have that history of his postings or comments interfere with their Map Changer contest, Edwards was chosen to be the one who actually asked for votes on the site. As he noted, "The politics of personal destruction have been amplified so much now by the Net that you need to go to extraordinary lengths to protect your privacy" (interview 2007).

The two campaigners received many replies to their pleas for votes from people on "Something Awful" who wanted to know about the ethics of the contest, how much the two were being paid to send out the Warner-related message, and other questions that reveal the paranoia many "Netizens" feel toward people seeking power. But, in the end, the request generated more than one hundred votes, which helped put them into the winner's circle.

Each district in the lower house of the New Hampshire legislature elects multiple representatives depending on its size. In District 26, for instance, Edwards received 3,558 votes, or 5 percent, finishing seventh out of twenty candidates. The ten candidates winning the greatest number of votes were entitled to a seat, so Edwards was sworn in as one of the youngest members of the state legislature. Meanwhile, in District 24, Fontas received 1,134 votes, or 22 percent. There were only five candidates running for the three seats in that district, so his total was enough to give him a seat. Even though he admits that he is a terrible blogger, Fontas still was proud enough of his victory that, in classic Millennial style, he posted the "obligatory mom and pop shot" on his blog the day he was sworn in. Within months of their victories, the two friends were speaking on the floor of the legislature, resisting entreaties from lobbyists, and capturing all the action for their friends on Facebook.

AS NEW HAMPSHIRE GOES, SO GOES THE NATION?

In 2006, Democrats took control of both houses of the New Hampshire legislature, along with the state's governorship, for the first time in 170 years. However, several factors suggest the possibility that what happened in New Hampshire in 2006 may not be the wave of the future in the rest of the country.

First, contrary to what took place in numerous other states, many of the Democratic legislative victories in New Hampshire occurred because large numbers of Republicans stayed home. Overall voter turnout in the state dropped by 6.8 percent, among the largest declines of any state in the nation that year (Committee for the Study of the American Electorate 2006). Second, the relatively small number of votes necessary to win election to the lower house of the New Hampshire legislature helps make the argument that these examples of Netroots victories in that state don't provide a model that can be duplicated in elections in larger constituencies or for higher offices, especially the presidency. To use the terminology of dot-com venture capitalists, it raises questions as to whether this business model can "scale" up to the size required for victories in bigger elections.

There is one more argument made against the idea that the future of politics will be found in online campaigning. This argument has less to do with scale and more to do with the level of political intensity of voters that are recruited online, rather than in person or through the mass media. Howard Dean's failure to win the Iowa caucuses in 2004 is the example that is most often cited. While the "open source" campaign that Dean designed found numerous new supporters, many of whom were counted as "ones," or hard core supporters, in the campaign's tracking process, Dean's actual vote total fell far short of expectations on the night that the caucuses were held. Even though insiders knew that Dean's support was falling fast in the weeks preceding the caucuses, especially after a withering barrage of attack ads from former House majority leader Dick Gephardt, Dean's third-place finish is often used to prove the notion that "'Netroots' don't vote" (Trippi 2004).

However, two powerful contrary trends suggest that the experience of the two Millennial New Hampshire state legislators will be replicated in the future and that those who ignore the new technology do so at their peril. One has to do with the economics and relative effectiveness of twenty-first century media and the other with significant changes in the demographics of the audience.

THE END OF TV CAMPAIGNING AS WE KNOW IT

The history of the evolution of political communications in America reveals that each new technological development does not completely displace the old ways of communicating. Instead, the new communication technology grows, over time, to become the more dominant form of campaigning—in much the same way that mammals eventually displaced reptiles as the more advanced life form. Radio overtook newspapers and precinct leafleting as the primary way of getting the candidate's message out in the 1930s. Even so, candidates today still spend a lot of money on their "ground game," or in-person voter turnout efforts. Depending on the race, some candidates also continue to buy newspaper ads. Television grabbed the dominant share of most campaigns' media expenditures in the 1960s, but almost every federal-level campaign still uses radio to reach particular voter segments.

The same pattern of displacement will cause television to lose its role as the primary medium for campaigns to get their messages out to voters in the near future. In 1965, when Lyndon Johnson was enacting the entire wish list of the Democratic Party, from Medicare to civil rights legislation to the War on Poverty, the Democratic Party could reach 80 percent of the country's prime demographic audience, 18- to 49-year-olds, with a sixty-second commercial played just three times on national TV. By 2002, achieving the same demographic coverage would have required 117 primetime commercials (Peers 2004). In the intervening years, the target demographic, which in 1965 was made up primarily of members of the Silent Generation, along with some aging members of the GI Generation, was replaced by a predominantly Gen-X set of viewers, many of whom had moved onto the Internet to get their news and information. When they did watch television, it wasn't to watch broadcasts for the masses, but more often satellite or cable programming targeted to their interests and frequently TiVo'ed to avoid commercials. By 2007, the audience became even harder to reach, as the first of the Millennials to enter that target demographic utilized the Net even more frequently as their primary source for news and information. The higher cost and lower impact of television had become more of a burden than any campaign could carry (New Politics Institute 2005).

The enormous advantage in the economics of campaigning via the Net compared to television means that it is only a matter of time until candidates who devote most of their energies, if not most of their money, to these new campaign tactics will gain the upper hand. Not only does the technology provide an economical way to reach voters, it does so with messages that are actually watched and heard and, if created properly, believed.

Nearly 80 percent of Americans are now online. About half of them are in the fast-growing group of broadband users (Barabak 2006; Rainie & Horrigan 2007). Over a third of Americans report that they spend more time online than they do watching television or listening to the radio (Barabak 2006). These numbers are even higher for the Millennial Generation, the first to be able to multitask by using all these media simultaneously and effectively (Strauss and Howe 2006). Broadcast technologies, requiring advertisers to interrupt the viewers' entertainment to sell them something they may not want, are simply not able to compete for the attention of a generation that expects communications to be authentic and relevant. History suggests that those who find ways to integrate the new technology with existing tactics to produce multi-faceted campaigns that reach all voters will be especially successful in future elections.

REACHING MILLENNIALS

The second trend arguing for the importance of online campaigning in the future is the increasing numbers of Millennials in the electorate. This emerging generation has a penchant for getting its information from the Net, especially on social networking sites.

Younger voters are twice as likely as others to use the Net, rather than newspapers, to get information about political campaigns. Thirty-five percent of younger broadband Internet users acquired most of their news about the 2006 elections online, compared to 57 percent who still obtained the bulk of their information from television. This is the lowest use of TV for information among all age groups, and its use continues to decline in importance among Millennials (Rainie and Horrigan 2007). If, as expected, these trends continue, the Net will become their primary source of information within the next several election cycles.

Adrian Talbott, co-founder and executive director of Generation Engage, summed up the potential that this shift in information-acquisition behavior has for increasing voter participation: "Young people are not apathetic. They don't suffer from lack of interest, but suffer from lack of access" (Mohammed 2006). Trying to find economical ways to reach and persuade younger voters, an age group whose lifestyle is much more mobile than those already in the workforce, has always been a problem for candidates. Yale graduate student David W. Nickerson demonstrated in 2002 that it took three dollars to get younger voters to the polls for every dollar spent to motivate those over twenty-five. It isn't that Millennials are any less susceptible to political messages, Dickerson showed; it was that the difficulty of reaching them made such efforts relatively uneconomical (Cannon 2007).

But the results of the 2006 election demonstrated that the use of social networking sites, such as MySpace, Facebook, and YouTube, dramatically lowers that cost. Now that most Millennials are connected at broadband speeds all the time, the technology arms race is on, with their information-gathering habits leading the way.

THE OPENING MOVEMENT OF THE NEW CAMPAIGN SYMPHONY

Survey research indicates that voters use media for two distinct purposes—to help them become aware of the candidates and to decide which ones to vote for. In general, voters use all varieties of media far more frequently as sources of awareness than as means of persuasion, or aids in decision making. Most voter behavior is based on party identification, candidate incumbency, and the individual's own ideology. Once voters know the identity of each party's candidates and/or their perceived ideological stances, they generally have sufficient information to decide for whom to vote. Voters are therefore less likely to invest further time in listening to persuasion arguments from candidates, regardless of the type of media through which those arguments are being made.

So it is not surprising that in the most recent midterm elections the importance of various media, as sources of both awareness and decision making, was quite similar. Overall, television, debates, newspapers, broadcast radio, and campaign materials from candidates, parties, and interest groups ranked highest as sources of political information and messages. But there was one important difference when it came to the Net. In 2006, for the first time, the Internet ranked high on the list of sources for information about political campaigns (Frank N. Magid Associates, December 2006). While it was not yet highly ranked as a means of persuasion, that result is likely to change in the coming years as well.

Indeed, a post-2006 election survey by the Pew Research Center for the People and the Press showed that the use of the Internet to acquire information about candidates among all Americans more than doubled between 2002 and 2006. Its use increased five-fold in the higher profile campaigns for the U.S. Senate. Sixty million people, or 31 percent of all Americans, reported going online in the 2006 campaign to gather information about the candidates or to exchange political views or both (Rainie and Horrigan 2007).

The differences in patterns of media usage between generations are even more striking. Television is considered about equally important as a source of awareness and persuasion information by all generations. However, older generations—Baby Boomers and, to a slightly lesser extent, Gen-Xers—place greater importance on more traditional media such as print, broadcast radio, and materials from candidates as sources of information for decision making than Millennials. Among the youngest generation, it is the Internet and, to an even larger extent, personal interaction with friends, parents, and siblings that has greater prominence, reflecting this generation's penchant for sharing and group decision making (Frank N. Magid Associates, December 2006).

There are also key differences in the way the generations use specific media within each broad media category. Older generations, especially Baby Boomers, who grew up with TV, are more likely than Millennials to use broadcast television news programming, both local and national, as sources for information and decision making. By contrast, Millennials are more likely to utilize relatively new types of TV programming, such as cable news and satirical or humorous shows, such as "The Daily Show" and "The Colbert Report," for these purposes. As John Fiske, a twenty-two-year-old Millennial law student in San Diego, put it, "Nobody caters to us"—adding that CNN, Fox News, and MSNBC "think they can attract young people by playing rap music at the beginning and end of their shows. We see right through it" (Dickey and Sullivan 2007).

While Millennials were far less likely to use traditional over-the-air broadcast news programming as a source of political information and persuasion in 2006, they were as likely as older generations to use the Internet web sites of broadcast and cable television channels, local and national, for these purposes. In other words, to the extent that Millennials continue to use the traditional broadcast media for political information and persuasion, they do so online and not over the air. Beyond this, when asked about the use of other types of Internet sites after the 2006 election, Millennials indicated that they used official and unofficial political web sites, videos on YouTube, candidate web sites, and social networking sites in far greater numbers than older generations—sometimes by ratios of as much as five or even ten to one (Frank N. Magid Associates, December 2006).

Understanding what the future of online political campaigning will look like, therefore, begins with understanding Millennials' penchant for social expression on the Net.

SHARING DEFINES A GENERATION

The desire to let the world know almost everything there is to know about their personal lives at any given moment is a defining characteristic of Millennials. Social networking sites such as MySpace and Facebook make it possible for Millennials to share their lives with many more people than anyone, in any other generation, could have possibly imagined.

Each person who joins a site's community gets a personal profile page or web site that can be customized (especially with personal photos) using the site's own tools or other widgets that the site allows the user to import. The underlying code for organizing each of these sites, extended markup language (XML), allows each of the key pieces of information on the site to be "tagged" and entered in the site's large relational database, where it can be linked to any other site. The links can be initiated by the user who visits a site and asks to become a "friend," or, in some of the more sophisticated applications, they can be suggested by common attributes such as tastes in music, school attended, or opinions about the opposite sex. Of course, to create that kind of interaction, a site or user has to take steps to attract attention, which often results in pictorial displays that older generations find disturbing if not downright dangerous. But for Millennials it just seems natural.

Fortunately for those seeking to reach them, Millennials have self-organized into overlapping friendship circles on social networking sites, which makes them easy to find. Increasingly, as the sheer number of Millennials has made these sites "must view" locations on the Net, many of the visitors have been members of older generations. Still, the relative age distribution of visitors to a given site provides a reasonable proxy for the actual age distribution of that site's users, which is a much more closely guarded piece of information. The site that started the social networking craze, friendster.com, had just over one million unique visitors in August 2006, of which only 26 percent were Millennials. By comparison, the college-oriented Facebook.com had nearly 15 million unique visitors that month, 34 percent of which were 18–24 years old (another 14 percent were ages 12–17). Meanwhile, a relatively new site, Xanga.com, was doing a good job of capturing its teenage target market, with 20.3 percent of its 8 million-plus unique visitors in the 12–17 year old age bracket (another 15.5 percent were 18–24). But those numbers pale in comparison to the number of friends on MySpace, which had almost 56 million visitors that same month.

Nevertheless, in the course of achieving its success, MySpace, like other such sites, has shown signs of aging. While 30 percent of its unique visitors were Millennials, the plurality of MySpace users, 40.6 percent, were 35–54 years old (Lipsman 2006c). No doubt the increasing interest of the site for parents, marketers, and even politicians hoping to get linked was making it a less attractive place for younger people to hang out. As baseball great Yogi Berra once said about a popular restaurant, "Nobody goes there anymore. It's too crowded."

Still, 30 percent of almost 55 million people represents over 33 million Millennial eyeballs, far more than any other site could offer to an aspiring politician. These Millennials, like many MySpace members, are not content to passively watch the world go by. According to Nielsen/NetRatings, MySpace users of voting age, not just Millennials, are three times more likely than non-users of the same age to interact online with politicians, and 42 percent more likely to watch politically oriented videos online (Balz, Cillizza, and Vargas 2007).

Since moving pictures are always more interesting than stills, it should have come as no surprise when three older Millennials struck gold in 2005 by combining the fundamentals of social networking technology with an easy to use flash video player application. Chad Hurley, Steve Chen, and Jawed Karim, three engineers at PayPal, a service that enables users to pay for products or make charitable contributions securely online, had found it hard to share videos they had created. Their solution was YouTube, and suddenly all one had to do was simply click on an onscreen image of the video from a web browser, thus shortening download times and significantly reducing the cost of creating and sharing video images. Originally launched in February 2005 as a way to enable online video auctions, the site soon became an overnight sensation. A year and a half later, the site was attracting 34 million unique visitors a month. Many of those users were heavily engaged in politics, which became the second most popular general type of channel, or topic cluster, on the site. (In 2006, the sixth most popular site on YouTube was one satirizing George Bush.) Just as television swamped radio in popularity by adding pictures to sound, YouTube achieved incredible growth by allowing people to share online not just text, photos, and audio, but full-motion video, regardless of quality.

By July 2006, 649 million videos had been streamed, or downloaded, from the site by over 30 million unique visitors (Lipsman 2006b). That placed the new site in third place among all U.S. video streaming sites, behind Yahoo! and MySpace. Six months later, YouTube visitors initiated almost one billion video streams, making the parent company, Google, the top web site for all video streaming activity on the Net. The 120 million worldwide visitors to YouTube in 2006 represented a 1,922 percent increase over the number of viewers the site had attracted in 2005 (Lipsman 2006a, 2007a). Not only does YouTube attract more viewers than any other online video site, but the site's average viewer spends more time browsing through the content than do visitors to the other, more text-oriented social networking sites (Jordan Hoffner interview 2007).

YouTube's growth in popularity created an almost insatiable demand for new content from amateur video bloggers. By significantly lowering the cost of creation and providing an inexpensive way for the aspiring artists to share their work, YouTube tapped into a rich vein of previously frustrated videographers. By September 2006, 6.1 million videos had been uploaded into YouTube's database, one million more than the previous month (Gomes 2006).

By the fall of 2006, there were about 500,000 user profiles on the site, a number that began to grow exponentially as the site hit critical mass at the end of 2006, according to Jordan Hoffner, a YouTube executive. Even though no one was required to have a personal profile on the site to view individual videos, the desire to become a part of this fast-growing community was hard to resist. Seventy percent of YouTube's profiles came from Americans, about half of whom were under twenty years of age. By one calculation, between the time of YouTube's conception and the end of August 2006, users spent the equivalent of

9,305 years on the site sharing videos of all kinds with one another (Gomes 2006).

POLITICAL ORGANIZING THROUGH SOCIAL NETWORKING

Because of Millennials' desire to share their ideas and experiences with others online, contacting them through the Internet is now an imperative for any politician who wants to reach them. Sixty-four percent of Millennials believe everyone in their group is equal, so they tend to make decisions together, with the leader managing a search for consensus rather than trying to dictate what their response should be. As a result, there are no Millennial "political bosses" who can deliver the entire generation. Each group of friends needs to be collectively convinced to support a particular cause or candidate. About two-thirds of all Millennials consider their friends the most important source of information on what's cool. Web sites on the Net come in second (with magazines, cable TV, and parents rounding out the top five). The key to reaching Millennials is clearly through their friends on the Net (Jack MacKenzie interview 2007).

When Millennials join the Netroots online, they are disproportionately more influential than the average citizen, precisely because they are so active in sharing their ideas and opinions with others. A 2004 study conducted by the Institute for Democracy, Politics, and the Internet at George Washington University found that fully 69 percent of those involved in politics online also met the Roper organization's definition of "'Influentials' or opinion leaders and trendsetters with their friends and neighbors" (Graf and Darr 2005). This stands in stark contrast to the general population, only 10 percent of which qualify as Influentials based on their tendency to share their ideas with others. Even among more prosperous and better educated Internet users, the percentage of Influentials doesn't exceed 13 percent. "If word of mouth is like a radio signal broadcast over the country, 'Influentials' are the strategically placed transmitters that amplify the signal, multiplying the number of people who hear it" (Keller and Berry 2003, 147–148).

Millennials and their social networks broadcast the strongest signal of all. In a typical month, MySpace members post almost 10 million blogs, 188 million bulletin board items, and 327,000 event notices. They are constantly messaging each other, with nearly five million Instant Message users exchanging 48 billion text messages on their cell phones and posting 11 billion messages on their computers every month. MySpace users are pretty good with a camera, too—uploading 220 million images or snapshots in a month and viewing 500 million video streams per month (Berman 2007). The fact that MySpace has the largest number of members of any social network site in America is precisely the reason Rupert Murdoch was willing to pay so much for the company—and why politicians can't wait to gain the attention and support of its members.

Former Vice President Al Gore gave Murdoch a sense of just how much traffic News Corporation could generate on MySpace by increasing the amount of political chatter between its members. To promote Gore's documentary *An Inconvenient Truth,* MySpace created a special community profile—complete with profile badges, downloadable trailers, and widgets that allowed viewers to calculate their own impact on global warming, while providing advice on what they personally could do to ameliorate those effects. Gore recorded a video interview with rap star Mos Def that was designed to "go viral," in the sense that viewers were encouraged to share the remarkable dialogue with their friends. Twenty-five thousand people became friends of the site in the first three days after its launch, growing to 65,000 after three weeks. Not only did this publicity help make *An Inconvenient Truth* the highest grossing documentary of 2006, it also generated 1,242,004,775 ad impressions—foretelling the amount of money MySpace could generate from this type of politically oriented programming in the future (Berman 2007).

MAKING AN IMPACT

After that experience, MySpace decided to create an entire portal, dubbed the "Impact Channel," devoted to providing its members an opportunity to interact with each other on selected current events. MySpace then agreed to let TV producer Mark Burnett use the site to find contestants for a proposed political show called "Independent." The idea was to have MySpace users "run for office" by submitting videos and conducting the kind of virtual campaign for votes that Mark Warner's Map Changer contest represented. Whether or not Burnett's idea becomes the first programming concept to leap from the Net to television, where the top 100 vote-getters would compete for a $1 million prize through a series of TV debates, its appeal was irresistible to MySpace CEO Chris DeWolfe. The show's concept "instantly clicked," he noted. "A lot of people think the younger generation doesn't care about politics, and we've just empirically seen that not to be true" (Menn 2007).

Every major 2008 presidential candidate has a political profile on MySpace's Impact Channel. If viewers like what they see, they can click on the candidate's donation widget (the only widgets that activate a contribution request permitted on MySpace), or they can drag a candidate ad onto their own page, creating what DeWolfe calls "a digital yard sign" (Williams 2007). When MySpace began promoting these profiles and driving traffic to the candidates' sites, it helped create the first command-and-control controversy of the 2008 presidential campaign.

Not surprisingly, the Barack Obama campaign, whose fundamental strategy was to build "a community around the idea that ordinary people can come together and effect change in the country," was the one that found itself at the center of the debate (Rospars 2007). Having waded into previously unexplored organizational waters, the campaign became embroiled in a dispute with its own supporters about just where to draw the line between the campaign's desire to control its message and the Netroots' desire for freedom to organize as they see fit.

The dispute's resolution provoked enough of a backlash in the blogosphere that Joe Rospars, Obama's "New Media" campaign director, felt compelled to explain what had happened. Rospars told readers of DailyKos and MyDD in a post on May 2, 2007, that when the senator made his official announcement, a volunteer, Joe Anthony, had already established a profile on MySpace in support of Obama's candidacy that had 40,000 friends linked to it. Even as the campaign created its own interactive official web site, it reached an agreement with Anthony to simply coordinate with and piggyback on his site on MySpace rather than creating a competing address there as well.

That unique arrangement was working fine until Impact Channel began publicizing the address and driving increasing amounts of traffic to it. Suddenly, Anthony was faced with the challenge of managing a web site with a growing list of over 160,000 friends—when he wasn't at his regular job as a paralegal in Los Angeles. Meanwhile, the Obama campaign was increasingly concerned about losing the ability to influence what Anthony was communicating on the site, especially when he changed the administrative password so that the Obama campaign could no longer gain access to it.

The conflict between bottom-up and top-down campaigning came to a head when Anthony, not unreasonably, asked to be compensated for his previous efforts before allowing the Obama campaign to take over the site. Although his asking price of $39,000 for the time he had spent building the site, plus potentially another $10,000, was cheap considering the number of friends he had generated for the campaign, Rospars decided to break off negotiations and exercise the campaign's site-ownership rights under MySpace's "public figure" policy. Jeff Berman, MySpace's vice president for public affairs, made the Solomonic decision to split the baby in this way: "We felt under the circumstances that Senator Obama had the right to the URL containing his name and to the official campaign content that was provided, but that the user should retain the basic elements of the profile, including the friends who had been accumulated" (Sifry 2007). The result satisfied no one. Anthony did not receive the compensation he had sought, and the Obama campaign was left to re-create its links to its MySpace followers, while also enduring the first hard-hitting criticism in the blogosphere for how the campaign treated one of its own.

At the end of the spat, Rospars's blog accurately summarized the current state of campaigns' readiness to embrace the chaotic world of online campaigning. "We're flying by the seat of our pants, and establishing new ways of doing things every day. We're going to try new things, and sometimes it's going to work, and sometimes it's not going to work. That's the cost and that's the risk of experimenting" (Rospars 2007).

If all of this uncertainty weren't enough to raise the level of anxiety of every campaign manager to new heights, MySpace decided to up the ante even further. Seeing a chance to drive an even greater amount of traffic to its site from video blogs, messages, event postings, and other politically related chatter, it decided to jump ahead of all the official caucus and primary states by holding an online primary for all its members on January 1 and 2, 2008. MySpace was confident that the results would indicate which presidential campaign was the most adept at the new way of campaigning, just as the candidates rounded the turn and headed to the real-life finish line in the technology arms race.

CHAPTER 10

Winning the Technology
Arms Race

THE HARDEST THING FOR those enjoying success is to abandon their perches on the mountain top and to go back down into the valley to look for new mountains to conquer. The rewards for doing so are neither certain nor easily obtained. The pressure to stay and collect the rewards for being on top is so intense that most organizations fail to embark upon the transition, let alone duplicate their successes on a different peak. The annals of corporate bankruptcy history are replete with former industry leaders such as the Philadelphia and Reading Railroad, Montgomery Ward, and the Packard Motor Car Co., who were unwilling and therefore unable to change to meet the demands of a new set of customers. Political history contains the names of extinct parties, such as the Federalists and the Whigs, who also failed to change with the times. Today, the challenge for both parties and their candidates is to find new ways to reach new voters with new messages, before their competitors beat them to the top of the next mountain and dominate the political landscape of the twenty-first century.

The challenge is made doubly difficult by the dynamic nature of American society. Immigrant populations are spreading throughout the country; families are moving out of traditional suburban and urban environments to find better schools and more open space in "ex-urban" communities and small towns; information technologies are creating a mosaic of "virtual communities," populated by those who share an affinity for a music genre or a hobby or even a political point of view (Kotkin 2006). The notion of stable political outcomes in a given location, let alone an entire country, in such an environment is becoming rapidly obsolete. Instead, the changes America is experiencing look more like the behavior of complex, adaptive systems that evolve and mutate, based on a continuous process of rapid responses to what is working at any given moment in time. In this environment, best described by the science of "chaos," the future will belong to those who learn to use information and communication technologies to enroll others in shaping a jointly envisioned future, rather than to attempt to control the outcome from the top.

In other words, the way to win the next political technology arms race will be to learn to let go and, to paraphrase Obi-wan Kenobi, "let the Force be with you."

SEEKING A WEB 2.0 TECHNOLOGICAL ADVANTAGE

The 2006 election results suggested the Republicans were having trouble mastering the new media. The YouTube-induced losses of George Allen and Conrad Burns cost Republicans control of the Senate, and those two elections were just the most prominent examples of Republicans' lack of awareness that the world of communication and media had substantially changed. According to campaign expenditure reports filed with the Federal Elections Commission (FEC), in the eighteen months leading up to the midterm election, the Democratic National Committee (DNC) and the Democratic Congressional Campaign Committee (DCCC) spent almost $7.4 million on web-oriented campaigning. Over the same period, the Republican National Committee (RNC) and its House campaign counterpart, the NRCC, spent $600,000 on such efforts. That meager expenditure represented only 6 percent of what the two Republican entities spent on consultants and related mass media strategies, while the Democrats spent about one dollar and fifty cents on web tactics for every dollar they spent with consultants.

The Republicans' aversion to interactive campaigning on the Net became even more evident when the first campaign fund-raising reports by the 2008 presidential prospects were filed with the FEC at the end of March 2007. Democratic candidates had raised $78.1 million, the Republican candidates only $50.6 million. Much of the Democratic Party's advantage came from the greater number of small donor contributions they were able to solicit and collect over the Net. Senator Barack Obama led all such efforts with $6.9 million raised online from over 50,000 donors (out of a total of more than 100,000 small donors). Almost one-third of all reported Democratic contributions came from online fund-raising. Meanwhile, the Republican candidates refused to share the percentage of their funds that had come from online donations, even with conservative allies.

For example, Robert Bluey posted a column on the conservative site TownHall.com on April 7, 2007, that summed up the problem for the Republicans. "In just a few years, the dominant liberal fund-raising site *ActBlue* has collected nearly $21.5 million, including about $4 million since last November. No conservative site comes close. Consider *ABC PAC*. It raised a little more than $300,000 last year, much of it coming through its *Rightroots* project geared toward conservative bloggers. . . . So far in 2007, ABC PAC's slate of 2008 presidential candidates—all of them Republican—has raked in a whopping $385.00. American" (Bluey 2007). As Joe Trippi commented on the comparative efforts of the two parties in building their Netroots activist infrastructure, "We [Democrats] built it and they [Republicans] didn't. Now it's paying big dividends" (Kornblut and Mosk 2007).

The fund-raising results ignited a spate of online hand-wringing by those in the Republican Party who had been urging their colleagues not to let the Democrats gain the advantage in the new campaign technology. Mike Turk, eCampaign Director for Bush-Cheney 2004, began the dialogue by pointing to the differences between Democrats and Republicans when it came to social networking:

> First, and most important, is the fact that we simply do not engage in the same type of activities online. . . . There just wasn't a lot of interest, among Republicans online, in social networking activities via the web. There was a lot of interest in social networking offline through house parties and such. That was illustrated by the fact that we had upwards of 5,000 to 8,000 Parties during our national party days (versus 2 to 3 thousand for MoveOn and the Dean campaign). Republicans were simply not as interested in virtual networking— they do most of it in the real world. . . . The trouble is not the Internet strategists, it is a party that doesn't believe its people will step up and participate if they are invited to do so. If you're cynical, you could make an argument that it is a party that doesn't trust its people enough to let them participate. (Turk 2007)

An example of the problem Turk cites received wide coverage in the blogosphere, before the full dimensions of the problem became clear with the candidate's FEC filings. On February 24, 2007, Todd Zeigler began a running commentary on the trouble John McCain campaign was having in getting conservative bloggers linked into their campaign:

> Mike Turk signed up for an account on McCain's social networking tool, *McCainSpace*, a while back. Due to the top-down nature of the campaign's online effort, accounts must be approved by a human administrator before they are made active. So far no joy for Turk: "It has been 14 days since I created my page, and it still has not been approved. I have received no rejection, no e-mail indicating there is a problem, and no request to change the content. There is simply stony silence." (Zeigler 2007)

Turk later decided to join Fred Thompson's nascent campaign for president. Zeigler made sure to contrast Turk's experience with two Democratic candidates' online operations:

> Contrast this with the Obama campaign's response to a site bug pointed out by Michael Arrington of Techcrunch. The bug was fixed within two hours of posting (although admittedly that bug was a little more explosive than the McCainSpace problems).
>
> Contrast this with the Edwards' campaign, where Elizabeth Edwards herself is engaging in blog discussions (including one on our blog).
>
> Having conference calls with bloggers is great. Truly listening to what they are saying is better. (2007)

Turk's commentary on the general problem Republicans have attracting the Netroots appeared shortly after this incident and provoked even more discussion among his conservative friends. Patrick Ruffini, who ran the Internet operations of the Republican National Committee in 2006 before joining the Rudy Giuliani campaign, disagreed with Turk's notion that the problem was the Republicans' aversion to social networking:

> The basic gist of the argument is that because Democrats embrace open systems online (blog comments, user generated content), they're

more successful and raise more money. This totally gets it back-wards. . . . When we're talking about raising money and generating email addresses, . . . your strategy is totally different. Look at *MoveOn*—an unqualified online success. It has no blog, just a mother-lode of email addresses. . . . Supporters are far more likely to interface with the campaign from a top-down email sent from headquarters than they are by having a peer-to-peer dialogue with the campaign. Blogs and email serve two entirely different purposes. Blogs generate buzz and influence the influentials; emails generate mass action. (2007)

Turk quickly posted a rejoinder, suggesting that Republicans contin-ued to be focused on advertising as a way of persuading voters while Democrats had moved onto the more important and broader task of marketing and branding, which he claimed was more important and effective in shaping consumer or voter behavior, especially in the longer run:

The Internet is the focal point of word-of-mouth marketing in the world, and the Republicans don't get that. . . . It is a difference between sender-receiver models and empowerment. . . . There is, without a doubt, a place for direction in campaigns. Direction, how-ever, is not the same as control. Republicans don't get that. I'm not sure why the GOP has more than its share of control freaks, but we do. We, as a party, tend to believe that everything can be scripted and micromanaged, and ignore every thing in nature that demonstrates otherwise. (2007)

Turk also made it clear that the Republican fascination with email as the focus of online campaigning was not only outdated, but woefully ineffective. He urged the party's candidates to adapt a much more inter-active approach for their Netroots campaign tactics:

What makes you successful online is not how many e-mails you can amass, but the quality of the people in the list. . . . Every single mes-sage can't drive them to a website where their only possible action is clicking the button the campaign shows them to send the message the campaign wrote to the recipient the campaign thinks is important. You absolutely want them to take that action, but what reasons are you giving them to stick around after they do? Are you allowing them to interact with other people? . . . Those activities [creating blogs, undertaking registration drives, etc.], that interaction, is the free pizza, Cokes and music with which you feed your volunteers. . . . Patrick [Ruffini] isn't advocating a strictly top-down model. Much of the GOP does. Much of the party is whistling past the graveyard. . . . At the same time the Republicans stress that they are falling behind, they decry and deny the things that make the two sides distinctly different. Many Republicans discount the level of involvement users have in social-networked Democrat sites, and then question why their model of command and control doesn't generate the same loyalty. (2007)

Turk closed his impassioned plea with a suggestion that it was time for Republicans to fundamentally rethink their strategy, but when Thompson supporters, under Turk's influence, initially floated the idea of running their campaign using more online tools than face-to-face inter-action, the notion was roundly criticized, even by such objective, non-partisan election analysts as Charlie Cook.

Meanwhile it was left for Ruffini to give his Republican readers some hope by hearkening back to campaign technology competitions of the past:

Republicans have always been the most innovative in communicat-ing to and activating their grassroots in political meaningful ways. First through direct mail. Then through talk radio. . . . After 2000, we had to relearn the art of grassroots campaigning the hard way after we got the stuffing kicked out of us by the unions in door-to-door organizing. The response was the RNC's 72 Hour Program, which turned the tables on the Democrats and totally changed the equation of grassroots politics. And just because we've relied on one set of media in the past, that doesn't mean the old playbook will con-tinue to work indefinitely. (2007)

It took Republicans fifty years after FDR demonstrated the power of radio before they pulled ahead of Democrats in the use of that medium for campaign purposes. It took them less than ten years after JFK's elec-tion to realize the potential of television and become masters of it in political campaigns. Their early lead in 2000 in the use of the Net to

energize voters, however, dissipated as soon as broadband became dominant. People no longer went online occasionally to check their mail and
read the latest gossip. Instead, Internet users, especially Millennials, were
plugged in constantly, checking what was new on their profiles as many
as fifty times a day.

Republicans seemed to be caught flat-footed by this phenomenon.
The 2007 second quarter fund-raising totals for the presidential campaigns continued to show much more enthusiasm for the Democratic
candidates than the Republicans. Not only had the top three Democrats
raised $133 million from their supporters compared to only $92 million
for the top three Republicans (not counting personal loans from candidates to their own campaigns), but the relative number of individual
donors who contributed indicated that the Democrats remained far
ahead in the use of the tools of online campaigning. Mitt Romney estimated the number of individual donors to his campaign at 80,000. That
didn't even match John Edwards's total of 100,000 donors, a base that still
left him in third place among Democratic candidates (Morain 2007). The
leader in this category was Barack Obama, whose campaign raised over
$31 million in just the second quarter of 2007, one-third of that amount
online. Obama's campaign clearly benefited from having one of the
developers of the Facebook platform, Chris Hughes, on board. Hughes
used his cutting-edge knowledge of social networking techniques to create a network of over 230,000 members at www.my.barackobama.com,
almost half of whom had already donated to the campaign online by just
the mid-point of the 2007 pre-primary campaign season.

Of course, the campaigns were far from over at that point, and which
party ultimately masters the art of online campaigning will not be known
until at least after the 2008 election. But the danger for the Republicans
is that the Net evolves at a much faster pace than broadcast media and
other communication technologies have evolved in the past. One has to
run at Internet speed to keep pace and doubly fast to catch up. It remains
to be seen if the inherent cultural and organizational biases of the
Republican Party will allow them to do that.

BREAKING THE REPUBLICAN'S VOTER BANK

Ruffini's comments about the Republican's seventy-two-hour
program, which focused on voter turnout, speaks volumes about the

willingness of Republicans to confront challenges and search for new ways of winning in the newly emerging civic era of American politics. The program was built upon a technology project called Voter's Vault, a sophisticated use of data-mining technologies that the Republicans first tested in a few Pennsylvania judicial races in 2003 and then used with incredible effectiveness in 2004. The technology uses artificial intelligence to look for connections in voters' personal profiles that might not otherwise be apparent. It requires the accumulation of large amounts of data about as many voters as possible, in order to allow the software to find patterns that are outside the normal distribution of behaviors or beliefs. A typical voter profile using these "micro-targeting" techniques will include more than 500 types of information about the individual, ranging from whether the person owns or rents a house to the type of car the person drives to whether or not the person also uses a snowmobile (and thereby might be less inclined to support environmental regulation) or how frequently the person attends church, and, if so, which one.

For instance, rather than accepting the fact that most African American voters are Democrats, Voter's Vault allowed the Republicans to find those individual African Americans whose particular interests on a given issue, such as education, health care, or abortion, might make them susceptible to being persuaded to vote for President Bush. The Republicans sent campaign mailings, emails, and automated phone messages, some from black leaders who supported Republicans on these issues, to those targeted voters in the days leading up to the 2004 election. As a result, the Republicans were able to cut into the Democrats' traditional margins among African Americans in the critical state of Ohio, which Bush ultimately won by only 118,601 votes. "Micro-targeting" technology was given credit for improving his margin among black voters in Ohio by 7 percentage points, enough to help swing the most pivotal state in the 2004 presidential election into the Bush column (Wallsten and Hamburger 2006).

The same technology was used with equally eye-popping results in New Mexico—one of only two states Bush carried in 2004 that he had failed to win in 2000. There the campaign focused on a segment of 19,000 Hispanic women whose children attended public schools. While this group, from the lower end of the socioeconomic scale, normally voted Democratic, the Bush campaign was able to determine that about half was

willing to support Bush solely because of his No Child Left Behind education legislation (Cillizza 2007). By enabling Bush to send campaign
messages on this issue to the 6,000 members of this micro-targeted segment who were most likely to vote, the technology helped Bush raise his
support among Latino voters in the state by 12 points between 2000 and
2004 (McKinnon 2007). He carried the state by just 5,988 votes.

After the election, Bush strategist Matthew Dowd described the
importance of the technology to Bush's reelection: "It gave us a way of
finding people we couldn't find before. We could get at Bush voters in
Democratic precincts, swing precincts, and other places we'd never been
able to look before" (Dreazen 2006).

The technology was developed by a nonprofit venture based on
expertise from scientists in Los Alamos, New Mexico, where the techniques were first honed for the nation's intelligence agencies. Later, banks
and phone companies were able to use the technology to see deviant patterns in credit card charges or calling patterns that suggested fraudulent
use of another person's identity. In politics, the same advanced statistical
techniques and neural networks can be used to look for connections in
voters' personal profiles that might not otherwise be apparent (Bryan
interview 2007).

Democrats were offered the opportunity to implement the technology
in August 2001, before the Republicans' own early trials and successes.
The proposal generated quite a bit of enthusiasm from those at the DNC
who heard about it under strict nondisclosure terms. After the meeting,
one staffer, Doug Kelly, said the technologies would enable the Democrats
to "beat the Republicans at their own game" (Bryan interview 2007). But
then the proposal began to encounter the normal obstacles that arise
when individuals experienced in older technologies are asked to give up
some of their control in favor of someone else's new idea.

In this case, the challenge was made doubly difficult by the financial
interests of those who were asked to make the decision at the DNC.
Some, such as Laura Quinn, who went on to found a consulting firm,
Copernicus Analytics, based on the technologies first presented to the
Democratic Party, stood to gain by incorporating the technology into
their own future consulting efforts rather than having it become the
intellectual property of the DNC. Indeed, once Howard Dean and his
team were selected to head the DNC, an independent effort to create

such a voter targeting capability was started by Quinn and Harold Ickes, who sought to raise over $10 million to fund a project they called Data Warehouse (Edsall 2006).

The resulting diffusion of capabilities and duplication of effort in creating the databases cost the Democrats the ability to keep pace with the Republicans, who were able to stay one step ahead as the technology evolved. Copernicus Analytics was able to deploy the technology in twenty-nine congressional contests in 2006. In the same year, the Republican equivalent, TargetPoint Consulting, had built upon its eighteen-state effort from 2004 to collect data on tens of millions of voters across the country. Republicans were far ahead in the quality of their data as well. While TargetPoint was working closely with the Republican National Committee to determine what campaign issues to emphasize in persuading "Tax and Terrorism Moderates" or "Downscale Union Independents" to vote Republican, Copernicus was just beginning to be able to identify voters based upon what they thought rather than where they lived (Dreazen 2006). Luckily for those involved on the Democratic side, the wave of political change that arrived in 2006 washed away almost all the evidence of their sins of omission and personal ambition.

A common mistake of those engaged in the technology arms race is to assume that the technology is intrinsically of strategic value. In fact, technology is only useful when its use meshes with the political strategy that a campaign or party has decided upon. As long as the Republicans were implementing Karl Rove's "divide and mobilize" strategy, Voter's Vault was a key asset in their victories. It was perfectly suited to an environment in which the two parties were divided in roughly equal ideological parts, and Independents could be persuaded to split their tickets based upon carefully targeted appeals. Mitt Romney even thought enough of the technology's value to hire the brain behind TargetPoint, Alex Gage, to work its magic for him in the Republican primaries (Cillizza 2007). But with the political environment of an idealist era coming to an end, Rove's strategy, and the technologies that supported it, will quickly lose much of its value in a general election.

In a civic political era, voters bond much more closely with one or the other political party, and are much more likely to vote based upon partisan appeals from members of their party. In such an environment, the right campaign technology is one that connects as many people as possible, as frequently as possible, to each other—a task for which social networks are ideally suited. Republicans placed themselves in danger of losing the technology arms race by fighting a new battle with ideas and technology from the previous war.

Politicians Jump on the
Web 2.0 Bandwagon

Whatever overall strategy the two parties eventually settle on, neither side could have missed the growing impact of campaigning online. During the early 2000 primaries, Senator John McCain surprised people when he was able to raise $7.5 million for his abortive presidential campaign, using the Net as a new source of funds. In 2004, the Dean campaign used Meetup.com to organize like-minded voters throughout the country. Then, when the campaign's momentum began to build, it designed software called GetLocal that customized Meetup for the size and peculiarities of a political campaign. The magic of the Net became apparent when all the Internet-stimulated participation began to produce campaign contributions in amounts, and from an array of contributors, that no one had ever seen before. In late June 2003, Dean stumbled badly on "Meet the Press" before formally announcing his candidacy in front of 35,000 supporters, 85 percent of whom viewed the announcement online. The campaign decided to underline its commitment to transparent politics by putting its internal second quarter fund-raising goal of $4.5 million on their web site for all to see. At that point, it had raised $3.2 million for the quarter. Within a week, Dean had raised $2 million more just in contributions that came over the Net. By the time the June 30 deadline arrived, the campaign's quarterly take had hit $7.2 million, with $829,000 coming from online contributions in the final day alone (Trippi 2004).

John Kerry, the ultimate winner of the primary war against Dean, learned the value of the Internet as a fund-raising tool well. Overall, he raised a startling $82 million from contributions generated over the Net, only to significantly dilute the impact of that remarkable achievement by plowing much of the proceeds into old-fashioned TV ads. This isn't to say that television can't still be relevant, but it can be even more useful when used as a platform for Internet strategies. In late 2006, when Senator Barack Obama was making noise as a potential presidential candidate, he appeared in a short video on ESPN just before a Monday Night Football game. He began by speaking very much like he was about to announce his candidacy, but spoofed the entire ritual by declaring instead his support for his beloved Chicago Bears. The video, both funny and authentic, had a much greater shelf life than just those few minutes on ESPN. It immediately moved onto YouTube and other sites, where it became an instant hit.

Another Democratic candidate, John Edwards, also proved to be a skilled Netroots campaign organizer. His social network site urged people to click on its "OneCorps" link, which echoed his overall campaign theme of the need to create "One America." The site's message, urging members to join with others to help rebuild parts of the nation most in need of help, such as New Orleans, was perfectly attuned to the service ethic that is a powerful motivator for Millennials.

Hillary Clinton, however, was trailing among Democratic Netroots voters, but not for lack of trying. Her official announcement that she was running for president generated 313,000 unique visits to her campaign's web site (Obama's announcement a month later generated 376,000 visitors to his site) (Lipsman 2007b). Right after the announcement, she offered to hold "wireside chats," echoing FDR in front of a crackling fire, with anyone who wanted to go online and ask her questions. But the campaign's culture of control and candidate management tripped up this initial effort when those who joined the chat realized that campaign staff members were screening the email submissions. Instead of transparently displaying all the emails all the time, as IMers were accustomed to, the Clinton campaign treated the event as more of a town hall format, where some people's questions were answered and others were not even posed to the candidate. That, along with Clinton's more moderate position on the war in Iraq, created early trouble for the campaign.

In effect, Clinton's efforts were built upon a client/server architecture approach, similar to the iPod model for music, which looked cool but really didn't enable the peer-to-peer communication architecture that builds community quickly. Her overall inability to freely embrace the free-form chaos of online campaigning eventually caused the campaign to lose its biggest asset—the appearance of inevitability—when her diminishing level of support among online contributors put her in second place in the early rounds of the 2008 "money primary."

Still, Clinton's online campaign far exceeded the efforts of most Republicans to activate support among the Netroots. Even though polls showed the political preferences of Internet users to be roughly equal between the parties (Pew Research Center 2007b), none of the web sites of the early Republican candidates attracted many enthusiasts. Most were essentially brochures dressed up with videos. Just as Turk noted in his critique, they contained no interactive features other than those asking for contributions and provided no reason for web surfers to return to the site each day, as social networkers enjoy doing.

While all the Republican campaigns felt obligated to create their own profiles on MySpace, Facebook, and other such sites, the party's candidates tended to balk whenever the medium threatened their control over the campaign's message. Even though the Democratic candidates had successfully navigated their way through a series of questions posed to them by video bloggers in CNN's initial YouTube debate, Republicans suggested that such a format would be beneath their dignity. Only when more Net-savvy Republicans, led by Patrick Ruffini, organized a "Save the Debate" coalition to shame them into participating did most of the candidates reluctantly agree to attend a rescheduled debate. The fact that all potential questions would be screened and therefore known in advance helped to overcome some of the candidates' initial qualms. But the Republicans' desire for tighter control of organizational activity, which had become part of that party's culture since Mark Hanna ran the McKinley campaign in 1896, continued to inhibit its candidates from truly embracing the power of the Net.

AND THE WINNER IS?

The Internet is constantly evolving and finding new ways to engage its users. Email, the original "killer application" that made dial-up so popular, has given way to Instant Messaging (IM), so much so that most Millennials consider email a quaint habit of their parents. Searching for information through sites such as Google and sharing photos online are applications that all generations are now comfortable using. In 2006, 8 percent of those who followed the campaign on the Internet, or about 5 million Americans, posted their own political commentaries on a web site or blog or forwarded a political audio or video file to someone they knew (Rainie and Horrigan 2006).

The latter activity is one that all campaigns now try to encourage. To date, the most likely form of video to "go viral" are humorous clips, akin to the often-annoying emails from supposed friends that contain jokes they just had to share. In the 2004 campaign, Jib Jab's cartoon sendoff of Bush and Kerry singing very different words to the tune of "This Land Is Your Land" was watched by 80 million people. Among the viewers were astronauts circling the earth in the International Space Station, making the satire the first instance of viral marketing to reach people in outer space (Gregg Spiridellis interview 2007).

Despite the success of such videos, it has been the subsequent rise of social networking sites filled with personal and authentic communication that has had the greatest impact. The technology that enables the ability of each "prosumer" to customize their profiles on social networking sites and become instant publishers of mashed-up content, including videos, is commonly referred to as a widget. These mini-computer programs have become increasingly sophisticated since Mark Warner's Map Changer contest in 2006. Facebook's newest platform allows users to choose from over 800 different widgets, which enable the user to do almost anything—playing Sudoku, creating a slide show of one's friends, or letting those friends listen to one's favorite music. As soon as all these widgets became available on Facebook's platform, its user population quickly jumped from 24 million to over 30 million, causing even MySpace owner Rupert Murdoch to remark of his newspapers' readers, "They're all going to Facebook at the moment" (Vara 2007).

The potential for the use of widgets in future campaigns could be seen in Reebok's 2007 Shoe Fight Contest. When visitors entered the contest to compete for the best new shoe design, they grabbed widgets from the Freewebs social networking site and moved them to their own profiles. The resulting design, including the Reebok logo widget, could be viewed by all friends linked to the contestant's site, who were then encouraged to vote for that design in head-to-head competition with others. The contest caused the advertising embedded in the widget to be virally distributed to millions of unique visitors to the contestant's profiles, or personal web sites. In addition, Reebok could automatically update the widget's content, with no intervention from the site's owner. As a result, Reebok gained access, via the web, to a de facto network of future customers (Cunningham 2007). This technology supercharges the type of campaign used by the two Millennial New Hampshire Map Changer winners with the power to provide every supporter the capability to run his or her own campaign, both online and offline.

Posting videos on web sites for others to see and share was a new and winning tactic in 2006, and it quickly became part of the standard arsenal of campaign weapons of all candidates. Today, the use of this tactic offers no particular strategic advantage to candidates. Moreover, adding content to a video web site that the campaign doesn't control can create problems, as Senator Obama so painfully learned. That incident and other similar experiences will eventually convince all presidential candidates to establish their own social networking sites where their campaigns can still use the power of peer-to-peer communications to create viral marketing campaigns, but ones that are aligned with the campaign's message. The most successful 2008 presidential campaigns will be those that are most effective at creating their own destination web sites with the power and attraction of social networking, so that the supporters of those campaigns can self-organize into multiple and overlapping networks of friends.

As candidate web sites become the core source of campaign interaction, a new breed of highly influential and highly motivated Millennials will undoubtedly use their superior social networking skills to build both Netroots and grassroots organizations, in numbers and with capabilities that twentieth-century political organizers could only dream about (Armstrong and Brundrett interview 2007). The candidate who combines the newest in online campaign technology with a message that attracts Millennial voters will not only win the technology arms race, but also the presidency of the United States—and partisan dominance in the civic era that is just around the corner.

PART THREE

❖❖❖ *The New American*
Political Landscape

CHAPTER 11

Triggering a New America

GENERATIONAL AND TECHNOLOGICAL changes that are sweeping the country will cause America to experience, in this decade, the third civic realignment in its political history. Indeed, the evidence from the last two elections suggests that the newest realigning era has already begun and is simply awaiting a decisive presidential election to be fully cemented into the dynamics of the body politic. Historically, an external event of major impact is the source of a major shift in the nation's psyche, and the realigning presidential election simply confirms the political implications of that change after the event has occurred.

Many Republicans, including Karl Rove, felt the attacks of September 11, 2001, would prove to be the triggering event for a realigning election in 2004 that would confirm Republican hegemony for four more decades. But while President Bush was reelected, it was by the smallest margin of any incumbent president in modern history; and more in-depth analysis suggests that if any realignment began to take shape in 2004, it was actually away from the Republicans and toward the Democrats. In fact, because the impact of 9/11 is likely to encourage the Democratically inclined Millennial Generation to vote in large numbers, the 2008 presidential election is more likely to be a realigning election that favors Democrats than one that keeps the Republicans in the White House.

The actual outcome of the next election, as well as the nature of the realignment the country will experience, depends on the nature and timing of the triggering event and the candidates' and the political parties' reaction to that event or series of events. We may be fortunate to find, in retrospect, that 9/11 was the only catastrophe the country needed to experience in order to set off the chain reaction of responses that will lead to the next realignment. Or Millennials, like other civic generations before them, may have to live through a series of even greater and more devastating shocks before the country is ready to move in a new direction.

What can be said with some certainty is that the type of crises the country experiences during this decade will create opportunities for major changes in the structure of our government and the policies it pursues. How well America responds to these crises will be determined, in part, by how well the two political parties handle the transition from the idealist era's politics of polarization and deadlock to a civic era of positive partisanship and government action. Furthermore, each party's success in making this transition will depend on the type of presidential candidate it chooses to lead it through the realignment, and the leadership skills the party's nominee brings to that party and to the task ahead. Those candidates who set a course based upon the attitudes and beliefs of our next generation of civic voters are the ones most likely to succeed in guiding the nation through the challenges it is sure to encounter.

PULLING THE TRIGGER ON THE NATION'S CONSCIOUSNESS

William Strauss and Neil Howe's analysis of American history asserts that the event which triggers a shift, or "turning," in the nation's mood occurs "two to five years after a new generation of children starts being born" (Strauss and Howe 1997, 100). While the notion that external events are somehow linked by a cosmic clock to the turning of the generational cycles may seem far-fetched, Strauss and Howe's distinction between what type of reaction such events cause in the nation's psyche based upon their generational archetypes seems to be uncannily accurate.

When triggering events occur as a newly vocal idealist generation begins to come of age, the result is what Strauss and Howe refer to as an "Awakening" or a rebellion against the morality of the existing establishment. The most recent example of this type of change in America's social direction was the cultural wars of the Baby Boomer era that began in the mid-1960s. The triggering event for that societal upheaval was the assassination of President John F. Kennedy on November 22, 1963. As with most triggering events, almost everyone alive at the time can remember precisely where they were and what they were doing when they heard that terrible news. Once Lee Harvey Oswald's bullets shattered the euphoria the nation had experienced throughout the 1950s, the nation seemed to unravel through a series of further violent events.

Some of the worst aftershocks included the "Bloody Sunday" police beatings of civil rights marchers in Selma, Alabama, in 1965, the urban riots of the late 1960s, and the assassinations of the Reverend Martin Luther King Jr. and Robert Kennedy in 1968. One Bobby Kennedy supporter recalls being unable to do anything in politics again after that event shattered his belief in the return of Camelot. "Every June 5th I stop for a few moments and remember how I believed in what America could be once—try to get some of that belief back—and, to use an old Boomer chestnut, 'keep on keeping on.' And I ask Bobby to forgive me—and my generation—for failing to pick up his torch" (Booth 2007). The political outcome of all that turmoil was a debate between those who wanted a return to law and order and traditional virtues and their opponents who insisted that only a greater degree of personal freedom and civil rights would heal the nation's wounds. As voting returns of the past four decades indicate, the forces of law and order and traditional values won the electoral debate more often than they lost.

By contrast, when a newly powerful civic generation starts coming of age, it is forced to react to triggering events that cause a societal and political crisis. This crisis leads to a reappraisal in how government is structured and what its role should be in people's lives. The civic generation's rebellion is against the morality of popular culture, not government, which it sees as a powerful institution to help shape, protect, and advance society (Strauss and Howe 1997, 2006).

The most recent civic generation's reappraisal of the role of government began with the terrorist attacks of 9/11. That event caused a new sense of vulnerability and danger to sweep the nation. A subsequent series of traumatic aftershocks reinforced the change in the nation's psyche. Hurricane Katrina raised the specter of environmental catastrophe, and the Bush administration's slothful and ineffective response to it created even more anxiety and unhappiness. Even as the nation continued to celebrate the heroism and patriotism of its fighting forces, a majority of the country united in opposition to the incompetence of those conducting the war in Iraq, its cost in American lives, and the callous treatment of some wounded service personnel from that war in veterans' hospitals. As a result, the focus of the most current upheaval, as it has been with earlier civic realignments, will be on how to improve the government's ability to protect and preserve the country and its citizens, not on the social issues that have defined our political debates in the last forty years.

A CBS/New York Times survey clearly indicates the increasing preference of many Americans for a more activist government. According to the March 2007 Pew Research Center report in which it is cited, the number of Americans preferring "a smaller government providing fewer services" dropped from 61 percent in 1996 to 45 percent in 2003. By contrast, support for a "bigger government, providing more services" rose from 30 percent to 42 percent over the same period. If what has happened in previous civic realignments holds true in the upcoming realignment, the public's endorsement of big government should increase even more.

IDEALISTS CHANGE THE NATION'S CULTURE

As these contemporary examples suggest, different types of events have triggered the awakenings that lead to idealist realignments and the crises that produce civic realignments. The 1828, 1896, and 1968 idealist realignments followed a rising rebellion by working-class and agrarian voters espousing traditionalist values against the dominant economic and cultural interests of those eras and generated major shifts in both economic policy and political mores.

The idealist realignment of 1828 was triggered by the "corrupt bargain" of 1825, following the previous year's presidential election that was ultimately decided by the House of Representatives. Despite the fact that Andrew Jackson finished first in both electoral and popular votes, John Quincy Adams became president after Speaker of the House Henry Clay, himself a presidential candidate, threw his support behind Adams. Whether in return or by coincidence, Adams later named Clay his secretary of state. The backroom dealing in the nation's capital crystallized the public's growing disenchantment with a political culture that seemed inbred and corrupt. Jackson's supporters depicted both Adams and Clay as "corrupt aristocrats who had undermined republicanism by an agreement that was immoral because it overturned the will of the people. Adams was denounced for his elitist education, his early association with European courts . . . and to crown it all, his purchase of a billiard table and chess set . . . for the White House" (Watson 1990, 91). Jackson won the next presidential election with 68 percent of the electoral vote and 56 percent of the popular vote, the largest margin of any nineteenth-century presidential candidate (Wilentz 2005).

The "mob" that celebrated Andrew Jackson's inauguration by reveling in rum while eating a 1,400-pound block of cheese on the White House grounds was considered the worst type of rabble by New England's banking and financial interests, which had grown strong in the first wave of America's industrialization. But those energetic and independent, if rough-hewn, celebrants were the backbone of the newly ascendant Democratic Party.

Throughout this idealist era, the Democrats, in contrast to the position that has generally characterized the party since the 1930s, advocated limited and decentralized government, especially at the national level. The Democratic Party of this era also tended to endorse traditional moral and religious values. Their Whig Party opponents, particularly the northern wing of that party, favored a more nationalistic approach that often advocated using government money to pay for improvements in the nation's infrastructure to aid business growth, while emphasizing a more contemporary conception of personal morality. Democrats were able to use Jackson's policies and the economic and cultural concepts they embodied to win six of the eight presidential elections from 1828 to 1856.

The same economic class conflict was brought to a boil by the Panic of 1893 and created a similar prairie revolt in the election of 1896. William Jennings Bryan led the forces of tradition against the culture of modernity that was threatening rural America's religion and values, as urban metropolises, considered hotbeds of sin and corruption, became an increasingly important part of American life. But by 1896, "America had become a nation of three forces: labor, agriculture, and industry. The spokesman of the new rising industrial order, of triumphant economic and political nationalism, was not Bryan, but McKinley" (Morgan 2003, 169). William McKinley won by dividing those who earned their livelihood from the soil or the minerals that lay beneath from those who worked in the growing cities of the Midwest and East. Sounding just like the Republicans of today, McKinley responded to Bryan's class-oriented appeals by tapping into America's growing patriotism and national pride: "My countrymen, the most un-American of all appeals observable in this campaign is the one which seeks to array labor against capital, employer against employed. It is most unpatriotic and is fraught with the greatest peril to all concerned. We are all political equals here—equal in privilege and opportunity, dependent upon each other, and the prosperity of the one is the prosperity of the other" (Morgan 2003, 179). In the last week of the campaign, McKinley became the first Republican to explicitly wrap himself in the flag, asking his supporters to fly it as a symbol of patriotism and, by implication, support for his candidacy (Cherny 1994).

By 1968, the almost total industrialization of America had made any agricultural revolt unlikely if not irrelevant. But the attempt by government to force the same working-class voters to give up their settled ways in order to achieve a more equitable distribution of economic and social benefits, especially across racial lines, helped to fuel the successful law-and-order campaign of Richard Nixon. Urban riots and antiwar marches reflected the nation's cultural divide as much, if not more, than its economic conflicts. The result was a split in the Democratic Party between those like George Wallace, whose populist ideas were a direct descendant from William Jennings Bryan, and those like Hubert H. Humphrey, whose liberalism sprang from the best impulses of Eleanor Roosevelt. Faced with these choices, the voters in 1968 elected to put a person in the White House who throughout his life identified as one of them, from his humble agricultural and lower-middle-class roots, to his extolling his wife's "good Republican cloth coat" in 1952, and to his assertion, during the first year of his presidency, that his policies reflected the values of America's "silent majority."

With that election the nation turned from LBJ's vision of building a "Great Society" to a focus on preserving its traditional cultural beliefs. First Nixon and then, much more boldly, Ronald Reagan built on the shift in the nation's mood to elevate social issues to the leading role in defining party allegiance. Economic conservatives were able to find common cause with social conservatives to enact an agenda in almost direct opposition to every element of the JFK/LBJ era's policy approach. The late twentieth-century shift from the New Deal civic era to the Republican idealist era led to the adoption of supply-side economics (instead of demand-side pump-priming), to the assertion of religious beliefs in public life (instead of an emphasis on a clear line between church and state), and, most recently, to a refusal to demand widespread public sacrifice in the form of reduced consumption or increased taxation, even in war time (instead of asking "not what your country can do for you, but what you can do for your country"). Today, the danger for the Republican Party is that an agenda perfectly suited for an idealist era may be completely out of sync with the country's mood as it enters another civic era.

HARD TIMES BUILD STRONG GOVERNMENTS

Beyond the similarity of the underlying economic and cultural class conflicts that fueled these idealist realignments, the triggering events were clearly less dramatic or consequential than those that have triggered America's previous civic realignments in 1860 and 1932. None of the idealist events come close to matching the two worst catastrophes the nation has experienced to date—the Civil War and the Great Depression. Both calamities were of such economic and social magnitude that voters demanded new leaders with new ideas and, above all, new governmental approaches to solve these overwhelming problems and put America back on track again.

While the 9/11 terrorist attacks and Hurricane Katrina certainly have led to an increased desire among most Americans for a strong and competent government to deal with the country's problems and sparked renewed interest in politics on the part of the Millennial Generation, those events by themselves may not have been of sufficient magnitude to have trigged the coming civic realignment. Either the attacks of 9/11 that precipitated the most recent turn of the nation's mood will go down as the mildest beginning of a crisis era that the nation has ever experienced, notwithstanding the loss of more than 3,000 lives, or those events will turn out to be only the first shock in a series of terrible shocks to follow. Either way, the country would seem to be headed for a crisis, or a series of crises, that will require all the energies of a civic generation such as the Millennials to overcome.

Furthermore, in the current global environment, the possible triggers for a political realignment are more varied and more complex than ever before. The next civic realignment conceivably could be triggered by an international crisis, perhaps even a nuclear war, a global environmental disaster, or a pandemic caused by today's vast increase in international trade and travel. In an earlier, more isolationist era, by rejecting foreign entanglements, America might have been able to avoid international crises—and their political consequences. But America's position in the world today makes such a course of action impossible for all but the diehard followers of Pat Buchanan to contemplate.

Environmental disasters and pandemics of fatal diseases might once have been interpreted as "acts of God," beyond the purview or remedy of government and the political process. But modern science puts responsibility for reacting to such events squarely on the shoulders of policymakers at every level of government. All these events, as well as the severe economic consequences that would flow from any one of them, are likely to produce political realignments of startling size and significance.

For instance, the country would not have to experience Al Gore's vision of apoplectic global warming or the sudden onslaught of a new ice age for this type of event to produce major economic and/or societal difficulties that would in turn cause major political damage. If, in fact, the increase in the number and strength of hurricanes that America experienced in 2005 is a foreshadowing of even more such seasons in the future, the experience we have already had with the aftermath of Katrina on the body politic might well foreshadow how environmental disasters could impact America's government. President Bush's popularity never fully recovered from his administration's response to the Katrina disaster.

But the more important long-term consequence can be seen in how quickly calls for government spending on infrastructure and improved government performance were heard from both sides of the aisle. Suddenly, it was popular again to think of government as a force to ameliorate poverty and distress. Even as the Bush administration continues to demonstrate its inability to rebuild New Orleans, large majorities in popular opinion in favor of a forceful and competent government response in times of emergency have not dissipated, especially among community-oriented Millennials (Frank N. Magid Associates, December 2006).

In addition, since Katrina, the public has demonstrated a newfound interest in the entire subject of global warming and its potential impact on the world's future. Al Gore's image has shifted from that of a Cassandra exaggerating the threat for his own political benefit to an Academy Award–winning visionary whose potential presidential candidacy is especially popular among Millennials. An increasingly concerned public eagerly reads the United Nation's reports on the implications of man-made global warming and the steps necessary to ameliorate its consequences. Even some parts of the evangelical forces within the Republican Party are crusading for the party to change its ostrich-like position and assume the mantle of "steward of the Earth" that the Bible says God placed upon mankind. Harvard's Institute of Politics survey research identifies a large segment of Millennials whom they call "religious centrists," whose concerns for the environment and the welfare of fellow human beings, coupled with their strong belief in God, distinguishes them from those along the traditional conservative/liberal dimensions. This cluster of attitudes is growing among Evangelicals of all ages, as the popularity of Pastor Rick Warren's teachings and his book *A Purpose-Driven Life* attests.

This desire for forceful government action was also immediately visible in the aftermath of 9/11. Overnight, that event changed the underlying beliefs of the American electorate about the importance and capability of the federal government, especially among Millennials. Sixty percent of college students, in a poll taken in late September 2001, said they had faith in the federal government to do the right thing all or most of the time, compared to only 36 percent who held that opinion in 2000. As Massachusetts pollster John Della Volpe put it, "The attacks of 9/11 totally changed the way the Millennial Generation thinks about politics. Overnight their attitudes were more like the Greatest Generation" (Cannon 2007, 25). When the first movie about 9/11, *United 93*, was shown in theaters in 2006, the distributors were surprised to find that the age group most interested in its depiction of the heroic actions of the passengers that prevented the plane from being flown into the U.S. Capitol was Millennials. That generation will lead a shift in attitudes toward the role of government that will have a dramatic impact on public policy as well.

The largest domestic cabinet department, the Department of Homeland Security, was willed into being within two years of 9/11 over the initial objections of President Bush, who was then very popular. Following a decline during the preceding eight years under a Democratic administration, the attack by Al Qaeda triggered an unrelenting growth in federal government employment that continues to this day, even apart from our involvement in Iraq. The fact that this buildup has occurred during the reign of the Republican Party, supposedly the advocates of small government, once again demonstrates the ability of external events to quickly trigger major changes in the political system. Almost certainly this chain reaction would be unstoppable if terrorists or a foreign government were to strike successfully on American soil again.

An ever more integrated world economy, besides threatening American jobs and lifestyles, also poses the possibility of a pandemic resulting from the spread of diseases, such as the avian flu from China or other newly economically vibrant countries in Asia. There still remains no completely effective vaccine for the avian flu, which is particularly terrifying because of its morbidity rate of almost 50 percent, coupled with the fact that an infected individual is contagious for days before developing symptoms. As the entire world scrambles to avoid such a pandemic, state governments in America have passed laws giving their governors the authority to quarantine people in their houses; the airline industry is demanding government insurance against the loss in profits a possible shut-down shutdown in international and domestic travel would cause; and new forms of intergovernmental cooperation are springing up around the world in an attempt to prevent the crisis from occurring.

In 2004, Hong Kong experienced a level of dramatic economic decline and public fear from a much more limited epidemic caused by the SARS virus, which provides a hint of the kind of economic and political upheaval that a real pandemic would create around the world. Indeed, when the last flu pandemic hit the United States right after World War I, the resulting shock and loss of economic vitality hastened the end of Woodrow Wilson's short-lived Democratic interregnum and, perhaps, delayed the arrival of progressive government for a decade. Meanwhile, candidates and political parties that have resisted the use of science to develop cures for diseases such as Parkinson's, based upon their religious beliefs, would quickly find themselves out of favor among voters if faced with such an overwhelming health and economic crisis.

All these forms of heightened governmental powers and activity are likely to be part of future scenarios that follow events of sufficient magnitude to trigger a civic realignment. Voters, especially Millennials with their generation's habit of sharing personal data of all types, will more readily accept the need for information to be gathered and shared by and between governmental entities in return for increased safety and security. The inevitable loss in privacy and freedom that has been a constant characteristic of the nation's reaction to any crisis that threatens America's future will more easily be accepted by a generation that willingly opts to share personal information with advertisers just for the sake of earning a few "freebies." After 9/11 and the massacres at Columbine and Virginia

Tech, Millennials are not likely to object to increased surveillance and other intrusions into their private lives if it means increased levels of personal safety. The shape of America's political landscape after a civic realignment is thus more likely to favor policies that involve collective action and individual accountability than the libertarian approaches so much favored by Gen-Xers.

THE PUBLIC IS RIGHT AGAIN

After the 2006 elections, voters were asked to think about the next two decades. They ranked events of sufficient magnitude to trigger a civic realignment as the most likely to occur in that time frame. A majority foresaw a "major terrorist attack such as 9/11" (57%) and "a major environmental disaster on the scale of Hurricane Katrina" (51%). Similar majorities expected the country to experience a "chronic, long-lasting war with no clear result, such as the Vietnam and Iraq wars" and "hyperinflation in which the price of goods and services rises far faster than the abilities of most people to pay for them" (52% each). Fewer, but still significant, were those worried about "an attack on the U.S. with nuclear weapons by a country like Iran or North Korea" (46%) and/or "a major health catastrophe such as the widespread epidemic of a potentially fatal disease" (41%). About a third of those surveyed were even willing to consider the possibility of the occurrence of such calamities as "a major economic collapse similar to the Great Depression of the 1930s" (38%), "a major world war such as World War II" (33%), and/or "a long struggle, like the Cold War with Communism, against other countries or ways of life" (31%) (Frank N. Magid Associates, December 2006).

There is broad agreement across generational lines about the likelihood of these events occurring. However, perhaps paralleling the experience of their GI Generation forebears, Millennials are somewhat more likely to forecast international crises, such as a nuclear attack, a world war, or a long international struggle similar to the Cold War. Meanwhile, those who have lived primarily in an idealist era, Gen-Xers and Baby Boomers, were more likely to predict the occurrence of domestic crises, such as a health catastrophe or an economic collapse.

Whether any of these predictions come true, of course, doesn't depend on the public's psychic powers but on the complex interaction of people and events that have yet to unfold. Still, the public's perception of whether their leaders are involved in preventing or mitigating the impact of disastrous events will affect how such leaders are treated, should the events occur as the public believes.

America is still assessing blame for what happened on 9/11. The continuing popularity of *The 9/11 Commission Report*, issued in 2004, and the enactment of all of its remaining recommendations as one of the first acts of the new Democratically controlled Congress in 2007 suggest that the public's willingness to engage in post-hoc retaliation remains as strong as ever. Clearly, if another terrorist attack occurs on American soil, those who failed to prevent it would likely suffer a similar fate as the Whigs in the 1850s or the Republicans in 1932.

But there is no absolute certainty about which political party will benefit from the current "crisis" era. On the one hand, the Democrats may gain from the American public's support for collective action such civic realignment events are likely to engender. And, indeed, survey research indicates that clear pluralities of Americans of all generations, but especially Millennials, believe that the Democratic Party is most likely to lead America in dealing effectively with these potential major crises (Frank N. Magid Associates, December 2006). However, Republican leadership traits of patriotic certainty and support of great causes may also be in demand if the nation experiences more catastrophes—in particular, if those events involve issues of safety and security. Which candidate each party chooses to represent it in the presidential campaign of 2008 and how that candidate structures his or her appeal to the nation will also play a key role in both the Democratic and Republican Parties' future success. More certain is the fact that new forms of government and new policy solutions to the nation's problems will be adopted as part of the country's recovery from whatever events await it.

CHAPTER 12

Who Will Party with Whom?

THE SHIFT IN PUBLIC OPINION that follows a triggering event can be quite dramatic. In the immediate aftermath of 9/11, as Americans rallied around their country and its commander-in-chief, more than two-thirds (68%) said the country was headed in the right direction. By November 2004, however, fewer than half of all Americans (45%) said they were satisfied with the country's direction. Since then, the satisfaction level of Americans with the state of their nation has moved steadily downward almost every month. In April 2007, less than a third of Americans were satisfied with the current state of affairs in the United States—an average of 28 percent across the major national polls taken that month (Greenberg, Carville, and Ipararraguirre 2007).

There is virtually no demographic variation in the perception that things in the United States are off track. Regardless of gender, age, race, socioeconomic status, or education, a large majority expresses dissatisfaction with the current state of American life. Democrats, of course, are least positive—about eight in ten Democratic identifiers are unhappy with the current situation in U.S. politics and society. But even a narrow plurality of Republicans also feels this way (46%) (Frank N. Magid Associates, May 2007).

This level of intense political discouragement is reminiscent of the beginning of earlier realignments. Voters' unhappiness with the status quo usually becomes evident before the country registers its final judgment on which of the two political parties it favors. Once that judgment is rendered in the course of at least one if not two presidential elections, with all the attendant emotion and involvement such contests bring to American politics, it establishes the relative standing of the two political parties for the next thirty to forty years.

The United States is headed for another of the cyclical realignments that have characterized the country's politics and elections throughout the past two centuries. Whether the specific realignment is idealist, as occurred in 1968, or civic, as we are about to experience, all these political makeovers have resulted in a significant alteration in the balance of competition between the nation's political parties. In all but one of the five previous realignments, the weaker of the two parties in the forty years before the realignment became the dominant party for at least the next four decades. Every realignment has also resulted in significant changes in the composition of each party's voting coalition, as important groups within society transferred their loyalties from one party to another, primarily to the benefit of the newly dominant party.

This state of flux in public opinion, and the stakes involved in responding correctly to possible shifts in the electorate, creates painful stress on each party's existing coalitions and ideological alliances. Normally, only a decisive intra-party fight between its potential presidential nominees can resolve the tension. The strategic choices each party makes as the Millennial Generation begins to assert itself in the electorate will therefore determine each party's success or failure for the next forty years.

Breaking Up Is Hard to Do

The hardest time to change strategic direction is when an enterprise or organization is doing well. Record companies ignored the rise of peer-to-peer distribution of digital music until the only option they could think of in order to hold onto their old business models was suing their disappearing customers. MTV rode Generation X's demand for a TV channel devoted to its music and lifestyle to the height of corporate success. But the cable network missed the turn in the market when Millennials asked for digital music on their PCs that they could mashup and share with their friends online. Broadcast television networks took note of the plight of their music industry brethren and began to experiment with new formats and new distribution platforms for their content, but only in carefully controlled experiments that didn't jeopardize their existing revenue streams.

Only a few visionaries in the entire media industry, like George Lucas, an evangelist for digital movie production, were willing to give up their past successes and embrace the new world order. For instance, when asked about the future of Hollywood at the "All Things Digital" conference in 2007, he issued this blunt assessment of the world he dominates: "The money doesn't exist. They borrow the money. The last thing you want to do is invest in the film business. It's the absolute worst. . . . It's not an economic model" (Mossberg and Swisher 2007). Earlier, his own company had bravely joined the Millennials' new world by putting clips from all six *Star Wars* movies on the Web (at starwars.com), with the express purpose of permitting visitors to remix them and post the results on any social networking site of their choosing. Jeffrey Ulin of Lucasfilm made the company's motivation to encourage mashups clear. It is "part of keeping the love of 'Star Wars' and the franchise alive. We're really trying to position ourselves for the next 30 years" (McBride 2007). Whether or not either political party has visionaries of the caliber of a George Lucas to guide them into a new Millennialist era remains to be seen.

Given the success of the Republican Party over the last forty years, the media-industry analogy would suggest that the GOP is more likely to have difficulty than the Democrats in making the changes necessary to be successful over the next forty years. And indeed, the blogosphere uproar over the Republican Party's presidential candidates' seeming lack of skills in organizing through social networks is evidence of these internal tensions and the resistance of some in the GOP to new campaign technologies. But the GOP's problems go much deeper, right to the heart of how well the beliefs of the Republican Party's core supporters match the attitudes of the emerging, and soon to be dominant, Millennial Generation.

To begin with, Democrats hold a clear lead in party identification within the electorate for the first time in decades. In June 2007, the nonpartisan Pew Research Center found that a majority of the country's voters identified as, or leaned toward, the Democrats (51%), while little more than a third (35%) said they were Republicans or leaned in that direction.

A report issued by the Democracy Corps, an organization supportive of the Democratic Party, elaborated on the significance of this shift in party identification in ways that every Republican strategist should read:

The Democratic advantage in party identification has reached 8.0 points, reflected in our 4,500 interviews conducted from December [2006] to March [2007]. That compares to 3.5 in the month leading up to the 2006 election upheaval—and compares to an average 2.0

points at the beginning of the last election cycle. This is a new period with a wholly new landscape. Further, Independents now break consistently for the Democrats by about 3 points, giving the Democrats an overall 11-point lead in party alignment. . . . At the same time, Democrats are feeling intensely about their identification as 31 percent identify as "strong" Democrats compared to only 21 percent "strong" Republicans. (Greenberg, Carville, and Ipararraguirre 2007, 2)

This Democratic resurgence is based almost entirely on the coming of age of the Millennial Generation; while the party identification of older Americans continues to be fairly evenly divided between the two major parties, Millennials identify as Democrats by a 1.75:1 ratio. There is almost no gender gap in the party identifications of Millennials: male and female Millennials are about equally likely to identify as Democrats (Frank N. Magid Associates, May 2007). By contrast, throughout most of the past several decades, Gen-X and Baby Boomer men leaned toward the GOP, while the women of those generations, more often than not, preferred the Democratic Party. There is also only a slight variation in party identification among Millennials between those attending a four-year college and those who do not (Harvard University Institute of Politics 2007).

The tendency of most Millennials to identify with the Democratic Party has severely aged the Republican base, threatening the party's chances for success in future elections. Citing data provided by GOP pollster Tony Fabrizio, Thomas Edsall wrote in the July 5, 2007, edition of the Huffington Post that "the median age of Republican voters has risen substantially over the past 10 years: in 1997, 28 percent were over 55; in 2007, 41 percent were. The percentage of Republicans between the age of 18 and 34 has dropped from 25 to 17, and those between 34 and 55 dropped from 44 percent to 40 percent. This suggests that, at least in the short run, Republican ranks face the threat of depletion." If the history of American political realignments is an accurate guide, that "run" will be longer than Edsall might think.

The last time the Democratic Party enjoyed a lead in party identification of the magnitude that it now enjoys was in the late 1960s, just before America's politics began to realign along idealist lines and away from the Democratic Party. Back then, about half of all American voters saw themselves as Democrats, a third as Republicans, and a fifth as Independents. That margin had held consistently since Franklin Delano Roosevelt's New Deal civic realignment nearly four decades earlier.

However, the Democrats stayed wedded to their New Deal base way too long. Unable to find new ways to reach new voters with new ideas, they stood by and watched as their lead in party identification over the Republicans shrank over the next twenty years. Eventually, it disappeared altogether, reaching parity with the GOP in 1994 when Republicans captured both houses of Congress. Meanwhile, the percentage of Independent identifiers within the electorate grew, until there were about the same number of Independents as either Democrats or Republicans.

As Democrats struggled to break the bonds of their base, the Republican Party was first able to dominate presidential and later congressional elections during the idealist era of the late twentieth century by building a coalition around new ideas and new ways of communicating them. Both southern white and northern blue-collar Democrats, the latter often called "Reagan Democrats," found Republican candidates closer to their attitudes on social issues than the "limousine liberal" beliefs of many national Democratic candidates. As a result, Democratic identifiers were more likely to desert their party than were Republicans. And Republicans used these issues to not only appeal to the large number of Independents and ticket-splitters who comprised the crucial swing voters in elections from the late 1960s through 2004, but also to solidify and grow their own base around the issues of "God, guns, and gays." The Republican Party built on this voting behavior advantage by capturing the dominant security and values concerns of the era and mastering the major communication technology of that time, television.

But as the United States moves toward another political realignment and a new civic era, Millennials' preferences for the Democratic Party are once again shifting the balance of political power.

Millennials have substantially more positive perceptions of the Democratic Party than of the Republican Party. In an early 2006 national survey, respondents were asked to indicate, on a five-point scale, if their attitudes toward each of the major political parties were favorable or unfavorable. A slightly larger number of Millennials said that their impressions of the Democratic Party were more positive than negative (31% vs. 26%). By contrast, a clear plurality of Millennials had unfavorable rather than favorable attitudes toward the Republican Party (42% vs. 18%) (Frank N. Magid Associates, January 2006).

The difference in attitudes toward the two parties among Millennials became even sharper after the Democratic victories in the 2006 midterm elections. In a June 9, 2007, Rasmussen Reports survey, Millennials rated the Democratic Party favorably as opposed to unfavorably by a 2:1 ratio (66% vs. 32%). At the same time, the Millennial Generation's rating of the Republicans was exactly reversed (32% favorable vs. 66% unfavorable).

Millennial attitudes toward the two parties appear to be a bit more firmly set in place than those of older generations as well. In a June 2007 Rasmussen Reports survey, only two percent of Millennials were not sure how to evaluate either party. By contrast, among older Americans, more than five percent were unable or unwilling to indicate whether their attitudes toward both the Democrats and Republicans are positive or negative.

Furthermore, for the first time in the last forty years, a plurality of an American generation is willing to call itself liberal. The Republicans pushed this term into political disrepute during the course of the current idealist era, and the Democrats did little to resurrect it. Ronald Reagan's ambassador to the United Nations, Jeanne Kirkpatrick, drove the point home in her keynote address at the 1984 Republican national convention. Kirkpatrick, a former Democrat, spoke interchangeably of the "new liberals" and "San Francisco Democrats," referring to the site of that year's Democratic convention. More obliquely, it called attention to what Kirkpatrick and many other Americans saw as effete liberal Democratic softness toward national security, crime, and social disorder.

But "the times, they are a changin,'" just as Baby Boomer musical idol Bob Dylan said. By early 2007, nearly a quarter of Millennials (24%) self-identified as liberal and fewer than one in five (17%) as conservative. An additional five percent of Millennials said they were progressive, an old label more recently adopted by centrist Democratic organizations such as the Democratic Leadership Council and the New Democratic Network to distinguish themselves from both the discredited liberals of their own party and the conservatives of the GOP. (And, indeed, most who do call themselves progressive are upscale, college-educated Democratic identifiers.) Nor was there any significant ideological difference in these attitudes between college and non-college Millennials. In both groups, self-perceived liberals outnumbered conservatives by similar margins (Harvard University Institute of Politics 2007). By contrast, in Generation X, conservatives outnumbered liberals by a 21 percent to 16 percent margin. Among Baby Boomers, the gap between self-perceived conservatives and liberals was even larger (30% vs. 14%) (Frank N. Magid Associates 2007).

Political behavior research has consistently indicated that once most individuals, and hence most generations, take on a party identification, they maintain it throughout their lives. As sociologist J. V. Namenworth noted, "Value orientations do not change much during a generation's life time. Committed during its early stages, a generation most often carried its value commitments into the grave" (Strauss and Howe 1997, 84). If the Democrats can maintain this initial generational allegiance during the next two presidential elections, they should gain a decisive electoral edge for decades to come.

Millennials themselves are beginning to recognize the pivotal importance and the Democratic leanings of their generation. A twenty-one-year-old from St. Paul, Minnesota, after participating in a June 2007 survey on politics, put it this way: "I think the Democratic Party is now realizing how big an impact my generation has, and they're trying to cater to that in some way. But the traditional Republican Party is still trying to get older votes, which doesn't make sense because there are so many more voters my age. It would be sensible to cater to us" (Nagourney and Thee 2007).

While realignments are spearheaded by the rise of a new, large generation that alters the existing balance of power between the parties, these changes do not come easily. As Strauss and Howe point out, there is always a gap of two generations between those in power and those entering young adulthood, creating strong tensions between the widely differing views of the two groups. Baby Boomers are the dominant voices in the base of both political parties, bringing their moralistic attitudes into debates over party platforms and candidates. Even the meanings of the words "liberal" and "conservative" have changed from their original economic context to one based on where people stand on the great debates of the 1960s—love and peace vs. law and order; civil and women's rights vs. traditional personal morality and adherence to natural, or even biblical, law. But those attitudes are not at all reflective of how the Millennial Generation sees the world. Like all civic generations before it, Millennials are destined to challenge each party's belief system and insist on a new set of values more reflective of their perspective on how the world should work.

AS MILLENNIALS GO, SO GOES THE NATION

Paced by the political beliefs of the Millennial Generation, Americans increasingly want and expect the federal government to both deal with and resolve a range of societal and economic concerns. In one national survey, voters were asked to indicate the likely importance of twelve specific issues in their 2008 presidential voting decision. About two-thirds indicated that four specific issues are likely to be very important in shaping their presidential preference: the war in Iraq (68%), health care and the economy (65% each), and national security/terrorism (63%). Smaller majorities also said they expected Social Security and Medicare (58%), government spending and the federal debt (57%), and taxes (52%) to be important to them in 2008. Less than half attributed great importance to immigration (49%), the environment (48%), economic inequality (39%), society's values and lifestyles (33%), abortion (31%), and racial and ethnic relations (30%) (Frank N. Magid Associates 2007).

There are significant generational differences on only a few issues. The aging Baby Boomer generation, not surprisingly, places far more importance on health care and Social Security. Millennials, more than other generations, regard the environment as a particularly important issue.

More striking is that Republican and Democratic identifiers have a clearly different sense of which issues are most important. In the words of political analyst and commentator Michael Barone, "One gets the impression that the Republican and Democratic primary electorates are living in two different nations—or the same nation that faces two very different threats." Barone writes of deep Republican concern with national security and terrorism and Democratic concern with the environment and climate change (Barone 2007).

But it goes beyond just those two issues. Voters who identify with the Democratic Party have a distinctive and different cluster of issues with which they are concerned in comparison with those who think of themselves as Republicans. For those who identify with the GOP, the cluster includes taxation and immigration in addition to national security and terrorism. For those who identify with the Democratic Party, the key issues of concern are the war in Iraq, the economy and the national debt, Social Security and Medicare, health care, and economic inequality as well as the environment (Frank N. Magid Associates 2007).

Regardless of which of these issues emerge as particularly important to voters by November 2008, Democrats appear to have the advantage on all but one. On issues such as the environment, Social Security, and Medicare, health care, economic inequality, and racial and ethnic relations, the Democrats are preferred more frequently than the Republicans by ratios of about 3:1. Even on taxation, an issue area of traditional Republican strength, the Democrats hold the edge by a statistically significant six percentage points (28% vs. 22%). Among Millennials, the Democratic Party is endorsed by ratios that are never less, and usually greater, than among the electorate as a whole.

Millennials even favor the Democrats on the one issue where the Republican Party continues to narrowly hold the advantage overall—national security and terrorism. Within the entire electorate, the Republicans have a slight edge over the Democrats (25% vs. 23%). And, among those voters who expect national security concerns to be very important in shaping their 2008 votes, the GOP margin over the Democrats is a statistically significant six percentage points (29% vs. 23%). However, among Millennials, the Democrats hold the edge on national security (28% vs. 23%) (Frank N. Magid Associates 2007).

The Democratic margin on all issues is particularly large among those voters who expect the 2008 election to be more important than other recent presidential elections. On the strong Democratic issues of the environment, Social Security and Medicare, health care, economic inequality, and racial and ethnic relations, the Democratic advantage over the GOP is about 4:1. Even on taxation, it is 1.7:1 (36% vs. 22%) among voters who expect the next presidential election to be especially important (Frank N. Magid Associates 2007).

Democratic activist and political writer Richard Reeves has compared what is happening now at the end of one political era to what happened at the end of another, nearly three decades ago:

> The politics we are seeing now, particularly in the Republican Party, really mark the end of the 28-year presidency of the cowboy actor [Ronald Reagan] who came riding out of the conservative

west in 1980. Like Franklin D. Roosevelt before him, Reagan reigned long after he left the White House. The New York liberal, I would argue, and so would many others, ran the country for at least 40 years. Both Roosevelt and Reagan governed by changing the way Americans viewed government itself. (Reeves 2007)

Of course, in many respects, Ronald Reagan's election and presidency served to cement into place much of what Richard Nixon's election had begun twelve years earlier. Still, Reeves does believe that the "end of the Reagan presidency" is likely to work to the advantage of the Democratic Party:

As Democrats did in the 1960s and 1970s, the Republicans have simply run out of agenda. Like the Democrats when the Roosevelt era finally ended, the Republicans are left with more candidates than new ideas. . . . At the end of the day, the end of the race, American politics are usually cyclical. One party runs out of energy and the other takes over until it runs out of energy. . . . so when the energy of the Reagan era is finally gone, the Democrats will probably find out how much they have after their desert years under a Reagan sun. (Reeves 2007)

Conservative columnist David Brooks echoes Reeves's views. In a piece entitled "Grim Old Party," he cogently describes the bind in which the Republican Party currently finds itself on most issues: "Democratic approaches are favored on almost all domestic, tax, and fiscal issues, and even on foreign affairs. The public, in short, wants change. And yet the Republicans refuse to offer that" (Brooks 2007).

THE REPUBLICAN PARTY IS NOT ALL OVER

However, while there is much to suggest a return to Democratic dominance, that outcome is not a sure thing. With the right candidate, and in the proper circumstances, the Republican Party could swim upstream politically and reestablish itself as the country's dominant political party. For this to occur, the Republican Party would need to reconstitute itself, as it did in the McKinley realignment of 1896. It would need to emphasize a different constellation of issues and attract a different voting coalition. Such fundamental changes are hard to undertake when things are going well. But luckily for its future prospects, the lack of popularity of its current president might just provide the Republican Party with the motivation it will need to undertake such wrenching reforms.

The May 14, 2007, editions of two of America's leading newsmagazines, *Newsweek* and *U.S. News & World Report*, both featured cover stories that focused on the presidential style of George W. Bush. The *U.S. News & World Report* cover asked the question in a pithy and colorful way: "Is he [Bush] resolute or delusional?" Each magazine suggested the possibility that history will eventually vindicate Bush, just as it vindicated Abraham Lincoln and Harry Truman, two other presidents who remained steadfast in their beliefs and actions during long and difficult wars.

But both magazines also indicated that, regardless of how Bush and his presidency are judged in the long run, present-day Americans have decidedly negative impressions of him. *U.S. News & World Report* cited presidential historian Robert Dallek's evaluation of Bush: "He may come across as a man of principle, but a great majority see him as stubborn and unyielding. . . . And everything he touches turns to dust" (Walsh 2007, 41). *Newsweek* commented: "George W. Bush may have thought he was following in the footsteps of Winston Churchill when he ordered the invasion of Iraq. But when things quickly turned sour, his show of resolve began to seem more foolhardy than wise. . . . Courage is also about learning from—and facing up to—your mistakes" (Thomas 2007, 28).

The negative appraisals of George W. Bush's presidency in the media are clearly reflected by a steady and sharp decline in the electorate's evaluation of his performance. In fact, since national public opinion surveys began to examine voter attitudes toward presidential performance in the 1930s, only one other president, Harry Truman, has registered a drop in his job approval ratings as steep as Bush's. Bush has the distinction of receiving the highest presidential approval rating ever recorded (a virtually unanimous 92% in an ABC poll conducted a month after 9/11). By the first half of 2007, however, Bush's approval rating had consistently fallen to around 30 percent, and two 2007 surveys (a mid-January CBS poll and an early May *Newsweek* poll) measured the public's approval of Bush's performance at only 28 percent. This represented a decline of 64 percentage points from its autumn 2001 high.

In addition, only Richard Nixon (23%, on the eve of his resignation, in 1974) and Harry Truman (22% in January 1952) received lower absolute performance ratings. Given the rate at which Bush's approval ratings have declined so far, it is certainly possible they will drop even lower during the remainder of his administration (Pew Research Center 2007c).

Bush has even lost ground among white Evangelical Protestants, a major component of the GOP's idealist-era success. In late 2004, three-quarters of white Evangelicals continued to give Bush a positive performance evaluation. However, by June 2007, white evangelicals were evenly divided in their appraisal of his presidency (44% approving vs. 45% disapproving).

Only among Republican identifiers, especially conservative Republicans, do majorities continue to approve of the job George W. Bush is doing as president; about two-thirds of all Republican identifiers (65%) rate his performance positively. The biggest problem standing in the way of the Republican Party making a major change in its agenda is that, at 74 percent, Bush's approval rating among conservative Republicans remains especially strong. This group makes up nearly two-thirds of all Republican identifiers and will provide a disproportionately large share of the votes in the 2008 GOP presidential primaries and caucuses that will help determine the future direction of the party (Pew Research Center 2007c).

The sharp division in appraisals of George W. Bush between the conservative base of the Republican Party and the rest of the electorate presents the same problem for the Republicans that confronted Vice President Hubert H. Humphrey and the Democratic Party in 1968. Some Republican strategists, such as pollster Tony Fabrizio, basically advocate the incremental-distancing strategy that Humphrey employed in that decisive year for the Democrats, in which the vice president (unsuccessfully, as it turned out) attempted to separate himself from President Johnson's unpopular Viet Nam policy. "If you want to win [Republican] primaries, it's still dangerous to be foursquare opposite the president. . . . You'll see some distancing now, but it will really start the moment we have a nominee . . . that will open the cracks and fissures" (Fineman 2007). In specific terms, Republican presidential candidates who follow this strategy would not openly criticize President Bush, but refer to him as infrequently as possible. Republicans who adopted

Humphrey's approach would tend to endorse most of Bush's policies, but promise to execute them better.

Other Republican strategists advocate that their candidates adopt tactics more like those of Senator Eugene McCarthy, a Democratic outsider in 1968. Conservative political columnist Jack Kelly seems to be offering that sort of advice. He maintains that George W. Bush has almost completely alienated the electorate, including many Republicans. According to Kelly, this should permit the eventual GOP presidential nominee to completely break from the president and chart a brand new course for himself and a newly reconstituted Republican Party (Kelly 2007).

William F. Buckley, the intellectual godfather of modern conservatism, joined Kelly by sharply criticizing the Iraq War and the Bush administration's conduct of it. By the spring of 2007, Buckley said Bush found himself in such a desperate position because of the war that "even if he [Bush] had invented the Bill of Rights, it would not get him out of this jam" (Hunt 2007). Earlier, Buckley had asked rhetorically about the negative impact that the Bush presidency may have on the fortunes and future of the Republican Party: "How can the Republican Party, headed by a president determined on a war he can't see an end to, attract the support of a majority of voters?" In his column, he confronted the worst-case scenario the question raised: "There are grounds for wondering whether the Republican Party will survive this dilemma" (Buckley 2007).

Finally, to complete the historical analogy to 1968, former Speaker of the House Newt Gingrich echoed the strategy Bobby Kennedy used to challenge the party's establishment in that realigning presidential election campaign four decades ago. Gingrich called for new ideas, many of them his own, to replenish an intellectually bankrupt party, even as he waited on the sidelines for much of the early campaign to see if his party wanted him to carry the message to the voters personally. Gingrich compared Bush's presidential performance to that of Jimmy Carter, someone described since 1980 by Republicans in pretty much the same terms that Democrats had used to describe Herbert Hoover in the 1930s and 1940s. Gingrich said, "You hire presidents, at a minimum, to run the country well enough that you don't have to think about it," clearly implying that George W. Bush had failed even that minimal standard (Fineman 2007).

In 1968, a disgraced president was forced to watch his own party's nominating convention on television from his Texas ranch, lacking any invitation to attend. Forty years later, the same fate could await George W. Bush. But the question remains, as Fabrizio points out, "Where do we hide the president?" (Fineman 2007).

Ignoring the elephant in the room (or in their case, the donkey) didn't help the Democrats address their ideological divisions in time to win the presidency in 1968, and it's unlikely to be an effective strategy for the Republicans in 2008. As V. O. Key so insightfully pointed out more than fifty years ago, voters tend to make their decisions in retrospect. It is not likely that the Republican Party will be able to completely escape from or neutralize the unpopular presidency of George W. Bush. The extent to which the GOP is able to do so at all will go a long way toward determining how it fares in the coming civic realignment. As any record company executive can attest, it's better to face up to the challenge and make the changes that need to be made in order to be successful earlier rather than later.

WILL DEMOCRATS SNATCH DEFEAT FROM THE JAWS OF VICTORY?

Because of their strongly held belief that things in the country are off course and, to a lesser degree, because they sense that the United States may be at a critical political crossroads, a clear majority of Americans (56%) believes that the 2008 presidential election will be "more important and crucial than other recent presidential elections." Potential voters who believe that an election really matters are more likely to turn out at the polls than those who believe that an election is routine or ordinary. The demographic profile of those voters who perceive that the 2008 presidential election will be especially crucial should work primarily to the advantage of the Democratic Party (Frank N. Magid Associates 2007).

While a majority of strong Republican identifiers (56%) and conservatives (58%) perceive the coming election to be especially important, perhaps recognizing that values and policies they hold dear are at stake, it is Democratic identifiers and groups oriented to the Democratic Party who hold this perception with particular force. Nearly three-quarters of Democratic identifiers (72%) and those labeling themselves liberals (73%), as well as two-thirds of both African Americans (65%) and Hispanics

(64%), believe that the 2008 presidential election will be particularly crucial. More than any other generation, the solidly Democratic Millennials also perceive that the first presidential election in which many of them will vote will be of major historical significance (61%) (Frank N. Magid Associates 2007).

As the United States moves toward its next civic political realignment, these attitudes provide the Democratic Party with one more advantage going into a critical realigning presidential election. In fact, the list of all of the Democrats' advantages is so long it would seem to make a Democratic victory inevitable. The list includes the Democrats' lead in party identification, especially among Millennials; negative attitudes toward President George W. Bush and the current condition of the country; alignment of public opinion on most issues with positions normally associated with the Democratic Party; and a perception that the Democrats will deal more successfully than the Republicans with most of the concerns likely to face the United States in coming years. In spite of these advantages, however, there are several potential barriers still standing in the way of Democrats' success.

The first is the mirror image of the Republicans' current political difficulties. With everything going so well for the Democratic Party, the danger exists that it will be unable to resist the cries from many in its base for a return to a version of liberalism associated with earlier generations. This approach would call for centralized, bureaucratic programs to deal with the nation's problems; an emphasis on social issues that the tolerant Millennial Generation and, indeed, most Americans feel no longer need to be the focus of political debate; and advocacy of an international policy that fails to recognize and confront this era's version of totalitarianism. After all, if victory is perceived to be inevitable, there is little reason to try to attract more voters or compromise party loyalists' beliefs in order to attract Independents and the voters of a new generation. But such an approach, built on the politics of the past and not of the future, could be fatal and deny the Democratic Party an opportunity to shape America's destiny in the civic era that's on its way.

Another danger for the Democrats is the possibility that the primary issue of concern in the 2008 election will be national security and terrorism, the only issue on which the Republican Party holds the advantage among the entire electorate (although not among Millennials).

Columnist Eleanor Clift, who generally leans toward Democrats, described how Republicans might use concerns over national security to overcome the many disadvantages they face. "Rudy Giuliani has figured out the formula for victory in '08. Elect a Republican, he says, and the country will stay on the offensive against terrorists. Elect a Democrat, and America will go back to playing defense in a kind of pre-9/11 oblivion. . . . If the election is framed as a choice between taking the fight to the enemy and sitting back a waiting for the terrorists to attack us again, the Democrats will lose. . . . It's a completely bogus choice, but unless Democrats take it on frontally and develop an effective offense, they'll doom themselves in '08" (Clift 2007).

Former U.S. senator and Democratic presidential candidate Gary Hart has also weighed in on the need for the Democrats to adopt a more proactive stance in support of both the military and multilateral approaches to the nation's foreign policy challenges:

> Security in this new century will be more international; what I call the security of the global commons. And it will require multinational collaboration on non-military levels. The new realities of proliferation of weapons of mass destruction, failed and failing states, mass south–north migrations, the threat of pandemics, climate change, and a host of similar destabilizing realities require imaginative new international cooperation. . . . Absent a new understanding of security and identification with achieving it, Democratic progressives will continue to be seen as anti-military and therefore anti-security. Consequently, when the nation feels itself to be endangered, it will always turn to conservative leaders. This cycle must be broken. (Hart 2007)

Two of the leading centrist Democratic veterans of the Clinton administration, Elaine Kamarck and William Galston, also called for a new set of foreign and national security policies that would be different from those of George W. Bush, but distinctive from the Cold War policies originally formulated by Harry Truman during America's last civic era and the Baby Boomer–driven fixation on Vietnam that became the defining moment of the last idealist-era realignment. All these Democratic commentators correctly point out that this new approach must meet the circumstances of a new international environment and the preferences of a rising new generation. And Clift underlined the importance of having the debate now, while the realignment is underway. "Once in a generation there is an opening for a national conversation that in more normal times doesn't occur."

But the biggest challenge confronting the Democratic Party is one that faces the Republican Party as well. How well each party meets this strategic imperative will define America's politics during the entire Millennialist era. If a party is to maneuver successfully amid the rapidly changing currents within the 2008 electorate and take advantage of the opportunities those changes present, it must nominate a presidential candidate with broad appeal beyond the Baby Boomer, ideologically driven base of that party. By sticking with what's familiar and what has worked at least on occasion in the past, that party would miss the opportunity of catching the "tide in the affairs of men, which, taken at the flood, leads on to fortune," as Shakespeare put it in *Julius Caesar*. Finding just the right combination of candidate characteristics required to lead and inspire the country through its next civic realignment will be the responsibility of the primary election voters in each party in 2008. Whichever party gets it right will win not only the presidency, but also the chance to lead America for decades to come.

CHAPTER 13

Who Will Lead the Realignment?

By mid-2007, Gallup survey research data suggested that the nation had reached a crisis in civic confidence of historic proportions. Reflecting frustration with the inability of the new Democratic leadership in Congress to accomplish more in ending the war in Iraq and the antipathy of the Republican base to the GOP congressional leadership's support for a bipartisan proposal on immigration, the job approval rating for that institution sunk to 14 percent, the lowest ever recorded in modern-day polling. President Bush's job approval ratings also continued to drop, damaging, as columnist David Broder put it, the "brand of the entire Republican Party" ("Meet the Press" 2007). In June 2007, just 19 percent of the public thought the country was headed in the right direction, close to the all-time low of 14 percent, recorded almost exactly fifteen years earlier (McKinnon 2007).

In their book *The Fourth Turning: An American Prophecy* (1997), William Strauss and Neil Howe predicted with uncanny accuracy exactly this scenario occurring at precisely this time period. Reflecting back on the eighty-year cycles of American history, they point out that, ironically, hostility to the nation's political system has always reached its peak right after a decade when the country is richer, more technologically sophisticated, and potentially more powerful militarily than ever before. In both 1860 and 1932, the country was pushed to examine its fundamental social contract by the force of a large and diverse generation, when a catalytic event triggered the two most significant political crises the country has ever faced. Strauss and Howe further predicted that during the first decade or so of the twenty-first century a crisis of similar magnitude would once again produce a "sweeping political realignment, as one faction or coalition capitalizes on a new public demand for decisive action. Republicans, Democrats, or perhaps a new party will decisively win the long partisan tug-of-war, ending the era of split government" (Strauss and Howe 1997, 275).

As in the past, how the crisis is resolved and how this next realignment turns out will depend a great deal upon the leadership of whoever is elected president in 2008. In the two previous civic realignments of 1860 and 1932, the country found among the various contenders for the presidency of the United States leaders who eventually became two of the country's greatest presidents. As America enters a critical turning point in its history, the 2008 presidential campaign will provide the electorate with a chance to find the next Lincoln or FDR among the candidates—someone who possesses the combination of personal qualities and political skills that will be required to lead the country through our next civic realignment.

LINCOLN'S AND FDR'S LEADERSHIP
CHANGED AMERICA

Even if the future is more kind to the country than Strauss and Howe's theory of generational cycles would suggest, the nation would still be well served to look for the qualities of a Lincoln or FDR to lead it. Lincoln's presidency was the beginning of many decades of electoral dominance for the Republican Party. His leadership saved the Union, at last ended the moral dilemma of slavery, and firmly established the United States as a centralized nation rather than a loose collection of states. Roosevelt's election ended seventy years of almost continuous Republican rule, leading to a period of nearly four decades during which Democrats won most elections and controlled government at the national level. In addition Roosevelt reoriented the role of American government in society and in the economy and the role of America in the world.

Both Lincoln and Franklin Roosevelt held office at times of obvious national crisis and trauma, the former as the country itself splintered and the latter during America's greatest economic and foreign crises. Once in office, the scale and scope of the challenges they faced provided Lincoln and FDR major opportunities for great achievements—leading some historians to suggest their greatness was driven by circumstance, not by personal characteristics. Presidential historian Robert Dallek has asked rhetorically if the presidents of the 1840s and 1850s couldn't have done more than they did to deal with the issues of slavery and sectionalism.

He also wonders if the presidents of the late nineteenth and early twentieth centuries couldn't have done a better job of helping to defuse the class tensions, economic dislocations, and ethnic conflicts stemming from the industrialization and immigration of that era (Dallek 1996).

Perhaps they could have. But, for example, as self-evident as it is in the America of the twenty-first century that slavery was morally abhorrent, that wasn't so clear-cut to many in the mid-nineteenth century, at a time when most southern and many northern whites perceived the abolitionists of that period as dangerous radicals. And, as Bill Clinton discovered early in his first term, when he proposed an extensive federal program to provide medical care for all Americans, it is often politically perilous for presidents to get ahead of public and elite opinion before the time is right. Circumstances can often be as much of a constraint on presidential greatness as an enabler.

Even when the economic, societal, and political circumstances that exist during an era of crisis provide an opportunity for achievement, they do not entirely account for presidential success. In February 1933, two weeks before Franklin Roosevelt was to take office, Giuseppe Zangara, an unemployed bricklayer, attempted to assassinate the president-elect, missing FDR and instead fatally wounding the mayor of Chicago, Anton Cermak. Presidential scholar Fred Greenstein posed the provocative question: "What would have happened to the country if Roosevelt had been killed and the vice-president-elect, John Nance Garner, had become president, instead of FDR?" Greenstein maintains that "few public figures were less equipped for restoring public confidence than the crusty Garner, who is best known for equating the vice-presidency to a pitcher of warm spit." He points to the possibility that if the United States "had been deprived of the political genius of FDR, it is far from impossible that [the United States] would have succumbed to authoritarian rule, or even dissolved as a political entity, as the Soviet Union did in 1991" (Greenstein 2000, 190–191).

As this example suggests, the right circumstances and opportunity are necessary but not sufficient conditions for shaping presidential greatness. In addition, the person who sits in the Oval Office must have the right set of skills and character traits that are the key determinants of presidential performance and leadership.

Abraham Lincoln demonstrated this skill and character when, early in his first term, he declined to rush headlong into conflict with the Confederacy. Eleven southern states began seceding from the Union almost immediately upon Lincoln's election, but he was careful to make certain his actions did not create the impression that he welcomed those developments or had any hand in their occurrence. Instead, he waited until South Carolina fired on Fort Sumter in Charleston harbor before he announced his intention to use military force to relieve the federal garrison at the fort. Not being precipitous or overly anxious made it easier for Lincoln to lead the country during the dark days that followed.

By contrast, the failure of Franklin Roosevelt's predecessor, Herbert Hoover, to see clearly what confronted him prevented him from taking decisive action to mitigate the initial impact of the Great Depression. The depth of Hoover's inability to comprehend the need to reverse his party's laissez-faire economic policies can be seen in his memoirs. Years after the Great Depression, he wrote that the apple peddlers that sprang up on street corners everywhere as desperate men struggled to earn a living represented a clever marketing device of the apple grower's association, who had "induced many people to leave their jobs 'for the more profitable one of selling apples'" (Black 2003, 211). Even as New York City's Central Park was turned into the largest "Hooverville," or shantytown, in America, Hoover refused to act. An entire generation of voters never forgave him or the Republican Party.

ABE LINCOLN'S AND FDR'S WINNING VISIONS

As defined by Ivan Rosenberg, a successful personal coach to the leaders of numerous organizations, leadership is the ability "to create the possibility of a future that isn't going to happen otherwise, and enroll others into taking action to fulfill that future" (Rosenberg interview 2007). Measured against this standard, Abraham Lincoln and Franklin Roosevelt, along with George Washington, have been the greatest leaders in the nation's history.

Robert Dallek's analysis of great presidents underscores the importance of the first part of this definition of leadership. "Every successful president has had vision, insight, or understanding. However illusory some of these dreams may have been . . . a clear and comprehensive grand design has been central to every significant presidential advance" (Dallek

1996, xx). Research by Warren Bennis, one of the nation's foremost authorities on leadership, suggests that only about 8 percent of the population has the inherent ability to inspire others to pursue alternative futures. But both Lincoln and FDR demonstrated the ability to enunciate a clear vision of America's future that attracted supporters and animated their quest for the presidency, long before they took office.

Of Lincoln, one editor in Peoria wrote in 1858, "Beyond and above all skill, was the overwhelming conviction imposed upon the audience that the speaker himself was charged with an irresistible and inspiring duty to his fellow men" (Charnwood 1996, 102). In describing his first meeting with Franklin Roosevelt, Rexford G. Tugwell, who later became a member of FDR's kitchen cabinet, wrote that it "was somewhat like coming into contact with destiny itself" (Davis 1985, 272).

Dallek observed that Lincoln's "triumph and greatness as a president rested principally on a clear confidence in the beliefs for which he stood. . . . Lincoln never lost sight of his fundamental aim: to preserve the Union and secure its existence as one nation. Seeing the United States as a test in self-government, 'the last best hope of earth,' Lincoln believed that its preservation was a crusade to save democracy for the world" (Dallek 1996, 13).

Central to his faith in American democracy was his belief in the immorality of slavery. Although tactical considerations did not permit him to announce Emancipation until after the Union military victory at Antietam in 1863, two years after the Civil War had begun, Lincoln never really lost sight of his ultimate goal of ending slavery in the United States. He made his opposition to slavery clear, against the advice of some of his Republican advisors, well before he was elected president. Lincoln believed that a "moral attitude of indifference to the wrongfulness of slavery . . . was, so to say, treason to the basic principle of the American commonwealth," and had to be wiped out rather than placated (Charnwood 1996, 107).

Speaking in 1856, Lincoln had declared that the United States "could not long endure half slave and half free." His Republican friends persuaded him never to say those words again or risk being labeled as an agitator for the dissolution of the Union. But by 1858, he decided to use that very thought in the opening of his famous debates with Senator Stephen Douglas, telling those who advised against it that "I would rather be defeated with this expression in my speech, and uphold and discuss it before the people, than be victorious without it" (Charnwood 1996, 110).

Even though Douglas was reelected to the Senate in 1858, the South ultimately refused to support his candidacy for president in 1860, based on his vacillating and temporizing positions over the years on an issue that could no longer be compromised. As a result, in 1860 Douglas became the presidential nominee of only the northern wing of the Democratic Party. With the national Democratic Party shattered, Lincoln, his new party, and his vision were chosen to lead the nation through its gravest crisis.

Franklin Roosevelt was famous for holding a multitude of positions at one time, many of them seemingly contradictory. In a February 1932 speech, Roosevelt attempted to appease the isolationist opinions of publisher William Randolph Hearst by distinguishing between economic internationalism, which FDR said he was for, and political internationalism, such as the League of Nations and the World Court, which he now said he was against, though he had been a member of the Wilson administration. Afterward, Walter Lippmann famously dismissed Roosevelt as a "slippery, unprincipled, amiable lightweight, 'carrying water on both shoulders . . . [and] too eager to please . . . to be a danger to anyone'" (Black 2003, 220). But Lippmann was among many observers who failed to distinguish between FDR's tactical maneuverings, as in this speech, and his deeply held convictions and radical vision for a completely different America.

Roosevelt recognized that he was breaking new ground and moving away from the beliefs and arguments of the past. In his 1932 address to the Commonwealth Club of San Francisco, he pronounced his vision of a decisively different and fundamentally expanded economic role for the federal government. Declaring that the exigencies of the Depression called for "a reappraisal of values," he said that the "task of government is to assist the development of an economic declaration of rights, an economic constitutional order" (Davis 1985, 370). This was the culmination of thoughts he had first expressed much earlier as he maneuvered for the Democratic Party's presidential nomination.

That vision ultimately brought Roosevelt the Democratic presidential nomination and then the presidency, as he overwhelmed his opponents and united a party divided for much of the previous decade over the social issues of the day. After the Democratic ticket's defeat twelve years earlier, when he had been the party's vice-presidential nominee, Roosevelt became intent on finding a vision for America's future that would unite southern Democrats, Catholic urban machine voters, and midwestern progressives. The economic crisis caused by the Great Depression provided him the opportunity to articulate just such a vision and to realign not only his party, but also the entire political structure of the country.

FDR carried 88 percent of the votes in the South and 64 percent in the border states. He received 61 percent of the vote in upper midwestern states that no Democratic presidential candidate had ever won and a similar margin in the rest of the Midwest and Pacific states. Herbert Hoover was able to remain relatively competitive only in the former Republican strongholds of the New England and Middle Atlantic states, but even in those regions FDR handily won the major urban centers (Black 2005). Roosevelt's vision of an economic New Deal struck such a chord with most voters that it spurred a vast increase in turnout and damped down any probability of a strong third-party challenge. Norman Thomas, the Socialist Party's presidential candidate, and presumably a likely focal point for economic protest voters, received less than three percent of the total popular vote in 1932, the third year of the Great Depression (Davis 1985).

How to Enroll a Country in a Civic Realignment

Both Abraham Lincoln and Franklin Roosevelt distinguished themselves by their abilities to connect at an emotional level with the bulk of the American people and, especially, a rising civic generation. This enabled them to fulfill the second aspect of Rosenberg's definition of leadership: the enrollment of others in the pursuit of one's vision of a vastly different future. Being born in a frontier log cabin and pulling himself from poverty to a position in the midwestern gentry gave Lincoln a set of life experiences that enabled him to identify with the rising power of American farmers and workers from a personal perspective. Although born to wealth and privilege, Roosevelt clearly saw the need to give "a New Deal" to the "forgotten man," and communicated that empathy with uncommon skill.

Enrolling the nation in support of a candidate's vision of the future requires a special combination of communication skills, political dexterity, and charismatic qualities that Lincoln and FDR possessed more than most presidents. Because the likelihood of their party's victory in a general election was high, both Lincoln and FDR had to work hard to outmaneuver factions within their parties to secure the nomination. Once in office, the political and communication skills that they demonstrated on the campaign trail, as well as their personal charisma, enabled them to lead their parties and the country through the crises that have always accompanied a civic realignment.

Great presidents differ from other, less successful, ones by using their enrollment skills to overcome the inherent constitutional limitations imposed upon them and their administrations. Theodore Roosevelt called the presidency a "bully pulpit," but Lincoln and Roosevelt's cousin, Franklin, surpassed even T.R.'s considerable skills in using "the powers of [the] office [to] assertively build and maintain public support, and establish a reputation among fellow policymakers as a skilled, determined political operator" (Greenstein 2000, 197). In comparing Lincoln's political skills with those of his initially more experienced Confederate counterpart, Jefferson Davis, several historians praise Lincoln's "feeling for the democratic medium in which he had to work, for its limitations, imperfections, and possibilities, proved akin to that of a great artist" (Morison, Commager, and Leuchtenburg 1977, 279). And FDR has been similarly lauded: "The Roosevelt presidency is laden with insights into how presidents can get results in an often intractable political system. Future presidents might well begin with the beginning, using the Hundred Days as a source of lessons on such matters as setting the agenda for congressional action, timing proposals, and even transforming a defeat into a seeming victory. . . . They would be equally advised to study FDR's international maneuvers, especially his patient, step-by-step alignment of the United States with the Western democracies in the period following Munich" (Greenstein 2000, 23).

Touching the electorate intellectually and emotionally is a major asset for a strong, successful presidency. Historians say that Lincoln and Franklin Roosevelt were, to use Greenstein's word, "shining" exceptions to the generalization that many presidents are not effective communicators. Whether their speeches were delivered on great public occasions as befit the oratorical and technological style of Lincoln's day or as fireside chats over the new medium of radio, each demonstrated a remarkable ability to speak directly to the American public and to mobilize them on behalf of their cause.

Clear speaking and writing were of particular importance to Abraham Lincoln, who declared himself "determined to be so clear that no honest man can misunderstand me, and no dishonest one can successfully misrepresent me" (Dallek 1996, 13). Evidence that Lincoln succeeded in doing just that can be found in a 1962 volume of essays, *Lincoln: A Contemporary Portrait*, which portrayed Lincoln, based solely on his writings and the description of him by others, in remarkably similar terms. The editors, historian Allan Nevins and novelist Irving Stone, said the result tempted them to entitle their book *United He Stands* (Dallek 1996, 13).

If anything, historians believe FDR was an even better communicator than Lincoln. "In his communication practices, as in much else, FDR provides a benchmark for his successors. His soaring rhetoric roused imaginations and stirred souls. He restored faith in a political system that Americans had few reasons to respect and rallied the nation and its allies in an epic conflict in which victory was by no means assured. . . . As a communicator, Roosevelt is to later presidents what Mozart and Beethoven have been to their successors—inimitable but endlessly inspiring" (Greenstein 2000, 22).

Closely related to the communication and political skills of great and successful presidents is their ability to rally public support for their goals and policies through personal magnetism. "The best of our presidents have always recognized that leadership required a personal connection between the president and the people, or that the power of the Oval Office rests to a great degree on the affection of the country for its chief" (Dallek 1996, xx). Today's pundits and pollsters examine the "likeability" of our presidential candidates, a pale imitation of real charisma.

Many of Lincoln's contemporaries described America's sixteenth president in quasi-religious, almost Christ-like terms. In part because of his melancholy appearance and tone and because of the sadness of his personal and political life, Lincoln was said to bear "the torments and moral burdens of a blundering and sinful people, suffer for them, and redeem them with hallowed Christian virtues" (Dallek 1996, 135).

Despite his personal embodiment of the nation's agony, Lincoln connected with the American people through his unique combination of rough-hewn honesty and wit. One visitor to the White House found "a man of unconventional manners, who, without the slightest effort to put on dignity, treated all men alike, much like old neighbors . . . who seemed to have time for a homely talk and never to press business" (Charnwood 1996, 172–173). His use of humor was described as his "opiate—a device to whistle down sadness." Lincoln himself said that a "funny story . . . has the same effect on me that I suppose a good square drink of whiskey has on an old toper; it puts new life into me" (Dallek 1996, 136–137). Lincoln's mixture of sad empathy, humor, and personal identification with the everyday people of his time enabled him to retain support for the Union's cause, even during its darkest hours.

Franklin Delano Roosevelt's ability to connect with the American people has been described in equally colorful and glowing terms. "Partly driven by his charm, ebullience, and natural self-confidence, he established an unmistakable hold on people everywhere. . . . His actions and programs . . . gained some measure of the credibility from the broad-shouldered, smiling, buoyant optimist with the up-tilted head offering reassurance that the nation would endure and prosper" (Dallek 1996, 141).

Like Lincoln, Roosevelt used both everyday metaphors and humor to gain support for his policies. After the 1940 election, he and Churchill met at sea and devised the concept of Lend-Lease to provide Britain the armaments it needed but couldn't afford to pay for. FDR explained this brand new policy upon his arrival home in a way every American could understand: "Suppose my neighbor's home catches on fire and I have a length of garden hose four or five hundred feet away. If he can take my garden hose and connect it up with his hydrant, I may be able to put out his fire. Now what do I do? I don't say to him before that operation, 'Neighbor, my garden hose cost me $15, you have to pay me $15 for it.'. . . I don't want $15. I want my garden hose back after the fire is over" (Black 2003, 605).

In a September 1944 radio address, Roosevelt jokingly responded to Republican charges that he had used a naval vessel to transport his dog: "Republican leaders have not been content with attacks on me, my wife, and my sons. No, not content with that they now include my little dog, Fala. Well, of course, I don't resent attacks, and my family doesn't resent attacks, but Fala does resent them. You know, Fala is Scotch and being a Scottie, as soon as he learned the Republican fiction writers in Congress and out [sic] had concocted a story that I had left him on the Aleutian

Islands and had sent a destroyer back to find him—at a cost to the tax-payers of two or three or eight or twenty million dollars—his Scotch soul was furious. He has not been the same dog since" (Black 2003, 1001). Though the use of this kind of humor, Roosevelt made his opponents an object of ridicule and further endeared himself to the American public.

On one level both Abraham Lincoln and Franklin Roosevelt were highly effective partisan politicians who valued and advanced the causes of their respective parties. Lincoln became the first Republican elected president, only four years after his party first nominated a candidate. FDR became only the second Democrat to be elected president in forty years and the first to win a majority of the popular vote in that period.

However, while both of the civic realigning presidents were more than capable practitioners of party politics and led their parties into long-term majority status, they were not shrill partisans. Especially during war, both Lincoln and FDR attempted to tamp down partisan struggles and to reach across party lines to unite Americans in common cause. As part of their efforts to enroll as many Americans as possible in their causes, both Lincoln and Roosevelt named members of the opposition party to important posts in their cabinets. Lincoln even nominated Andrew Johnson, a Union Democrat from the secessionist state of Tennessee, as his running mate in 1864. This ability to be positive partisans while continuing to place the nation's interest above politics was one of the key reasons both presidents were able to generate so much affection and support from so many Americans.

What Voters Look For in a Great President

Given the pivotal importance of Lincoln and Roosevelt in U.S. history, it is hardly surprising that the characteristics of the two great presidents who led civic realignments are reflected in the expectations of the American people about presidential leadership. When survey respondents are asked to indicate the qualities that characterize a great president, it is almost as if they are looking at portraits or biographies of Lincoln and FDR.

At a time when an idealist era is coming to an end and a civic era is unfolding, Americans place greatest importance on successful governmental activism and far less on issues and ideological specificity. The U.S.

electorate wants a president who can inspire the nation to accept his or her vision of America's future. After the midterm elections in 2006, voters pointed to "an ability to reach across party lines" (83%) and "a willingness and ability to organize the government to resolve major problems" (82%) as the two characteristics they were most interested in when deciding for whom to vote for president in 2008. These characteristics were followed closely by ones associated with the capacity to enroll others in that vision in order to make it come true: "an ability to understand the needs of and relate to the majority of the American people" and "an ability to successfully guide the economy and keep America prosperous" (79% each). The president's role as the leader of the free world causes the electorate to also look for "a willingness and ability to take on and effectively deal with major security and international concerns" (78%) and "an ability to earn the respect of foreign countries and create alliances to further America's goals" (76%). The next most important aspects of a presidential candidate, "a willingness to break new ground and not remain tied to the beliefs and policies of the past" (70%) and "an ability to communicate clearly and mobilize public opinion to achieve his goals" (66%), once again capture the leadership skills of vision and enrollment that Lincoln and Roosevelt so aptly demonstrated. But reflecting the country's lack of interest in ideology as an idealist era ends, the least important characteristic mentioned was "a strong and clear philosophy or set of beliefs" (62%).

While all these traits are important to a majority within all generations, it is particularly important to note that the more action-oriented and socially inclined Millennials, in comparison to older generations, place greater importance on the ability of a president to utilize government to resolve major problems. Millennials are significantly less likely to rate the possession of a strong, clear philosophy as a crucial presidential attribute (Frank N. Magid Associates, December 2006).

PICKING AMERICA'S NEXT
CIVIC PRESIDENT

In 2008, the presidential primaries and the general election will provide America's voters with an opportunity to evaluate all the candidates against these traits of presidential greatness. Perhaps the eventual winner will be a Democrat, such as Hillary Clinton, John Edwards, Barack Obama, Bill Richardson, or Al Gore, or a Republican like Rudy Giuliani,

John McCain, Mitt Romney, Mike Huckabee, or Fred Thompson. Whoever that victorious candidate turns out to be, he or she will most likely be the one who demonstrates the courage to transcend the approach to issues and political style of past generations in order to make an appeal to the aspirations, hopes, and beliefs of the Millennial Generation.

The reward for that display of political courage will be the rare opportunity to produce a fundamental and long-lasting change in the United States. By articulating his or her vision for a different future for our country and enrolling a broad coalition in support of that vision, the winning candidate will fundamentally alter the nation's politics and, even more important, its public policy. This will fulfill the prophecy of Strauss and Howe, who, in 1997, predicted that the winner of the realigning election of this decade "will now have the power to pursue the more potent, less incremental agenda about which they had long dreamed and against which their adversaries had darkly warned" (Strauss and Howe 1997, 275).

While we do not yet know the identity of the individual who will earn the opportunity to lead America's next civic realignment, the American people have clearly indicated the kind of leader they would like to find among the current crop of presidential candidates. If fortune once again smiles on the United States, the presidential choice the country makes in 2008 will prove to be as wise as the selections of a plain-speaking small-town lawyer from Illinois in 1860 and an eloquent patrician from upstate New York in 1932.

CHAPTER 14

Rebuilding America's Civic
Infrastructure

HISTORICALLY, civic realignments have led to the
renewal and expansion of American governmental institutions. The first
civic restructuring that occurred during what Strauss and Howe call the
Revolutionary generational cycle was led by America's first civic generation, born between 1742 and 1766, and included Thomas Jefferson,
Alexander Hamilton, James Madison, John Paul Jones, and Abigail Adams
among its members. After providing much of the leadership during the
American Revolution, the voices of this republican generation were the
key to the ratification of the Constitution. And their service in the nation's
first cabinet turned that visionary document into living proof of the power
and practicality of a democratic system of government.

Strauss and Howe maintain that there was no actual civic generation
in the Civil War generational cycle that followed the Revolutionary
cycle—the only incomplete cycle in our history. Nevertheless, the first
two decades that followed the Civil War had many of the attributes of a
true civic era: a major economic expansion accompanied by substantial
economic equality, acceptance of large-scale immigration, and a lessen-
ing of concern with social issues such as women's rights and substance
abuse. Unfortunately, there was no large civic generation in place to
restrain the tendencies of the next generation, who came into power with
the largest generational landslide victory in U.S. history. In the congressional elections of 1868, the generation of Ulysses S. Grant defeated one-
third of the incumbent members of Lincoln's generation (Strauss and
Howe 1997). The ultimate result of this generational transfer of power was
the political compromise of 1877, which formally ended Reconstruction
with the election of Republican Rutherford B. Hayes and set back the

cause of racial equality for more than a century. Even so, it wasn't until the next idealist era of the 1890s and the first decade of the twentieth century that Jim Crow laws were firmly established and lynching reached its historical peak.

Despite this major mistake, by saving the Union and firmly establishing the United States as a centralized nation rather than a loose collection of states, the Civil War-era civic realignment did lead to the revitalization of existing governmental institutions and the establishment of new ones. Republican programs designed to win the political allegiance of western states overturned the prohibition against federal economic intervention that had been the dominant political philosophy since the Jackson administration in the previous idealist era.

The Great Depression provided America's next civic generation, the GI generation, with the opportunity to reshape the U.S. government to fit the realities of the modern industrial age. The civic ideas of the Progressives, which were not fully acceptable during the previous idealist era, were welcomed and embraced in the 1930s by a Democratic president, who had the full support of the large, new GI Generation. Progressives argued for the introduction of industrial-age planning and expertise into government. This meant establishing a strong, centralized federal government to house the nation's best experts, who would decide the best course for public policy to take, based upon an objective examination of the available data. The desired result of this new approach to governance would be a predictable outcome that workers and investors alike could rely upon.

Based on this philosophy, FDR created a multitude of new agencies, each designed to bring national purpose to the major commercial activities of the country. With the outbreak of World War II and the subsequent Cold War, those same concepts of centralized expertise exercising full command and control over the enterprise were used to successfully execute a global war and then a foreign policy designed to contain Communist expansion. And when the men of the GI Generation traded their military khakis for gray flannel suits and marched off to jobs that were designed to limit any deviation on their part from practices dictated from on high, these concepts became embedded in American corporate enterprise.

Today's corporate world searches for ways to undo this industrial-age legacy by flattening its layers of management, encouraging innovation and individual enterprise, and assuring a steady flow of communication and information from those working most closely with the enterprise's customers. At the same time, America's government remains locked in institutional structures created during the last civic realignment nearly eighty years ago.

RESHAPING GOVERNMENT
TO SUIT MILLENNIALS' TASTES

The next civic realignment will cause these structures and the way our democratic form of government functions to change. The beliefs and behaviors of the Millennial Generation will reshape how government policy is made and how it is administered. Millennials constantly interact with each other using peer-to-peer communications. They have a strong orientation toward the needs of their circle of friends as well as the larger community. Both these characteristics will play a key role in producing a distinctive Millennialist approach to government, and it will be as different from today's federal government as FDR's centralized, progressive approach was from the laissez-faire, hands-off approach he inherited.

Millennials are likely to endorse an administrative approach that decentralizes the administration of government, even as it expands government and its functions. The country's first glimpse of this new approach came during the Clinton administration, when Vice President Al Gore led an initiative to "reinvent government." Under the taskforce's leadership, the federal government cut its workforce by 20 percent and helped to bring the nation's budget into balance. At the same time, leaders of that effort pursued several strategies to move policy administration out of the marble halls of the federal government and into the hands of those on the front lines of government service.

Elaine Kamarck, who first headed the initiative, suggests in her 2006 book *The End of Government as We Know It* that beyond simply reinventing government to make it more efficient and accountable, twenty-first-century governments at all levels will need to accomplish their agendas through markets or networks. Governments have been particularly successful using a market approach in environmental policy, for instance, with state bottle bills that provide incentives for recycling and the establishment of cap-and-trade regimes that establish a price for pollution and thus create incentives for the private sector to reduce greenhouse gas emissions.

Network approaches to government require central agencies to reach out to local organizations, many of them faith-based, non-profit organizations, to deal with problems of human behavior and family support. Successful programs to reduce the nation's welfare rolls by finding jobs for unemployed mothers and to encourage organized after-school activities are just two examples of using ordinary citizens, who are most knowledgeable about the specific conditions and challenges in their communities, to accomplish the objectives of a central government (Kahn 2003).

Attempted first by the Clinton-Gore administration and then by George W. Bush's President's Management Agenda (PMA) program, these "reinventing government" efforts have more often been met with resistance and opposition from those in power than with praise from the public in an idealist era. Legislators, jealous of their prerogatives to set priorities based on their personal agendas, and constituent groups, determined to preserve their influence and insider perquisites that they worked so hard to establish in the old regime, have for the most part successfully resisted executive branch attempts to drag government into the twenty-first century.

REINVENTING GOVERNANCE IN A CIVIC ERA

This will all change as civic-era Millennials assert their beliefs on how America's government should be designed. The characteristics of this civic generation will move the debate beyond the question of how to administer government programs to the more fundamental question of how decisions should be made and by whom. Instead of debating how to reinvent government, the country will debate how to reinvent its governance.

Most Millennials believe that the opinion of each member of a group carries equal weight. They tend to make decisions based on consensus, with leadership focused on forming and shaping that consensus (Jack MacKenzie interview 2007). Since they have learned to search for expertise on the Net, they tend not to believe in the authority of a few elite experts. Instead, they place their faith in the wisdom that comes from the combined opinions of all their friends, or in members of a network.

Stories that glorify top-down planning and centralized control are therefore not likely to engage their imaginations. For instance, Millennials don't think of NASA's successful moon landing in 1969 or even the Allies landing on the beaches of Normandy in 1944 as great examples of how to harness the power of government to accomplish difficult tasks. Dispersed participatory structures, such as Google or Wikipedia, are the brands they think of when asked to name information sources they trust. And it is from these models that "Millennialists" will draw their inspiration for reshaping America's government.

Sergey Brin and Lawrence Page created Google when they were graduate students at Stanford. Their goal was to design a better search engine than those that were popular in 1998, such as Yahoo! or AltaVista. Earlier search engines attempted to use experts' opinions on the best sites on the Net for a particular subject, combined with the frequency that the words being searched appeared on a given site, to present the results of the user's query. The system was easily gamed, so users found themselves digging through pages and pages of search results to find the one that might actually provide the answers they were looking for. Brin and Page decided the solution was to rely instead on the wisdom of every Internet user to determine which answer would most likely satisfy the user's needs.

This idea, the PageRank algorithm, was described in their 1998 research paper "The Anatomy of a Large-Scale Hypertextual Web Search Engine": "Google interprets a link from Page A to Page B as a vote, by Page A, for page B. Google assesses a page's importance by the votes it receives. But Google looks at more than sheer volume of votes or links; it also analyzes the page that casts the vote. Votes cast by pages that are themselves 'important' weigh more heavily and help to make other pages 'important' " (qtd. in Surowiecki 2004, 16). In other words, by trusting that the opinions of every Internet user, when aggregated, would produce a result most likely to meet the needs of the next person interested in finding out about a given topic, Google created one of the most valued resources in the world. Google is constantly updating its search algorithms, under a veil of complete secrecy, to make sure its results truly reflect every click on the Web every day; but the core of the enterprise's success remains its trust in the wisdom of crowds.

The same logic, albeit with a very different organizational model, is behind the phenomenal success of Wikipedia. Launched by Jimmy "Jimbo" Wales on January 15, 2001, Wikipedia attracted 164,675,000 unique visitors within five years—each one of them looking for information from the 5.3 million articles available at the site (Deutschman 2007). While any page can be added or edited by anyone who wishes to, more than 75,000 volunteer editors, using a completely transparent "edit history" for that page, police acts of vandalism or questionable insertions. The result is a product whose size dwarfs the 120,000 subjects available from the experts recruited by the editors of *Encyclopedia Britannica*. And, according to at least one study, the wisdom of the group is about equal to that of the experts. Wikipedia's error rate is 3.9 errors per article compared to 2.9 for *Britannica* (McNichol 2007).

Jimbo Wales made his political agenda clear in an "open letter to the political blogosphere" posted on Independence Day 2006, announcing the launch of a new web site, Campaigns Wikia, "aimed at being a central meeting ground for people on all sides of the political spectrum who think that it is time for politics to become more participatory, and more intelligent":

> Campaigns have been more about getting the television messaging right, the image, the soundbite, than about engaging ordinary people in understanding and caring how political issues really affect their lives. . . . Blog and wiki authors are now inventing a new era of media, and it is my belief that this new media is going to invent a new era of politics. If broadcast media brought us broadcast politics, then participatory media will bring us participatory politics. . . . The candidates who will win elections in the future will be the candidates who build genuinely participative campaigns by generating and expanding genuine communities of engaged citizens. (Wales 2006)

Unlike the vast and opaque enterprise that Google has spawned, just five employees of the Wikipedia Foundation administer Wikipedia. A classic Generation X libertarian, Wales was determined to eliminate any hint of bureaucracy or control from his creation. "When you build a social network, you're asking people to use your facilities to build a community. If you have a lot of secret mechanisms that regulate your site, people aren't going to feel comfortable. It's about building trust" (McNichol 2007, 103). Rebuilding that kind of trust in government will require adopting the same values of transparency and participation that have made Wikipedia so beloved in so short a time.

OPEN UP AND DECIDE FOR YOURSELF

Given Millennials' values and behaviors and the technologies they love, the principle thrust of efforts to reshape governance in the United States in the upcoming civic era will feature the creation of open structures that attempt to maximize the number of people who participate in the policymaking process. Exactly what form these structures will take depends on what type of crisis triggers the need for a stronger, more trustworthy government.

The popularity of "American Idol," which allows Americans to text-message their opinions on who should be the next recording star, is often cited as the model for how Millennials will want to run government in the future. Under this scenario, Millennialist public-policy decision making would involve the increased use of the mechanisms of direct democracy, namely the initiative, referendum, and recall. However, these reforms reflect idealist-era beliefs and are actually less likely to find favor in the new civic era than they have in the past.

The idea of direct democracy came into existence as Progressive reforms in the idealist era of the early twentieth century. They were used only rarely during the New Deal civic era that began in the 1930s, but have enjoyed a revival in popularity during the most recent idealist era. In 1978, the adoption of Proposition 13 by the voters of California created an explosion in the use of the citizen initiative throughout the country. Almost 250 such proposals were put to the voters in states across the country from 1975 to 1984. The idea's popularity continued to climb, with over 300 ballot questions voted upon from 1985 to 1994, and more than 360 from 1995 to 2005 (Matsusaka 2005a). Californians also used another instrument of direct democracy, the recall, with a vengeance in October 2003. The state's voters removed Democratic governor Gray Davis from an office to which he had been reelected less than a year earlier and replaced him with Republican Arnold Schwarzenegger. Since then, recall efforts have been launched against the Democratic governor in Louisiana and the Republican governor of Nevada.

John Matsusaka, who heads the Initiative and Referendum Institute at the University of Southern California, argues that the use of these instruments of direct democracy produces public policy more reflective of popular opinion and deals more effectively with problems confronting society than current governance structures. Matsusaka maintains that a careful comparison of the impact on public policy in states and cities that permit citizen initiatives with those that do not demonstrates that governments influenced by even the possibility of a citizen initiative are more likely to adopt policies that the majority favors (Matsusaka 2004). He uses the same basic defense against those who attack the idea of uninformed voters making public policy that Jimbo Wales uses to defend Wikipedia: "By the law of large numbers, aggregating the opinions of a million voters can give a very accurate estimate of an underlying parameter even if each individual's chance of knowing the parameter is small" (Matsusaka 2005a, 193).

The public tends to agree with his arguments. In 2003, Americans were asked which method, legislative enactment or voter adoption, was most likely to produce "laws in the public interest." Two-thirds of the respondents thought voters would do the best job; only 20 percent selected the legislature. Today, over 70 percent of Americans approve of direct democracy at the state and local level, and a majority favor the introduction of the initiative process for the federal government as well (Matsusaka 2005b).

The emergence and increasing use of peer-to-peer, Internet-based communication technology also provides new opportunities to deal with the potential problem of uninformed voters. The ability to create virtual online worlds holds the promise of providing an easy and entertaining way for voters to become better informed without interfering with events in the "real world" at all. These sites, such as Second Life, represent the convergence of online chat rooms, social networking sites, and massive multiplayer games like World of Warcraft. Each person who signs on to the site creates his or her own avatar, or virtual 3D character. Unlike static, two-dimensional social networking sites, in virtual environments the actions of each user's avatar influences the behavior of every other avatar that it comes in contact with. Users are free to experiment with alternative personalities, engage in what might otherwise be prohibited behavior, and interact with other avatars in a variety of settings.

The concept is already being tested for its potential value by major American corporations. IBM and Cisco have hundreds of employees wandering around Second Life looking for customers and potential employees (Wagner 2007). IBM owns 50 "islands" (in reality, servers) in this virtual world, using them for lectures and group discussions, which their employees' avatars can participate in online even as they continue their work in real life (Bulkely 2007). Hewlett-Packard, Microsoft, and Verizon, among others, have participated in cyber-world job fairs where prospective new hires present their avatar to a virtual interviewer who determines if they should be invited back for a real-life interview (Athavaley 2007). As with earlier reinventing government initiatives, the federal government will soon be experimenting with these business practices as well.

Just as the SIM series of games permitted an entire generation to experiment with building new and better worlds, government will be able to create "islands of ideas" on which engaged citizens can experience the consequences of their policy choices. Then, when the game is up, each participant can vote for the policy that has demonstrated the most likelihood of producing the results he or she favors. The use of such large-scale, virtual life environments to experiment with alternative policy choices will have to wait until computing and software systems have the capacity to handle the simultaneous participation of millions of people. But by the time the nation is ready to experiment with such an approach, the computing power will be ready for the implementation of these ideas and other forms of governance that reflect Millennials' beliefs and values.

Millennialist Incrementalism

Despite continuing technological advancements, even in the long run, those advocating the adoption of direct democracy at the national level are unlikely to be successful. For one thing, it is hard to imagine a crisis of sufficient magnitude that would create both a major collapse in the public's faith in representative democracy and a desire to have everyone involved in deciding what to do about it. And without almost unanimous support for the need for such a radical change in our national system of governance, direct democracy proponents would not be able to overcome the fears at both ends of the political spectrum that the implementation of these new institutions would threaten their political power. Nor would an idea with such strongly Millennialist characteristics find much support among Boomers or Gen-Xers. Instead, it is more likely that the public's continuing frustration with the foibles of the legislative process, especially in times of great national need, will lead to incremental changes in how democracy functions in a "Millennialist" era—very similar to the way FDR eventually triumphed in his efforts to implement Progressive ideas in the last civic era.

Results from state initiatives in the 1990s suggested that liberals would have the most to lose from letting the people decide matters directly. Voters, in that idealist era, showed a decided preference for reducing government spending, moving spending from distant state governments to local municipalities, and switching revenue out of general taxes to fees paid for by users of the service. Of even greater concern for liberals, state initiatives in the same era pushed their states to permit capital punishment and limit abortions by minors, as well as imposing term limits on state legislatures (Matsusaka 2005a).

But the outcomes of more recent ballot initiatives suggest that the nature of policy choices by voters is changing to reflect more current civic-era values. There were 204 propositions on the ballot in 37 different states in 2006 (up from 162 in 2004). Voters in the various states rejected almost all attempts to impose tax and spending limits and approved every single bond issue put before them. Voters in the red state of South Dakota overturned a legislative ban on all abortions, and the notion of requiring parental notification before a minor could have an abortion went down to defeat in both Oregon and California (Initiative and Referendum Institute 2006).

In sum, the history of direct democracy at the state and local level suggests that the institution of federal citizen initiatives and referenda won't favor any particular ideology, only the majority's point of view. Those results, however, will only reinforce opposition to the idea of direct democracy from Americans who have been taught the importance of respecting minority rights.

Furthermore, older generations, concerned about Millennials' tendency to reject people and opinions from anyone not cool enough to be included in their clique, are not likely to embrace the idea of direct democracy either. Millennials could easily fail to listen to all points of view before making a decision, especially when the generation's relative size causes their opinions to dominate the debate. Older generations, particularly Gen-Xers, would be particularly sensitive to the danger that Millennials could end up imposing a dictatorship of the majority on the rest of the country.

Many advocates of direct democracy point to the writings of James Surowiecki, such as *The Wisdom of Crowds*, to support their point of view. The three conditions that he postulates must be present for the judgment of a group to be better than that of a selected group of experts, however, actually undermine the argument for participatory democracy when placed in a Millennial context. Surowiecki's first requirement is that the group must be diverse to ensure that its thinking will encompass all possible answers or ideas for the problem at hand. Despite its racial and ethnic diversity, the cliquish behavior of many Millennials presents a potential problem in devising a solution that meets this condition. The same problem applies to his second condition, which requires that each member of the group be fairly independent of all other members. And even Millennial-era technologies such as Wikis, which help to meet Surowiecki's third condition—that there be some way to aggregate all the local expertise for consideration by the entire group—are not immune from criticism from members of other generations (Surowiecki 2004).

Jaron Lanier, a classic Baby Boomer who coined the term "virtual reality" in the 1980s, warned against putting too much faith in aggregations of opinions without personal attribution and accountability in his essay "Digital Maoism: The Hazards of the New Online Digital Collectivism." "What we are witnessing today is the alarming rise of the fallacy of the infallible collective. Numerous elite organizations have been swept off their feet by the idea. They are inspired by the rise of the Wikipedia, by the wealth of Google" (Lanier 2006). Later he underlined his concern about putting too much faith in the opinions or wisdom of crowds. "I don't like people pretending something better than themselves exists in the computer. This is a great danger. . . . You get a bunch of people together on a project, and they quickly become anonymous. They contribute to some sort of computer-mediated phenomenon, and treat the results as an oracle" (qtd. in Blume 2006).

These kinds of intergenerational and ideological conflicts, as well as the historical resistance of Americans to enact significant change in the constitutional institutions of the federal government, make the adoption of the practice of direct democracy at the federal level in the near future extremely unlikely. Of the twenty-seven amendments to the U.S. Constitution, and the seventeen added since the adoption of the Bill of Rights, only five have related to the structure of the national government. Of those, only the Seventeenth Amendment, which provided for the direct election of U.S. senators, altered the governance system of our representative democracy.

It is not entirely coincidental that this amendment was passed and rat-ified in the second decade of the twentieth century, the high point of that idealist era. Calls for direct democracy are heard most frequently in times of political gridlock that characterize such eras. By World War I, over twenty states had provided for implementation of the initiative and refer-endum and fourteen for the recall of governmental and judicial officials. More than two-thirds of the states had enacted the direct primary election for party nominations. In a perfect description of the ethos of idealist eras, the historians Morison, Commager, and Leuchtenburg portray the early twentieth-century Progressives who pushed this idea as "fundamentally moralists [who] assumed that most of the failings of government could be ascribed to Bad Men—bosses, vested interests, 'malefactors of great wealth'—and assumed, too, that if only Men of Good Will would devote themselves to public service, all would be well. Progressivism had a touch-ing faith, too, in mechanical contrivances; [Woodrow] Wilson once said that the 'short ballot was the key to the whole problem of the restoration of popular government in this country" (1977, 508–510).

But the use of the mechanisms of direct democracy declined sharply with the beginning of the civic era after the New Deal realignment of the 1930s. At the same time, positive attitudes toward the ability of the fed-eral government to represent the will of the people and to serve the com-mon good reached their peaks in the 1950s and early 1960s, the last decade of that civic era. At the time, that optimism seemed well founded. Even during periods of divided government in that era, Congress passed and presidents signed into law appropriations for such significant initia-tives as the Marshall Plan, the interstate highway system, and the space program, as well as, in 1957, the first civil rights act enacted since Recon-struction. If history is any guide, America will experience the same type of positive government action during the civic era that lies ahead, leading to a decrease in support for the further expansion of the tools of direct democracy.

Even so, Millennials will be extremely influential in bringing the con-cepts of authentic or transparent government into more common practice than we experience today. For instance, Jaron Lanier, though a fierce critic of Wikipedia, also celebrates the individualism of social networking sites such as MySpace, and defenders of Wikipedia point out the strong role that the individual plays in its editing process. Furthermore, the evolving world of online politics may well contain an inherent antidote to the problem of unfettered aggregation and lowest common denominator outcomes. "The ecology of social media is balanced by the presence of other applications such as blogs and social networking where individuality and cooperation are alive and well. . . . By using a mix of social media, communities can benefit both from the wisdom of crowds and the wisdom of individuals" (Mejias 2006).

The first steps in the use of technology to enable increased citizen involvement and participation in policymaking, while still preserving the constitutional role of representative legislative bodies, have already been taken in the very conservative but tech-savvy state of Utah. Politicopia. com, a "virtual town square" founded by Republican Utah legislator Steve Urquhart, "where Utahans could debate issues coming before the legislature," was used to influence the debate in the state's 2007 legislative session. Technologically, Politicopia operates in a very Millennialist manner, being "based on a user-controlled Wiki system that allows anyone to join the discussion. Unlike activist groups such as MoveOn.org, it does not push an agenda other than open discussion." Andrew Rasiej, founder of the Personal Democracy Forum and a strong advocate for more openness in government, points out an important difference between chat rooms and political Wikis. Capturing one of Surowiecki's conditions for using the wisdom of crowds to make decisions, he says, "Politicopia is more of a repository of ideas and discussions where issues can be debated and information can be added over time." Voters leave behind "both a record and an aggregation of voices to define an issue." Urquhart unwittingly captured the other two Surowiecki conditions as he underlined the keys to Politicopia's success: "It only works if it's a broad pool of people, not just techies or one party or another. . . . It has to be bottom up. The people have to have the tools and ability to set the agenda" (Martelle 2007).

The political impact of the site did not break down along traditional conservative and liberal lines either. The online debate moved the chamber in a conservative direction when it convinced several key legislators to vote for the adoption of a school voucher program that passed by only one vote. But it also pushed the legislature toward a liberal decision by rejecting a proposal to have Utah directly challenge the *Roe v. Wade* abortion ruling.

The result put Utah "at the vanguard of the future of American politics in the twenty-first century," according to Rasiej, "where town halls, policy debates and civic involvement will happen on Wikis, blogs, video-sharing and social networking sites." Despite its "bleeding edge" character, Politicopia.com was warmly received by the legislature. "It moved the needle. . . . It helped improve the dialogue," said Urquhart. "I think that's what a lot of us are yearning for in politics these days." His colleague Steve Sandstrom agreed: "I think we're on the verge of something new. . . . It was intelligent, thoughtful and produced a consensus. It was pretty neat" (Martelle 2007). By embracing "voter-generated content," Politicopia.com helped take the country down a new path, which will enhance public participation in policymaking and thereby strengthen our system of democratic governance.

The way in which public policy is made in America will change significantly as a result of the influence of Millennials on our next civic realignment. While this doesn't mean that the instruments of direct democracy will suddenly be used to displace the role of Congress, the process of making public policy will take advantage of new peer-to-peer communication technologies to more fully inform the nation's citizens and to increase their continual participation in the debates as they occur. A suggestion from an ideologically diverse and bipartisan group of members of Congress might become the first step along this path. The group wants all proposed legislation posted on the Internet seventy-two hours before debate, in order to "harness the collective intelligence of thousands of Americans" (Harwood 2007).

Having become engaged, Americans will also be more likely to participate in the administration of their government and the implementation of whatever policies are adopted. Exactly what policies this new process will ultimately produce will be determined by the nature of the events that trigger America's next realignment and the influence of the Millennial Generation on the solutions that are designed to deal with the consequences.

CHAPTER 15

Public Policy in a Millennial Era

As the challenges facing America evolve, the rhythm of generational cycles, reinforced by technological change, generates new ideas on how government should respond. Dissatisfaction with the status quo rises to the point where the public demands a wholesale restructuring of governmental institutions only about once every eight decades, or every "fourth turning," to use Strauss and Howe's terminology. But other aspects of public policy require more frequent fine-tuning to bring them in line with the public's changing attitudes and beliefs. As Millennials assert their primary electoral role over the next twenty years, the center of America's public policy debate will shift off its current liberal/conservative, Baby Boomer–dominated axis to focus on finding new ways to balance national purpose with individual involvement and decision making.

The fundamental question in American public policy is almost always about where to draw the line, or, more accurately, redraw the line, between the competing values of individual liberty and community and between the desire for both national order and local flexibility. While idealist eras are more concerned with the first tension, civic-era debates tend to focus on the latter. As a result, the expansion and contraction of policies favoring either personal liberty or community coherence have moved in harmony with the dynamics of generational change.

These same tensions will frame the debate over acceptable solutions to our country's problems in the Millennial civic era we are now entering. Old debates over social issues will fade into the background, and new questions about America's social unity and global competitiveness will move to the forefront. Proposals that are able to synthesize the two competing claims of national priorities and individual flexibility will become the preferred answers to the challenges America will face in the next two decades.

WHERE WE STAND DEPENDS ON
WHERE WE SIT IN HISTORY

The tension between individual liberty and community cohesion has been part of America's political debate since the discovery of the New World. When the ideologically driven Pilgrims landed in the New World to escape religious persecution, they established a community with clear rules about what would be considered acceptable personal behavior, with draconian consequences for those who didn't obey. In our most recent idealist political era, Republicans argued consistently for expanding personal liberty in the economic sphere and restricting individual freedom in one's private life, while Democrats tended to argue from exactly the opposite point of view. Republicans asserted the importance of individual initiative in growing the economy, while Democrats denounced the resulting lack of economic equality and social justice. The outcome was either deadlock in our public policy debate that postponed doing anything about most major problems, or solutions so weakened by the nature of the compromises that they accomplished little in the long run.

The second enduring tension in the country's policy debates has been over where to draw the line between individual and states' rights, on the one hand, and the safety and security of our public spaces on the other. In the civic era that followed the American Revolution, the Constitutional Convention was convened in part to strengthen the federal government's ability to impose order on its citizens and thus to counter the chaos that followed the adoption of the Articles of Confederation. The resulting document produced a brilliant system of checks and balances to protect against the possibility of autocratic imposition of too much order by an unconstrained executive. But its adoption was only secured with a promise that the Congress would approve amendments providing strong protections for individual rights as its first order of business. Echoes of that same debate are heard today in arguments over provisions of the Patriot Act that attempt to draw the line between individual privacy and the need to ferret out those among us who might be plotting the next terrorist attack. The events of 9/11 not only heralded the beginning of a new civic era, they also secured both the passage and the reenactment of the security provisions of the Patriot Act—an outcome that satisfied most of the public, if not partisans on both sides of the issue.

Exactly where the United States decides to draw the line along these two fundamental continuums over the next few decades will be heavily influenced by the nature of the challenges the country faces. When the nation's security is threatened by a foreign power, the focus of political debate shifts to the structural changes needed to preserve the union. Attempts to assert the primacy of individual rights, or even the importance of state's rights, are quickly put down by a rising chorus from a new civic generation. When times are good the country feels free to indulge itself in debates over moral or social issues, egged on by the rising power of an idealist generation. But when the crisis is economic in nature, the reaction falls midway between these extremes. In hard times, policy debates focus on the right division of roles and responsibilities between government and individuals in achieving a return to economic prosperity.

The 2007 Senate debate on immigration reform reflected this dynamic. As lingering concerns from 9/11 continued to shift the nation's mood out of an idealist era into a civic era, issues of order and community assumed a primary role in the debate, despite the pleas from immigrant right's groups to focus the discussion on the plights of families impacted by the proposal. Republicans, egged on by talk radio, demanded that even tougher requirements, designed to ensure the security of our borders and the integrity of employers' hiring practices, be added to the bill before they would even consider a more Millennialist, inclusive approach to the problem. The second priority of the proposal was to address the economic consequences of immigration. In determining who would be allowed to enter the United States in the future, the grand bargain on immigration between conservative Republican and liberal Democratic senators placed the highest priority on the skills and potential economic contributions of immigrants. This represented a major departure from prior immigration reform efforts, which tended to focus on the idealistic notion of reuniting families of those who had already entered the country. While Democratic proponents of the bill also attempted to address the issues of individual liberty and local flexibility for those already here illegally, their efforts came to naught. Despite the support of two-thirds of Americans of every political persuasion for the overall approach, the fissures within each party's caucus exposed by this issue demonstrated just how difficult it will be to devise acceptable, civic-era solutions in a Congress still motivated to pursue ideological agendas from an idealist era (Hook 2007).

As the newest civic realignment evolves, the center of America's public policy debate will continue to shift away from an emphasis on individual rights and public morality toward a search for solutions that benefit the entire community in as equitable and orderly a way as possible. Majorities will coalesce around ideas that involve the entire group in the solution and downplay the right of individuals to opt out of the process.

A MILLENNIAL ERA PUBLIC POLICY AGENDA

Millennials will demand fundamental changes in America's health care and educational systems as the first step in restoring America's economic competitiveness with the rest of the world and in enhancing economic equality in the country. These new programs will simultaneously devolve decision making to individual citizens and connect the work of each local community to accomplish national goals. This decentralized, integrated approach is neither traditionally liberal nor conservative in its conception. Instead, Millennialist public policy is focused on results, eschewing ideology for pragmatic leadership. As Yoda taught Luke Skywalker, "Try not. Do. Or do not. There is no try" (Lucas and Brackett 1980).

Economic theories that attempt to justify today's level of income inequality as a natural result of individual entrepreneurialism and education will be discarded in favor of more collectivist approaches. On economic policy, "restoring a decent sense of proportion, reviving a sense of community in the workplace, and strengthening the middle class (which they perceive as weak and endangered) will be the lifelong agenda for this generation" (Strauss and Howe 2007, 168).

When faced with a choice between exuberant economic growth and the preservation of the environment for future generations, Millennials will choose environmentalism every time. A unilateralist approach on global warming, as with any other foreign policy issue, does not appeal to Millennials, who have been taught to "play nice" since they were toddlers. They will want the United States to get involved in processes that include as many countries as possible in finding an answer that benefits the entire world. Solutions that synthesize this new emphasis on the importance of the larger community with processes that involve everyone in achieving the goal will find the most favor with the public in a Millennial civic era.

As a result, the best ideas for dealing with our nation's problems will spring initially from bipartisan, or even "post-partisan," coalitions that reflect the end of an idealist era and the beginning of a more civic-era political orientation. Later, whichever party best adapts to the new political era will become the primary source of innovative public policy. Elements of these new solutions, which are producing better outcomes at a lower cost, are already visible at the leading edge of a new civic era. Each success provides a preview of the changes all of America will experience in the coming decades.

MILLENNIALS ARE UP TO THEIR INTERNET EYEBALLS IN DEBT

Individual Millennials are fairly confident about how they will personally fare in the future, especially with regard to economic concerns, such as having a fulfilling career (46%), holding good jobs (43%), being financially well-off (39%), having a sufficiently high-quality education (51%), being able to afford a home (40%), having access to health care (36%), and retiring comfortably (36%) (Frank N. Magid Associates, January 2006). The facts, however, suggest that it will take all of their optimism and more to overcome the economic hardships that await them. Indeed, the high costs of housing, health care, and education has led many to speculate that this generation may well see its standard of living decline from that of its parents. Whether that prediction comes true or not, there is no question that the unwillingness of those currently in power to invest in the infrastructure needed to preserve the country's economic competitiveness will saddle Millennials, individually and collectively, with large financial obligations throughout their lifetimes.

The size and scale of the debt that Baby Boomers will leave to future generations of Americans is unprecedented. It is so large that the administrations of both Boomer presidents have shied away from publishing the actual numbers. Gene Sperling, Bill Clinton's chief economic advisor, took the calculations out of an appendix to the 1994 budget document, and John Snow, as soon as he replaced Paul O'Neill as George W. Bush's secretary of the treasury, did the same thing ten years later. While he was secretary, O'Neill had the Treasury Department calculate the difference between the government's future income and expenditures over the expected lifetime of those alive today, assuming no changes in net tax rates in the future. The resulting "fiscal gap" was calculated at $45 trillion, or $51 trillion if the costs of the new Medicare drug benefit were factored in. Since then, the number has grown to $66 trillion (Kotlikoff and Burns 2005).

The numbers appeared in draft editions of Bush's 2004 budget message to Congress but were removed before the official document was printed. To pay off this amount by the time the Millennial Generation ends its economic life would theoretically require a doubling of today's federal income tax rates. Of course, there is no reason why all of America's debts must be paid by any particular deadline, and no such policy is likely to be advocated by any politician. But there is no question that tax rates and taxable receipts will have to go higher as the country's debts become too large to manage otherwise during the next two decades.

As in past civic eras, the tax increases that are adopted will be designed to reduce economic inequality by asking those most able to pay to contribute the most. With today's economic wealth skewed to older generations, future tax policy may well represent an intergenerational conflict between Millennials and Boomers, with Gen-Xers, as always, caught in the middle.

President Bush's recent venture to reform or privatize Social Security, depending on one's point of view, was the opening round of this attempt to achieve some kind of fiscal reckoning. Millennials listened to the debate over Social Security's future in the 2004 presidential election and concluded that they shouldn't count on receiving today's level of benefits when they retire. While a majority of Americans supported leaving Social Security as it is currently designed, Millennials favored changing the system to allow individual investments in the stock market, even at the risk of losing some of their money, by a 52 percent to 39 percent margin. Indeed, 70 percent of young people surveyed after the election were concerned that Social Security would not provide them the benefits they would need upon retirement—and 63 percent were equally concerned about the benefits their parents would receive (Harvard Institute of Politics 2005).

Despite those beliefs, Boomer and Silent Generation concerns about the reliability of future streams of retirement income, amplified by the lobbying efforts of the AARP and its union allies, won this first fiscal intergenerational battle. Over time, such victories will become harder and harder for older generations to achieve.

To Our Good Health

The next fiscal fights are likely to be over Medicaid, the government health care system for the indigent, and Medicare, the nation's health care system for those over sixty-five years of age. As Barry Bosworth, among other analysts of America's fiscal policy, pointed out, "The focus has been on Social Security reform when in fact the problems with Social Security are pretty minor. . . . Either you have to cut benefits or increase taxes. . . . The real problem with aging costs is in health care, where the cost increases are much larger" (Kamenetz 2006, 174).

Health care premiums have gone up 73 percent since 2000, and total spending on health care in the United States is projected to reach 20 percent of the nation's gross domestic product (GDP) as early as 2015 (Furman 2006). Government pays 45 percent of the nation's health care bill. Medicare cost $278 billion in 2003, ten times more than in 1970, even after adjusting for inflation. Today, that cost represents 2.6 percent of the nation's GDP and it is projected to rise to 4.7 percent by 2030. The Congressional Budget Office (CBO) estimates that, with the added cost of the recently enacted drug benefit for seniors, spending on Medicare per beneficiary will grow 57 percent by 2014. Projecting out to the end of this civic era, the CBO predicts health care costs for Medicare and Medicaid will rise to 22 percent of GDP by 2050. Since the *total* expenditures by the federal government have only exceeded 20 percent of GDP once in the last fifty years, the rising cost of health care is clearly unsustainable in the long run (Osborne and Hutchinson 2004; Kotlikoff and Burns 2005).

These statistics make it clear that our nation's health care system is badly in need of reforms that will lower its overall cost without jeopardizing the quality of care that Americans choose to pay for. A system that provides coverage based on an individual's employment status is badly out of sync with the country's need to indulge Millennials' proclivity for trying multiple jobs before finding one that fully engages their talents. Furthermore, a system that provides tax benefits to those lucky enough to have jobs with health care benefits, while denying tax advantages to the more vulnerable participants in the labor market, will offend Millennials' sense of equity and fairness. The answers to these problems will not be found by making the government the sole payer of our health care bill, as much as liberal Baby Boomers may continue to dream of instituting such a system. Nor is the answer to be found in health savings accounts and other forms of individual initiative favored by conservatives. Instead, Millennialist health care reforms will focus on government policies that blend the power of individual learning and responsibility with national requirements and priorities.

Millennials' penchant for looking out for the well-being of the group and treating everyone equally will focus the first round of health care reform on the problem of the uninsured. Each 2008 Democratic presidential candidate has felt obligated to present their version of a comprehensive plan to address this problem, even though only about 15 percent of Americans lack such coverage in any given time period. But it's a very real problem for Millennials, 30 percent of whom are without coverage (Kamenetz 2006).

Despite his reticence to raise the subject, the outline of a civic-era answer to this problem can be found in the bipartisan solution adopted by the commonwealth of Massachusetts with the support of its former governor, GOP presidential candidate Mitt Romney. That plan contains a requirement that every individual buy health insurance, just as every driver is required by their state government to have liability insurance for the car they own. It also provides a state subsidy for those who can't afford insurance, a concept endorsed by 61 percent of Millennials (Harvard University Institute of Politics 2007). Democratic presidential candidate John Edwards incorporated the very same idea in his health care proposal, as did California's Republican governor, Arnold Schwarzenegger. Not surprisingly, it is also the option most likely to satisfy Millennials' orientation toward community and shared responsibility. Once in place, this reform will set off a natural chain of events leading to the resolution of the larger problem of the cost of health care in America.

A critical consequence of an individual health care insurance mandate is the creation of the largest possible pool of people for insurance companies to cover. In actuarial terms, this maximum-size pool leads to a decrease in the cost per person for providing such coverage, which is the next step in lowering the overall cost. Millennials' yearly health care costs average $1,800 per person, compared to $5,000 for the average Boomer. An individual mandate would bring those lower costs into the pool, instead of one-third of Millennials contributing nothing to the risk calculations of insurance companies (Kamenetz 2006).

Furthermore, an "individual responsibility" reform will have to expand the Health Insurance Portability and Accountability Act's (HIPAA) prohibition on insurance companies' use of an individual's pre-existing condition to determine insurability. This often-abused business practice will have to be completely prohibited once everyone is required to carry insurance. Eliminating that pernicious behavior will, in turn, blow up the obstacle to information exchange that HIPAA's rules on the sharing of electronic medical records created and open up a floodgate of sharing, further reducing the escalating costs of health care.

Another part of the solution to lowering the nation's health care bill is to create more knowledgeable consumers of medical care. In most markets, when cost and quality become widely known, prices tend to come down as each participant's choice informs the next decision of others. So far, this learning characteristic has been absent in the health care market, because most consumers know neither the price nor the quality of the treatments they receive. Experiments with systems designed to remedy the problem have shown dramatic results. Health Dialog, a Boston-based company devoted to the idea of what it calls "collaborative care," provides its members with a full briefing on the complexities of any medical decision an individual must make. Its CEO, George Bennett, asserts that based on his company's experience, shared decision making could cut Medicare costs by 30 percent, or roughly $11.7 trillion, and simultaneously increase patient satisfaction (Kotlikoff and Burns 2005).

Already, large employers and major health care insurers are banding together to find ways to share this type of information with their employees or clients. However, to be truly effective, such databases will need to know as much as possible about health outcomes for every American, which will require congressional action. Legislation to establish a legal and technical framework for an online records system that would guarantee medical care providers access to patient files has been introduced in both houses of Congress with bipartisan support.

The next step will be to extend the ability to share medical information to the community at large, with each individual's permission, of course. Even today, web sites that enable individuals to share their medical histories and swap information on treatment alternatives and costs are among the most popular Internet destinations. In the future, widgets will encapsulate authoritative health care applications on treatments, costs, and outcomes that can be accessed and distributed online. Soon, people will use social networking technology to share their problems with fellow sufferers, compare doctors and treatments, and seek out medical solutions that most appeal to them.

These comprehensive health care information databases that promise to reduce the cost of health care will be favored, rather than feared, when Millennials bring their unique sense of privacy to the discussion. Most Millennials try not to reveal embarrassing personal facts to their peers, despite the generation's reputation for exhibitionism (Strauss and Howe 2007). Sixty-nine percent of today's 18- to 24-year-olds believe people should be concerned that personal information posted on their social networking profiles might "come back to haunt them sometime in the future" (Harvard University Institute 2007). At the same time, Millennials are happy to share information about themselves that they think might help others. Medical databases that identify best practices and the lowest prices for a wide range of treatments without revealing personal medical histories provide just the right blend of privacy protection and community benefit for Millennials to feel comfortable sharing the real cost and quality of health care treatments with their friends.

The Rand Corporation estimated that a fully implemented national health care database could save the country $346 billion a year in administrative costs—a significant share of the nation's annual $2 trillion health care bill (Alonso-Zaldivar 2006). The savings that flow from these efforts will be used by Millennial-influenced governments to create a new U.S. health care system that will provide more universality in health care insurance and greater equity of treatment. One way or the other, Millennials will seek to find ways to creatively avoid intergenerational conflict by taking care of the needs of everyone in the community—their aging parents and grandparents and the children of the next generation.

EDUCATION FOR ALL, ALL FOR EDUCATION

However, the problems of financing the nation's health care bill is less of an immediate concern to individual Millennials than the problem of paying off their personal debts from the cost of higher education, which has been rising faster than inflation for the last thirty years. As Anya Kamenetz, author of *Generation Debt,* points out, "An astonishing 44 percent of dependent students from families making over $100,000 a year borrowed money for school in 2002. Credit card debt is higher for the middle class than for the poor" (7). In the last decade, the annual volume of federal student loans has tripled to $85 billion. Two-thirds of four-year college graduates have not paid off those loans, with an average individual debt load of about $23,000 in 2004 (18).

Compounding the problem is the failure of our nation's high schools, particularly those in urban America, to graduate the number of students needed to generate economic growth at a rate anywhere near enough to pay off all these debts. Nationwide, only 38 percent of high school freshmen eventually enroll in college and, due in part to its high cost, only 18 percent graduate within 150 percent of the allotted time to earn a degree. Only 29 percent of African Americans and just 10 percent of Hispanic Americans earn a baccalaureate degree by age twenty-nine. Between 50 and 60 percent of ninth graders in many urban school districts drop out before earning a high school diploma (Kazis, Vargas, and Hoffman 2004).

Before Millennials could even talk, the value of an education, from preschool through college, has been drilled into them by their parents. "Over seven in ten of today's high school students say they are aiming for a four-year college degree, and at least that share of all races and ethnicities agree that a college degree confers 'respect'" (Strauss and Howe 2007, 211). Unfortunately, Millennials' parents and grandparents have not maintained the investments in America's public schools needed to achieve that outcome. The result is a dangerous decline in the ability of an urban high school to produce its most important product—a senior who has the skills and knowledge needed to go on to college. Only half of today's high school graduates are prepared for college-level work (Kamenetz 2006). And those graduates who are able to enroll in college discover that the cost of such an education continues to grow beyond their abilities to pay for it.

Unlike health care policy, the solution to large drop-out rates in our public high schools, as well as the poor quality of education students receive there, will not be found by listening to today's political debate. Calls for higher standards and curriculum reform are well meaning but miss the importance of the individual student's motivation and the broader culture that is so crucial in determining a student's success. Charter schools and other attempts to decentralize the administration of the educational experience are a logical response to these cultural challenges, but too many deal only with the freedom of administrators to explore new ideas and don't provide that same freedom to their students. Meanwhile, many urban school systems have been turned over to the local mayor in order to provide accountability for improving schools through the political process. The results from these reforms in school governance haven't produced outcomes that are significantly better for the students involved, despite endless rounds of curriculum reform and testing.

But urban high schools that produce educated seniors ready to tackle college do exist. One of the most successful models was created by Dennis Littky and Eliot Washor in Providence, Rhode Island. Their Metropolitan Regional Career and Technical Center (MET) program delivers the same outcomes for urban youth that affluent suburban schools provide to their students. Without lowering academic standards, MET schools have reshaped the rituals and routines of traditional public high schools in order to build the level of "identity and aspiration" each student needs to succeed. The model works because its decentralized approach integrates all three components of student achievement—academics, personal motivation, and the confidence and skills to navigate the cultures of college and the private sector where economic opportunity awaits them—into one child-centered effort (Ross and Plastrik 2007).

Just as social networks succeed by enabling users to generate the content they are most interested in consuming, the MET program starts by finding the subject matter each student is most interested in learning. Then it builds an individualized learning plan for what each student must know to earn a diploma and get accepted to college. A group of about sixteen students, called a student advisory, stays together throughout four years of high school with one teacher-advisor, who takes ultimate responsibility for each member of the group's academic and social success. Advisories are combined into a community of no more than 130 students so that the level of adult supervision prevents any child from slipping between the cracks. To build both motivation and an understanding of the real world that awaits them, students regularly leave school to participate in unpaid internships that last anywhere from eight weeks to a full year—producing project results that reflect both the students' interests and the basic skills they need to master for academic success (Ross and Plastrik 2007). Every element of the model addresses Millennials' preferred way of learning by actively engaging them in a continuously changing set of experiences within an environment that provides both safety and encouragement.

The model is both scaleable and portable. For instance, in 2000, Doug Ross, former assistant secretary of labor in the Clinton administration, founded a publicly funded charter school, University Preparatory Academy, in the heart of Detroit. It used the MET model to promise parents that 90 percent of its entering class of sixth graders would graduate from high school, and 90 percent of those high school graduates would then go on to college. This guarantee not only attracted a swarm of eager students but also funding from a Republican benefactor, who conditioned his gifts of a new middle and high school facility on Ross meeting those targets. No academic conditions were placed upon the selection of the school's student body, which was made up entirely of minorities, 70 percent of whom were poor enough to qualify for the federal free lunch program (Finley 2006). Seven years later, University Prep is set to graduate 94 percent of its first senior class, all of whom have been accepted into a post-secondary educational institution upon graduation (Pratt 2007b). And University Prep provides this radically different and successful educational experience at a lower cost per student than more traditional public schools—$8,300 per pupil compared to $10,300 in the Detroit Public Schools (Finley 2006).

The political reaction to this track record of success has slowly begun to change as the country moves from one era to another. In 2004, Bob Thompson, the retired Republican businessman who provided the facilities for University Prep on a $1 per year lease, offered to donate $200 million to establish fifteen other K–12 charter schools in Michigan that would make the same 90 percent/90 percent guarantee that University Prep did. After initially signaling support for the idea, the mayor of Detroit, Kwame Kilpatrick, and the governor of Michigan, Jennifer Granholm, both Democrats, backed away when the Detroit Federation of Teachers brought 3,500 people to the state capitol to protest this threat to their job security. But the Republican legislature passed the bill anyway, and it became law without the governor's support (Ross and Plastrik 2007).

By 2007, the political mood had changed. Mayor Kilpatrick issued an endorsement of his education policy transition team's recommendation to establish fifty charter schools in Detroit, even as the school district made plans to close sixty of its own facilities that no longer had a population that could or wanted to use them. The mayor gave a classic civic-era explanation for his change of heart, saying his responsibility was to all

Detroit's children, not just those in its public school system. Still, the two representatives from the Detroit Public Schools (DPS) on his transition team voted to oppose that particular recommendation. The school board president, Jimmy Womack, played the race card in his public comments: "If there is so much support for charters, why not put them in West Bloomfield [a predominantly white upper-middle-class suburb of Detroit]?" (Riley 2007). But schools in West Bloomfield were not failing their students at nearly the same rate as Detroit schools. Doug Ross could only shrug his shoulders at this continued blindness of the educational establishment: "Why is the discussion about DPS losing its monopoly? . . . What about the students?" (Pratt 2007a).

That is the same question aroused parents will be asking every politician as America demands a makeover of its educational system. By a margin of 38 percent to 29 percent, Millennials believe America's educational system would be better if parents had more freedom to choose which schools their children attended (Harvard University Institute of Politics 2007). Social networks, "mommy blogs," and other forms of peer-to-peer communications will spread the word about models that produce superior results at lower costs and provide the aggregating mechanism for a new, decentralized, parent-controlled, educational decision-making system. Armed with new information on graduation and college acceptance rates of America's high schools, parents will choose the type of education they want for their child, with the money following the child to the school they have selected, not to the school district they live in. The subsequent invigoration of our system of public education will diminish the use of more conservative approaches, such as school vouchers and home schooling, while incorporating the concepts' focus on parental control and choice. The result will be a system of public education that mirrors the egalitarian and community orientation of a Millennial civic era.

GETTING A TROPHY FOR SERVING AMERICA

The desire to provide civic generations with the opportunity to go to college has been the inspiration for reforms to our system of higher education throughout American history. In 1786, Thomas Jefferson urged his friend George Wythe to "preach, my dear Sir, a crusade against ignorance; establish and improve the law for educating the common people"

(Kamenetz 2006, 15). During the Civil War, Senator Justin Smith Morrill of Vermont successfully sponsored legislation to create land grant colleges to "promote the liberal and practical education of the industrial classes." Almost exactly eighty years later, FDR signed the Servicemen's Readjustment Act, better known as the GI Bill, which provided full tuition grants and family stipends to eight million demobilizing veterans of World War II, further broadening higher education opportunities (Kamenetz 2006). This cycle of expanding the federal government's role in providing higher education opportunities for civic generations is about to come full circle again. Over the next twenty years, the high cost of a college education, coupled with Millennials' desire to serve their community, will create the political conditions for the creation of a program of citizen service, the Millennial Generation's signature contribution to America in the twenty-first century.

The seeds of this new federal program were sown by an earlier bipartisan coalition that came together to pass the National and Community Service Trust Act of 1993. The law created three programs—Senior Corps, AmeriCorps, and Learn and Save America—each of which was designed to encourage Americans to volunteer to provide service to their community. Originally a pet project of President Clinton, the concept survived partisan attacks and ideologically driven criticism throughout an idealist era, even as the ranks of volunteers continued to swell. Between 1974 and 1989, the percentage of Americans over the age of sixteen who provided volunteer services to their communities fell from 23.6 percent to 20.4 percent. Since then, as Millennials became old enough to participate in the program, the overall percentage of volunteers rose to a high of 28.8 percent in 2005, with a slight drop to 26.7 percent recorded in 2006. Much of this rise in participation is attributed to a doubling of the percentage of volunteers in the 16–24 year old age bracket between 1989 (13.4 percent), when only individualistic Gen-Xers and no Millennials were in this cohort, and 2006 (26.4 percent), when the entire age range was made up of Millennials (Corporation for National and Community Service 2007).

This increased participation in organized volunteer programs is only a small part of Millennials' overall dedication to the idea of service to their communities. Community service was a rare experience for high school Gen-Xers in 1984, but, according to the U.S. Department of Education, participation rates have tripled since then. Over 80 percent of

Millennials performed some type of community service while in high school. Seventy percent of college-age Millennials report having recently performed some type of voluntary community service, and an astounding 85 percent consider it an effective way to solve problems facing the country. (An even higher percentage, 94 percent, considers volunteer service an effective way to deal with challenges in their local community [Harvard University Institute of Politics 2004].)

Today, proposals for some form of universal national service inevitably run up against objections from Gen-Xers who see no value in promoting the general welfare through mandatory personal sacrifice, and from religious Baby Boomers, who see it as a Trojan horse designed to have government impose a secular set of values on the nation's youth. At the same time, 80 percent of Americans support the idea that the federal government should "guarantee at least two years of college for every qualified American who wants to attend" (DLC 2006, 25). A program that links such subsidies to the performance of community service will be supported by a majority of Americans when Millennials' belief in the inherent value of giving something back to their community permeates the nation's political consciousness.

The first beneficiaries of this new program will be community colleges and universities that will need to vastly expand their physical capacities to meet the overwhelming demand for a college education from America's largest generation. While it won't happen soon enough to help Millennials escape the high cost of college, the resulting expansion in the supply of classrooms and faculty will lead to an eventual reduction in tuition costs when the drop in demand from the next, smaller generation forces each college to compete for a dwindling pool of applicants.

The impact on the cost of higher education will be only one of the benefits the country receives from this signature Millennialist initiative. Through citizen service, those young people who do not choose to serve in the military will have a chance to do meaningful work in a community. Just as real-world experiences proved to be a critical element in the success of MET high school students, the universal acquisition of these skills by future generations will help the country improve its overall economic competitiveness.

Above all, national service will create a bonding and values-reinforcing experience almost as powerful as the GI Generation's service in the

Armed Forces did three generations ago. In the same way that World War II boot camps helped to break down America's ethnic and racial silos, twenty-first century experiences of working together for a common goal will institutionalize Millennial values of family, responsibility, and diversity as "American values" for future decades. The opening scene of the enormously popular movie *The Lion King* celebrates these values, as animals of every type gather at Pride Rock to herald the birth of a future king. So, too, will Millennials tell their children and their children's children about the help they received from the government in recognition of their service to the nation (Pacheco 2000).

MILLENNIALS THINK GLOBALLY, ACT LOCALLY

Having grown up with the Internet, Millennials are more connected to the world than any other generation in our nation's history. Seventy percent of Millennials attending a four-year college program and 59 percent of all 18- to 24-year-olds have already traveled outside the United States. As a result, their attitudes on globalization, which they favor overall (37 to 20 percent), demonstrate a level of sophistication beyond what their ages might suggest. They are positive about globalization's impact on the culture and educational system of the United States, by about a 2:1 margin, but are almost evenly divided on its impact on our economy and the health and well-being of U.S. citizens. These same 18- to 24-year-olds express slightly negative opinions of globalization's impact on the environment and the political system of the United States (Harvard University Institute of Politics 2007).

Millennials bring a unique perspective to environmental and national security debates that sees the relationship of foreign policy to domestic policy concerns in ways that many politicians in the United States do not. For instance, in March 2007, 18- to 24-year-olds ranked global warming and other environmental issues among the five most important issues the nation needed to address. In fact, by a margin of 68 percent to 11 percent, those interviewed felt protecting the environment should be just as high a governmental priority as protecting jobs (Harvard University Institute of Politics 2007). Millennials favor environmental protection even at the cost of economic growth by a somewhat wider margin than any other generation (43% for Millennials vs. 40% for

Gen-Xers and 38% for Baby Boomers), hardly surprising, given the emphasis this issue received in their favorite childhood television programs, such as "Barney" and "Sesame Street" (Frank N. Magid Associates, May 2007). As a result, future presidents, who will have to wrestle with increasing demands from other countries for the United States to join the fight on global warming with tough regulations, will find enthusiastic supporters for more drastic action among this increasing force in the electorate.

Meanwhile, surveys just prior to the 2006 elections showed "the national security issue that most concerned voters was not terrorism or even Iraq—it was America's dependence on foreign oil. The country has concluded that this dependency lies at the intersection of a number of critical problems on national security, the economy and the environment" (Rosner 2006, 20). After the election, 47 percent of voters under thirty cited Republicans' failure to deal with the high cost of energy and gas prices as their top concern about GOP congressional candidates, ten points higher than any other issue. Blogs and other nontraditional media reinforced this concern by continuing to expose the connection between those who try to prevent governmental regulation to protect the environment and their company's economic stake in avoiding such restrictions. As a result, a majority of Americans now agree with the proposition that "the goal of cleaner energy and more fuel efficient cars would be achieved today if big oil and their political friends did not stand in the way" (Quinlan and Bocian 2006, 2). And 88 percent express support for proposals that would "require energy companies to invest record profits in alternative energy or pay a tax that will be used to fund alternative energy research" (DLC 2007, 25). These changing attitudes will unleash a floodgate of regulation and government intervention designed to simultaneously improve America's national security and protect the earth's atmosphere—both goals dear to a Millennial's heart.

Even as older generations fight over the right balance between government mandates, cap-and-trade market-based approaches, and voluntary efforts to prevent global warming and reduce America's consumption of foreign oil, Millennials will favor policies that mandate individual responsibility in the achievement of these national priorities. The matched pair of liberal and conservative female co-eds in PBS's 2007 documentary "Generation Next" who found common ground in creating a campus-wide recycling program would happily support rules requiring such efforts by every one of their peers. Similar support will be found among Millennials for government requirements that every household replace its incandescent light bulbs with fluorescent ones, and that all utilities use more renewable energy sources in generating electricity, even at a higher cost to the consumer. Using individually generated power to "get off the grid," buying more fuel efficient cars, purchasing "C" products that are certified as using less of carbon resources, and telecommuting rather than driving to work are all best-effort behaviors that Millennials will want rewarded with tax breaks and other incentives.

Because of the generational-defining events of 9/11 and the intra-generational killings at Columbine High School and Virginia Tech, Millennials are especially concerned over issues of safety and security. But, once again, their attitudes on this issue do not fall neatly into categories, such as "hawk" or "dove," used to characterize Boomers' or Gen-Xers' political attitudes. Among Millennials surveyed in 2007, 24 percent cited the war in Iraq as the most important foreign policy issue, followed by 17 percent who wanted the United States to first deal with the genocide in Darfur, Sudan. Only 6 percent named the war on terror as their highest-priority global concern. But, reflecting the anxiety of their times, 40 percent of those surveyed felt followers of Islam were more prone to violence than believers in other religions, and almost half were unsure of the loyalty of Muslims living in the United States (Harvard University Institute of Politics 2007). Furthermore, Millennials are the generation least perturbed by any potential restrictions on civil rights or invasions of privacy that might have occurred in fighting the war on terrorism (Strauss and Howe 2007). Having grown up in an age of amber alerts, tough airport screening procedures, and the use of metal detectors at school entrances, Millennials are willing to put up with restrictions on individual liberties in exchange for a greater feeling of personal safety.

At the same time, Millennials are interested in a multilateral, reasoned approach in dealing with the nation's enemies, rather than a more unilateral, militaristic strategy. By a 3:1 margin, they believe the United States should let other countries and the United Nations take the lead in solving international crises. While a slim majority agreed that the United States should take unilateral action to stop Iran's development of nuclear weapons, less than 4 percent are in favor of using unilateral economic sanctions or military force to stop the genocide in Darfur. Even though 39 percent of 18- to 24-year-olds surveyed felt the United States was not doing enough about this problem, their preferred solution (34 percent) was to have the United States continue to work through the United Nations.

By a 61 percent to 13 percent margin, Millennials believe it is important for the United States to be respected in the world, and most feel that goal can best be achieved through moral leadership, not military force. Only 14 percent are in favor of the U.S. incurring significant military casualties in order to spread democracy and freedom, and 64 percent disagree with this neo-conservative approach to dealing with global challenges (Harvard University Institute of Politics 2007). Instead, Millennials bring to the world's stage their strong beliefs in the importance of working things out in ways that take into account the needs of each member of the group.

THE WORLD IS FLAT—DEAL WITH IT

Despite the political outcry in the 2006 election over the impact of free trade on domestic jobs, Millennials are more likely to favor government policies that help individuals cope with the impact of globalization on their personal economic well-being than ones designed to try to halt what they see as the inevitable integration of an increasingly flat world.

Wage insurance is a leading-edge example of this type of program. Workers over fifty years old who have been displaced by the rapid changes in manufacturing due to technological innovation and globalization are paid half the difference between their new and old salaries for two years. By subsidizing lower wages associated with the first job displaced workers can find, the program has been shown to boost workers' long-term earnings while cutting the average length of unemployment by 4.4 percent. A bipartisan coalition in the Senate, led by Montana Democrat Max Baucus and Minnesota Republican Norm Coleman, wants to expand coverage to everyone over forty years old and include those in the service industry, not just manufacturing (Hennessy-Fiske 2007). Republicans in the House have so far tended to follow President Bush's lead in actually trying to cut the modest efforts already in the law, based upon continued adherence to an idealist-era, free-market ideology. But that opposition will soon crumble as Millennial attitudes make wage insurance, or "Income Security," as common a feature of America's socioeconomic landscape as unemployment insurance and Social Security became in our last civic era.

A second, more radical proposal, likely to gain favor as more and more Millennials face the realities of tomorrow's workplace, is designed to change America's educational system so that it trains young people for jobs that are the hardest to ship overseas. As former Federal Reserve vice-chairman Alan Blinder points out, "It isn't how many years one spends in school that will matter [for future economic success], it's choosing to learn the skills for jobs that cannot easily be delivered electronically from afar" (Wessel and Davis 2007). Blinder estimates that 30 to 40 million American jobs could be outsourced to people not living in the United States using the same information technology that makes social networking so popular. He suggests that when the full impact of this economic transformation is felt ten to twenty years from now, the resulting outcry from highly educated, politically involved people will make such an educational system makeover inevitable.

Whether it's education or health care, energy policy or the environment, the way democracy functions or how we approach the world, no part of government will be untouched by the changes Millennial beliefs will bring to our public policy debate. The tectonic plates undergirding America's current political landscape are beginning to shift. The resulting cataclysm will wash away the current politics of polarization and ideological deadlock, putting in place a new landscape of collective purpose and national consensus that involves individuals and communities in solving the nation's problems. While such an outcome is hard to imagine before the shift actually occurs, especially for the inherently divided, pessimistic, and cynical generations now in positions of power, the evidence of the desire for such a change among much of the American public, especially Millennials, is clear. The battle lines between those locked in the dogmas of the past and those ready to present something new to the American public are already forming. Because of the sheer size of the Millennial Generation and its greater facility with new information and communication technologies, their attitudes and beliefs will overwhelm defenders of the status quo and reshape American politics for decades to come.

References

Abcarian, R., and J. Horn. 2006. "Underwhelmed by It All." *Los Angeles Times*. August 7.

Alonso-Zaldivar, R. 2006. "Bill Seeks National Medical Records System." *Los Angeles Times*. August 13.

Andersen, K. 2007. "1848: When America Came of Age." *Time*. March 28.

Anderson, C. 2006. *The Long Tail*. New York: Hyperion.

Armstrong, J., and M. M. Zúniga. 2006. *Crashing the Gate: Netroots, Grassroots, and the Rise of People-powered Politics*. White River Junction, Vt.: Chelsea Green Publishing.

Athavaley, A. 2007. "A Job Interview You Don't Have to Show Up For: Microsoft, Verizon, Others Use Virtual Worlds to Recruit; Dressing Avatars for Success." *Wall Street Journal*. June 20.

Atkinson, R. D. 2005. *The Past and Future of America's Economy: Long Waves of Innovation That Drive Cycles of Growth*. [Northampton, Mass.]: Edward Elgar.

Babaloo [pseud.]. 2007. "CA-11: McNerney Activist Falls on Hard Times." *Daily Kos*. http://www.dailykos.com/story/2007/4/9/193456/8587. Accessed July 10, 2007.

Baender, P. 1992. *A Hero Perched: The Diary and Selected Letters of Nile Kinnick*. Iowa City: University of Iowa Press.

Balz, D., C. Cillizza, and J. A. Vargas. 2007. "Tommy Thompson Opens GOP Bid." *Washington Post*. April 4.

Barabak, M. Z. 2006. "Campaign '08 Preview: Podcasting Politicians." *Los Angeles Times*. July 21.

"BarackObama.com Most Popular among Younger and African-American Audiences; Hillary Clinton Attracts Visitors from Higher-Income Households." 2007. Comscore news release. http://www.comscore.com/press/release.asp?press=1363. Accessed July 10, 2007.

Barone, M. 2007. "Red Nation, Blue Nation." *Real Clear Politics*. http://www.realclearpolitics.com/articles/2007/06/red_nation_blue_nation.html. June 11. Accessed July 10, 2007.

Bendavid, N. 2007. *The Thumpin': How Rahm Emanuel and the Democrats Learned to Be Ruthless and Ended the Republican Revolution*. New York: Doubleday.

Berman, J. 2007. "The Future of Digital Content." Speech delivered at the Center for Telecom Management Executive Round Table, University of Southern California, Los Angeles. March 8.

Black, C. 2003. *Franklin Delano Roosevelt: Champion of Freedom*. Cambridge, Mass.: Perseus Books.

Bluey, R. 2007. "Online Fundraising Advantage: Dems." Townhall.com. http://www.townhall.com/columnists/RobertBluey/2007/04/07/online_fundraising_advantage_dems. April 7. Accessed July 10, 2007.

Blume, H. 2006. "Online Q and A with Jaron Lanier." *Boston Globe.* June 25.

Booth, J. 2007. "Bobby." *Scholars and Rogues.* http://www.rawstory.com/showoutarticle.php?src=http%3A%2F%2Fscholarsandrogues.wordpress.com%2F2007%2F06%2F05%2Fbobby%2F. June 5. Accessed July 10, 2007.

Bowers, C. 2007. "Edwards and Obama: A MyDD-Dailykos Generation Gap?" *MyDD.* http://www.mydd.com/story/2007/3/16/51430/5162. May 16. Accessed July 10, 2007.

Britt-Gibson, J. 2007. "What's Wrong with This Picture?" *Washington Post.* March 19.

Brooks, D. 2007. "Grim Old Party." *New York Times.* April 28.

Buckley, W. F. 2007. "Iraq Threatens GOP Future." *New York Sun.* April 30.

Buffa, D. W., and M. A. Winograd. 1996. *Taking Control: Politics in the Information Age.* New York: Holt.

Bulkely, W. M. 2007. "Playing Well with Others: How IBM's Employees Have Taken Social Networking to an Unusual Level." *Wall Street Journal.* June 18.

Burnham, W. D. 1970. *Critical Elections and the Mainsprings of American Politics.* New York: Norton.

Campbell, A., P. E. Converse, W. E. Miller, and D. E. Stokes. 1960. *American Voter.* New York: Wiley.

———. 1966. *Elections and the Political Order.* New York: Wiley.

Cannon, C. M. 2007. "Generation 'We'—the Awakened Giant." *National Journal Group* 39, no. 10 (March 9): 20.

Center for the Study of the American Electorate. 2006. "Bush, Iraq Propel Modest Turnout Increase Ending 12 Year Republican Revolution: Dems Higher Than GOP for the First Time Since 1990." Washington, D.C.: American University.

Chait, J. 2007. "How the Netroots Became the Most Important Mass Movement in U.S. Politics: The Left's New Machine." *New Republic.* May 1.

Charnwood, G. R. B. 1996. *Abraham Lincoln.* Lanham, Md.: Madison Books.

Cherny, R. W. 1994. *A Righteous Cause.* Norman: University of Oklahoma Press.

Cillizza, C. 2007. "Romney's Data Cruncher." *Washington Post.* July 5.

Clift, E. 2007. "Here's the Formula for Victory in '08." *Newsweek.* May 18.

Cole, J. 2004. "Now Is the Time to Start Studying the Internet Age." *Digital Future Report: Surveying the Digital Future, Year 4.* 99–100. http://www.digitalcenter.org/downloads/DigitalFutureReport-Year4-2004.pdf. Accessed July 10, 2007.

Committee for the Study of the American Electorate. 2005. "Turnout Exceeds Optimistic Predictions: More Than 122 Million Vote." http://www.third?-way.com/press/release/9. January 14. Accessed July 10, 2007.

Corporation for National and Community Service. Office of Research and Policy Development. "Volunteering in America: 2007 State Trends and Rankings in Civic Life." April. http://www.nationalservice.gov/about/role_impact/performance_research.asp#VIA. Accessed July 10, 2007.

Cresscourt, J. 2007. "The Fourth Turning, Part II—Rise of the Anti-Boomers: Millennial Generation 1, Imus 0." *Yahoo Finance Groups.* http://finance.groups.yahoo.com/group/gang8/message/11565. May 11. Accessed July 10, 2007.

Croly, H. 1912. *Marcus Alonzo Hanna, His Life and Work.* New York: Macmillan.

Cunningham, C. 2007. "Millennials and the Media." Presentation given at the University of California at Los Angeles. April 18.

Dallek, R. 1996. *Hail to the Chief: The Making and Unmaking of American Presidents.* New York: Hyperion.

Davis, K. S. 1985. *FDR: The New York Years, 1928–1933.* New York: Random House.

Delaney, K. J., and M. Karnitschnig. 2007. "Viacom v. Google Could Shape Digital Future." *Wall Street Journal.* March 14.

Deutschman, A. 2007. "Why Is This Man Smiling?" *Fast Company.* April.

DeVries, W. P., and L. Tarrance. 1972. *The Ticket Splitter: A New Force in American Politics.* Grand Rapids, Mich.: W. E. Erdemans.

Dickey, J., and J. Sullivan. 2007. "Generational Shift in Media Habits." *Mediaweek.* http://www.mediaweek.com/mw/departments/columns/article_display.jsp?vnu_content_id=1003544293. February 12. Accessed July 10, 2007.

Dickinson, T. 2007. "The Enemy Within." *Rolling Stone.* http://www.rollingstone.com/politics/story/13883484/national_affairs_the_enemy_within. March 20. Accessed July 10, 2007.

DLC. 2006. "Voter Attitudes on Globalization." *Blueprint Magazine* 2006, no. 5.

Dreazen, Y. 2006. "Democrats, Playing Catch-up, Tap Database to Woo Potential Voters; Copernicus Crunches the Numbers." *Wall Street Journal.* November 2.

Edsall, T. B. 2006. "Democrat's Data Mining Stirs an Intraparty Battle." *Washington Post.* March 8.

Fineman, H. 2007. "GOP Runs Far from President Bush." *Newsweek.* May 15.

Finley, N. 2006. "University Prep Gives Michigan a Model for School Success." *Detroit News.* January 1.

Fox, J. 2003. "What Does This Mean for Politics in California and the Nation?" Talk delivered at the Post Mortem Conference on the California Recall, University of Southern California, Los Angeles. November 14.

Furman, J. 2006. "Our Unhealthy Tax Code." *Democracy: A Journal of Ideas* 1 (Summer): 45–56.

Galston, W. A., and E. C. Kamarck. 2005. "Third Way Releases Groundbreaking Report: The Politics of Polarization." http://www.third-way.com/press/release/9. October 6. Accessed July 10, 2007.

"Generation Next." 2007. PBS broadcast. January 7.

Goldstein, P. 2007. "Network Fear: The Net as Copilot." *Los Angeles Times.* March 27.

Gomes, L. 2006. "Will All of Us Get Our 15 Minutes on YouTube Video?" *Wall Street Journal.* August 30.

Graf, J., and C. Darr. 2005. "Political Influentials Online in the 2004 Presidential Election." Institute for Politics, Democracy, and the Internet, Graduate School of Political Management, George Washington University, Washington, D.C. http://www.ipdi.org/UploadedFiles/influentials_in_2004.pdf. February 5. Accessed July 10, 2007.

"Greatest Shows of All Times: The Ultimate List of the Best 50 TV series (Just Try to Guess What's No. 1!)." 2002. *TV Guide.* May 4–10.

Greenberg Quinlan Rosner Research. 2005. "The Democrats, Moment to Engage." http://www.democracycorps.com/reports/index.html. June. Accessed July 10, 2007.

————. 2006. "The Meltdown Election: Report on the 2006 Post-election Surveys." http://www.democracycorps.com/reports/analyses/Democracy_ Corps_ November_15_2006_DC-GQR_Memo.pdf. November 15. Accessed July 10, 2007.

Greenberg, S., J. Carville, and A. Ipararraguirre. 2007. "The New Partisan Landscape: Republicans versus the Rest of America." Greenberg Quinlan Rosner Research. http://www.greenbergresearch.com/index.php?ID=1933. April 12. Accessed July 10, 2007.

Greenstein, F. I. 2000. *The Presidential Difference: Leadership Style from FDR to Clinton.* New York: Free Press.

Hart, G. 2007. "What It Means to Be Secure." *Huffington Post.* http:// www.huffingtonpost.com/gary-hart/what-it-means-to-be-secur_ b_49455.html. March 28. Accessed July 10, 2007.

Harvard University Institute of Politics. 2005. "Spring 2005 Top Line Data." http://www.iop.harvard.edu/research_polling.html. Accessed July 10, 2007.

————. 2007. "The 12th Biannual Youth Survey on Politics and Public Service." http://www.iop.harvard.edu/pdfs/survey_s2007_topline.pdf. April 17. Accessed July 10, 2007.

Harwood, J. 2007. "Washington Wire: A Weekly Report from The Wall Street Journal's Capital Bureau." *Wall Street Journal.* June 22.

Healey, J. 2003. "Apple's Online Music Store Sells 25 Million Downloads." *Los Angeles Times.* December 16.

Hennessy-Fiske, M. 2007. "Aid Plan for Unemployed Gains Support." *Los Angeles Times.* April 9.

Hook, J. 2007. "Large Majority Supports Giving Path to Citizenship." *Los Angeles Times.* June 13.

Huffstutter, P. J. 2006. "Smile, Politicians! You're on YouTube." *Los Angeles Times.* September 4.

Hunt, A. R. 2007. "Republicans Shaken by Bush Presidency: Albert R. Hunt (Update 1)." *Bloomberg.com.* http://www.bloomberg.com/apps/news?pid= newsarchive&sid=aQmm_Syi7itQ. May 15. Accessed July 10, 2007.

Imbornoni, A. 2007. "Women's Rights Movement in the U.S.: Timeline of Key Events in the American Women's Rights Movement." http:// www.infoplease.com/spot/womenstimeline1.html. Accessed July 10, 2007.

Initiative and Referendum Institute. 2006. University of Southern California School of Law. "Election Results 2006." *Ballotwatch* 5 (November). http:// iandrinstitute.org/BW%202006–5%20(Election%20results-update).pdf. Accessed July 10, 2007.

Jacobson, G. 2007. "Polarized Politics and the 2004 Congressional and Presidential Elections." *Political Science Quarterly* 120:2 (Summer): 199–218.

Jamieson, K. H. 1992. *Packaging the Presidency: A History and Criticism of Presidential Campaign Advertising.* New York: Oxford University Press.

Kahn, L. S. 2003. *Results at the Edge: The Ten Rules for Government Reform.* Lanham, Md.: University Press of America.

Kamarck, E. C. 2006. "Assessing Howard Dean's Fifty State Strategy and the 2006 Midterm Elections." *Forum* 4 (3): Article 5.

Kamenetz, A. 2006. *Generation Debt: Why Now Is a Terrible Time to Be Young.* New York: Riverhead Books.

Karnitschnig, M. 2006. "Viacom Discovers Kids Don't Want Their MTV Online." *Wall Street Journal.* August 29.

Kazis, R., J. Vargas, and N. Hoffman. 2004. *Double the Numbers: Increasing Postsecondary Credentials for Underrepresented Youth.* Cambridge, Mass.: Harvard Education Press.

"KDKA, First Commercial Radio Station." 2007. IEEE Virtual Museum. http:// ieee-virtual-museum.org/collection/event.php?taid=&id=3456885&lid=1. Accessed July 10, 2007.

Keeter, S. 2006. "Election '06: 'Big Changes in Some Key Groups.'" Pew Research Center Publications. http://pewresearch.org/pubs/93/election-06-big-changes-in-some-key-groups. November 16. Accessed July 10, 2007.

Keller, E., and J. Berry. 2003. *The Influentials: One American in Ten Tells the Other Nine How to Vote, Where to Eat, and What to Buy.* New York: Free Press.

Kelly, J. 2007. "Silver Lining in GOP's Dark Cloud." *Real Clear Politics.* http://www.realclearpolitics.com/articles/2007/06/silver_lining_in_dark_cloud_ha.html. June 9. Accessed July 10, 2007.

Key, V. O. 1955. "A Theory of Critical Elections." *Journal of Politics* 17 (February): 3–18.

———. 1960. *The Responsible Electorate: Rationality in Presidential Voting, 1936–1966.* Cambridge, Mass.: Belknap Press.

Kornblut, A. E., and M. Mosk. 2007. "Obama's Campaign Takes in $25 Million." *Washington Post.* April 5.

Kotkin, J. 2006. "Presenting . . . The New Economic Map of America." *The American* (November/December): 31–36.

Kotlikoff, L., and S. Burns. 2005. *The Coming Generational Storm: What You Need to Know about America's Economic Future.* Cambridge, Mass.: MIT Press.

Ladd, E. C. 1978. *Transformations of the American Party System: Political Coalitions from the New Deal to the 1970s.* New York: Norton.

Lanier, J. 2006. "Digital Maoism: The Hazards of the New Online Collectivism." *Edge.* http://www.edge.org/3rd_culture/lanier06/lanier06_index.html. May 30. Accessed July 10, 2007.

"The Lincoln/Douglas Debates of 1858." 2002. Robert R. McCormick Tribune Foundation. http://lincoln.lib.niu.edu/lincolndouglas/. Accessed July 10, 2007.

Lipset, S. M., ed. 1978. *Emerging Coalitions in American Politics.* San Francisco: Institute for Contemporary Studies.

Lipsman, A. 2006a. "Worldwide Internet Audience Has Grown 10 Percent in Last Year, According to Comscore Networks." London: Comscore. www.comscore.com/press/release.asp?press=1242. March 6. Accessed July 10, 2007.

———. 2006b. "MySpace Leads in Number of U.S. Video Streams Viewed Online, Capturing 20 Percent Market Share; Yahoo! Ranks #1 in Number of People Streaming." Reston, Va.: Comscore. http://216.239.51.104/search?q=cache: EGcHpUYVFpoJ:www.comscore.com/press/release.asp%3Fpress%3D1015+myspace+leads+streams&hl=en&ct=clnk&cd=1&gl=us. September 27. Accessed July 10, 2007.

———. 2006c. "More Than Half of MySpace Visitors Are Now Age 35 or Older, as the Site's Demographic Composition Continues to Shift." Reston, Va.: Comscore. http://www.comscore.com/press/release.asp?press=1019. October 5. Accessed July 10, 2007.

————. 2007a. "Bolstered by Youtube.com, Google Ranks as Top U.S. Streaming Video Property in January, According to comScore Video Metrix." Reston, Va.: *Comscore*. www.comscore.com/press/release.asp?press=1264. March 21. Accessed July 10, 2007.

————. 2007b. "Barack Obama.com Most Popular among Younger and African American Audiences: Hillary Clinton.com Attracts Visitors from Higher-Income Households." Reston, Va.: Comscore. http://www.comscore.com/press/release.asp?press=1363. April 5. Accessed July 10, 2007.

Love, J. 2004. "Political Behavior and Values across the Generations: A Summary of Selected Findings." *AARP*. http://www.aarp.org/research/reference/publicopinions/aresearch-import-886.html. July. Accessed July 10, 2007.

Lubell, S. 1952. *The Future of American Politics*. New York: Harper.

Lucas, G., and G. Brackett. 1980. "The Empire Strikes Back: Ben and Grover's Star Wars Universe." http://www.benandgrover.com/scripts/ep5_ss.txt. Accessed July 10, 2007.

Manning, T., B. Fields, and C. Roberts. n.d. "The Millennial Generation: The Next Generation in College Enrollment." Charlotte, N.C.: Central Piedmont Community College Center for Applied Research. http://www.cpcc.edu/planning/studies_reports/studies_reports.htm. Accessed July 10, 2007.

Martelle, S. 2007. "Site Cedes Power to People." *Los Angeles Times*. June 18.

Matsusaka, J. G. 2004. *For the Many or the Few: The Initiative, Public Policy, and American Democracy*. Chicago: University of Chicago Press.

————. 2005a. "Direct Democracy Works." *Journal of Economic Perspectives* 19, no. 2 (Spring): 185–206.

————. 2005b. "The Eclipse of Legislatures: Direct Democracy in the 21st Century." *Journal of Public Choice* 124: 157–177.

Mayhew, D. 2002. *Electoral Realignments: A Critique of an American Genre*. New Haven: Yale University Press.

McBride, S. 2007. "Make-It-Yourself 'Star Wars.'" *Wall Street Journal*. May 24.

McGinniss, J. 1969. *The Selling of the President 1968*. New York: Trident Press.

McKinnon, J. D. 2007. "Bloomberg Move Fuels '08 Buzz." *Wall Street Journal*. June 20.

McNichol, T. 2007. "Building a Wiki World." *Business 2.0*. March.

"Meet the Press." 2007. "Rep. Luis Gutierrez (D-IL) and Pat Buchanan Debate Immigration Reform." June 24. http://www.msnbc.msn.com/id/19354560/. Accessed July 10, 2007.

Mehren, E. 2006. "Congresswoman-elect Sets Her Own Terms." *Los Angeles Times*. November 26.

Mejias, U. A. 2006. "Social Media and the Networked Public Sphere." *Ideant*. http://ideant.typepad.com/ideant/2006/07/social_media_an.html. July 20. Accessed July 10, 2007.

Menn, J. 2007. "MySpace Users May Run for Office." *Los Angeles Times*. April 25.

Mohammed, M. 2006. "Web Could Give New Voters a Choice." *Los Angeles Times*. November 5.

Morain, D. 2007. "Raising $32.5 Million, Obama Far Outpaces Rivals, Sets Record." *Los Angeles Times*. July 2.

Morgan, H. W. 2003. *William McKinley and His America*. Kent, Ohio: Kent State University Press.

Morison, S. E., H. S. Commager, and W. E. Leuchtenburg. 1977. *A Concise History of the American Republic.* New York: Oxford University Press.

Mossberg, W., and K. Swisher. 2007. "Mastering a New Tool: George Lucas on Circus vs. Art." *Wall Street Journal.* June 18.

Nagourney, A., and M. Thee 2007. "Young Americans Are Leaning Left, New Poll Finds." *New York Times.* June 27.

National Women's History Project. 2007. *Living the Legacy: The Women's Rights Movement 1848–1998.* http://www.legacy98.0rg/move-hist.html. Accessed July 10, 2007.

New Politics Institute. 2005. "Fundamental Shifts in the U.S. Media and Advertising Industries." http://www.newpolitics.net/files/ShiftsinMediaand Advertising.pdf. November. Accessed July 10, 2007.

Newton, J. 2007. [Blog.] http://p2pnet.net/story/11777. March 27. Accessed July 10, 2007.

Nie, N. H., S. Verba, and J. R. Petrocik. 1976. *The Changing American Voter.* Cambridge, Mass.: Twentieth Century Fund.

"The Odd Attack on Dean." 2006. *The Nation.* http://www.thenation.com/doc/ 20061211/editors. December 11. Accessed July 10, 2007.

Osborne, D., and P. Hutchinson. 2004. *The Price of Government: Getting the Results We Need in an Age of Permanent Fiscal Crisis.* New York: Basic Books.

Pacheco, P. 2000. "Lion King Los Angeles." *Playbill* 12: 22–26.

Paulson, A. 2007. *Electoral Realignment and the Outlook for American Democracy.* Lebanon, N.H.: University Press of New England.

Peers, M. 2004. "Buddy, Can You Spare Some Time?" *Wall Street Journal.* January 26.

Pew Research Center. 2000. "Some Final Observations on Voter Opinions." http://people-press.org/reports/print.php3?ReportID=20. December 21. Accessed July 10, 2007.

———. 2002. "Generations Divide over Military Action in Iraq." http:// people-press.org/commentary/display.php3?AnalysisID=57. October 17. Accessed July 10, 2007.

———. 2004. "A Global Generation Gap: Adapting to a New World." http://people-press.org/commentary/display.php3?AnalysisID=86. February 24. Accessed July 10, 2007.

———. 2005. "The Dean Activists: Their Profile and Prospects." http://people-press. org/ reports/display.php3?ReportID=240. April 6. Accessed July 10, 2007.

———. 2007a. "A Portrait of Generation Next: How Young People View Their Lives, Futures and Politics." http://pewresearch.org/pubs/278/a-portrait-of-generation-next. January 9. Accessed July 10, 2007.

———. 2007b. "Public Knowledge of Current Affairs Little Changed by News and Information Revolutions: What Americans Know, 1989–2007." http://people-press.org/reports/display.php3?ReportID=319. April 15. Accessed July 10, 2007.

———. 2007c. "Thompson Demonstrates Broad Potential Appeal: Bush Approval Falls to 29%—Lowest Ever." http://people-press.org/reports/display.php3? ReportID=334. June 4. Accessed July 10, 2007.

———. 2007d. "Trends in Political Values and Core Attitudes: 1987–2007." http://pewresearch.org/pubs/434/trends-in-political-values-and-core-attitudes-1987–2007." March 22. Accessed July 10, 2007.

Phillips, K. 1990. *The Politics of Rich and Poor: Wealth and the American Electorate in the Reagan Aftermath*. New York: Random House.

Pinkus, S. 2003. "Los Angeles Times Poll." Talk given at the Post Mortem Conference on the California Recall, University of Southern California, Los Angeles. November 13.

Poniewozik, J. 2006. "When Politics Goes Viral." *Time*. November 6.

Pratt, C. 2007a. "Charter Schools a Growing Threat to DPS." *Detroit Free Press*. May 25.

———. 2007b. "School Succeeds Where Others Fail." *Detroit Free Press*. May 25.

Puzzanghera, J. 2007. "Google Canvasses for Political Ads." *Los Angeles Times*. March 25.

Quinlan, A., and M. Bocian. 2006. "Clean Energy: Key to America's Future Economy." Greenberg Quinlan Rosner Research. http://www.greenber gresearch.com/articles/1726/2170_CleanEnergy0806.pdf. August 23. Accessed July 10, 2007.

Quinn, M., A. Semuels, and D. C. Chmielewski. 2007. "Apple Seeks to Unchain Melodies." *Los Angeles Times*. February 7.

Rainie, L., and J. Horrigan. 2006. "Election 2006 Online." Pew Research Center. http://www.pewinternet.org/pdfs/PIP_Politics_2006.pdf. January 17. Accessed July 10, 2007.

Reeves, R. 2007. "The End of Reaganism." *Real Clear Politics*. http://www. realclearpolitics.com/articles/2007/06/the_end_of_reaganism.html. June 2. Accessed July 10, 2007.

Riley, R. 2007. "Kilpatrick Seeks Charter Schools for Good of City: Mayor Wants School Options." *Detroit Free Press*. March 28.

Robertson, A., S. Garfinkel, and E. Eckstein. 2000. "Radio in the 1920s: Emergence of Radio in the 1920s and Its Cultural Significance." *Meet Me at the Third Annual Chicago Radio Show*. http://xroads.virginia.edu/~ug00/30n1/ radioshow/1920radio.htm. May 1. Accessed July 10, 2007.

Rosenof, T. 2003. *Realignment: The Theory That Changed the Way We Think about American Politics*. Lanham, Md.: Rowman & Littlefield.

Rosner, J. 2006. "A New Vision of Security." *Blueprint Magazine* 5. January 4. http://www.dlc.org/ndol_ci.cfm?contentid=254152&kaid=124&subid=307. Accessed July 10, 2007.

Rospars, J. 2007. "Our MySpace Experiment." *My.BarackObama.com Community Blogs* http://my.barackobama.com/page/community/post_group/ObamaHQ/CvSl. May 2. Accessed July 10, 2007.

Ross, D., and P. Plastrik. 2007. "There's a Proven Way to Educate Urban Kids Successfully—But It's Not Coming to a Neighborhood Near You Any Time Soon." *Innovation Network for Communities*. http://www.in4c.net/index.asp. April. Accessed July 10, 2007.

Ruffini, P. 2007. "Do Democrats Own the Internet?" http://www. patrickruffini.com/2007/04/08/do-democrats-own-the-internet/. April 8. Accessed July 10, 2007.

Schatz, A. 2006. "In Clips on YouTube, Politicians Reveal Their Unscripted Side: Rival Posts 'Gotcha' Videos in Tight Montana Race." *Wall Street Journal*. October 9.

Schlesinger, A. M. Jr. 1986. *The Cycles of American History*. Boston: Houghton Mifflin.

Schlesinger, A. M. Sr. 1922. *New Viewpoints in American History*. New York: Macmillan.

Semuels, A., and M. Quinn. 2007. "Fans, Labels Are Split on Unlocked Music Plan." *Los Angeles Times*. February 8.

Shafer, B. E. 1991. *The End of Realignment?: Interpreting American Electoral Eras*. Madison: University of Wisconsin Press.

Short, J., and O'Brien, K. n.d. "MP3.com and the Future of the Music Industry: MP3.com Case A: Pre-IPO Background, Industry Note Version 2." London Business School.

Shuler, H. 2006. Interview by Candy Crowley. "Broken Government." Television broadcast. "CNN Newsroom." October 24.

Sifry, M. 2007. "The Battle to Control Obama's MySpace." http://techpresident.com/node/301. May 1. Accessed July 10, 2007.

Slevin, P. 2006. "Kansas Republicans Cut and Run—To Become Democrats." *Washington Post*. October 19.

Smith, E. 2007. "Sales of Music, Long in Decline, Plunge Sharply." *Wall Street Journal*. March 21.

Smith, G., S. Keeter, and J. Green. 2006. "Religious Groups React to the 2006 Election." *Pew Research Center Publications*. http://pewresearch.org/pubs/99/religious-groups-react-to-the-2006-election. November 27. Accessed July 10, 2007.

Standage, T. 1998. *The Victorian Internet*. New York: Walker.

Steinberg, B. 2006. "'Law and Order' Boss Dick Wolf Ponders the Future of TV Ads (Doink, Doink)." *Wall Street Journal*. October 18.

Strauss, W., and N. Howe. 1991. *Generations: The History of America's Future, 1584 to 2069*. New York: Morrow.

———. 1997. *The Fourth Turning: An American Prophecy*. New York: Broadway Books.

Strauss, W., and N. Howe, with P. Markiewicz. 2006. *Millennials and the Pop Culture: Strategies for a new Generation of Consumers in Music, Movies, Television, the Internet, and Video Games*. N.p.: Life Course Associates.

Streeter, T. 2007. http://xroads.virginia.edu/~ug00/30n1/radioshow/1920radio.htm. Accessed July 10, 2007.

Surowiecki, J. A. 2004. *The Wisdom of Crowds: Why the Many Are Smarter Than the Few and How Collective Wisdom Shapes Business*. New York: Doubleday.

Szalai, G. 2007. "Big Media Has Less Sway on Internet." http://www.hollywoodreporter.com/hr/content_display/news/e3i96671211ab37012854ddbec57715c8b0. Accessed July 10, 2007.

Telegeography Research. 2007. "Global Traffic, Bandwidth and Pricing Trends and Wholesale Market Outlook." Paper presented to the Pacific Telecommunications Council, Honolulu. January 14. http://www.telegeography.com. Accessed July 10, 2007.

Thomas, E. 2007. "The Truman Primary." *Newsweek*. May 14.

Trippi, J. 2004. *The Revolution Will Not Be Televised*. New York: HarperCollins.

Turk, M. 2007. "The GOP Online." *Kung Fu Quips*. April 9. http://www.kungfuquip.com/archives/679. Accessed July 10, 2007.

Twenge, J. M. 2006. *Generation Me: Why Today's Young Americans Are More Confident, Assertive, Entitled—and More Miserable Than Ever Before*. New York: Free Press.

Vara, V. 2007. "Facebook Gets Help from Its Friends." *Wall Street Journal*. June 22.

Vranica, S. 2007. "On Madison Avenue, a Digital Wake-up Call." *Wall Street Journal*. March 26.

Wagner, M. 2007. "Using Second Life as a Business-to-Business Tool." *Information Week Blog*. http://www.informationweek.com/blog/main/archives/2007/04/using_second_li_2.html. April 26. Accessed July 10, 2007.

Wales, J. 2006. "An Open Letter to the Political Blogosphere." Wikia.com. http://campaigns.wikia.com/wiki/Mission_Statement. April 6. Accessed July 10, 2007.

Wallsten, P., and T. Hamburger. 2006. "The GOP Knows You Don't Like Anchovies." *Los Angeles Times*. June 25.

Walsh, K. T. 2007. "A Sinking Presidency: The President Still Exudes Confidence, But His Ship of State Is Taking on Water—Fast." *U.S. News and World Report*. May 14.

Watson, H. L. 1990. *Liberty and Power: The Politics of Jacksonian America*. New York: Hill and Wang.

Webb, J., and J. Tester. 2006. Interview by Tim Russert. November 19. "Meet the Press." NBC.

Wessel, D., and B. Davis. 2007. "Pain from Free Trade Spurs Second Thoughts." *Wall Street Journal*. March 28.

Whicher, G. F. 1953. *William Jennings Bryan and the Campaign of 1896*. Boston: D. C. Heath.

White, T. H. 1961. *The Making of the President 1960*. New York: Pocket Books.

Wilentz, S. 2005. *Andrew Jackson*. New York: Henry Holt.

Williams, A. 2007. "The Future President on Your Friends List." *New York Times*. March 18.

Wingfield, N., and E. Smith. 2007. "Jobs's New Tune Raises Pressure on Music Firms." *Wall Street Journal*. February 7.

York, E. B. 2007. "Hot Topic Goes Beyond the Pale." *Los Angeles Business Journal*. January 15–21.

Zeigler, T. 2007. "Is the McCain Campaign Listening to Bloggers?" *Bivings Report*. http://www.bivingsreport.com/2007/is-the-mccain-campaign-listening-to-bloggers/. February 24. Accessed July 10, 2007.

Index

AARP, 90–91, 252
ABC PAC, 176
abolitionism, 42–43
abortion: ballot initiatives on, 242; decline in use of, 78–79, 81, 82; Millennial attitudes toward, 99; polarization over, 115–116; state discourse on, 245; in 2006 election, 132, 137–138; in 2008 election, 210
Abramoff, Jack, 136
ActBlue, 176
Adams, Abigail, 233
Adams, John Quincy, 194
Adaptive Generation, 26. *See also* Silent Generation
"Adventures of Ozzie and Harriet, The" (television program), 72–73
advertisements and advertising: attack type, 130–131, 154, 155, 162; Burns's use of, 137; decline in television political, 162–164; funding for "Red to Blue" campaign, 120–121, 124; Internet potential for, 153–155; radio as medium for, 58–59; of Shea-Porter's candidacy, 126; on stem cell research issue, 133
affirmative action programs, 95–96
African Americans: data mining as technique to target, 181; drop-out rates of, 257; on interracial

relationships, 95; Jim Crow laws and, 43, 234; shift to Democratic Party, 19; 2008 election's importance and, 216–217
age: attitudinal changes and, 88–91; immigration attitudes and, 96–97; party identification and, 206. *See also* children and childrearing practices; generations and generational cycles; elderly people; youth vote
agriculture vs. industrialization, 195–196
AIDS, 98
Alabama: civil rights march remembered in, 11–14, 193
Albright, Madeleine, 134
"Alice" (television program), 74
Allen, George, 134–135
"All in the Family" (television program), 74, 78
"All Things Digital" conference (2007), 205
AltaVista, 237
Altmire, Jason, 120
amber alerts, 81, 120, 265
America First, 100
"American Idol" (television program), 87, 239
American Independent Party, 37–38
American Indians, 46
American (Know-Nothing) Party, 42

American Temperance Society, 40
AmeriCorps, 260
Amos, Tori, 145
Andersen, Kurt, 6–7
Anderson, Kylee, 148
"Andy Griffith Show, The" (television program), 73
Anthony, Joe, 172–173
Anthony, Susan B., 41
Apple, 143, 148–149, 154
Armstrong, Jerome, 157–161
Arno, Peter, 60
Arrington, Michael, 177
Articles of Confederation, 248
ArtistDirect, Inc., 149
AT&T, 141
attitudes. *See* public opinion and attitudes; voters' attitudes; *specific generations (e.g., Millennial attitudes)*
Avalon (film), 69–70
avian flu, 200
awakening, use of term, 192–193

Baby Boomer Generation: childhood environment of, 68–70; civil rights movement and, 45; conservative vs. liberal gap in, 209; cultural wars and, 3, 192–193; debt of, 251–252; demographics of, 26, 69–70; divisions of, 2; media usage of, 166; Millennials compared with, 4; moralistic views of, 209; Moses Generation compared with, 13–14; music identified with, 86; party identification of, 206; pop culture's reflection of, 72–73, 84–85, 151; post-2006 election predictions of, 201; retirement concerns of, 252; surveys of, xiv–xv
Baby Boomers' attitudes: differences between parties and candidates, 105; foreign affairs, 101–102, 104; global warming, 5; Iraq War, 5; music, 151;

optimism, 82, 92; religion, 89; self-centered, 83; sexuality, 97; 2008 election issues, 210; 2006 election results, 138; voluntarism, 262; voting, 90–91; women's roles, 98
"Bachelor Father" (television program), 73
Backstreet Boys, 85
"Barney" (television program), 264
Barone, Michael, 210
Baucus, Max, 266–267
Beatles, 151
Bennett, George, 255
Bennis, Warren, 223
Berelson, Bernard, 88
Berman, Jeff, 173
Berra, Yogi, 168
Bertelsmann corporation, 145
Best Buy, 144–145
Biloxi Blues (play and film), 67
bipartisanship: community service and, 260–263; health care solution and, 254, 255–256; Millennialist agenda and, 250–251; post-9/11 expansion of, 115; wage insurance program and, 266–267. *See also* partisanship; party identification
birth control: changing attitudes toward, 99; decline in use of, 78–79, 81, 82. *See also* abortion
Birth of a Nation, The (film), 43
birthrates: generations compared, 69–71, 78–79; GI Generation and, 26; Millennial Generation and, 26, 67
Blackberries, 114
Blanchard, Jim, ix, 62
Blinder, Alan, 267
blogs and blogosphere: email compared with, 178; increased importance of, 138, 175–180; on Map Changers contest, 158–159; McNerney's 2006 campaign and,

129–131; on MySpace and command-and-control controversy, 172–173; problems with conservative, 177–178; Tester's 2006 campaign and, 135–137

"Bloody Sunday" remembrances, 11–14, 193

Bloomer, Amelia, 41

Bluey, Robert, 176

"Bob Newhart Show, The" (television program), 74, 75

Bosworth, Barry, 253

Boyda, Nancy, 122

"Brady Bunch, The" (television program), 73

Briand, Aristide, 88

Brin, Sergei, 237

Britt-Gibson, Justin, 95

Broder, David, 21, 220

Brokaw, Tom, 66

Brooks, David, 212

Brown, H. Rap, 44

Brown, Sherrod, 132

Brown v. Board of Education, 45

Brundrett, Trei, 158

Bryan, William Jennings: in currency debate, 54–57; in evolution vs. creationism debate, 41–42; Gore compared with, 113; McKinley compared with, 195–196; nomination of, 32; Tester compared with, 136

Buchanan, Pat, 44, 198

Buckley, William F., 215

Buffa, Dudley, x

bumper stickers, 80

Burnett, Mark, 171–172

Burns, Conrad, 136–137

Bush, George H. W., 47

Bush, George W.: attitudes toward, 107, 118, 199; data-mining technologies and, 181–182; election and reelection of,

105–106, 114, 116, 191; failures of, 193–194, 213–216, 218, 220; federal debt and, 251–252; Limbaugh's audience and, 63; military actions of, 102–103; response to Hurricane Katrina, 198; role of government under, 47, 236; satires of, 169, 187; televised debates of, 62; votes for, 115–116, 117. *See also* Iraq War

businesses: digital-based, 144–147, 204–205; social networking used by, 240–241; transitions in, 174–175. *See also* Internet; *specific companies*

Butch Cassidy and the Sundance Kid (film), 150

California campaigns and elections: propositions and referenda in, 80, 239–240, 242; recall petition in, 63–64, 239; 2006 winning candidate in, 127–131

campaign funding: alternatives to massive amounts of, 126–131; Map Changers contest and, 158–161; number of donors and, 129; online appeals for, 163–165, 176–180, 184–186; 2006 election, compared, 124–126, 175; widgets for, 172

Campaigns Wikia, 238

Carmichael, Stokely, 43–44

Carter, Jimmy, 115, 215

Carville, James, 124

Casey, Bob, Jr., 131–132

CBS radio, 58

CDs: declining sales of, 147, 148–149; MP3 format compared with, 144–145

celebrities, 60, 64

cell phones: IMing on, 83–84, 171, 186; text messaging on, 83–84, 87, 171, 239

Center for the Digital Future, 142, 154

Cermak, Anton, 222

Chafee, Lincoln, 132

Champiou, Ken, 63

chaos theory, 175

charisma, 228

"Cheers" (television program), 74, 75

Chen, Steve, 168–169

Chiachiere, Ryan, 4

Chicago (film), 60

Chicago Herald and Examiner, 55

Chicago Times, 52–53

Chicago Tribune, 16, 53

children and childrearing practices: abuse and exploitation of, 81; environments of generations, compared, 67–71; Millennials in context of, 5–6, 81–84; pop culture's reflection of, 72–81. *See also* marriage/family/children values

Churchill, Winston, 88, 229

Cisco, 240–241

citizen service program, 261–263

Civic Generation: description of, 5–6, 25; Joshua generation as, 14; Revolutionary, 233. *See also* civic realignments; GI Generation (Greatest Generation); Millennial Generation (b. 1982–2003)

civic infrastructure: balancing individual and national goals in, 247; crisis of confidence in, 220–221; direct democracy and, 239–241; engaging citizens in revitalizing, 226–230; historical perspective on, 233–235; incremental changes in, 241–246; leadership and vision for, 221–226; reshaping of, 235–238

civic realignments: attitudes toward foreign affairs in, 100–101, 102–104; attitudes toward political institutions in, 36–38;

characteristics of, summarized, 28, 233–234; civic infrastructure and, 233–235; control of government in, 35–36; crises as triggers of, 197–201; cultural change as trigger of, 194–197; dominant pop culture rejected in, 151, 193–194; economic disparities issue in, 38–40; economic role of government in, 46, 47–49, 94–95; election of 1860 as, 6, 16, 18; election of 1932 as, 6, 7, 16, 18; election of 1928 as signal of, 116–118; engaging citizens in, 226–230; idealist realignments compared with, 27–29, 30; immigration issues in, 42, 44–45, 96–97; inclusivity in, 41, 45–46, 95–97, 249; leadership and vision in, 221–226; national consciousness as trigger of, 192–194; partisanship in, 105–108, 114; party coalitions in, 31–33; polarization of voters in, 115–116, 131; precursors to, 48–49, 137–139, 140; presidential leadership in, 230–232; public policy issues in, 42–46; public's predictions of, 201–202; reinventing governance in, 236–238; sexual issues in, 97–99; social issues in, 40–42; technology appropriate to, 183–184; third-party movements in, 38; voter engagement in, 31, 33–34. *See also* Civil War realignment (1860s); New Deal realignment (1930s); Millennialist realignment (2000s)

Civil Rights Act (1964), 12

civil rights movement: emergence of, 45; political context of, 43–44; politicians' remembrances of, 11–14, 193

Civil War, 197, 223, 224. *See also* Civil War realignment (1860s);

Lincoln, Abraham; slaves and slavery

Civil War realignment (1860s): compromise of 1877 in, 233–234; control of government in, 35; economic disparities in, 39; economic growth in, 6–7; economic role of government in, 47–48; immigration issues in, 44; leadership in, 221–223; party coalitions in, 31–32; period of, 19; political, social, and technological context of, 23–24, 220–221; racial issues in, 45; vision of, 223–226; voters engaged in vision of, 226–230; voter turnout in, 31; women's rights in, 41

Clay, Henry, 194

Cleveland, Grover, 38

Clift, Eleanor, 218–219

Clinton, Bill: community service program of, 260; contact with, x; health care plan of, 222; impeachment inquiry against, 111–112; on 1998 election results, 112–113; role of government under, 47, 48, 235–236; televised appearances of, 64

Clinton, Hillary Rodham, 3, 11–12, 154, 185–186

CNN: Millennials' view of, 166; political identification of, 52; on 2000 election, 114; on 2006 election, 122, 133, 135; YouTube debate of, 186

Cohen, Ted, 146–147

"Colbert Report, The" (television program), 166

Cold War, 68, 101, 234

Cole, Jeff, 142, 154

Coleman, Norm, 266–267

collective action, 104, 243. *See also* community/group values; United Nations

Columbine High School shooting, 81, 200–201, 265

Commager, Henry S., 244

communication technologies: approach to, xv–xvi; development of, 140–144; incoming new as overlapping fading older, 162–164; music sharing and, 144–148; peer-to-peer pressure in, 148–151; political context of, 1, 114; power shifts and, 151–152; as precursors to realignments, 48–49, 50; producer and power in, 133, 152–155, 245–246. *See also* film and movies; Internet; media; newspapers; peer-to-peer (P2P) communication technologies; radio; social networking technologies; telegraph; telephone; television

community/group values: dangers of, 243; in Edwards's campaign, 185; health care solution based in, 255–256; historical perspective on, 248–250; individual goals balanced with, 247; of Millennials, 83–84, 94–95; service and voluntarism in, 84, 260–263; trust in wisdom of, 237–238, 239–240; of 2006 Democratic candidates, 120–122. *See also* friends and friendships; peer-to-peer (P2P) communication technologies

community service initiative, 260–263

computers: direct links among, 142–144; movies and television programs on, 140, 150–151; ripping music on, 148; video editing on, 154. *See also* email; Internet; peer-to-peer (P2P) communication technologies; social networking technologies

Conrad, Frank, 58

consensus as goal, 96–97, 236

conservatism: appropriate sexual
behavior in, 97; idealist and civic
realignments from, 28–29, 30;
identification with, decline in,
208–209; polarization and,
115–116, 131; portrayals on
sitcoms, 77; radio used in, 63–64;
realignment theory and, 17; voters'
turn against, 107
Cook, Charlie, 179
Coolidge, Calvin, 47, 58–59
Coopersmith Self-Esteem Inventory,
79–80
co-parenting concept, 71
Copernicus Analytics, 182–183
copyright laws, 146–148, 156–157
Cosby, Bill, 77–78
"Cosby Show, The" (television
program), 77–78
Cosgrove, Vicki, 128
"Courtship of Eddie's Father, The"
(television program), 73
Cox, James, 58
creationism vs. evolution, 41–42
Cruise, Tom, 84
Culkin, Macaulay, 71
culture: of Baby Boomers, 3,
192–193; change in, as trigger of
civic realignments, 194–197; of
conservative right, 113. *See also*
pop culture
currency and monetary policy, 54–57

DailyKos blog, 135, 160, 172
Daily Pantagraph (Bloomington, Ill.),
52, 53
"Daily Show, The" (television
program), 166
Dallek, Robert, 213, 221–222,
223–224, 228, 229
Darfur, Sudan, 265–266
Darrow, Clarence, 42
Darwin, Charles, 41–42

Daschle, Tom, 115
data-mining technologies, 181–184
Data Warehouse project, 183
Dauman, Philippe, 156
Davis, Artur, 11
Davis, Gray, 63–64, 239
Davis, Jefferson, 227
Dean, Howard: campaign funding
and, 124–126; fifty-state and
Netroots strategies of, 118–119,
121, 124; micro-targeting
technology and, 182–183;
presidential campaign of, 104,
155, 157, 162; social networking
of, 184
DeanNation blog, 157
debt: of Baby Boomers, 251–252;
education, 256–257; health care,
253–256
Defenders of Wildlife Action Fund,
130
Democracy Corps, 205–206
Democratic Party: of Andrew
Jackson, 195; as "big government"
party, 48; campaign funding of,
124–126, 175–176; currency
debate of 1896 and, 55, 56–57;
demographics of, 18, 21, 117; on
direction of country, 203; divisions
in, 196, 216, 225; eras of
dominance of, 15–16; FDR's
leadership and vision for, 221–226;
Gore's campaign and, 113; idealist
and civic realignments and, 27–28,
30; micro-targeting technology
and, 182–183; Millennials' leaning
toward, 105–108, 138, 205–210;
Netroots and fifty-state strategies
of, 3–4, 118–119, 121, 124,
175–176; polarization and,
115–116, 131; as soft on security
and crime, 101–102, 208; 2008
election and, 210–212, 216–219;

2006 election wins of, 121–137.
    See also "Red to Blue" (R2B)
    campaign; *specific candidates*
"Designing Women" (television
    program), 74
Detroit: model school in, 259–260
Detroit Federation of Teachers, 259
Devil Wears Prada, The (film), 84–85
Dewey, Tom, 16–17
DeWolf, Chris, 172
Diamond, Jon, 149
"Dick Van Dyke Show, The"
    (television program), 75
digital businesses, 144–147, 204–205.
    See also MP3 format
Digital Millennium Copyright Act
    (DMCA), 147, 148–149
digital video recorders (DVRs),
    153–154
digital yard sign concept, 172
direct democracy: blog dedicated to,
    135, 172; concept of, 239–241;
    conditions necessary for, 242–243;
    context of call for, 244; limits of,
    241–242
direct mail, 179
diseases, 98, 133, 200
divorce, 69, 71, 75, 78–79
Dobbs, Lou, 44
door-to-door canvassing, 130, 136, 179
Douglas, Stephen A., 51–53,
    224–225
Dowd, Matthew, 182
drug and substance abuse, 40, 67–68,
    75
Dukakis, Michael, 62
Dylan, Bob, 208

eBay, 143
economic disparities: in civic vs.
    idealist realignments, 38–40;
    governmental assistance in
    overcoming, 94–95; in Millennialist

realignment, 250; tax issues and,
    252; 2008 election and, 210, 211;
    2006 Democratic candidates on,
    122, 127, 132–133
economy: currency debate and,
    54–57; debt and, 251–257; dynamic
    context of, 174–175; generations
    compared, 67–68; government's
    role in, 46–49, 94–95; immigration
    issues linked to, 44, 249; as issue in
    2008 election, 210, 211; optimism
    about, 82–83, 92, 138; Panic of
    1893 and, 195; public's predictions
    about, 201; realignments linked to
    crises in, 19, 197–201; shifting
    power equation in, 151–152. *See
    also* Great Depression
Edsall, Thomas, 206
education: gender equality in, 83;
    integration of, 45; in Millennialist
    realignment, 250, 256–260; of
    Millennials, 80–81, 82; Millennials'
    optimism about, 92; motivation key
    to, 258–259; parental roles in, 260;
    party identification by, 206. *See also*
    schools
education, college: community
    service for tuition for, 261–263;
    debt due to, 256–257;
    encouragement of, 260–261; for
    jobs that can't be outsourced, 267
Edwards, Andrew, 158–161
Edwards, Elizabeth, 177
Edwards, John, 3, 155, 177, 180, 185,
    254
"8 Simple Rules for Dating My
    Teenage Daughter" (television
    program), 79
Eisenhower, Dwight D., 36, 48,
    108
elderly people: religiosity of, 89;
    voting behavior of, 91
election of 1822, 113

election of 1824, 31, 194

election of 1828: control of government after, 34–35; cultural change after, 194–195; economic disparities after, 38; economic role of government after, 46–47; electoral realignment in, 16, 18; immigration issues after, 42; party coalitions in, 31; social issues in, 40–41; voter turnout in, 31, 34. *See also* Jacksonian realignment (1828)

election of 1840, 34

election of 1844, 50–51

election of 1848, 6

election of 1852, 31, 34

election of 1856, 31

election of 1858, 51–53

election of 1860: as civic realignment, 6, 16, 18; control of government after, 35; Democratic divisions in, 225; economic disparities after, 39; economic role of government after, 47–48; immigration issues after, 44; party coalitions in, 31–32; political, social, and technological context of, 6–7, 220–221; voter turnout in, 31, 34. *See also* Civil War realignment (1860s)

election of 1864, 34

election of 1872, 34

election of 1876, 35

election of 1880, 38

election of 1892, 31, 34

election of 1896: communication technology in, 54–57; control of government after, 34–35; divisions evident in, 195–196; economic disparities after, 39; economic role of government after, 46–47; electoral realignment in, 16, 18; ethnic and racial issues after, 43; evolution vs. creationism after, 41–42; immigration issues after, 42;

interests and party dominance in, 15; voter turnout in, 31, 34, 57; women's rights after, 41. *See also* late-nineteenth-century realignment

election of 1900, 34

election of 1912, 35, 38

election of 1916, 35

election of 1920, 58

election of 1924, 31, 34

election of 1928: communication technologies in, 59; economic disparities after, 39; 2004 election compared with, 116–118; voter turnout in, 31, 116–117

election of 1930, 35

election of 1932: as civic realignment, 6, 7, 16, 18; communication technologies in, 59; economic disparities after, 39; economic role of government after, 48; immigration issues after, 44–45; party coalitions in, 32; political, social, and technological context of, 220–221; social issues in, 40; vote distribution in, 226; voter turnout in, 31, 34. *See also* New Deal realignment (1930s)

election of 1934, 112

election of 1936, 31, 59–60

election of 1946, 16

election of 1948, 16–17, 31, 34, 38

election of 1954, 36

election of 1956, 31, 36

election of 1958, 36

election of 1960: split-ticket voting in, 36; televised debate of, 61–62, 179; voter turnout in, 31, 34

election of 1964, 19, 31

election of 1968: communication technologies in, 62; control of government after, 34–35; cultural context and aftermath of, 196–197;

economic disparities after, 39; economic role of government after, 46–47; electoral realignment in, 16; ethnic and racial issues after, 43–44; party coalitions in, 33; Paulsen's campaign in, 90; political dynamics after, 20–21; voter attitudes toward political institutions in, 37; voter turnout in, 31, 34, 116. *See also* Republican realignment (1960s)

election of 1972, 34, 36, 37

election of 1986, 113

election of 1992, 38, 116

election of 1994, 63, 106

election of 1996, 7, 34, 116

election of 1998, 111–113

election of 2000: advertising money in, 155; communication technologies in, 62, 179–182, 184; early signs of realignment in, 113–114; polarization in, 116; popular vote vs. electoral vote winners in, 35; third-party candidates in, 38; voter turnout in, 117; youth vote in, 87

election of 2002, 106–107, 117, 165

election of 2004: advertising money in, 155; antiwar activists and, 104; Bush's narrow margin in, 191; communication technologies in, 181–182, 184; Dean's "open source" campaign in, 162; Democratic divisions after, 118–119; Millennials' votes in, 105–106; 1928 election compared with, 116–118; partisanship in, 117–118; polarization in, 115–116; Social Security debate in, 252; voter turnout in, 31, 116–117; youth vote in, 87, 105–106

election of 2006: ballot initiatives in, 242; campaign funding in, 124–126; foreign oil issue in, 264; implications for future, 175, 201–202; micro-targeting technology in, 183; Millennials on political parties after, 208; Millennials' votes in, 105–106; party identification in, 105–106; as signal in coming realignment, 118–123, 137–139, 140; social networking technologies in, 158–162, 164–165, 188; voters' attitudes in, 37, 117; voters' media use in, 165–167, 186–187; voter turnout in, 31; winning campaigns in, 126–137; youth vote in, 87, 105–106, 135, 137

election of 2008: changing field for, 154–155; developing trends in, 121–123; eligibility to vote in, 87–88; fund-raising in, 175–180; issues central to, 210–212, 254–256; online unofficial primary of, 173; voters' focus on, 216–217. *See also* Millennialist realignment (2000s)

election of 2008, predictions about: civic president, 231–232; future dominance of winners, 7–8; online presence, 188; realignment, 191–192; voter turnout, 31

election of 2008, presidential candidates: "Bloody Sunday" remembrances and, 11–14; challenges for Republican, 213, 214–215; evolution vs. creationism debate, 42; first commercial to go viral, 154; immigration issues, 44; social networking of, 2–3, 172, 184–186. *See also specific candidates*

election of 2010, predictions about, 107

election of 2012, predictions about, 31

electoral politics: characteristics of, 1; "critical" elections and, 17; cyclical pattern of, 14–16; dealignment and disaggregation in recent, 22; incumbents and voter behavior in, 165; midterm elections in, 111–113; social networking as challenge to, 2–3. *See also* campaign funding; political campaigns; political parties; realignments; *specific candidates and elections*

email: blogs compared with, 178; IMing as replacing, 186; as killer application, 141–142; parent-child communication via, 83; Republican approach to, 178–179; role in 2006 winning campaign, 129; screened for Hillary's wireside chats, 185

Emancipation Proclamation (1863), 224

Emanuel, Rahm, 119–122, 124, 127, 128

EMI Group, 145, 149

eMusic.com, 149

Encyclopedia Britannica, 238

Endangered Species Act (1973), 130

energy issues, 264. *See also* environment; global warming

entertainment industries: digital video recorders (DVRs) and, 153–154; Internet as channel for, 142–143; new technologies in, 140. *See also* film and movies; music; television

environment: disasters in, 198; in Millennialist realignment, 250; overpopulation's effects on, 78; public's predictions about, 201–202; reinventing public policy on, 235–236; think globally, act locally concept and, 263–266; 2008 election and, 210, 211; 2006

California candidate's focus on, 127–131. *See also* global warming

equality: campaign messages about economic, 137; in consensus and decision making, 236; among friends, 170; gender, 83, 92, 95–96, 98; public policy to foster, 94–95, 253–254; racial, 43, 95–96, 137, 233–234

ESPN, 184–185

ethnicity and ethnic issues: in civic vs. idealist realignments, 42–46; data mining as technique to target, 181; drop-out rates and, 257; future campaign messages about, 137; generations compared, 66–67; Millennials' inclusivity and, 41, 45–46, 95–97, 249; Millennials' optimism about, 82–83; 2008 election and, 210, 211, 216–217; in 2006 Senate campaigns, 134–135, 136

evolution vs. creationism, 41–42

Exorcist, The (film), 78

Fabrizio, Tony, 206, 214, 216

Facebook: NewsFeed feature of, 159–160; Obama's use of, 3, 180; political organizing via, 159–161; popularity of, 84; role of, 64–65; sharing as central to, 167; 2008 presidential candidates' profiles on, 186; users of, 168; widgets of, 187

FairPlay (Apple), 148

"Fala speech" of FDR, 229–230

family. *See* marriage/family/children values

"Family Affair" (television program), 73

"Family Ties" (television program), 77

Farley, James, 59

"Father Knows Best" (television program), 72–73

Federal Elections Commission (FEC), 175–176

Federal Regulatory Commission, 58

feminism, 40–41. *See also* gender

film and movies: adapting to changes in, 204–205; alternative ways to view, 140, 150–151; on children as gifts, 79; on children as savages, 78; coming-of-age theme in, 84–85; email touted in, 141–142; emergence of talkies, 60; on Gen-X kids, 71; of Millennials, 84–85; MySpace promotion of, 171; on 9/11, 199; on suburbanization, 69–70. *See also* video clips; *specific movies*

Filson, Steve, 128, 129

FinalCutPro (software), 154

Fiske, John, 166

Florida: campaigns and elections in, 114

Fontas, Jeffrey, 158–161

Ford, Gerald, 115

Ford, Harold, 137

foreign affairs: collective action in, 104; GI Generation and, 100–101; as issue in 2008 election, 210, 211, 217–219; Millennials' engagement with, 103–104; multilateral, reasoned approach to, 265–266; retreats from, 68; think globally, act locally concept and, 263–266. *See also* globalism; security, U.S.

Forward Together web site, 158, 159–161

Fox, Michael J., 77, 133

Fox News Channel, 52, 114, 152, 166

Franklin, Bonnie, 75

Frank N. Magid Associates, x, xiv–xv

free trade issues, 266

Freewebs, 187

Friedman, Milton, 77

"Friends" (television program), 76–77

friends and friendships: in coming-of-age movies, 84–85; conversations with, 83–84; equality among, 170; political information gathered from, 166; reshaping civic infrastructure in context of, 235–236; sharing among, 167–170. *See also* community/group values; peer-to-peer (P2P) communication technologies

friendster.com, 168

Gage, Alex, 183

Galston, William, 115, 218

Gamez, Martha, 131

Garner, John Nance, 222

Garrison, William Lloyd, 42–43

Gates, Bill, 152

gay rights, 98, 137–138

gender, 117, 206

gender equality, 83, 92, 95–96, 98

Generation Engage, 164–165

Generation Me, 5–6

"Generation Next" (television program), 84, 264–265

generations and generational cycles: allegories of, 4; approach to, xiii; assumed changes within single, 88–91; biblical, 13; childhood environments and, 68–71; distinctions among, 1–2; dynamic types of, 5–6; gap of, 209; issues in 2008 election and, 210; as key to political realignment, 24–26; media usage differences by, 166; Obama's allusion to, 13–14; party identification by, 206; patterns of, 25–26, 66–68; pop culture's reflection of, 72–81, 84–86; Revolutionary, 233. *See also* Adaptive Generation; Civic Generation; Idealist Generation; Reactive Generation

Generation X: childhood environment of, 68, 70–71; conservative vs. liberal gap in, 2, 209; demographics of, 70–71; Goth look and, 86; juvenile delinquency among, 81; media usage of, 166; Millennials compared with, 4, 81–82, 87, 151; music identified with, 5, 86, 156, 204; as nomadic generation, 14; party identification of, 106–107, 206; pop culture's reflection of, 73–77, 84–85; post-2006 election predictions of, 201; self-esteem of, 79; as television viewers, 163

Gen-X attitudes: cynical individualism, 83; differences between parties vs. candidates, 105; foreign affairs, 104; government, 93; Millennials, 5–6, 242; optimism, 82, 92; religion, 89; 2006 election results, 138; voluntarism, 261, 262; women's roles, 98

Gephardt, Dick, 162

GetLocal (software), 184

GI Bill of Rights, 48, 261

GI Generation (Greatest Generation): birthrate and, 26; childhood environment of, 69; civic involvement of, 234; civil rights movement and, 45; coming-of-age impact of, 24–25; description of, 6; Joshua generation compared with, 13–14; Millennials compared with, 66–68, 151; music identified with, 86; pop culture's reflection of, 72–73, 74, 84–85; as television viewers, 163

GI Generation attitudes: foreign affairs, 100–101, 104; religion, 89; voting, 90–91; women's roles, 98

Gingrich, Newt, 112, 113, 215

Giuliani, Rudy, 177, 218

Gleason, Jackie, 72

globalism: centrality of, 266–267; complexity of, 197–198; increased focus on, 247; as issue in 2008 election, 217; Millennials' attitudes toward, 103–104, 263–266; pandemics and, 200; public's predictions about, 201–202. *See also* foreign affairs; security, U.S.

global warming: Baby Boomers' vs. Millennials' attitudes toward, 5; in Millennialist realignment, 250; public concerns about, 198–199; reinventing public policy on, 235–236; think globally, act locally concept and, 263–266; widgets for calculating, 171

God and religion, attitudes toward: of Baby Boomers', 89; care for Earth based in, 199; historical perspective on, 248; Obama's references to, 13–14; political party shifts and, 117; stem cell research issue and, 132–133; 2004 election and, 115–116

"God Gap," 117

gold vs. silver debate, 54–57

Goldwater, Barry, 12, 19, 29, 101

Google: cross-generational use of, 186; organization of, 237; political consultant seminars of, 154; as reliable source, 237; as verb, 146; Viacom's suit against, 156–157; YouTube owned by, 153, 156, 169

Gore, Al: Blackberry of, 114; global warming concerns of, 171, 198–199; mentioned, x; presidential campaign of, 113–114, 155; "reinvent government" initiative of, 47, 235–236; televised debates of, 62; votes for, 117

government: civic generation's reappraisal of, 193–194, 198–201; debt of, 251–252; decentralization and expansion of, 235; divided vs. unified control of, 34–36; economic role of, 46–49, 94–95; fairness and accountability of, 133–134; FDR's vision for, 225–226; incremental changes in, 241–246; as issue in 2008 election, 210, 217; Millennials' optimism about, 93, 94–95; reinvention of, 235–238; surveillance by, 200–201; 2006 Democratic candidates' optimism about, 122, 138; voters' attitudes toward, 36–38, 203–204. *See also* civic infrastructure; political institutions; public policy
Graduate, The (film), 84–85
Granholm, Jennifer, 62, 259
Grant, Ulysses S., 233
grassroots organizing: Netroots combined with, 119, 127–131; online fund-raising to support, 159–161; Republican strategies of, 179–180
Great Depression: devastation of, 197; GI Generation and, 68, 234; leadership and vision in countering, 221–226. *See also* New Deal realignment (1930s)
Greenback Party, 38
Green Party, 38
Greenstein, Fred, 222, 227
"Grey's Anatomy" (television program), 150
Griffin, Robert, ix
Griffith, Andy, 73

Hackett, Paul, 132
Hagel, Chuck, 134
Hall, Arsenio, 64
Hamilton, Alexander, 233

Hanks, Tom, 141
Hanna, Mark, 55–57, 186
Harding, Warren G., 47, 58
Hardy, Andy, 84–85
Harry Potter series, 4
Hart, Gary, 218
Hathaway, Anne, 84
Hayes, Rutherford B., 35, 233–234
health care: Clinton's plan for, 222; "collaborative" type of, 255; as issue in 2008 election, 210, 211; in Millennialist realignment, 250, 253–256; Millennials' optimism about, 92; 2006 Democratic candidates' optimism about, 122
health care insurance mandate, 94–95, 254–255
Health Dialog company, 255
Health Insurance Portability and Accountability Act (HIPAA) (1996), 255
health savings accounts, 254
Hearst, William Randolph, 53, 55, 225
Hewlett-Packard, 241
High School Musical (film), 85
Hill, Baron, 120
Hispanics, 181, 216–217, 257; data mining as technique to target, 181; drop-out rates of, 257; 2008 election's importance and, 216–217
Hitler, Adolf, 67
Hoffman, Dustin, 84
Hoffner, Jordan, 169
Home Alone (film), 71
homeownership, 92
Homestead Act, 32, 47–48
homosexuality, 97–98, 115, 137–138
"Honeymooners, The" (television program), 72
Hong Kong: SARS virus in, 200
Hoover, Herbert, 40, 59, 116, 215, 223, 226

Hot Topic (stores), 86
households: Internet access in, 142, 153–154, 164; radios in, 58, 59; televisions in, 61
Howe, Neil: current political crisis predicted by, 220–221, 232; on generational types and politics, 25–26, 151; on generation gap, 209; on generations, xiii, 5–6, 14; on Generation X, 70; on government restructuring, 247; on Millennials' optimism, 82–83; on Revolutionary generational cycle, 233; on social values, 68; on triggering events, 192
Hughes, Chris, 180
humor, 228–230
Humphrey, Hubert, 29, 62, 196, 214–215
Hurley, Chad, 168–169
Hurricane Katrina, 47, 185, 193, 197, 198

IBM, 143, 240–241
Ickes, Harold, 183
Idealist Generation: description of, 5–6, 25; Moses Generation as, 14. *See also* Baby Boomer Generation
idealist realignments: attitudes toward political institutions in, 36–38; attitudinal and behavioral patterns in, 89–90; characteristics of, summarized, 28; children raised in, 67–68; civic realignments compared with, 27–29, 30; control of government in, 34–35; cultural change in, 194–197; economic disparities issue in, 38–40; economic role of government in, 46–47; party coalitions in, 31–33; public policy issues in, 42–46; social issues in, 40–42; third-party movements in, 37–38; voter

disengagement in, 33–34; voter turnout in, 31. *See also* Jacksonian realignment (1828); late-nineteenth-century realignment; Republican realignment (1960s)
"I Love Lucy" (television program), 72
immigrants and immigration: in civic vs. idealist realignments, 42, 44–45, 96–97; congressional failure to act on, 220; dynamic generations preceded by, 26; generations compared, 66–67; laws on, 43, 45; Millennials and consensus on, 96–97; shift to Democratic Party, 19; talk radio and, 63–64; 2008 election and, 210; 2007 Senate debate on, 249; in 2006 election, 135, 136, 137–138
Imus, Don, 4
inclusivity: future campaign messages about, 137; Millennials' support for, 41, 45–46, 95–97, 249
"Income Security" program, 266–267
Inconvenient Truth, An (film), 171, 198
incrementalism, 242–246
Independents: end of era for, 114; increased number of, 21, 36, 90; party identification and, 106, 207; technology's usefulness and, 183; television's role in appeals to, 62; voter turnout and, 116. *See also* split-ticket voting; third-party movements
Indiana: campaigns and elections in, 120
individualism: cynical type of, 83; historical perspective on, 248–250; national goals balanced with, 247; privacy issues and, 161, 200–201, 255–256, 265; schools and, 257–260; in social networking technologies, 244–245

industrialization vs. agriculture, 195–196
Influentials, 170
information technologies, 174–175. *See also* communication technologies
Inherit the Wind (play and film), 42
Instant Messaging ("IMing"), 83–84, 171, 186
Institute of Politics (Harvard University), 87
Internet: advertising on, 153–155; analyzing traffic on, 150–151; analyzing voter use of, 165–167; broadband access to, 142–143; centrality of, 64–65; client/server vs. networking architecture on, 185; consensus seeking and, 236; health care database on, 255–256; individualism of, 244–245; as information source, 164, 166; Lincoln-Douglas debates available on, 53–54; Millennials' attitudes toward, 138, 142–144, 148–150, 151, 164–165, 167–170, 200, 256; potential of, 140–144, 152; producers of, 152–155; 2000 election news on, 114; word-of-mouth marketing via, 178. *See also* blogs and blogosphere; email; peer-to-peer (P2P) communication technologies; Netroots; search engines; social networking technologies; *specific sites*
Internet Privacy Protection (IPP) companies, 149
Internet Protocol (IP), 141
Iowa: campaigns and elections in, 122, 158–159, 162
iPods, 140, 148–149, 150, 154
Iran, 265–266
Iraq: 1998 events in, 112

Iraq War: Baby Boomers on, 5; changing attitudes toward, 102–103, 121, 193–194; congressional failure to end, 220; conservative critique of, 215; Fox News on, 152; Millennials' attitudes toward, 5, 103–104, 265; optimism about, 138; public's predictions about, 201–202; in 2008 election, 210, 211; in 2006 election, 126–127, 132; wounded soldiers from, 47; youth vote and, 87
Islam, 265

Jackson, Andrew, 31, 56, 194, 195. *See also* Jacksonian realignment (1828)
Jacksonian realignment (1828): control of government after, 34–35; cultural change in, 194–195; economic disparities after, 38; economic role of government in, 46–47; immigration issues after, 42; party coalitions in, 31; social issues in, 40–41; voter disengagement in, 34; voter turnout in, 31
Jacksonville Sentinel (Ill.), 52, 53
Jamieson, Kathleen Hall, 59–60
Jefferson, Thomas, 233, 260
Jerry McGuire (film), 79
Jib Jab, 187
Jim Crow laws, 43, 234
job fairs, 241
Jobs, Steve, 149
Johnson, Andrew, 230
Johnson, Lyndon B., 48, 163, 196–197, 214–215
Jones, John Paul, 233
"Julia" (television program), 73
Julius Caesar (Shakespeare), 219
juvenile delinquency, 81

Kagan, Steve, 122

Kamarck, Elaine, 115, 125, 218, 235–236

Kamenetz, Amy, 256–257

Kansas: campaigns and elections in, 99

Karim, Jawed, 168–169

KDKA radio, 58

Kelly, Doug, 182

Kelly, Jack, 215

Kennedy, John F.: assassination of, 192–193; on missile gap, 13, 101; Obama on, 12; television appearance of, 61–62, 179

Kennedy, Robert, 193, 215

Kentucky: campaigns and elections in, 137

Kerrey, Bob, 134

Kerry, John: cartoon spoof of, 187; Millennials' support for, 105–106; online fund-raising of, 184; presidential campaign of, 155; revelations about, 134; Swift Boat ads against, 155; votes for, 115, 117

Key, V. O., 17, 106, 216

Kilpatrick, Kwame, 259–260

King, Martin Luther, Jr., 11, 12, 193

Kinnick, Nile, 100–101

Kirkpatrick, Jeanne, 208

Kline, Phill, 99

Kobylt, John, 63

Kryzinski, John, 24–25

Ku Klux Klan (KKK), 43

Ladd, Everett Carll, 21

Lanier, Jaron, 243, 244–245

LANS (local area networks), 143

late-nineteenth-century realignment: communication technologies in, 54–57; control of government after, 34–35; cultural change in, 194, 195–196; currency debate preceding, 54–57; economic disparities after, 39; economic role of government after, 46–47; ethnic and racial issues after, 43; evolution vs. creationism debate after, 41–42; immigration issues after, 42; party coalitions in, 32; voter turnout in, 31; women's rights after, 41

"Laugh In" (television program), 62

"Law and Order" (television program), 151

Lazarsfeld, Paul, 88

Lazarus, Emma, 44

League of Nations, 68, 225

Learn and Save America, 260

"Leave It to Beaver" (television program), 72–73, 74

Lend-Lease concept, 229

Leno, Jay, 64

Letterman, David, 64

Leuchtenburg, William E., 244

Levin, Carl, ix

Levinson, Barry, 69–70

Lewinsky, Monica, 112

Lewis, John, 11

liberalism: appropriate sexual behavior in, 97; idealist and civic realignments from, 28–29, 30; identification with, increase in, 208–209; Millennials' identification with, 107; polarization and, 115–116, 131; realignment theory and, 17; state initiatives juxtaposed to, 242; 2008 election's importance and, 216–217

Limbaugh, Rush, 63

Lincoln, Abraham: domestic policies of, 32; 1858 Senate campaign of, 51–53, 224–225; election of, 6–7, 19; historical reappraisal of, 213; leadership of, 221–223, 230–231;

role of government under, 47–48; vision of, 223–230. *See also* Civil War realignment (1860s)

Lincoln-Douglas debates, 51–53, 224–225

Lindbergh, Charles, 100

Lion King, The (film), 263

Lippmann, Walter, 225

Littky, Dennis, 258–259

Lockshin, Matt, 129, 131

Loebsack, David, 122

Lolita (film), 78

Lord of the Flies (film), 78

Lost Generation (1920s), 86

Lubell, Samuel, 24

Lucas, George, 204–205

lynchings, 43, 234

"macaca" comment, 134–135

MacKenzie, Jack, 151, 153

MacMurray, Fred, 73

Madison, James, 233

Map Changer contest, 158–161, 162

marriage, 69, 70, 71, 98

marriage/family/children values: community service goal and, 263; of generations, compared, 68–71; of Millennials, 98; pop culture's reflection of, 72–81

"Married . . . with Children" (television program), 76

Marshall Plan, 101

"Mary Tyler Moore" (television program), 74, 75

mashed-up content: adapting to, 204; of music, 86; of Obama ad, 154; of *Star Wars* clips, 205; of videos, 136–137, 187

Matsusaka, John, 239–240

Mayhew, David, 21–22

McCain, John, 177, 184

McCainSpace, 177

McCarran-Walter Immigration and Nationality Act (1952), 45

McCarthy, Eugene, 215

McCaskill, Claire, 132–133

McCloskey, Pete, 128

McGinniss, Joe, 61–62

McKinley, William, 54, 55, 56–57, 186, 195–196. *See also* late-nineteenth-century realignment

McNerney, Jerry, 127–131

McNerney, Michael, 127–128

McPhee, William, 88

media: adapting to changes in, 204–205; as intermediator, 53–54; for masses, 57–60; producers in, 152–155; voters' use of, 165–167. *See also* communication technologies; film and movies; Internet; newspapers; radio; television

Media Defender, 149

Medicaid, 253

Medicare, 210, 211, 252, 253, 255

Medill, Joseph, 54

"Meet the Press" (television program), 184

Meetup.com, 184

metadata and tagging, 159–160, 167

Metropolitan Regional Career and Technical Center (MET), 258–259

Michigan: campaigns and elections in, ix–x, 62, 259–260

Microsoft, 241

micro-targeting technology, 181–184

Middle Atlantic: elections in, 226. *See also specific states*

Midwest, upper: elections in, 122–123, 226; realignments, 20, 23, 32–33. *See also specific states*

military: alternative to service in, 262–263; foreign affairs attitudes and, 100–104; integration of, 45; Millennials' attitudes on use of, 265–266

Millennial Cycle (ca. 1967–2050), 25

Millennial Generation (b. 1982–2003): appeal of "Red to Blue" candidates to, 120–121; childhood environments of, 5–6, 68–69, 71, 78–84; debt faced by, 251–252; declining music purchases of, 147, 148–149; demographics of, 26, 66–67, 81–82, 95–96; description of, xi, 1–2; economic power equation and, 151–152; education of, 80–81, 82; as focus point for 2006 candidates, 127–128; GI Generation compared with, 66–68; health care coverage of, 253, 254; Internet vs. television use of, 163–164; Joshua generation compared with, 14; limits of, 243; music identified with, 85–86, 204; music industry lawsuits against, 147–148; parental relationships of, 83; party coalitions of, 33; party identification of, 105–108, 138, 205–210; political centrality of, 210–212; political organizers' approach to, 170–173; pop culture's reflection of, 77–78, 84–85; positive behavior and lifestyle of, 81–83; post-2006 election predictions of, 201–202; public policy agenda of, 250–251; self-esteem of, 79–80; surveys of, xiv–xv, 2; voting eligibility of, 7–8, 34, 87–88, 164–165. *See also* Millennialist realignment (2000s); Millennials' attitudes

Millennialist realignment (2000s): community service in, 260–263; crises and government response as trigger of, 197–201; debt issues in, 251–252; Democratic Party's future in, 216–219; difficulties in adapting to, 204–210; direct democracy in, 239–241; early signs of, 111–114; education issues in, 250, 256–260; engaging citizens in, 226–230; environmental issues in, 250; generational and technological triggers of, 191–192; global issues in, 266–267; health care issues in, 250, 253–256; incremental changes in, 241–246; leadership of, 220–221, 231–232; Millennials' centrality to, 210–212; national consciousness as trigger of, 192–194; polarization in, 115–116; presidential leadership for, 230–232; public policy agenda of, summarized, 250–251; public's predictions of, 201–202; Republican Party's future in, 212–216; reshaping civic infrastructure in, 235–238; think globally, act locally concept in, 263–266; 2008 election's importance in, 216–217; 2004 election as precursor to, 116–118; 2006 "Red to Blue" campaign and, 119–121; 2006 election as tipping point for, 118–119

Millennials' attitudes: abortion, 99; community orientation, 83–84; community service and voluntarism, 84, 260–263; consensus-based decision making, 96–97, 236; direct, open democracy, 239–241; education, 257, 258, 260; email, 186; gender, 98; globalism, 103–104, 263–266; global warming, 5; governance and civic infrastructure, 235–238;

government's role, 48–49, 94–95,
199–201; homosexuality, 97–98;
immigration, 96–97; inclusivity, 41,
45–46, 95–97, 249;
incrementalism, 241–246; Internet
freedoms and sharing, 138,
142–144, 148–150, 151, 164–165,
167–170, 200, 256; Iraq War, 5,
103–104, 265; military force,
265–266; multitasking, 164; 9/11,
199–200; optimism, 82–83, 91–94,
251; political parties, 3–4,
105–108, 207–208; politics and
political institutions, 92–94, 107;
presidential characteristics,
231–232; P2P technology, 140,
144–148; religion, 89; sexuality,
97–99; Social Security debate, 252;
social welfare, 94–95; 2008
election, 210–212, 217; United
Nations, 265–266; U.S. Congress,
107. *See also* equality
Miller, Harris, xvi, 134
Milliken, William, ix, 62
minimum wage issues, 132–133
missile gap concept, 13, 101
Missionary Generation (1890s), 86
Missouri: campaigns and elections in,
132–133
money, 54–57. *See also* campaign
funding
Montana: campaigns and elections in,
133, 135–137
Moore, Mary Tyler, 74, 75
Morison, S. E., 244
Morissette, Alanis, 145
"morning-after" pill, 99
Morrill, Justin Smith, 261
Morrill Act (Land Grant Colleges),
32, 47–48, 261
Morrison, John, 135–136
Morrison, Paul, 99
Morse, Samuel F. B., 50–51

Mos Def, 171
Mott, Lucretia, 40–41
MoveOn.org, 104, 178, 245
MP3.com, 144–146
MP3 format, 144–151. *See also* iPods
MSNBC, 114, 166
MTV, 5, 156, 204
Murdoch, Rupert, 152, 171, 187
music: declining purchases of, 147,
148–149; DRM-free, 149; of
Millennials, 85–86. *See also* peer-
to-peer (P2P) communication
technologies
music industry: adapting to changes
in, 204; peer-to-peer technology
in, 140, 144–148. *See also* CDs;
MP3 format
MyDD blog, 135, 172
MySpace: Impact Channel of,
171–173; individualism of,
244–245; Murdoch's purchase of,
152, 171, 187; online unofficial
primary of, 173; popularity of, 2,
5, 84; potential of, 64–65, 153;
sharing as central to, 167; traffic on,
170–171; 2008 presidential
candidates' profiles on, 3, 172–173,
186; users of, 168; video streaming
capability of, 169
"My Three Sons" (television
program), 73

Nader, Ralph, 38
Namenworth, J. V., 209
name recognition, 60
Napster, 2, 146–148
narcissism, 5–6
National Abortion Rights Action
League (NARAL), 132
National and Community Service
Trust Act (1993), 260
national consciousness: as trigger of
realignment, 192–194

National Organization for Women (NOW), 41

National Partnership for Reinventing Government, x

national service program, 261–263

National Woman Suffrage Association, 41

NATO (North Atlantic Treaty Organization), 101

"NBC Dateline" (television program), 81

NBC radio, 58

Nelson, Ricky, 73

Netroots: coining of term, 157; Democratic advantage doubled by, 125–126; dynamic context of, 174–175; fund-raising via, 176–180, 184–186; Millennials' influence in, 170–171; potential of, 186–188; reaching youth vote via, 138, 164–165; Republicans as outsiders to, 175–176, 180–184; scaling up from state to national campaigns in, 162; 2006 House midterm elections and, 119, 127–131; 2006 Senate midterm elections and, 132–137; state races and, 157–161

Nevins, Allan, 228

New Deal realignment (1930s): civic infrastructure of, 234; communication technology in, 59–60; control of government after, 35–36; economic disparities after, 39; economic role of government after, 48; engaging voters in vision for, 226–230; foreign affairs attitudes in, 100–101; immigration issues after, 44–45; independent voters after, 36; leadership in, 221–223; limited number of referenda in, 244; party coalitions in, 32; party identification in, 19, 207; period of, 19; political, social,

and technological context of, 7, 220–221; public policy after, 20; rejection of, 196–197; social issues in, 40; studies of, 17; vision in, 223–226; voter attitudes toward political institutions in, 37; voter turnout in, 31

New Democratic Network, 208

New Hampshire: campaigns and elections in, 161–162; Netroots' role in, 126–127, 158–161

Newhart, Bob, 74, 75

Newman, Paul, 150

New Mexico: campaigns and elections in, 137, 181–182

News Corporation, 152, 171

newspapers: on gold vs. silver debate, 55; on Lincoln-Douglas debates, 52–53; news acquired via Internet vs., 164; on 1948 election, 16; political advertising in, 163; political affiliations of, 51–52

Newsweek magazine, 213

Newton, Huey, 44

New Yorker magazine, 60

New York Morning Journal, 55

Nextel, 157

Nickerson, David W., 165

"Night Court" (television program), 74

Nike, 153–154

9/11 Commission Report, The, 202. *See also* September 11, 2001

Nissan, 155

Nixon, Richard M.: law-and-order campaign of, 44; negative appraisals of, 214; policies of, 196–197, 212; television appearances of, 61–62, 179. *See also* Republican realignment (1960s)

No Child Left Behind Act (2001), 182

North Atlantic Treaty Organization (NATO), 101

North Carolina: campaigns and
elections in, 119–120
Northeast: elections, 122–123, 226;
realignments, 20, 23, 31–33. *See
also specific states*
'N Sync, 85
nuclear war, 201

Obama, Barack: appeal to Millennials,
3; "Bloody Sunday" remembered,
11, 12–14; ESPN appearance of,
184–185; fund-raising of, 175–176,
180; mashup ad of, 154; social
networking embraced by, 3,
172–173, 177, 188
O'Brien, Kevin, 136
occupations and careers: Millennials'
optimism about, 92, 253; portrayals
in sitcoms, 73–75; of 2006
Democratic candidates, 120–122;
wage insurance in, 266–267
Ohio: campaigns and elections in,
132, 137, 181
"One Day at a Time" (television
program), 75
O'Neill, Paul, 251
optimism: economy, 82–83, 92, 138;
education, 92; government, 93,
94–95, 122, 138; health care, 92,
122; Iraq War, 138; national
security, 138; occupations and
careers, 92, 253; politics and
political institutions, 92–94, 107,
122, 138; racial issues, 82–83;
sexual freedom, 92, 97–99; social
issues, 82–83, 92–94, 138
Order of the Star Spangled Banner, 42
Oregon: campaigns and elections in,
242
Oswald, Lee Harvey, 192–193

Pacific Coast: elections, 226;
realignments, 33. *See also specific states*

Pacific Railway Act, 47–48
PACs (political action committees),
158–161
Page, Lawrence, 237
Pakman, David, 149
Panic of 1893, 195
Pariser, Eli, 104
Parkinson's disease, 133
partisanship: in civic realignments,
105–108, 114; process in, 115–116;
technology's usefulness and, 183;
tempering of, by FDR and
Lincoln, 230; in 2004 election,
117–118. *See also* bipartisanship;
party identification
"Partridge Family, The" (television
program), 73
party identification: changing role of,
21, 204; decline, in 2004, 116; in
idealist vs. civic realignments, 27,
90; inversion of, 19, 20, 22–23; as
lifelong, 209; Millennials' views on,
105–108, 138, 205–210; popular
vote margins linked to, 17–18; shift
toward Democratic, 105–108, 138,
205–207; social issues in defining,
196–197; 2008 election's
importance and, 216–217; in 2004
election, 117–118; voter behavior
based on, 165, 183–184. *See also*
bipartisanship; partisanship; political
parties
Patriot Act (2001), 248
patriotism: attitudes toward, 103;
McKinley's use of, 195–196; of
2006 Democratic candidates,
120–122, 130–131
Paulsen, Pat, 90
Paulson, Arthur, 22–23
PayPal, 168
PBS network, 84, 132, 264–265
PCs. *See* computers
Pearl Harbor attack (1941), 100–101

peer-to-peer (P2P) communication technologies: adapting to, 204–205; analyzing use of, 150–151; attempts to counter, 146–148; educating voters via, 240–241; emergence of, 140, 142–146; Millennials' embrace of, 2, 148; persistence of, 148–150; producers in, 152–155; reshaping civic infrastructure in context of, 235–236. *See also* community/group values; friends and friendships

Pelosi, Nancy, 119, 120

Pennsylvania: campaigns and elections in, 120, 131–132, 181

Perlman, Rhea, 75

Perot, Ross, 38, 116

Perry, Matthew, 76–77

Person of the Year award (2006), 153

Phillips, Kevin, 39

Phillips, Mackenzie, 75

phones. *See* cell phones; telephone

photographs, 171, 186

Pilgrims, 248

Pleshette, Suzanne, 75

Plessy v. Ferguson, 43

Podesta, John, 112

political action committees (PACs), 158–161

political campaigns: centrality of social networking in, 170–173; changing field for, 154–155; command-and-control controversy in, 172; decline of television-oriented, 162–164; four M's in (money, media, message, messenger), 118, 124–126, 131, 137; revising formula for successful, 137–139, 140; television teaser of coming, 184–185; top-down vs. bottom-up approach to, 157, 173, 177, 178, 179, 185; voters' use of media in, 165–167; widgets' potential for, 187–188. *See also* advertisements and advertising;

campaign funding; electoral politics; grassroots organizing; Netroots; *specific candidates and elections*

political campaign techniques: digital yard sign, 172; direct mail, 179; door-to-door canvassing, 130, 136, 179; online organizing, 157–162, 188; pamphlets, 56; town hall events, 56–57

political institutions: Democratic congressional victory and optimism about, 122, 138; hostility toward, 220–221; in idealist vs. civic realignments, 27; incremental changes in, 241–246; Millennials' optimism about, 92–94, 107; voter attitudes toward, 36–38. *See also* civic infrastructure; government; political parties

political parties: altering balance of, 204; coalitions of, in realignments, 31–33; extinct, 174; increased differences perceived between, 105–108, 117–118; issues in 2008 election and, 210–211; media consultants of, 154–155; rise and fall of, 11–29; voter attitudes toward, 90–91. *See also* electoral politics; party identification; *specific parties*

Politicopia.com, 245–246

politics: adapting to changes in, 205–210; attitudinal and behavioral patterns in, 89–90; compromise of 1877 in, 233–234; dynamic context of, 174–175; Internet potential for, 153–155; Millennials' centrality to coming, 210–212; Millennials' optimism about, 92–94; Netroots as disrupting, 126–131, 132; polarization of, 115–116, 131. *See also* electoral politics; political campaigns

Pombo, Richard, 127–131

pop culture: civic generation's rejection of dominant, 151, 193–194; generational cycles reflected in, 72–81; sexuality in, 97–98. *See also* film and movies; music; television; radio

population growth, 26, 78–79. *See also* birthrates

Populist era (1890s), 4

Populist Party, 37

Prairie West region, 20, 22–23. *See also specific states*

presidency and presidential leadership: citizens' expectations of, 230–231; engaging voters in vision of, 226–230; Lincoln and FDR as models of, 221–223, 230–231; Lincoln's and FDR's visions for, 223–226; midterm elections and, 112–113; popular vote margins and, 17–18; 2008 election and, 231–232

President's Management Agenda (PMA), 236

privacy issues, 161, 200–201, 255–256, 265

Progressive Party, 35, 38, 234, 244

progressivism, 208. *See also* direct democracy

Prohibition, 40

Protestants, evangelical, 117, 214. *See also* God and religion, attitudes toward

P2P. *See* peer-to-peer (P2P) communication technologies

public opinion and attitudes: activist government, 193–194, 198–201; Bush, 107, 118, 199, 213–215; direction of country, 203–204; efficacy of politics, 92–94; foreign affairs, 100–104; great presidents, 230–231; immigration, 66–67, 96–97; inclusivity, 41, 45–46, 95–97, 249; patterns of, 88–91; presidential leadership, 222; religion, 89; sexuality, 97–99; social welfare policies, 94–95; 2008 election issues, 210–212; U.S. Congress, 220. *See also* voters' attitudes

public policy: attitudes toward children reflected in, 80–81; in civic vs. idealist realignments, 20, 27, 42–46; community service and, 260–263; debt issues and, 251–252; direct democracy and, 239–241; economic equality and, 94–95; education issues and, 250, 256–260; environmental issues in, 250; global issues in, 266–267; health care issues and, 250, 253–256; historical perspective on, 248–250; inclusivity fostered in, 41, 45–46, 95–97, 249; individual vs. community/national goals in, 247–250; liberal to conservative shift in, 23; locus of developing, 235–236; Millennial-era agenda on, summarized, 250–251; think globally, act locally concept in, 263–266

Qaeda, Al, 199

"Queer Eye for the Straight Guy" (television program), 97

Quinn, Laura, 182–183

"Q" scores, 64

race and racial issues: in civic vs. idealist realignments, 42–46; Millennials' demographics and, 66–67, 95–96; Millennials' inclusivity and, 41, 45–46, 95–97, 249; Millennials' optimism about, 82–83; portrayals on sitcoms, 77–78; 2008 election and, 210, 211; 2004 election and, 117; in 2006 Senate campaigns, 134–135, 136; suburbanization and, 70–71 racial equality: future campaign messages about, 137; government promotion of, 95–96; post–Civil War setback for, 43, 233–234

radio: advertising on, 58–59, 163; emergence of, 57–58; FDR's use of, 59–60, 179, 185; movies juxtaposed to, 60; presidential addresses on, 58–60; television juxtaposed to, 61. *See also* talk radio

Radio Act (1927), 58

railroads and railroad development, 56–57

Rasiej, Andrew, 245–246

Reactive Generation, 25. *See also* Generation X

Reagan, Ronald, 47, 62, 113, 196, 211–212

Reagan Democrats, 33, 207

realignments: components of, 17–20; differences among, 27–29; economic disparities issue in, 38–40; economic role of government in, 46–49, 94–95; generational archetypes linked to, 5–6; generational changes as key to, 24–26; party coalitions in, 31–33; political, social, and technological context of, 1–2, 6–7, 23–24, 220–221; precursors to, 50, 87–88; public opinion shifts in, 203–204; public policy issues in, 42–46; signs of, 111–114; social issues in, 40–42; triggering events of, 192–194; voter attitudes toward political institutions in, 36–38; voter engagement in, 33–34; voter turnout in, 31. *See also* civic realignments; idealist realignments; realignment theory

realignment theory: archetypes and, 27–29; challenges to, 20–23; electoral patterns and, 14–16;

emergence of, 16–17; reformulation of, 23. *See also* realignments

recall petition, 63–64, 239

Recording Industry Associates of America (RIAA), 147–148, 150, 156–157

Redford, Robert, 150

Redstone, Sumner, 156–157

"Red to Blue" (R2B) campaign: analysis of, 124–126; description of, 119–121; success of, 121–123

Reebok, 187–188

Reeves, Richard, 211–212

referenda and propositions: as direct democracy, 239–240; implications of, 242; recall petition and, 63–64, 239; on school bonds, 80; voter turnout linked to, 132–133; World War I–era, 244

religion. *See* God and religion, attitudes toward

Republican Party: ability to adapt, 205; currency debate and, 55–57; on direction of country, 203; emergence of, 19; eras of dominance of, 15–16, 118; idealist and civic realignments from, 27–28, 30; identifiers and voters of, 18, 21, 207; impeachment inquiry of, 111–112; on liberalism, 208; Lincoln's leadership and vision for, 221–226; micro-targeting technology and, 181–182, 183; "missile gap" and, 101; as party of "big oil" party, 264; as party of small government, 199–200; as party of strong military, 217–218; polarization encouraged by, 115–116, 131; portrayals on sitcoms, 77; scandals of, 132, 134, 136; 72 Hour Program of, 179,

180–181; social activism of, 108; social networking's challenge to, 175–184; television and radio use of, 62, 63–64; 2008 election as opportunity for, 212–216; 2008 election issues and, 210–212; voters' turn against, 106–108

Republican realignment (1960s): attitudinal and behavioral patterns in, 89–90; characteristics of, 20–21, 22–23; control of government after, 34–35; cultural change in, 194, 196–197; economic disparities after, 39; economic role of government after, 46–47; ethnic and racial issues after, 43–44; foreign affairs attitudes in, 101–102; hopes for prolonging, 191; independent voters after, 36; individualism vs. community values in, 248; party coalitions in, 32–33; party identification in, 207; period of, 19; underlying context in, 24; voter turnout in, 31; women's rights after, 41

Revolutionary generational cycle, 233, 248

Rhode Island: campaigns and elections in, 132; model school in, 258–259

Richardson, Bill, 12

Richardson, Eileen, 147

Rightroots project, 176

Riordan, Richard, 63

Risky Business (film), 84–85

Ritter, John, 79

Robert McCormick Foundation, 54

Robertson, Michael, 144–145, 146

Rocky Mountain region: realignments, 20, 22–23, 32. *See also specific states*

Roe v. Wade, 78, 245

Rogers, Will, 59

Romney, George, ix, 62

Romney, Mitt, 180, 183, 254

Roosevelt, Eleanor, 196

Roosevelt, Franklin D.: election of, 7, 39; GI Bill of, 48, 261; immigration issues and, 45; leadership of, 221–223, 230–231; legacy of, 212; military draft and, 100; radio used by, 59–60, 179, 185; successor to, 16–17; supporters of, 24; vision of, 223–230. *See also* New Deal realignment (1930s)

Roosevelt, Theodore, 46, 54, 108, 227

Rosemary's Baby (film), 78

Rosen, Hillary, 147, 150

Rosenberg, Ivan, 223, 226

Rospars, Joe, 172–173

Ross, Doug, ix, 259, 260

Rove, Karl, 118, 183, 191

Rowling, J. K., 4

Ruffini, Patrick, 177–178, 179, 180, 186

Rutgers University: women's basketball team of, 4

Ryan, Meg, 141

Sandstrom, Steve, 246

San Francisco Examiner, 55

Santangelo, Michelle, 148

Santorum, Rick, 132

SARS virus, 200

"Saturday Night Live" ("SNL") (television program), 64, 153

"Save the Debate" coalition, 186

Savich, Peter, 86

"saynotopombo" blog, 129–131

Schlesinger, Arthur, Jr., 17

Schlesinger, Arthur, Sr., 17

Schlessinger, Laura, 71
schools: charter type of, 80–81; drop-
out rates of, 257–258; homosexual
teachers in, 97–98; individually
focused models of, 258–260;
shootings in, 81, 200–201, 265;
sports in, 83; voluntarism aspect of,
84, 260–261. *See also* education
Schulman, Dan, 141–142
Schumer, Charles, 119, 131–133
Schwarzenegger, Arnold, 64, 239,
254
Scopes monkey trial, 41–42
search engines, 237. *See also* Google;
Yahoo!
Second Life, 240–241
security, U.S.: Democratic
congressional victory and optimism
about, 138; individual vs.
community in debates on, 248–249;
Millennials' attitudes toward,
103–104; think globally, act locally
concept and, 263–266; as 2008
election issue, 210, 211, 217–219.
See also foreign affairs; globalism
segregation, 43, 45
Seinfeld, Jerry, 76, 97
"Seinfeld" (television program), 76, 97
Selective Service Act (1940), 100
Selma (Ala.): "Bloody Sunday"
remembrances in, 11–14, 193
Senior Corps, 260
September 11, 2001: activist
government reappraised after,
199–200; attitudes toward
patriotism after, 103; bipartisanship
after, 115; evaluation and report
on, 202; immigration issues and,
44; long-term effects of, 191–192,
193–194, 197, 203; Patriot Act in
wake of, 248; U.S. attention to
world events after, 68; youth vote
increased after, 87

"Sesame Street" (television program),
264
72 Hour Program, 179, 180–181
sexual abuse, 81
sexual freedom, 92, 95, 97–99
Shakespeare, William, 219
Shalala, Donna, 112
Shaw, George Bernard, 88
Shea-Porter, Carol, 126–127
Sheehan, Cindy, 104
Shoe Fight Contest (Reebok),
187–188
Shop Around the Corner, The (film),
141–142
Shrum, Bob, 155
Shuler, Heath, 119–120
Sidarth, S. R., 134–135
Silent Generation: childhood
environment of, 69; civil rights
movement and, 45; description of,
26; music identified with, 86; on
religion, 89; retirement concerns
of, 252; as television viewers, 163;
voting attitudes and behavior of,
90–91; on women's roles, 98
"silent majority" concept, 196
SIM games, 241
Simon, Bill, 63
Simon, Neil, 67
situation comedies (sitcoms), 72–78
Skype (company), 143
slaves and slavery: abolitionist
agitation and, 42–43; economic
disparities and, 38, 39; leadership
and vision in ending, 45, 221–223,
224–225; in Lincoln-Douglas
debates, 51–53
Smith, Al, 19, 59, 117
Snow, John, 251
social class, 19, 23–24. *See also*
economic disparities
social issues: in civic vs. idealist
realignments, 27, 40–42;

diminished focus on, 247; dynamic context of, 174–175; generational differences in, 67–71; Millennials' optimism about, 82–83, 92–94; polarization over, 115–116; public's predictions about, 201–202; realignments linked to crises in, 19, 197–201; 2008 election and, 210, 217; in 2006 election, 137–138; welfare policy and, 94–95

Socialist Party, 226

social networking technologies: analyzing use of, 150–151; centrality of political organizing via, 170–173, 184–186; dynamic context of, 174–175; failure to recognize, 156–157; first electoral test of, 2–3; as fund-raising advantage, 175–180; health care and, 256; individualism of, 244–245; Map Changers contest and, 158–161; necessity for using, 64–65, 205; organizational model of, 237–238; outsourcing jobs and, 267; popularity of, 83–84; potential of, 184, 186–188, 240–241; producers in, 152–155; reaching younger voters via, 138, 164–165; Republicans challenged by, 175–184; sharing as central to, 167–170; 2006 Democratic strategies and, 133–137; voters' personal commentaries on, 186–187. *See also* blogs and blogosphere; *specific sites (e.g., Facebook)*

Social Security, 210, 211, 252

"Something Awful" forum (comedy web site), 160–161

Sony, 145

South: elections, 122–123, 225, 226; realignments, 19, 20, 22–23, 31–33. *See also specific states*

South Dakota: campaigns and elections in, 242

Southwest: realignments, 33. *See also specific states*

Spanish-American War (1898), 54

Sperling, Gene, 251

split-ticket voting: end of era for, 114, 118; increase in, 21, 36, 90; technology's usefulness and, 183; television's role in, 62. *See also* Independents; third-party movements

Stanton, Elizabeth Cady, 40–41

Star Wars (film series), 205

State's Rights Party, 38

stem cell research, 132–133

Stewart, Jimmy, 141–142

Stone, Irving, 228

straight-ticket voting, 117–118. *See also* partisanship; party identification; political parties

Strauss, William: current political crisis predicted by, 220–221, 232; on generational types and politics, 25–26; on generation gap, 209; on generations, xiii, 5–6, 14; on Generation X, 70; on government restructuring, 247; on Millennials' optimism, 82–83; on Revolutionary generational cycle, 233; on social values, 68; on triggering events, 192

substance abuse, 40, 67–68, 75

suburbanization, 69–72

Sullavan, Margaret, 141–142

Surowiecki, James, 242–243, 245

Swift Boat ads, 155

Taft, William H., 47

tagging and metadata, 159–160, 167

Talbott, Adrian, 164–165

Talent, Jim, 132–133

talking points, 52

talk radio, 63–64, 179, 249
Tancredo, Tom, 44
TargetPoint Consulting, 183
Tauscher, Ellen, 128
tax issues: ballot initiatives on, 242;
Democratic congressional victory
and optimism about, 138; federal
debt and, 251–252; micro-targeting
on, 183; in 2008 election, 210
"Taxi" (television program), 74
Techcrunch, 177
technological developments: context
of usefulness of, 183–184; growth
patterns of, 51; political
realignments linked to, 23–24;
vacuum tube, 57–58. *See also*
communication technologies;
specific technologies
teenage pregnancy, 81, 82
telegraph, 51–57
telephone, 55–56, 83, 141. *See also*
cell phones
television: adapting to changes in,
204; campaign advertising dollars
on, 155; decline of campaigning
via, 162–164; early political use of,
61–62, 179; as information source,
164, 166; Internet's impact on, 152;
as platform for online strategies,
184–185; skipping commercials on,
153–154
television programs: child sexual
abuse highlighted on, 81; Clinton's
appearance on, 64; gays in, 97;
generational cycles reflected in,
72–78; Nixon's appearance on, 62;
online recruiting for proposed,
171–172; political identification
of, 52; P2P technology and,
150–151
temperance, 40
Tennessee: campaigns and elections
in, 137

Terminator, The (film), 64
terrorism, war against: Burns's
comments on, 136; governmental
role reappraised in, 199–200;
individual vs. community in
debates on, 248–249; Millennials'
attitudes toward, 104; privacy issues
in, 248, 265; public's predictions
about, 201–202; as 2008 election
issue, 210, 211, 217–219
Tester, Jon, 135–137
Texas Association of College
Technical Educators, 79
text messaging, 83–84, 87, 171, 239
"That Girl" (television program), 75
think globally, act locally concept,
263–266
third-party movements, 37–38,
90–91. *See also* Independents;
specific parties
"This Land Is Your Land" (song),
187
Thomas, Marlo, 75
Thomas, Norman, 226
Thompson, Bob, 259
Thompson, Fred, 177, 179
Three Men and a Baby (film), 79
"Three's Company" (television
program), 79
Tilden, Samuel, 35
Time magazine, 153
Title IX, 83
TiVo, 146, 153, 163
TownHall.com, 176
traditionalists' attitudes, 37
triggering events concept, 50,
192–194
Trippi, Joe, 155, 157, 176
Truman, Harry, 16–17, 45, 213, 214,
218
tsunami metaphor: concept of, 111;
small changes and big effects in,
140–144; source of, xv–xvi

Tugwell, Rexford G., 224
Turk, Mike, 176–177, 178–179, 186
Turner, Nat, 43
Tweed, William Marcy "Boss," 137
"tweeny" pop, 86
Tweeten, Andy, 136–137
Twenge, Jean M., 5–6

Ulin, Jeffrey, 205
United 93 (film), 199
United Nations: global warming reports of, 198–199; Millennials' attitudes toward, 265–266; support for, 101
University Music Group, 145
University Preparatory Academy (Detroit), 259–260
Urquhart, Steve, 245–246
U.S. Congress: Bush's post-9/11 speech to, 115; Democratic-controlled (1968–1994), 20–21; Millennials' attitudes toward, 107; 2006 Democratic takeover of, 121–137, 138, 220. *See also* U.S. House of Representatives; U.S. Senate
U.S. Constitution: Seventeenth Amendment, 243–244; Eighteenth Amendment, 40; Nineteenth Amendment, 41; Twenty-first Amendment, 40; Twenty-sixth Amendment, 69
U.S. Department of Homeland Security, 199
U.S. House of Representatives: impeachment inquiry of, 111–112; Selective Service Act of, 100; 2006 Democratic takeover of, 121–131, 138, 220
U.S.-Mexico border fence, 96–97
U.S. News & World Report magazine, 213

U.S. Senate: immigration debate in, 249; 2006 Democratic takeover of, 131–137, 138, 220
U.S. Supreme Court, 114, 147
user-generated content: of amateur videographers, 169–170; as campaign weapon, 133; possibilities of, 152–155; Utah example of, 245–246. *See also* peer-to-peer (P2P) communication technologies; social networking technologies
USS *Maine,* 54
Utah: campaigns and elections in, 245–246

Vandenberg, Arthur, 101
Van Dyke, Dick, 75
Verizon, 241
Viacom, 156–157. *See also* MTV
video clips: easy-to-use application for, 168–170; producers of, 153–155; viral potential of, 187–188. *See also* YouTube
videographers, 169–170
video stalkers concept, 136
Vietnam War, 101–102, 104, 214, 218
Villas, Phil de ("parkridge47"), 154
viral: use of term, 130, 154, 187–188
viral marketing, 155, 171, 178, 187
Virginia: campaigns and elections in, 133–135
Virginia Tech shooting, 81, 200–201, 265
Virgin Mobile USA, 141
Voice Over Internet Protocol (VOIP), 143, 150
Volpe, John Della, 199

voluntarism, 84, 260–263
voters: attitudinal and behavioral
    differences among, 89–90;
    changing demographics of, 117;
    eligibility of younger generation,
    7–8, 24–26, 34, 87–88, 164–165;
    engaged in leader's vision,
    226–230; gathering information
    on, 158; Internet's reach of,
    163–164; media usage of, 165–167,
    186–187; micro-targeting
    technology and, 181–183; online
    recruitment and intensity of, 162;
    political engagement of, 33–34, 50,
    192–194; as producers of news,
    152–155; sorting out of, in 2000
    and 2004, 115–116. *See also*
    generations and generational
    cycles; referenda and propositions
voters' attitudes: consensus across, in
    2006 elections, 138–139; on
    differences between political
    parties, 105–108, 117–118; on
    direct democracy tools, 240; on
    economic disparities, 38–40; on
    government and political
    institutions, 36–38; on great
    presidents, 230–231; on ideology,
    165; on immigration, 135;
    persistence of, by generation,
    89–91; on schools and education,
    80–81; on social issues, 40–42;
    studies of, 17; on 2008 election's
    importance, 216–217. *See also*
    public opinion and attitudes
Voter's Vault project, 181–182, 183
voter turnout: attitudes toward
    political institutions and, 37;
    ballot referenda/propositions
    and, 132–133; campaign debate
    intensity and, 57; declines in,
    21–22, 116; Democratic wins in
    New Hampshire and, 162;

information-acquisition behavior
    and, 164–165; in realignments, 31,
    34, 116–117; Republican 72 Hour
    Program and, 179, 180–181; in
    2006 Senate elections, 135, 137
voting rights, 11, 41, 43, 45
Voting Rights Act (1965), 11

wage insurance program, 266–267
Wales, Jimmy "Jimbo," 237–238,
    240
Wallace, George, 37, 196
Wall Street Journal, 151
Warner, Mark, 157, 158–161
Warner Music Group, 145
Warren, Rick, 199
wars. *See* Iraq War; terrorism, war
    against; World War I; World War II
Washington, George, 100, 223
Washington, D.C., 43, 140
Washor, Eliot, 258–259
Web 2.0. *See* social networking
    technologies
Webb, Jim, xvi, 133–135
WebNoize Conference, 147
wedge issues, 42
Wendt, George, 75
West: elections, 123; realignments, 31,
    32–33. *See also specific states*
Westinghouse, George, 57–58
Wetterling, Patty, 120
Whig Party, 50–51, 195
widgets: for global warming
    questions, 171; for health care
    information, 255–256; for Map
    Changer contest, 160; for mashed-
    up content, 187; for political
    donations, 172; potential of,
    187–188
Wikipedia, 237–238, 240, 244–245
"Will and Grace" (television
    program), 97
Wilson, Pete, 64

Wilson, Woodrow: election of, 35; FDR and, 225; New Freedom policies of, 46–47; radio address of, 58; on "short ballot," 244; World War I pandemic and, 200
Wisconsin: campaigns and elections in, 122
Wizard of Oz, The (film), 4
"WKRP in Cincinnati" (television program), 74
Wolf, Dick, 151
Womack, Jimmy, 260
Women's Christian Temperance Union, 40
women's rights, 40–41, 74
women's roles: compared by generations, 69–71, 78; Millennials on, 98; in sitcoms, 72–78
word-of-mouth marketing, 178. *See also* viral marketing
World Economic Forum, 151–152
World of Warcraft, 240
World War I, 68, 100, 200, 225
World War II: changing response to, 100–101; civic infrastructure during, 234; GI Bill after, 48, 261; GI Generation and, 68; portrayals in sitcoms, 74
Wythe, George, 260

Xanga.com, 168
XML (extended markup language), 167

Yahoo!, 169
Young Americans for Freedom (YAF), 101
youth vote: eligibility of, 7–8, 24–26, 34, 87–88, 164–165; party identification of, 106–107; technologies central to, 138, 164–165; in 2006 elections, 87, 135, 137. *See also* Millennial Generation (b. 1982–2003)
YouTube: Allen's mistakes highlighted on, 134–135; analyzing traffic on, 151, 153; anti-Hillary ad on, 154; creation of, 168–169; Democratic debate on, 186; Google's purchase of, 153, 156, 169; Imus on, 4; as information source, 167; mashup video of Burns on, 136–137; Obama on, 3; plea for stem cell research on, 133; popularity of, 2, 5, 152; potential of, 65, 153; "SNL" clips on, 153; users of, 169–170
You've Got Mail (film), 141–142

Zangara, Giuseppe, 222
Zeigler, Todd, 177

About the Authors

MORLEY WINOGRAD is the executive director of the Center for Telecom Management at the University of Southern California's Marshall School of Business. He is also the president and CEO of Morwin, Inc., a government reform consulting company. He served as senior policy advisor to Vice President Al Gore and director of the National Partnership for Reinventing Government (NPR) from December 1, 1997, until January 20, 2001. He is co-author of *Taking Control: Politics in the Information Age*. His comments on technology, politics, and government reform have appeared in numerous magazines and newspapers. Winograd earned a Bachelor of Business Administration from the University of Michigan in 1963 and attended law school there as well.

MICHAEL D. HAIS retired as vice president, Entertainment Research, at Frank N. Magid Associates, where he conducted audience research for hundreds of television stations, cable channels, and program producers in nearly fifty states and more than a dozen foreign countries. Prior to joining Magid in 1983, he was a political pollster for Democrats in Michigan and served as an assistant professor of political science at the University of Detroit. He received a B.A. from the University of Iowa, an M.A. from the University of Wisconsin at Madison, and a Ph.D. from the University of Maryland, all in political science.